Web Programming

Building Internet Applications

Third Edition

Chris Bates

Sheffield Hallam University

John Wiley & Sons, Ltd

Copyright © 2006   John Wiley & Sons Ltd, The Atrium, Southern Gate, Chichester,
West Sussex PO19 8SQ, England

Telephone (+44) 1243 779777

Email (for orders and customer service enquiries): cs-books@wiley.co.uk
Visit our Home Page on www.wiley.com

Reprinted October 2006

Other Wiley Editorial Offices

John Wiley & Sons Inc., 111 River Street, Hoboken, NJ 07030, USA

Jossey-Bass, 989 Market Street, San Francisco, CA 94103-1741, USA

Wiley-VCH Verlag GmbH, Boschstr. 12, D-69469 Weinheim, Germany

John Wiley & Sons Australia Ltd, 42 McDougall Street, Milton, Queensland 4064, Australia

John Wiley & Sons (Asia) Pte Ltd, 2 Clementi Loop #02-01, Jin Xing Distripark, Singapore 129809

John Wiley & Sons Canada Ltd, 22 Worcester Road, Etobicoke, Ontario, Canada M9W 1L1

Wiley also publishes its books in a variety of electronic formats. Some content that appears
in print may not be available in electronic books.

Library of Congress Cataloging-in-Publication Data:

Bates, Chris (Chris D.)
  Web programming : building internet applications / Chris Bates. – 3rd ed.
    p. cm.
  Includes bibliographical references and index.
  ISBN-13: 978-0-470-01775-3
  ISBN-10: 0-470-01775-9 (pbk. : alk. paper)
  1.   Internet programming. 2. Web sites – Design.   I.   Title.
  QA76.625.B38 2006
  006.7'6 – dc22

                              2006004492

British Library Cataloguing in Publication Data

A catalogue record for this book is available from the British Library

ISBN-13: 978-0-470-01775-3 (P/B)

Typeset in 10/14 Weiss by Laserwords Private Limited, Chennai, India
Printed and bound in Great Britain by Bell & Bain, Glasgow
This book is printed on acid-free paper responsibly manufactured from sustainable forestry
in which at least two trees are planted for each one used for paper production.

Contents

List of Figures

List of Tables

Preface

This book is about implementing Web sites on servers and on browsers. Take a quick look at the contents and you'll see chapters which discuss XHTML, Dynamic HTML, JavaScript, Perl, CGI scripting, PHP and more. Now look around the computing shelves of any bookshop and you will see they are groaning under their load. Most of that load seems to be made of books which cover those same topics. The difference is that I am providing an introduction to a number of different technologies. Other authors tend to look at one subject in the tiniest detail. If you need to learn about building some Dynamic HTML then you could easily find yourself buying three or four expensive books and only using a few chapters from each. That is not a problem for full-time dedicated Web developers. However, for novices starting out on the process of learning Web technologies it really is overkill. This book introduces a range of ideas, but leaves the real nitty-gritty detail to others.

Since the second edition of this book was published, much has changed on the Web, yet much has stayed the same. New ideas such as Blogs have appeared and have transformed the ecostructure of the Web. Technologies have come and gone at a rapid rate. Web sites appear, may be widely use and disseminated more widely through Blogs and forums and then suddenly disappear without trace. Web surfers have no way of guaranteeing that a site which they visit today will be available tomorrow. Despite this tendency towards change, many Web sites stay *in situ* for years on end, growing and evolving, but always there.

This is a book about those technologies, which are used to create and publish Web sites. Technologies, which, furthermore, have stood the test of time. That is why *Web Programming* is now in its third edition. There was nothing wrong with the earlier editions, but things have moved on and the book needs to keep up.

So what has changed in the book? Well, there is more coverage of the `CGI.pm` Perl module which is now the standard way to handle CGI requests if you are a Perl programmer. Remaining on the server I have removed some rather token material about ASP and Java, two technologies which have changed an awful lot in the last five years and which are well catered for elsewhere. What I have mostly done is to add things which I think matter. These include more JavaScript. When I wrote the first edition, the role and future of JavaScript on the Web looked insecure. It was being assailed by Java applets and Flash animations. Nowadays Java has moved from the Web client to the server, applets are very rare and, where they are used, they are marginal rather than central to a site. Flash was briefly used everywhere, annoyed many people, and now seems to have mostly disappeared. JavaScript can be annoying but is widely used for form validation so I have given it a much fuller treatment. When I wrote the previous edition of this book, PHP was the new kid on the block. Now it is one of the most popular programming languages out there. I have added a lost more coverage which I hope does justice to the language, and its developers.

This book grew out of my experience in teaching Web development at Sheffield Hallam University in the UK. My students needed a good practical book which taught them how to do the programming but left the theory to other classes. They wanted something which they could use in the laboratory over a whole semester but which did not contain too much material that they would never use. In a series of lab classes, the only information that the students wanted had to be *relevant*: they did not have the time to work out what was important and what was not.

Looking at the available texts it was clear that no single volume met the needs of lecturers and students alike. Those which tried, tended to rush past the difficult subjects such as introductory Perl while laboring over easier topics such as introductory HTML. The only answer was to create a custom-made booklet which would meet my needs and those of my students, so I started writing. After a while the booklet had grown far beyond my initial vision and was turning into a book, and it kept on growing. The Web has so many important technologies which colleagues, academic reviewers and others insisted *had* to be covered. Usually I agreed wholeheartedly and, where I did not, I was probably too open to persuasion.

This book is the result. It is a practical, hands-on sort of book which will help you to get the job done. It is suitable for use in many teaching and training situations but will also work as a teach-yourself manual. On its own it will probably not turn you into the world's greatest Web developer, but it will certainly give you the best possible start. I hope you enjoy learning about (and using) this stuff as much as I have enjoyed writing about it.

THE INTENDED AUDIENCE

Let us consider the intended audience for a moment: a mixture of students and professional developers. The book is ideally suited as support to a series of practical laboratory classes at either undergraduate level or on Masters courses for non-specialists. Developers who suddenly find that they have to implement an interactive Web site using technologies which are new to them, will find much in this book that is useful. A third audience is composed of those who already know a little about developing Web sites but are not totally confident in what they are doing. Some of this group will have done a lot of HTML using WYSIWYG environments, such as Dreamweaver or FrontPage, and now want to understand what is happening *behind the scenes*; others will have no Web coding experience and want to start.

I assume that readers have a certain level of technical ability. A background which includes a bit of programming and some knowledge of networks and file systems would help with some of the content, but neither is essential. I have tried, though, to be gentle. Each idea is introduced and explained and there are examples throughout the text that you can try out on your own.

I will be honest right away and say that programming the Web is hard; learning about it requires patience and dedication, but can be infinitely rewarding.

There is a lot of theory in this book but there is a lot more "doing". I hope that when you have tried some of the pieces of code or worked through the exercises you will start to ask *why* the Web works as it does. You can then go to some of the resources I have listed at the end of the book, which include just as much detail as you can handle. Once you start to really work through this book and implement the ideas within it you may notice that it is not a comprehensive resource. Each of the technologies that I discuss has been the subject of any number of thousand-page tomes. These give you absolutely all of the detail on the workings of each technology but they often lack context. In this book I have given enough detail to build all but the most complex e-commerce site. To coin a phrase, 80% of programmers use just 20% of the facilities in their chosen system. I have concentrated on the 20% for which you will actually find a use.

Throughout the book you will find exercises and questions. Some involve programming and some involve thinking. Many of the thought exercises relate directly to facts taken from the text, but others are more abstract. You will be expected to wonder about the why and how of the Web. I have not supplied any answers to the exercises. Those which involve writing code can often be answered in a variety of ways: there are no perfect programs. The thought exercises often do not *have* answers. Which leaves the factual questions. The answers to these are to be found in the text preceding the question. Giving sample answers would be like rewriting the book in ultra-brief form. If you cannot answer a question that is probably a sign that you should go back and read the chapter again (and again) so that it makes sense.

Finally, some of the examples I give are simple and some are trivial. What you will soon notice is that many apparently very complex Web sites use just these simple ideas. You will gain more practical skills from a full understanding of simple examples rather than from a partial understanding of overly complex systems.

TYPOGRAPHY

I have used a number of different typefaces throughout this book. Each has a particular meaning. I have also structured some parts of the book, especially definitions of code, to clarify the meaning of the content. It is important that you understand what I have done, otherwise you may end up writing code that does not work.

First of all code is written in a monospaced Courier font. This is done to distinguish it from the descriptive text within the book. Here is an example of some HTML code:

```
1    <html>
       <head>
         <title>A Minimal HTML document</title>
       </head>
5
       <body>
         <h2>Some text...</h2>
         <p>A sample paragraph showing formatting and
         followed by a line across the screen.
10       <hr />
       </body>
     </html>
```

Notice that it is clearly different from normal text. The keywords from the language under discussion are highlighted in bold text. In some chapters, such as those discussing Perl, embedded strings are displayed in a serif font. Code samples presented like this can often be used directly in functioning programs.

Second definitions of terms appear as **bold monospaced Courier**. Again, these stand out from the text but the use of **bold** text indicates that they are *not* functional code. You cannot type the definitions straight into a program and expect them to work. Here's a definition of a typical HTML tag followed by an explanation:

<ol [type=1|a|A|I|i] [start=n] [compact]> ... </ol>

An ordered list has a number instead of a bullet in front of each list item.

- HTML tags are all surrounded by angled brackets (< and >). Where you see these brackets used in HTML, they are part of the code and must be reproduced in your programs.
- Tags which, in the jargon, *close* HTML elements, always include a slash (/).
- Many HTML tags and programming constructs, have optional attributes. Because these are optional you can *choose* to use one of them if you so desire. Throughout this book these optional attributes are listed inside square brackets ([ ]). The square brackets are not part of the HTML code and *must* be omitted from your pages.
- Optional items in lists are always separated by short vertical lines (|). These lines are not part of the HTML code and *must* be omitted from your programs.
- Many of the HTML tag and style definitions include an ellipsis (...). These are used to indicate places where you should add your own text. For instance <h1> ... </h1> might become <h1>A HEADING</h1> in your page.

- The letter n is used to indicate a place where you must enter a numerical value, usually in the definitions of HTML elements which have variable size, and programming functions which require parameters.

If you are unsure about the use of any of these elements, try these two things.

- Look at the sample programs throughout the book and see how I have used the tags and attributes. This should give you some pointers about what you can, and cannot, do inside your HTML.
- Write some code, load it up in a browser if it is HTML, or run it from the command-line if it is Perl, and see what happens. During the testing and development process, especially with HTML, very little can go seriously wrong so try things out. It won't hurt. Honestly!

CONTACTING THE AUTHOR

I would be delighted to hear from readers of this book. It is my first attempt. Or perhaps it is now my second, since there is so much additional material in this new edition. Whichever is the case, I hope it will not be the last, and I am sure there are things that I can improve in the future. Anyone who teaches will tell you that education is a dialogue in which teacher can learn from pupil just as pupil learns from teacher. Not everything in this book will make sense; you may have problems with exercises or with changing technologies and standards. I would be happy to discuss those things with you.

I have a Web site which contains material related to this book at:

```
http://homepages.shu.ac.uk/~cmscrb/
```

which I use mostly as a way of communicating with my students. More information, exercises and errata will appear there too.

If you want to send me e-mail I will try to respond as quickly and accurately as I can. My email address is:

```
c.d.bates@shu.ac.uk
```

CHRIS BATES
Sheffield, UK

Acknowledgments

First, let me thank the colleagues and students who have used and commented on earlier editions of this text. I am particularly grateful to Peter Scott for looking through the Perl, CGI, and PHP chapters, and to Hugh Lafferty for his comments on the XML sections. The Web development course on which I taught when I wrote the first edition is now run by Samir Al Khayatt. Samir has been the driving force for simple examples and clear explanations in my writing, for which I am, again, grateful.

I would like to thank the technical reviewers including Paul Hanna, Martin Hanneghan, Gill Windall and Nik Blessis for their kind and useful comments.

Although writing a book is an essentially solitary occupation, normal life continues unabated. I'm really fortunate that my wife Julie and our daughters, Sophie and Faye, are willing to live with a writer. They let me chase strange syntax errors until 3 a.m. or spend sunny Sunday afternoons reading specification documents instead of going for a walk in the park. Their support and love has been as central to the creation of the second edition as it was to the first. It cannot be said too often: Julie, Sophie and Faye I love you all.

C. D. B.

Introduction

This book is an introduction to some of the basic technologies for creating and processing content on Internet Web sites. It is not meant to be a comprehensive guide to any of the areas covered, there are plenty of those available if you need them, but it should provide enough information for the majority of readers. If you find that you want more information, better tutorials or the comprehensive coverage that so many authors favor nowadays, you are directed to the computing shelves of your nearest bookshop. I have attempted to introduce a number of technologies which when combined make an interesting and user-friendly Web site. Hopefully throughout the text there are enough examples to get you started with each of them.

If you are thinking about creating a Web site then you are probably planning to use a lot of text and some images to make it lively, and possibly a sound clip or two. What about building a dynamic and interactive multimedia extravaganza? Sounds intimidating, doesn't it? There are many complex ways of doing these things which require that you be a fully paid up Geek before you begin. There is also a much simpler approach called *dynamic HTML*, a mix of standard HTML and simple JavaScript, to help you out. It will significantly reduce the development workload and DHTML is supported by all of the popular browsers. This means that you can create leading-edge Web sites without needing to use things like plug-ins or Java applets.

The Web is no longer just a way of presenting information on a computer screen. Being realistic, it has not been for a number of years now. Many commercial sites include some way of getting information from a browser and back to their server. The usual way of doing this is by writing small programs called scripts which run on the server. The process uses a protocol called the Common Gateway Interface or *CGI* for short. Does this book cater for CGI developers? You bet it does, but to be realistic if you're going to develop any sort of

CGI script then you *have* to understand at least something about programming. It is not *so* complicated that it has to be left to the people with computer science degrees and years of experience in the internals of complex programming languages like C++ or ADA, but it *is* complicated. Having said all of that, with a little bit of patience, plenty of hard work, and some thought, many people can write effective server-side scripts.

Web server scripts can be written in almost any programming language. I've chosen to include two languages: Perl and PHP. Perl is probably not the easiest programming language but people from many different backgrounds pick it up quickly enough if they get the right support. The important thing about Perl is that it is perfectly suited to CGI scripting, although it has lots of other uses too. PHP looks very similar to Perl but with a lot of complex syntax removed. It is a phenomenally popular language with libraries available which cover just about any Web development task you can name. It is possible to argue that PHP is now so widely used that it is the single most important technology in this book. PHP works with any Web server but can be optimized to run with Apache using an extension to that server. The interesting thing about PHP is that its growth has happened almost unnoticed by the wider computing community. It is rarely mentioned in the media, yet it is used by millions of sites around the World. PHP is an underground phenomenon which just cannot be ignored.

Those of you interested in CGI scripting should be able to cope with the HTML and JavaScript in the book. Even if you're new to the field you can soon learn what you need to know. But you may want to add more to your site: collecting data about users, creating tailored Web pages, or accessing databases and file systems. Some of these are relatively trivial tasks, as you'll see later, others are at the complicated end of the programming spectrum. If you're keen to learn and willing to work through the examples and exercises even the hardest of these scripts should not prove too difficult.

One technology that I cannot ignore is Extensible Markup Language, XML. This is like HTML after a trip to the gym,[1] it's a way of formatting almost any data so that many applications can handle it. And, fortuitously it just happens that many Web browsers can process or display XML files. With XML, data from spreadsheets, reports, databases, or even applications like CAD packages can be displayed on Web sites. It can be amended and stored in a variety of ways. The computer industry has been looking out for something like XML for a long time. In this book I will give you a taste of what it is and how it can be used and show you a few scripts that let you add the power of XML to your Web site.

Chapter 17 gives you the chance to implement a large system based around an imaginary problem. You can cherry-pick the parts that you choose to do: for instance you may not have access to CGI and database facilities. Whichever part(s) you try should give you a feel for what Web development is all about today. And before anyone asks, no, I don't have a

---

[1] OK, not really, although the analogy will do for now.

sample solution. There are as many correct (and good) Web sites for any customer as there are developers building those sites.

One more thought, don't dive straight into the most complex parts. Each of the main chapters has some exercises to help you *learn*. Once you have done the learning you will be able to apply your new knowledge, but not before. That is obvious when someone says it, but take a look around the Web: it is a mess of broken links, bad coding, and sites that are permanently *under construction*. It is better to know what you are doing, take your time over it and produce an exemplary Web site than to rush in and create something quick but dirty. Surveys suggest that Web sites, especially commercial ones, have just one chance to attract surfers. Make the most of that chance and you will get repeat visits. If you are building business sites then repeat visits equal repeat sales. Customer loyalty starts from that first ever download.

1.1 HTML, XML, AND THE WORLD WIDE WEB

What is HTML and what is it for? First of all, the acronym HTML means *Hypertext Markup Language*. HTML is a method of describing the format of documents which allows them to be viewed on computer screens. HTML documents are displayed by Web browsers, programs which can navigate across networks and display a wide variety of types of information. HTML pages can be developed to be simple text or to be complex multimedia extravaganzas containing sound, moving images, virtual reality, and Java applets. Most Internet Web pages lie somewhere along that continuum, being mostly text but with a few images to add interest and variety.

The Internet is a global phenomenon which can provide documents from servers across the world to browser clients which can be in any location. If documents are to be readily exchanged across such a vast and complex network, some sort of global protocol is required which allows that information to be viewed anywhere.

The global publishing format of the Internet is HTML. It allows authors not only to use text, but also to format that text with headings, lists, and tables, and to include still images, video, and sound within the text. Readers can access pages of information from anywhere in the world at the click of a mouse-button. Information can be downloaded to the reader's own PC or workstation, printed out or e-mailed on to others. HTML pages can also be used for entering data and as the front-end for commercial transactions.

It is probably also worth briefly mentioning what HTML is not. It is not a programming language – you cannot write an HTML program and expect anything to happen. It is not a data description language – the HTML that you write will not tell anyone anything about the structure of your data, although XML will add those capabilities should you choose to use them. Finally HTML is not really very complicated – although the creators of WYSIWYG authoring tools would like you to think that it is.

> **NOTE** *Using HTML forces a separation between content and formatting. You can readily change how your pages will look without having to change what they say.*

1.1.1 A Little Bit of History

The idea of hypertext and hyperlinked documents has been around for a while. In order to be practical it required the implementation of a number of technologies which began to come together in the 1980s, an early example being the HyperCard information management system from Apple. HTML itself was developed by Tim Berners-Lee when he worked at CERN, the European center for particle physics. The phenomenal success of HTML as a format was due to the Mosaic browser developed at NCSA, the US super-computing center, and the simplicity of the language itself.

Mosaic was the result of a US government funded research project and was distributed free of charge. Much of the functionality that we now see in the Netscape Navigator browser in particular, has evolved directly from the early Mosaic browser so that, although Mosaic itself is no longer in development, its influence lives on.

HTML is an application of something called SGML, the Standardized General Markup Language. SGML grew from a number of pieces of work, notably Charles Goldfarb, Edward Mosher and Raymond Lorie at IBM who created a General Markup Language in the late 1960s. In 1978 The American National Standards Institute (ANSI) set up a committee to investigate text processing languages. Charles Goldfarb joined that committee and lead a project to extend GML. In 1980 the first draft of SGML was released and after a series of reviews and revisions became a standard in 1985.

The use of SGML was given impetus by the US Department of Defense. By the early 1970s the DoD was already being swamped by electronic documentation. Their problem arose not from the volume of data, but from the variety of mutually incompatible data formats. SGML was a suitable solution for their problem – and for many others over the years.

Many people mistakenly believe that the Internet and World Wide Web are the same thing. In fact the Internet has been growing for a long time and supports a number of TCP/IP based protocols. Standards exist for sending e-mail (SMTP), Usenet news (NNTP), and file transfer (FTP), alongside a variety of indexing and searching mechanisms such as Gopher and Archie, now obsolete. The 1990s has seen explosive growth in the use of networked computing and the Internet, based in large part upon the growth of homepages on the Web. These homepages are attractive to authors and readers because they are written in HTML and can be formatted in a wide variety of appealing ways.

To be successful, the Web depends on Web page authors and browser vendors sharing the same conventions for HTML. Commercial vendors such as Netscape (e.g., frames) and

Microsoft (e.g., banners) have attempted to develop proprietary tags so that certain text formatting can only be seen on their browser. Such developments are both unwelcome and unlikely to succeed against the libertarian and anarchic framework of the Web. Where a development is seen to be both popular and widely useful, such as Netscape's frame tag or some of Microsoft's Dynamic HTML developments, it will be accepted into a revision of the HTML standard. Where tags are either too system specific or lack technical merit they tend to fall into disuse. There is little point in developing a Web site using fancy formats which visitors cannot see with their browser.

HTML standards (called recommendations by W3C) are created by a group of interested organizations and individuals called W3C. There have now been three official HTML standards: version 2.0 was released in 1994 and remains the baseline for backwards compatibility and should be supported by all browsers and authoring tools; version 3.2 was released in 1996 with many useful additions; version 4.0 was ratified towards the end of 1997 and slightly amended in late 1999. Although many books have been published based around the HTML 3.0 specification, this version was never officially released by W3C. When you create your new documents try to stick to using HTML 4.0 – all of the major browsers will soon support it and relatively few Web surfers use the older versions of browsers.

> **NOTE**
>
> The HTML 4.0 specification document from W3C says:
>
> ... HTML documents should work well across different browsers and platforms. Achieving interoperability lowers costs to content providers since they must develop only one version of a document. If the effort is not made, there is much greater risk that the Web will devolve into a proprietary world of incompatible formats, which will ultimately reduce the Web's commercial potential for all participants.

HTML has been developed so that a wide variety of client systems should be able to use information from the Web: PCs and workstations with graphics displays of varying resolution and color depths; cellular telephones; handheld devices; devices for speech for output and input; computers with high or low bandwidth; and cable-television systems. Authors, especially those developing commercial Web sites need to be aware of all of these. Excluding anyone from using a site means excluding customers – fancy Web pages are very nice but surely counter-productive if they lead to a smaller growth in the customer base than might have been expected. Having said that, there is no excuse for ignoring the standards. If authors had not implemented the new tags as they were ratified by W3C we wouldn't have tables and forms, or stylesheets, or a myriad of other useful formats. The whole Web surfing experience would surely be poorer for these omissions.

1.1.2 XML: The Future of the Web

HTML has, literally, changed the way that we look at and present information. There is now a clear distinction between content and format and new rules for designing and laying-out content are evolving. It is now clear that images, still or moving, and sound can become part of the reader's experience and yet HTML is unsatisfactory in a number of ways:

- advanced Web sites which rely upon the latest tags or use scripting and programming languages to animate the Web page are unusable by many people with disabilities,
- the Web remains largely the preserve of people using the English alphabet. More support is required for different character sets and for different approaches to document preparation,
- many types of content cannot be expressed in conventional alphabets. Most mathematics and much hard science and engineering require different notations. These need to be processed in different ways to conventional text and often cannot be included in HTML documents except as inline images.

Fortunately the limitations of HTML have been widely recognized and are being solved. The most important of the solutions is XML, *Extensible Markup Language* which is a grammar (or set of rules) for creating other markup languages. The power of XML comes from allowing Web designers to specify their own tags to meet their own needs. A site developer who uses a unique data type or wants to express a particular idea in a Web page can create their own specification and use it in on the Web.

Here is a quick example showing how XML includes lots of information which is lost when HTML is used:

HTML	XML
`<h1>Car</h1>`	`<h1>Car</h1>`
`<h2>Make</h2>`	`<make>Ford Mustang</make>`
`<p>Ford Mustang</p>`	`<seats>5</seats>`
`<h2>Seats</h2>`	`<speed units="mph">70</speed>`
`<p>5</p>`	
`<h2>Top Speed</h2>`	
`<p>70 m.p.h.</p>`	

Browsers have recently started to appear which support XML. Microsoft lead the field here with Internet Explorer, version 7 of which is in beta as I write. This has good support for XML and in fact its parser is available for use by other applications. XML may soon become a ubiquitous data format on the PC desktop.

The W3C consortium has already specified a markup language which can be used to express and format mathematical expressions, and other markup grammars are available for multimedia and for describing chemical structures. Combining these markup languages with stylesheets and scripting provides a powerful set of tools, especially for developers inside large organizations. Much complex data can now be presented inside Web pages for consumption either internally or for use by those outside the organization.

HTML is also changing. A new standard has recently been released called XHTML. This brings together the strict rules applied to XML markup and conventional HTML tags. Section 3.6 provides a brief guide to converting your HTML 4 Web page into XHTML. This is important because the intention is that all browsers and servers will move to supporting XHTML. HTML is not compliant with the XHTML standard in a number of ways but with care it *can* be.

1.1.3 Hypertext

As the name suggests, hypertext is more than simply text. Text is two-dimensional and linear; it flows from one place to another. The meaning that we extract from text is often multi-dimensional, with the words that we read able to trigger associations or set us off on tangential thoughts. Many novelists, poets, and playwrights have tried to place the multiple dimensions of meaning directly into the text. Whether authors such as Thomas Pynchon or William S.Burroughs succeed as they de-construct the novels they write, while writing them, is a matter of debate. What is obvious is that their techniques cannot usefully be applied to non-fiction material where clarity of meaning and intent is so important.

Factual material is definitely non-linear and seeks to break out of its two constraining dimensions. Factual material can break boundaries and make new connections for readers: some of you will have read the previous paragraph and wondered what I was writing about and why I was bothering; others will be intrigued by the references to Pynchon and Burroughs and will want to seek out more information; while anyone who has read and enjoyed *Gravity's Rainbow* or *Junkie* may be inspired to read those works instead of this!

Hypertext lets the author add diversions and dead-ends into a piece of work. If this were a hypertext document I would have been able to include links to pieces about Pynchon or theories of writing. Anyone inspired to go down one of those diversions could easily have done so. This is a technical document and there will be many occasions on which I will want to explain terms and ideas in more detail, but to do so would break the narrative flow. If I include such explanations they will be footnotes to the main page, which may reduce their significance. In a hypertext document I would be able to divert interested readers towards peripheral, yet important, information.

Conventional academic or technical writing includes a bibliography so that the keener reader knows where to look for more information. A hypertext document can include a link directly to those sources. In effect such links can be used to include many documents within one framework.

The final benefit of hypertext is that it lets the author create links within a document. Often when reading technical books meanings, ideas, and links occur to the reader. To follow up such ideas the reader has to search back through the whole book to find the information needed to complete a thought. With the modern computer textbook weighing in at around the 800 page mark, looking for a single paragraph becomes nearly impossible, even if a good index has been included.

RULE OF THUMB

When done well, hypertext is a powerful aid to presenting, finding and using information. When done badly it can obscure meaning, mask content, and make documents unusable.

1.1.4 Styles versus Formatting

Anyone who has used a WYSIWYG[2] word processor for any significant document preparation has at some point formatted text. When many people use a word processor they re-enter the formatting information each time that they use it. This is time-consuming and can easily lead to inconsistencies, especially in large documents. A much more effective way of formatting text is to use styles. A style is a set of formatting commands which can be applied to any text. For instance, the style of a paragraph in a word processor might be:

- font: 10 point Arial
- text fully justified
- indent left 2cm
- line-spacing 1.5 lines
- 12 point space after paragraph.

By highlighting text and applying a style to it I can easily use lots of formatting information at the same time. If I decide that I prefer a Times New Roman font to the Arial, I can alter the entire text of the document simply by changing the way that the style is set up. This will work without affecting the formatting of other elements such as headings or footnotes.

HTML presents text in a very different way. The page author simply specifies which style should be used for a piece of text but has no control over how that text will actually appear. This approach to formatting has been used for quite a number of years on text-processing systems such as UNIX groff, nroff, TeX, and LaTeX. Sections of the document are surrounded

[2]What You See Is What You Get: screen content is formatted as exactly as possible to the printed version.

by macro commands which specify what style is required but not how that style should look. The actual styles are formatted separately in *macro* packages. This allows a certain degree of flexibility in the formatting of the text as the same document can be made to look radically different simply by using a different macro package. This approach particularly appeals to scientists, who may submit a paper to a number of conferences or journals knowing that they can easily format it to suit the style of whichever one accepts their work for publication.

In fact, this book was prepared using LaTeX and I made very few creative efforts to format the text. I relied upon the pre-existing sets of formatting commands that came with the LaTeX distributions I use. I simply decide that something is a paragraph and the system will try its best to typeset a beautiful paragraph for me.

Some of the more highly configurable browsers actually allow the reader of the document to change the way that the different styles look. Thus, formatting is controlled more by the reader than the author. Later we will examine stylesheets, a method by which authors can provide absolute formatting information.

It is important that users can define how text styles are presented by their browser because of the accessibility issues that I have already, briefly, mentioned. Many people who use computers to view documents have visual problems of different types. It is important that they can adjust the look of text so that they can actually read it. Sometimes even those who do not have such impairments will want to reconfigure a style for their own reasons, they may find the default style lacking in æsthetic pleasure or, more commonly, the background, colors and images make a particular configuration unusable.

RULE OF THUMB

Formatting is best achieved through the use of styles. Where absolute formatting, such as choosing individual fonts within the text, is used, authors should be careful about readability and æsthetics.

1.1.5 Relative Positioning

The HTML approach to styles is carried over into the positioning of material on the screen. As each object is placed on the screen it is placed relative to items already placed, or to any containers such as frames or tables which might be holding the item. The WYSIWYG approach places objects in an absolute position on the page, within reasonable constraints. HTML browsers cannot know the structure of the whole document in advance. HTML documents arrive in pieces, separately, across the network and those pieces can only be placed once they and surrounding sections have arrived. A word processor has the whole of the document available before it starts to place items onto the page.

An additional problem for HTML browsers is that the position an item can take on the screen depends upon the area available to the browser. A browser may be using the whole screen or only a small part of it. The location of items depends upon the area available for viewing.

RULE OF THUMB

Whenever possible use relative rather than absolute positioning. Let the viewing software perform the page layout: it's designed to do just that and is likely to be better at it than you.

1.1.6 HTML Authoring Tools

There are many tools available to help in the creation of HTML documents. Some of these are useful to all authors, especially tools which create image maps, identify the hexadecimal values of colors or combine individual GIFs into moving images. There is another category of tool which I regard as less helpful. These are the programs which are used to write actual HTML. These tend to operate exactly like typical PC word processors. The user enters text and then selects a style to apply to that text. Tools usually let the author add hyperlinks and images by entering data in popup boxes.

The more sophisticated authoring programs provide preview facilities which purport to show how the finished page will look. Unfortunately HTML is not a WYSIWYG system, it cannot be for the reasons outlined earlier. Therefore, the best that automated tools can provide is a sort of What You See Is What You *Might* Get. The tools must make assumptions about what you are trying to achieve.

Of course, software developers are always trying to improve their products. HTML authoring tools are no exception. Tools such as FrontPage from Microsoft and Dreamweaver from Macromedia bear little relation to the editors of even a couple of years ago. They include good support for scripting languages such as JavaScript, and have libraries of scripts than can be used *straight out of the box*. In many circumstances, such as when creating the typical Web *homepage*, an authoring tool is more than adequate. However, there are a number of good reasons for learning all about HTML even if you mostly use a tool.

For straightforward Web sites an authoring tool will usually provide acceptable HTML, but not always. These tools can only be as good as their developers and can make mistakes. The question then arises of how the code can be corrected: the tools cannot be used to correct the broken code because it was the tool which broke the HTML in the first place. You can leave the code as it is – large areas of the Internet are littered with broken HTML. If you understand HTML then you have the knowledge to examine the code and correct any mistakes that the tool made. Of course this leaves the problem of what happens when your corrected version of the code is loaded back into your WYSIWYG editor. The code may be rejected, flagged up as incorrect, or automatically adjusted back into the broken format that the editor expects. Frankly the process is fraught with potential pitfalls.

If you try to write more complex Web sites, possibly using frames or tables to format the site, then an automated tool is not usually going to be of any use. Your apparently simple desire to use a different format is likely to fall outside of the parameters that the editor finds acceptable. Do not despair though: as this book shows, HTML is fairly simple and you can build complex sites quite easily with a bit of practice.

For anyone who is going to build a truly dynamic Web site there is no alternative to writing HTML by hand. Dynamic sites use CGI scripts or Active Server Pages to actually build the pages on the server. These are then sent to the browser and may be unique for every user on every visit to the site. On static sites the pages are simply stored on a server and always look the same. You might wonder what is the point of building pages dynamically. Well, it gives users a more *personal* experience. You might build a large site in which users can choose to see only links to topics that interest them; your site might be commercial, with order forms, or you might have so much data that creating static pages is impractical. In all of these cases writing scripts which run on the server is your only option.

1.1.7 MIME Types and Multimedia Content

In the early days of HTML the content of Web pages was simply text based. Support for the viewing of still images began to be incorporated in one of the early versions of the Mosaic browser and since 1993 there has been development in moving the Web towards a fully multimedia environment. Web pages can now contain any of the following (incomplete) list:

- text that is formatted, colored, and structured
- still images in any graphics format
- sound
  - typically as WAV or AU files
  - MIDI files
  - CD quality audio stored in MPEG compressed format
- moving images
- animated GIFs
  - QuickTime movies made using Apple technology
  - MPEG compressed video
  - Shockwave movies created using Director from Macromedia
- files for download using file transfer protocol
- Java applets.

How, then, does the browser recognize the type of data it is receiving, and having recognized it how does it process the data correctly? The answer is MIME.

Multipurpose Internet Mail Extensions

The solution to recognizing and handling file types is not Web specific; in fact, Web browsers use a technology which was around for a number of years before HTTP (Hypertext Transfer Protocol) was designed. In the 1980s scientists at Carnegie-Mellon University in the USA recognized that e-mail users wanted to share more than plain text files. File sharing had always been done via FTP with the sender uploading the file onto an FTP site and then e-mailing the IP address of that server to the recipients. They would use FTP to download the file from the FTP server. This was not an ideal solution as it relied upon both sender and receiver having sufficient computer knowledge to cope with command-line FTP.

MIME simplifies the process. The formatted file is attached to the e-mail and when the server transmits the message it also sends information about the type of the attached file. The receiving software uses this type information to handle the attachment. For instance if the attachment was compressed using GNU-zip, the mail program would launch GNU-zip to uncompress the message.

Web browsers do exactly the same thing. When they get a MIME-compliant file they decode the MIME information and use it either to process the file themselves or to launch an external application to process the data for them.

Helper Applications

The actual Web browser can process only a limited range of data types. It can display images in GIF, JPG, PNG, or XBM formats, cannot process sound, and has no compression utilities. Therefore to process almost any multimedia data the browser needs some help. This is provided by helper applications and plug-ins. Helper applications are ordinary programs such as PKZIP or the Microsoft Windows media player which the browser can call upon for help.

Plug-ins are small applications which handle specific data types and which may either run as stand-alone applications or embedded within the browser. Generally when a software house devises a new multimedia type for the Web it will sell the authoring tool but give away the viewer for free. This is done for good commercial reasons: the easiest way to get authors to use the format is to make viewing the data easy for readers. Similarly once authors adopt a format it is important that readers can quickly, and cheaply, acquire the means to view their pages.

The free viewer model was developed by Adobe with their Portable Document Format tools Acrobat, the authoring tool, and Acrobat Reader, the viewer. Although authors must pay to buy tools to create PDF documents anyone can download the document viewer free of charge. In fact the Adobe PDF viewer is given away on the cover disks of many computer magazines.

Plug-ins are available for all of the popular data types such as QuickTime and Shockwave. Some data types which require plug-ins are international standards. An example of this is the

MPEG series which specify compression for video and audio. A range of freeware, shareware, and try-before-you-buy tools are available from Internet sites for creating, editing, and using MPEG data. The ready availability of such tools has led to the increasing popularity of these formats, especially MP3, which is being used on many Internet sites to supply CD quality music from a variety of sources.

EXERCISES

1. Briefly outline the early history of the World Wide Web.
2. Can you think of three advantages to using a common data format such as XML? What about some disadvantages?
3. What are the main Internet application protocols?
4. What is the role of the W3C?
5. List some reasons for using hypertext when creating technical documentation.
6. Why are organizations such as W3C so keen to emphasize the separation of data and its formatting?
7. Compare and contrast relative and absolute positioning of content.
8. While HTML authoring tools may aid the beginner they can create more problems than they solve. Why are such tools almost inevitably obsolete as soon as they appear?
9. What is MIME?
10. Assess the validity of the following statement:

    Within 50 years the era of the printed word will be over. On-line presentation, multimedia data, virtual reality worlds, and as yet undreamt-of new technologies will have too many advantages. The printed book cannot survive.

PART I

HTML

Hypertext Markup Language

2.1 BASIC HTML

Websites are often powerful and complex applications yet they are based upon such a simple and straightforward markup language that almost anyone with a moderate amount of knowledge can produce them. The principle which underpins HTML is to take some structured content, usually a mixture of text and images, and then add formatting instructions to it. The Web browser uses that formatting information to correctly process the content. The processing may take the form of display on the screen, sending it to a printer or reading the page aloud to a visually impaired user.

That is just like word processing really, the big difference being that we can directly edit the formatting information *in situ*. In a word processor, formatting is done using binary control codes which are not legible to, or suitable for editing by, humans. The formatting codes within a Web page are all written in plain text. One of the most important features of Web documents is that they contain *hyperlinks* which let readers navigate to other documents. Again these are entered as simple plain text. All of the complex processing needed to locate, download and display the linked page is performed transparently by the browser.

In this chapter I will show you how to write standard HTML to create well-structured Web pages which can be linked to build rich and enjoyable Websites.

The most primitive Web pages contain just text, possibly with a few hyperlinks. You will still see sites around the Web which are formatted just as pages were in the mid 1990s. These sites are often trying to impart information and their developers regard presentation as a secondary attribute. I think of such markup as basic HTML – the sort of thing that we were writing before the Web became interactive and multimedia. I will describe some of the more visual parts of HTML later but let us start off by learning about the simplest types of Web page.

2.1.1 Tags

Any formatted text document is composed of a set of elements such as paragraphs, headings, and lists. Each element has to be surrounded by control information which tells the presentation or printing software when to switch on a piece of formatting and when to switch it off. In HTML, formatting is specified by using *tags*. A tag is a format name surrounded by angle brackets. End tags which switch a format off also contain a forward slash. For instance, the following example sets the text to the style h1 and switches that style off before processing any more of the document:

```
<h1>Text in an H1 style</h1>
```

See the preface details for typefaces used in this book, and their meanings.

A number of points should be noted about HTML tags:

- tags are delimited by angled brackets: <h1>;
- they are case sensitive: <HEAD>, <head>, and <hEaD> are not equivalent. In HTML up to version 4 tags were not case sensitive. XHTML *is* case sensitive and, furthermore, tags must be in lower case letters;
- each element is terminated by an end tag. There are a few exceptions to this rule – generally elements which never contain content. Those elements which act differently will be identified when all of the components of XHTML are described later in this chapter;
- some characters have to be replaced in the text by *escape sequences*. If < was not *escaped* the software would attempt to process anything that followed it as part of a tag. Therefore if you want to include such a character in your code you must replace it with the escape sequence. There is more on all of this in Section 2.3;
- white space, tabs, and newlines are ignored by the browser, they can be used to make the HTML source more readable without affecting the way that the page is displayed. Actually they are not ignored, but multiple white spaces are replaced by a single space, while newlines and tabs are treated as spaces;
- if a browser does not understand a tag it will usually ignore it.

2.1.2 Structure of an XHTML Document

All XHTML documents follow the same basic structure. They have a head which contains control information used by the browser and server and a large body. The body contains the content that displays on the screen and tags which control how that content is formatted by the browser. The basic document is:

```
1    <html>
         <head>
             <title>A Minimal XHTML document</title>
         </head>

5
         <body>
             <h1>The Largest Heading</h1>
             <p>A sample paragraph showing formatting and
             followed by a line across the screen.</p>
10           <hr />
         </body>
     </html>
```

If you copy that code into a plain text file and save it as `test.html` you will be able to open it in a Web browser. Despite its apparent simplicity when viewed, this document contains several important features which need a little explaining for novices.

The entire document is surrounded by `<html>` ... `</html>` which tell the software that it is now processing HTML. Most Web browsers can display a number of types of content. At the very least they are able to display plain text and HTML. Documents which are stored with a `.html` extension to their file name are automatically treated as HTML files. If, for some reason, the page as saved using some other extension such as `.txt` the browser would start to read the file and when it came across something like HTML tags it would switch into HTML mode. Magically, your incorrectly named file would display as you intended. Similarly if your page was not enclosed in `html` tags, the page might be displayed as plain text with both content and formatting information on display. Web browsers are amazingly tolerant pieces of software.

If you already know something about XHTML you will now be howling that the sample document does not include an XML declaration or a Document Type Declaration. These are pieces of control information which most browsers don't currently expect to see. They are introduced in Section 3.5 once everyone has gained some HTML coding experience.

RULE OF THUMB

Although current versions of Web browsing software are tolerant of errors, future versions are not guaranteed to behave in the same way. If you want the pages you create to be viewed in the future make sure that you format your content according to the W3C recommendations.

The Web page has <head> ... </head> and <body> ... </body> sections. All of these tags are compulsory in all HTML documents that you write because of their central role in structuring the page.

Commenting Your Pages

Programmers are always encouraged to document their code through the use of *comments*. A programmer might create a working program today, see it used for months or years and then have to make changes to it. Many programming languages are fairly cryptic and if the program is complex even the original author can struggle to understand what the code is meant to do. Programming languages include a mechanism called the comment that lets developers write plain text inside their code files. This plain text is used to describe what the program does and, sometimes, how it works. It is a good idea to add comments to your HTML files. Possibly they are not needed when you are writing simple pages, but they certainly are when you start to introduce some of the advanced ideas shown in this book such as JavaScript, styles and multiple layers.

Comments in HTML documents are the same as those used by SGML and XML. Comment tags start <! and end with >. Each comment can contain as many lines of text as you like. If the comment runs over a number of lines, each must start and end with -- and must not contain -- within its body. Here's an example:

```
1    <! -- this is a comment --
     -- which is continued --
     -- here -- >


5    <! ---- >
```

Comments can be placed in either the head or body of your documents, although it seems sensible to use them as near to the feature which you are describing as possible. Good practice in programming is to use comments to describe *what* the code does rather than *how* it works. A programmer might modify the way that the code performs at a later date but they will still want the same outcome from it.

Here is one idea that you can use even as a novice HTML developer. In the head of your documents include some simple *version control* information. Software developers often place some comments which give:

- the name of the application
- a description of the purpose of the code in the file
- the name of the author
- the original creation date
- a version number
- copyright information.

I would advise you to get into the habit of doing the same thing in your Web pages. I suggest placing this information into the head section simply because it is about the file and is not intended to be displayed within the browser. Here's an example:

```
1   <html>
      <head>
        <title>Bill Smiggins Inc.</title>

5       <!-- Version Information --
        -- File: index.html --
        -- Author: Chris Bates --
        -- Creation: March 17th, 2001 --
        -- Last Modified: June 6th, 2005 --
10      -- Description: This is the introductory page on the --
        -- new corporate Web site. The layout by Chris Bates --
        -- Copyright: All material on this page is copyright --
        -- Bill Smiggins Inc. For more information see --
        -- document BS_copy03v2.Doc --
15      -->

      </head>
      <body>
        <h1>Bill Smiggins Inc. </h1>
20      <h2>About our Company... </h2>
        <p>This Web site provides clients, customers,
        interested parties and our staff with all of the
        information that they could want on our products,
        services, success and failures. </p>
25    </body>
    </html>
```

2.1.3 The Document Head

This is a brief introduction to the document head. More detail is given in Section 3.5. The document head holds control information to be used by browsers and servers. When you are just starting to write Web pages you really don't need to know what that information is, or how it is used. Actually many people never use any of the head tags except for `title` which is mandatory. As you browse the Web take a look at the source code of a few pages. You are more than likely going to find that, where control information is provided, it was placed there by a WYSIWYG editor without the author knowing!

The only tag that most authors insert in their head sections is the title.

<title> ... </title>

All HTML documents have just one title which is displayed at the top of the browser window. The title is also used as the name in bookmark files and on search engines.

To see the effect of the `title` tag look at the example of a simple Web page in Section 3.5.

The head of the document can be used to import stylesheets, files containing scripting code, for example written in JavaScript, or information about the document itself. Information about the document is called *metadata* which means data about data. You will learn more about all of these uses of the document head as you work through this book.

2.2 THE DOCUMENT BODY

I am going to concentrate on the most commonly used, or useful, tags here. There are other tags and plenty of sources of information describing how to use them. If you need more detail I advise you to go to those sources.

2.2.1 Blocks

HTML documents are structured as blocks of text, each of which can be formatted independently. A block has no meaning outside the context of a particular document. When you format some text as, for instance, an h2 heading, you are simply telling the browser what combination of font and color it should apply to the text. You are *not* defining something which can be used in searching or in creating indices. This is radically different to using a word processor. In that application, when you describe something as a level two heading, you are saying something about its role within the document. Word processors use information about things such as heading levels in their tools for outlining and the creation of tables of contents. When you read Section 3.6 you will discover that this is gradually changing as the HTML recommendation evolves into something which has wider applicability than simple Web page formatting.

The two major blocks of text in HTML documents are the paragraph and the heading. Almost all text and images in your documents will be part of either a heading or a paragraph. The exceptions are lists and tables which we will consider later.

<p [align="left"|"center"|"right"]> ... </p>

Most text is part of a paragraph of information. Every paragraph has to be explicitly tagged within the source of the document. Each paragraph can be aligned on the screen either to the left (the default option which does not need specifying), the right, or centered. Like so many things in computing, HTML tags are English words or are derived from variants of them. However, notice the spelling of *center*, HTML uses standard American English spelling rather than the British English version. Fortunately for non-English speakers, HTML has been designed to support content written in many languages and which uses many different font types. Chapter 15 takes a look at how you can *internationalize* the content of your pages.

HTML processors ignore all white space in your source documents except for spacing between words. This means that tabs, newlines, and paragraphs are not formatted as you would expect: in fact any of these that are encountered in your source code get converted into a single space character. Any spaces that you place between words will also get converted into a single space in the displayed document. To display more than one whitespace you generally use an *escape sequence*. These are described in Section 2.3, for now it is enough to know that wherever you want to place an extra whitespace character you should use the non-breaking whitespace sequence . There will be many times when you will want to use padding in your documents but you don't want to add lots of escape sequences. In these cases you should create formats in a stylesheet. Stylesheets are described in Chapter 3.

If you align a paragraph either to the right or in the center of the screen, always specify that the next paragraph is aligned to the left. Not all browsers automatically return to the default value.

```
<h1 [align="left"|"center"|"right"]> ... </h1>
<h2 [align="left"|"center"|"right"]> ... </h2>
<h3 [align="left"|"center"|"right"]> ... </h3>
```

These three are the different levels of heading that are commonly used. In fact, HTML has six levels of heading but these three are enough for most purposes. As with paragraphs they can, optionally, be moved horizontally across the screen although this should be done with care. Most readers will expect headings either in the center or on the left of the screen and putting them to the right may be confusing. All headings require an end tag.

The largest heading is <h1> which should be used for main titles. Often these will be the same as the title of the document as given in the <head> section of the page. Use <h2> and <h3> for subsections of the document. If you find that you need more levels of heading it may be a good idea to restructure your Web site into more, smaller, pages rather than present a cluttered monolithic site.

HTML elements often have *attributes*. These are items which affect the way that the element operates but are not, strictly, part of its content. The heading tags can be aligned on the screen to the left, to the right or in the center of a line. In this case each heading tag has an attribute called align which can be set to left, center, or right. In this case the attribute is optional; if it is left out the browser will, by default, align all items to the left.

In Western languages, text looks best if you left align it. If you try to center everything on the screen, the effect is slightly unnerving. You should try to make the visitor's experience of your Web site as pleasant as you can – that way they may come back again.

 All attributes have to be placed inside quotation marks. That is one of the changes which were introduced with XHTML. Most browsers will attempt to process documents where attributes are not quoted but they often struggle with styles and scripts. Use quotes and the browser will do a much better job of displaying your page.

Using attributes to control how content appears on the screen is easy to do but it is very inflexible. You will see when I discuss stylesheets that these provide many more options and that they work well with numerous different types of device. Aligning a paragraph to the right may be futile if your document is being displayed on the screen of a mobile phone which is only two hundred or so pixels across. Ideally your formatting should be flexible enough that each device displays the document to the best of its ability. For now simply be aware that there are better options and that you will soon meet them.

```
<hr [align="left"|"center"|"right"][size="n"][noshade] [width="nn%"]></hr>
```

This places a horizontal line across the screen. These lines are used to break up the page and give it a little structure. However, they should be used sparingly as too many lines waste valuable screen *real-estate* and detract from the content.

The options determine how the rule will be displayed. It can be aligned but, by default, is centered on the screen. The `size` option specifies the thickness of the rule in pixels, `noshade` draws the rule as a single thick line rather than giving it the default three-dimensional appearance. The width of the line is best given as a percentage of the available screen size. This means that if the browser window is resized the rule will resize in a logical manner. The percentage length should be placed inside quotes like this: `<hr width="50%"></hr>`.

Reducing Elements

The `<hr>` element can never contain anything. Putting text or images inside a horizontal rule is a meaningless idea. This means that the end tag always follows immediately after the opening one. XHTML lets you use a simpler form for clarity and conciseness: `<hr />`. Notice the format of the reduced element. The tag contains the name of the element followed by a forward slash. To improve readability, a space can be placed between the element name and the slash. The most common mistake when using this form is to place the slash before the name, this creates a closing tag which is not what you want.

All elements which are *empty* can be reduced in this way. I will point out the most important as we go along but you should be aware that elements such as <p /> or <h1 /> can also be reduced.

2.2.2 The Basic Web Page – A Worked Example

Throughout the book I am going to show you lots of working code. This code is *not* meant to be the greatest, most optimal code you will ever see. It demonstrates the ideas and principles which I am describing. Where appropriate I have included a screenshot of the output which the code produces. As you look through the book you will see screenshots which are taken using Microsoft Windows, Apple Macs running OS X and the GNU/Linux operating systems. I would encourage you to try the code and see for yourself that it works. This will give you good practice at structuring your code and it will give you the opportunity to play around by altering, removing and adding items to see what effect that has.

 NOTE *Almost none of the code in this book is in any way dangerous to your system. In fact I would be very surprised if there is anything in here which will damage any system. You might find that some things such as the JavaScript can crash your Web browser if you type them in wrongly, but it can easily be restarted. Don't be afraid, play around, it's the only way you'll find out what works.*

The following code is a typical example of the sort of thing you will find scattered through the book. Usually I will not introduce them as their function and purpose should be clear from the context in which they appear. This example should be used as the basis of your first Web page.

```
1   <html>
      <head>
        <title>Bill Smiggins Inc.</title>
      </head>
5     <body>
        <h1>Bill Smiggins Inc.</h1>
        <h2>About our Company...</h2>
        <p>This Web site provides clients, customers,
        interested parties and our staff with all of the
10      information that they could want on our products,
        services, success and failures.</p>
        <hr />
        <h3>Products</h3>
```

```
  <p align="center">We are probably the largest
  supplier of custom widgets, thingummybobs, and bits
  and pieces in North America.</p>
  <hr width="50%" />
 </body>
</html>
```

15

2.3 TEXT

The text on an HTML page can be altered in a number of ways: the actual font used can be changed to attempt to force the browser to use a specific font and the look of the text can be changed for emphasis. Web page authors who are worried about issues of usability and who want to create pages which work across different types of device frown upon the elements in this section. It is a really good idea to use styles wherever possible. The forthcoming XHTML 2 Recommendation even suggests that the `style` attribute will disappear, to be replaced by a new element. Unfortunately many HTML editing tools still use the elements and attributes listed here so the chances are that you will come across these at some point. Be aware that whenever you are able to write your code by hand, or if you have user-configurable tool, you should use styles.

Figure 2.1 The basic Web page

<basefont size="n">

lets you specify a minimum font size for basic text but not for headings. The size argument takes an integer from 1 to 7.

<font size="[+|-]n" color="#rrggbb">

sets the font size relative to either the default value or to any size set by <basefont>. Absolute font sizes can be forced by using an integer from 1 to 7; relative font sizes are set by using +/- 1 to 7.

The color of the text is set with the color argument. This takes a hexadecimal value which represents the amounts of red, green, and blue in the chosen color. The easiest way to discover the hexadecimal number which you need is to use a piece of software. Several of these *color choosers* are available for free download from sites around the Internet. For more information on using colors see Section 2.7.

The following code sample and Figure 2.2 show what this looks like in practice:

```
1   <html>
        <head>
            <title>Changing Font Sizes</title>
        </head>
5       <body>
            <h1>Changing Font Sizes</h1>
            <basefont size="3">
            <p>Here is some text in size three
            <p>And here is some <font size="7">larger</font>
10              <font size="+3">t</font>
                <font size="+2">e</font>
                <font size="+1">x</font>
                <font size="-1">t</font>
            </basefont>
15      </body>
    </html>
```

<b> ... **</b>**
<i> ... **</i>**
<strong> ... **</strong>**
<tt> ... **</tt>**
<sub> ... **</sub>**
<sup> ... **</sup>**

Altering the appearance of text can subtly change its meaning. If text is in a bold typeface then it is often read with added emphasis. When you are writing Web pages

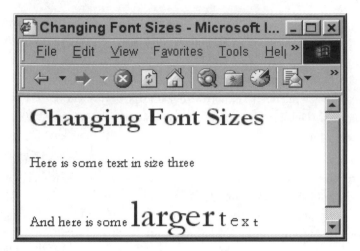

Figure 2.2 Changing font sizes

which present information you will need to use standard typographical methods of changing the appearance of text.

These should all be used with care as they can make the text unreadable. For instance you may want to emphasize something such as a warning or a special offer on a commercial site. The best way to do that is often by using color; using something such as bold font may make the text difficult to read which in turn may cause visitors to pass on, ignoring your message. On the other hand browsers on platforms such as mobile phones or PDAs, or browsers which are used by the disabled, may not be able to display your colors. These browsers depend upon the standard text formatting commands, as shown here, to change the way that they display content.

The bold and italic tags should be self-explanatory. The <strong> tag is used as a form of emphasis, usually rendered as a bold-faced font. The browser will choose an alternative if bold is not available. Therefore use <b> when you want a bold-face and <strong> to ensure the text is always emphasized. The <tt> tag lets text be rendered using a monospaced font to simulate typewriter output which can be useful if you want to include program code, for instance, on a Web page. Finally <sub> renders text as a subscript, <sup> as superscript. These can be useful when rendering mathematics although browsers are now starting to provide support for the MathML maths markup language or symbols such as @ or ©.

```
1   <html>
      <head>
        <title>Font Variations</title>
      </head>
```

```
 5     <body>
           <h1>Font Variations</h1>
           <p>We can use <b>simple</b> tags to <i>change</i> the
           appearance of <strong>text</strong> within <tt>Web
           pages</tt>. Even super<sup>script</sup> and sub<sub>
10         scripts</sub> are <em>supported</em></p>
       </body>
    </html>
```

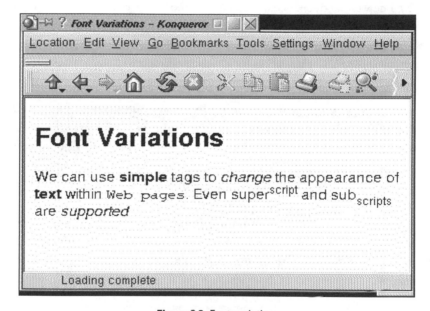

Figure 2.3 Font variations

**
</br>**

    forces a line break within a passage of text where a paragraph is not desirable. On complex pages it is sometimes useful to put a <br> before and after tables, lists, or <hr> as this simplifies rendering for the browser.

<pre> ... </pre>

    Sometimes you will want to include ready-formatted text on a Web page, for instance program code, recipes, or poetry. Inside a <pre> tag the text is only wrapped when the source has a line break and tabs or multiple white spaces are not converted to a single space.

`&amp; &lt; &gt; &quot;   &copy;`

These are character escape sequences which are required if you want to display characters that HTML uses as control sequences. When HTML finds a character such as < in the text of a page, it treats it as an instruction. Therefore you cannot display such a character simply by using it in your page. Instead you must use one of the alternatives shown here. All of these replacement sequences start with an ampersand, &, and are terminated with a semicolon.

Although double quotes usually display normally, this behavior is not guaranteed, it is safer to use `&quot;` which always behaves correctly. If you want to force a white space where one would not be used by default, you should use ` `. Figure 2.4 shows the effect of these sequences. These escape sequences are case-sensitive. A fuller list of escape sequences is given in Appendix D although it is not comprehensive since there are many thousands of sequences for Unicode characters.

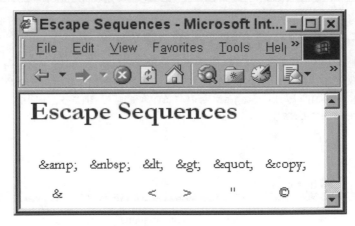

Figure 2.4 Escape sequences

RULE OF THUMB

Make your text easy to read by judicious use of different font styles. Remember that you will have to use text formatting to try to convey ideas such as humor or irony. Even simple font styling can make a lot of difference to the way that large blocks of text read on the screen. Reading from a screen is not like reading from a page so make it simple for your visitors.

2.3.1 Text Formatting – A Worked Example

```
 1   <html>
        <head>
           <title>Bill Smiggins Inc</title>
        </head>
 5      <body>
           <h3>Placing Orders</h3>
           <p> You can place <strong>orders</strong> via our
           <font color="#121212"> Web site</font> or by using the
           <font size="+2">telephone</font> if you <i>must</i>.
10         Call in person for orders &lt; 50 dollars.<br/> <i>&quot;
           We are always ready to help &quot;</i></p>

           <h3>Our Address</h3>
           <pre>
15            Unit 5,
              Tax Havens Industrial Estate,
              Enterprise City, USA
           </pre>
        </body>
20   </html>
```

2.4 HYPERLINKS

The power and flexibility of HTML comes from the simple method it uses to link documents together. The importance of the hypertext concept was introduced in Section 1.1.3, if you skipped by the introduction you might want to go back and read that now. A single tag is used for all types of links between pages. Links should be used freely within documents where they either add to the understanding of the work or can be used to reduce download times. It is better to have many links to medium sized documents containing about a screenful of information, rather than forcing readers to download a single massive document. When structuring a Web site always consider that even in these days of widespread high-speed DSL connections many users will be accessing your site via 56 Kbps modems. If a page takes a long time to download these users will go elsewhere for their information or business.

`<a href="address"> ... </a>`

The link tag has three sections: the address of the referenced document, a piece of text to display as the link, and the closing tag. The link text can be formatted using any of the text formatting options. Hypertext references, the `href` part of the tag, can be: links to documents or services at other Internet sites; links to documents within

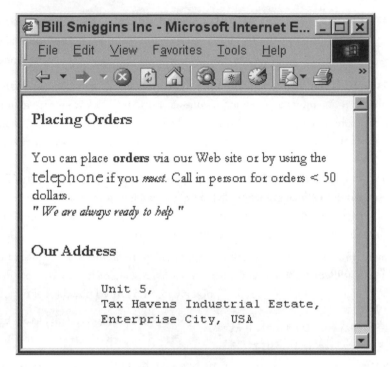

Figure 2.5 Formatted text

the same Web site; or links to a specific part of either the current page or another page. For example:

`<a href="pagetwo.html">Next Page</a>`

links to another page in the same directory. The browser displays Next Page on the screen and highlights it so that readers know it is a hyperlink. Usually this highlighting takes the form of displaying the link in blue text and underlining it.

`<a href="http://www.somesite.co.uk/index.html">Some Site</a>`

links to another Web site. This time Some Site is displayed and highlighted.

You should make the descriptive text meaningful and useful. One of the two examples I have just given is perhaps more useful than the other. The link to the next page of the document is highly context-sensitive. It depends upon the reader knowing where they are within your document. Generally this will be the case, but if someone had arrived on the third page of your document via an external link from another Web site they might need more information to help them navigate. Instead of *Next page* you could structure your document in sections and have the link be something like *Accounting Practices*.

Some Web developers use the URL of a page as the descriptive text when connecting to external sites. This works when you are linking to the top level of a site but how useful would this be:

```
www.somesite.co.uk?SID=ag2423e&SRC=23&D=050610
```

Descriptive text is important because screen readers, for example, will read it to a blind user. If the text is clear, meaningful and simple they will be able to navigate around. You may think that you will never get a blind user on your site but developing Web sites which can be used under even the most taxing of conditions means developing sites which are straightforward for every user.

A sample hyperlink is shown in Figure 2.6.

Figure 2.6 Hyperlinks

2.4.1 Relative Paths

Whenever possible relative, rather than absolute, paths should be used in hypertext links. If you want to know more about the terms relative and absolute you should consult any good reference on the UNIX operating system for a full explanation. This is a simplified guide for the timid. This description of paths uses Figure 2.7 as a template.

Basically an absolute path gives the full system path of a file. For instance, a specific file on a UNIX system could be referenced as:

```
/home/chris/public_html/writing/index.html
```

but if I were already looking at the /home/chris/public_html directory, that reference might become:

```
./writing/index.html
```

The current directory is indicated by the single dot at the start of the path. HTML uses the UNIX style of forward slashes as separators in directory paths. If I wanted to access an

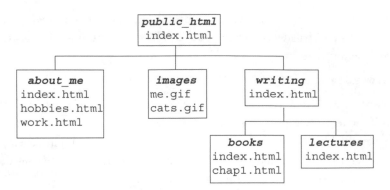

Figure 2.7 Sample site map

image in directory/home/chris/public_html/images from the writing directory I would use:

> ../images/cats.gif}

The pair of dots at the start of the path is used to indicate that a file is in the parent directory of the current one, i.e., the one *above* it in the directory tree and hence the directory which contains it. Complex paths can be created so that, for instance, a link can be created between index.html in the lectures directory and work.html in about_me, like this:

> ../../about_me/work.html

Why go to all of this trouble? Well, if you developed your Web site on your home PC you might store all files on your C drive. At first sight it would seem sensible to give the full path of each file in every link:

> c:\My Documents\webpage\inxx.html

That's fine on the local machine but what about when you transfer your Web site over to the server? The files will be placed in a totally different directory. The server may not even *have* a C drive! In fact, Your PC may not have one either, but the same principle applies to all directory structures. None of your carefully constructed links will work. Using relative paths means that the Web site can be moved from computer to computer and it will still all work perfectly.

NOTE   *All file paths in HTML use a forward slash. You might be used to using backslashes in your operating system, take a little care to get it right in your Web pages. If you do not, your site will simply not be usable.*

2.4.2 Uniform Resource Locators

Web browsers can be used to access several different services across the Internet. So that the browser knows how to process the incoming data, each service type is identified by a different URL. The commonest services that you might link to are FTP, Usenet news, and other HTML pages. All use the same format of:

```
type://host.domain/path/file
```

where `type` can be FTP, news or HTTP. A fuller description of URLs is given in Chapter 16.

2.4.3 Linking to Specific Sections

Linking to a specific section of a document is a straightforward process, but if you have many links they can become confusing. Therefore, it is a good idea to liberally sprinkle comments around these definitions so that you can maintain the code. A link has an address component and a target.

`<a href="#target"> ... </a>`

> The start of the link simply requires an address to which the browser should jump. The address is prefixed by # and has to be given a name that is unique for that document.

`<a name="target"> ... </a>`

> The target of the jump requires just the target name.

`<a href="./nextpage.html#target"> ... </a>`

> This type of link is used to go to a specific section of another document.

> Here is an example of linking to sections of a document. In the file `car.html` we might have this text:

```
As well as the <a href="./engines.html#engine"> engine </a>, cars
have <a href="#wheels"> wheels </a> ...
```

The targets would be formatted as follows:

in cars.html:

```
<a name="#wheels"> Wheels </a> are quite important
to cars.
```

in engines.html:

```
<a name="#engine"> Noisy, oily things</a> under the
<a href="./car.html#hood"> hood</a>.
```

RULES OF THUMB

Whenever possible use relative rather than absolute links. If you move a Web site to a different server or a new directory you will not have to change all of the links that you have made. Use hyperlinks to structure your site into a number of small/medium sized packets of related information. Minimize download times wherever possible.

2.4.4 Linking to Other Pages – A Worked Example

The file containing the start of the link contains

```
1   <html>
      <head>
        <title>Bill Smiggins Inc</title>
      </head>
5   <body>
        <h3>Linking to Another Page</h3>
        <p>Bill Smiggins is, of course a multi-national business.
        We even have overseas offices, well, <em>an</em> overseas
        office. If you are nearer to <i>that</i> Web server please
10      <a href="http://www.smiggins.co.uk/index.html">click here</a>.
        </p>
        <hr />
      </body>
    </html>
```

The file which is the target of the link contains nothing special. All of the work is done at the start.

```
1   <html>
      <head>
        <title>Bill Smiggins Inc</title>
      </head>
5   <body>
        <h1>Bill Smiggins Inc</h1>
        <h2>Overseas Branch</h2>
        <p>Welcome to the British Web server
        <hr width="50%"/>
10      <h2>About our Company...</h2>
```

```
        <p> This Web site provides clients, customers, interested
        parties and our staff with all of the information that
        they could want on our products, services, success and
        failures.</p>
15      <hr />
        <h3>Products</h3>
        <p align="center">We are probably the largest supplier of
        custom widgets, thingummybobs, and bits and pieces in North
        America and here in the European Union.</p>
20      <hr width="50%" />
    </body>
</html>
```

This shows that the link from the first page leads us to a second page. This second page may even be on a different server. The hyperlinking mechanism sorts it out for us.

2.5 ADDING MORE FORMATTING

That is the basics out of the way. Given what you already know you can go and build complex and informative Web sites. There is obviously more to the Web than hyperlinked content. That is where its origins lie but today Web surfers expect sites to have carefully structured content which is formatted in interesting ways. They, and we, expect that using the Web will be fun if nothing else.

It is now time to learn how to start adding color and life to a Web page. We will start by formatting data in the simplest way, the list, using tables to structure complex data before adding color and multimedia objects such as sound, applets, and animations. Finally, in this chapter I will show you how to add forms to your Web site which you can use to acquire data from users that you can send back to a Web server for detailed processing.

2.6 LISTS

One of the most effective ways of structuring a Web site or its contents is to use lists. Lists may be for something as simple as supplying a piece of information or for providing a straightforward index to the site, but could become highly complex. As an example, a commercial Web site may use pictures of its products instead of text in hyperlinks. These can be built as nested lists to provide an interesting graphical interface to the site.

HTML provides three types of list: the basic bulleted list, a numbered list, and a definition list. Each has a different use but generally the definition list is the most flexible of the three as it easily incorporates images and paragraphs of text while keeping an obvious structure.

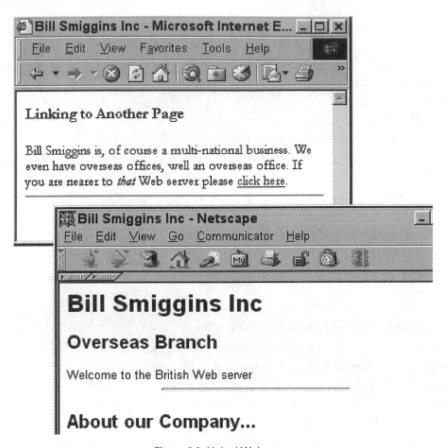

Figure 2.8 Linked Web pages

`<li> ... </li>`

The ordered and unordered lists are each made up of sets of list items. Elements of a list may be formatted with any of the usual text formatting tags and may be images or hyperlinks. The closing tag is required under the rules of XHTML, browsers which do not support XHTML will simply ignore it. Not using it will cause problems in the future as browser software becomes less tolerant of non-standard code.

`<ul [type="disc"|"square"|"circle"] [compact]> ... </ul>`

The basic unordered list has a bullet in front of each list item. List elements have to be placed within a list. A set of `<ul> ... </ul>` elements go inside a single `<li>`

. . . </li> element. Bullets do not have to be small filled-in circles. Browsers support
different types of bullet which can be specified by the type attribute. If you want to
minimize the amount of space that a list uses then add the compact attribute.

<ol [type="1"|"a"|"A"|"I"|"i"] [start="n"] [compact]> ... </ol>
An ordered list has a number instead of a bullet in front of each list item. Different
numbering schemes can be specified depending upon preference. A list can number
from any value that you desire: the starting value is given by the start attribute. As
with the unordered list, all items in an ordered list must be enclosed within <li> . . .
</li> tags.

Probably the most often used of the three list types is the unordered list. Each element
starts with a bullet point. Here is a simple example.

```
1   <html>
      <head>
        <title>Bill Smiggins Inc</title>
      </head>
5     <body>
        <h1>Product Lines</h1>

        <ul type="disc">
          <li>Widgets, sizes 2 to 12</li>
10        <li>ThingummyBobs for families and the single
          person</li>
        </ul>
      </body>
    </html>
```

<dl [compact]> ... </dl>
Definition lists are different from the previous types in that they do not use list items to
contain their members. Elements within a definition list are either items being defined
or their definitions.

<dt> ... [</dt>]
Definition terms mark items whose definition will be provided by the next data definition. They can be formatted using any regular text formatting. The closing tag is
optional, as it is assumed once a <dd> tag is reached.

<dd> ... [</dd>]
Definitions of terms are enclosed within these tags. The definition can include any
text or block formatting elements. The text of a definition is usually rendered indented

and on the line below the preceding item. Hence <dd> can be used outside a definition list to provide conventionally indented text, although this is not guaranteed to work in all browsers.

RULE OF THUMB

Lists provide a simple formatting option which can be used in many situations. They are easily understood and should be used instead of complex image maps on sites which require fast access and navigation.

2.6.1 Lists – A Worked Example

The basic unordered list and the numbered list are fairly intuitive to anyone who has used a word processor. Almost everyone will, at some point, have created a list of items or the outline of an essay or report using them. What about the definition list, though? That's not quite so easy to understand. The following code shows all three lists in action and, hopefully, you will see from its structure that the definition list is actually a very powerful construct with many applications.

```
1   <html>
        <head>
            <title>Bill Smiggins Inc</title>
        </head>
5   <body>
    <h2>Two simple lists</h2>

    <h3>Products</h3>
    <ul>
10      <li>Widgets, sizes 2 to 12</li>
        <li>ThingummyBobs for families and the single
        person</li>
    </ul>

15  <h3>Deadlines</h3>
    <ol>
        <li>Place your orders before 4:00 p.m. for next
        day delivery</li>
        <li>Order by midnight for next New Year</li>
20  </ol>
```

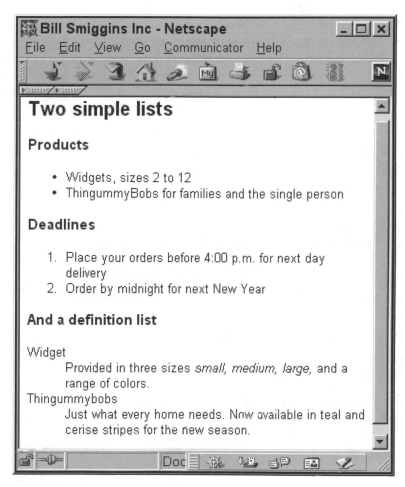

Figure 2.9 Lists

```
        <h3>And a definition list</h3>
        <dl>
            <dt>Widget</dt>
25          <dd>Provided in three sizes <i>small, medium,
            large</i>, and a range of colors.</dd>
            <dt>Thingummybobs</dt>
            <dd>Just what every home needs. Now available in
            teal and cerise stripes for the new season.</dd>
30      </dl>
        </body>
    </html>
```

2.7 USING COLOR AND IMAGES

Why are some Web pages attractive and pleasant to use while others are just a visual turn-off? It is simply that some page authors make good use of colors and images on their Web sites, while others think that either more is better or that images get in the way. The reason that people enjoy surfing the Web is that it is a mixed medium with text, images, and multimedia content.

Color is essential to the Web experience; it brings pages alive and takes them beyond the mundane. Color is also dangerous and must be used carefully. Some cautionary examples leap to mind: those Web sites that would like to be *dangerous* and so use red text on a black background which does not make for a pleasurable reading experience; and sites using white text on a dark background which sometimes prints out as blank pages.

Color can be used in a number of places on a Web page: the background can be colored, individual elements can be altered, and links which are already colored can have their colors adjusted.

To change the colors of links or of the page background, hexadecimal values are placed in the <body> tag or altered in the sylesheet. It is important to realise that people visiting your site may expect hyperlinks to be blue and visited links to turn purple. Altering these can seriously compromise the usability of your site.

```
1   <body bgcolor="#nnnnnn" text="#nnnnnn" link="#nnnnnn"
    vlink="#nnnnnn" alink="#nnnnnn">
```

The vlink attribute sets the color of links visited recently, alink the color of a currently active link. The six figure hexadecimal values must be enclosed in double quotes and preceded by a hash (#).

The colors of page elements can be altered by using the color modifier. For instance, to change the color of an individual heading you could use:

```
<h2 color="#ababab">My Heading</h2>
```

and within a table the table headers could be colored by:

```
<th bgcolor="#ababab">
```

RULE OF THUMB

Color is important to the Web experience but must be used wisely. Generally, subdued autumnal or pastel colors work best. Do not choose a set of colors that are too close together: many people set their monitors to view only 256 or 16,000 colors. Your site may look nice on your flashy 32 million color set-up but become ugly and monochrome on your visitor's display.

2.8 IMAGES

Images are the second aspect of a pleasant Web experience. The problems with images are legion if they are not used wisely. First, experienced or impatient Web surfers often switch image loading off by default, on their browsers. If your site relies on an image to get important information across, these people may never see it. Second, loading images is a slow process and if you use too many, or your images are too large, the download times can easily become intolerable.

Browsers display a limited range of image types. You can only guarantee that GIF and JPG will be displayed everywhere, although more and more browsers are now able to display the PNG format, which was intended as a free replacement for the GIF format when that was copyrighted. If you want high-quality, good compression, and lots of colors use JPG, for instance when displaying photographs. Generally, though GIFs are more common as they tend to be smaller files, lots of software can manipulate them – and can be animated.

<body background="URL"> ... **</body>**

> sets the background of your page to use the given image. Images are tiled (repeated) to fill the available space by default. If you want to use a single image across the width of a page make it 1281 pixels wide then it cannot be tiled horizontally. This is a useful technique if you have an image with a differently colored left edge and want a classy looking page. Background images tend to work best in pale greys and browns, but if they are too complex they may hide the text.

<img src="URL"|"name" height="n" width="n" [alt="string"] [align="top"|"center"|"bottom"] [usemap="URL"] />

> displays an inline image, that is an image which appears in the body of the text rather than on a page of its own or in a spawned viewer program. The height and width of the image, in pixels, tell the browser how much space to allocate to an image when displaying a page. Some browsers also use these to shrink/stretch images to fit, but generally it is safest to use the correct sizes for the image.

 It is important that you provide a piece of text to be displayed if the image is not loaded, the alt attribute is used for this purpose. Text and speech based browsers will handle this alt text to aid users understand the structure of your pages.

By default, any text which follows an image will be aligned alongside its bottom edge. You can alter this so that the first line of text displays alongside the center or top of the image. Once the text wraps it will continue below the image. If you want to be sure that a block of text is shown next to an image you must use a table. To display an image without text, make it into a paragraph:

```
<p align="center"><img src="./mygif.gif" alt="Myself"></p>
```

This is one case in which it is important to end the paragraph properly. The usemap attribute is used in image mapping which is explained below.

```
<a href="URL">text message</a>
<a href="URL"><img src="filename"></a>
```

images can also be viewed on pages of their own. The first example uses an ordinary hypertext link but the URL should point to the image file, giving its name and type, e.g. mypic.gif or mypic.jpg. In the second case we are using an image as the link to another image. This can be useful if you want to display a page of thumbnail images and allow the reader to choose which ones to view full-size. This is one way of speeding up the loading times of graphically intensive sites.

Image maps are probably the most complex, yet most visually satisfying, method of navigating around a Web site. An image map is a large picture which has areas that the reader can click with a mouse. Each clickable area provides a hypertext link. The image map has two parts: the image and a map.

```
<img src="URL" usemap="URL">
```

tells the browser to display the source image and to map the second URL, the image map, onto it.

```
<area shape="circle"|"rect"|"poly"|"default"
href="URL" coords="string" alt="string">
```

creates a clickable area on an image map. The alt text in this case is displayed by the browser as an indicator for the reader of where the link goes. If you do not supply an alt, your image map is invalid and may not be displayed. The meaning of href should be clear: it is the destination of the link. The clickable area can have one of four shapes. Each shape is defined by coordinates, pairs of integers which give locations on the image in pixels:

- The default location does not require coordinates and is used to indicate what happens if the user clicks outside of the mapped areas. Each image map can have only one default.
- A rect has four coordinates which are paired. The first pair defines the top left corner and the second pair the bottom right corner of the area.

- A `circle` is defined by its center and its radius. The center is given by a pair of values, the radius by a single value. Therefore this requires just *three* values in the coordinate string.
- A `polygon` is made from a set of coordinates with the last pair listed being joined to the first to complete the shape.

An example image map with the mapping in the same file as the image link might look like this:

```
1   <img src="./mappic.gif" usemap="#main_map"
          height=30 width=50 />

    <a name="#main_map">
5
        <map name="main_map">
            <area shape="rect" href="./images/img1.jpg"
                    alt="Image One" coords="0,0,25,25">
            <area shape="rect" href="./page1.html"
10                  alt="Page One" coords="26,26,50,50">
            <area shape=default href="./page32.html"
                    alt="Page 32">
        </map>
    </a>
```

RULE OF THUMB

Image maps load slowly and are almost impossible to use if the designer gets them wrong. It is very easy to send readers to the wrong location or to hide the links within the image so that users cannot find them. Strangely, perhaps, a complex image map can be almost more usable if readers are navigating using the `alt` *text instead of the images.*

Many sites achieve the same effect more simply by making a complex image from a set of smaller, simpler ones. Each smaller image then acts as its own hyperlink. If you do this, switch the borders off on your images.

2.8.1 Images – A Worked Example

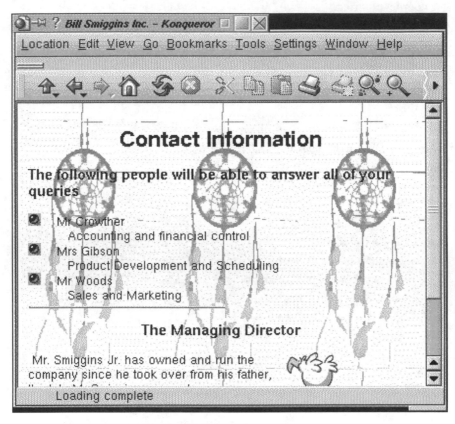

Figure 2.10 Using colors and images

```
1   <html>
      <head>
        <title>Bill Smiggins Inc.</title>
      </head>

5
      <body bgcolor="#000000" background="./Dream.gif"
      text="#000000">

        <h1 align="center">Contact Information</h1>
10      <h3>The following people will be able to answer all
        of your queries</h3>
```

```
        <dl>
            <dt><img src="./bullet.gif" alt="bullet">   
15          Mr Crowther</dt>
            <dd>Accounting and financial control</dd>
            <dt><img src="./bullet.gif" alt="bullet">   
            Mrs Gibson</dt>
            <dd>Product Development and Scheduling</dd>
20          <dt><img src="./bullet.gif" alt="bullet">   
            Mr Woods</dt>
            <dd>Sales and Marketing</dd>
        </dl>
        <hr width="50%" />
25
        <h3 align="center">The Managing Director</h3>

        <img align="right" src="./boss.gif"
            textalign="top" alt="The Boss">
30      Mr. Smiggins Jr. has owned and run the company since he
        took over from his father, the late Mr Smiggins, several
        years ago.
    </body>
</html>
```

EXERCISES

Basic HTML

1. What are HTML tags? How do the tags that switch a format on differ from those which switch it off?
2. Which tags and sections must *all* HTML documents contain?
3. How is a comment shown in HTML?
4. What is the difference between `<title>` ... `</title>` and `<h1>` ... `</h1>`?
5. Create an empty HTML file containing just the head and body sections with no content. Store this in your new directory as `template.html`. You can use this as the basis of all your pages. As you learn more about file headers you can easily update this template file.

6. Try putting a `title` and an h1 level header into an HTML file. Save the file as `test.html` remembering to use the `.html` extension. Now try to open the file inside your favorite Web browser. If you cannot do that using the `open` command of the `file` menu, read the documentation that came with your browser.

Formatting

1. How can page content be formatted horizontally across the screen?
2. Why does the browser ignore white space and newline characters in the source text for your page?
3. List the formatting options that are provided for plain text. How can the font size be changed using basic HTML rather than a stylesheet?
4. Discuss the differences between relative and absolute paths in hyperlinks.
5. When should you use relative hyperlinks, and when are absolute hyperlinks needed?
6. A hyperlink can be used to move around within a single page rather than to load another page. How is this done?
7. Open your `test.html` file, from the previous section, inside an editor. Add some paragraphs of text and h2 and h3 headers. Open the file in your browser to check how it looks. Pretty dull isn't it? Well that was how everything on the Web looked back in the early 1990s!
8. Try changing the font size for individual page elements. What effect do the emphasis tags have?
9. Now try changing the colors of some of those page elements. Use the chart in appendix C to help. Try using both hexadecimal values and the proper names of the colors.
10. Create a second page called `test2.html` in the same directory as `test.html`. Try to make a hyperlink in each one so that you can swap backwards and forwards between the two files.
11. Add a link from one of your files to a site you have used on the Web. Go on-line and test this link.
12. This final exercise is for anyone who is still confused about absolute and relative hyperlinks. Edit `test.html` and `test2.html` so that the links between them are like this:

```
<a href="c:/mypages/test.html">link text</a>
<a href="c:/mypages/test2.html">link text</a>
```

Try the links again in your Web browser. Now move the files to a temporary directory. Don't copy them, make sure they are moved. Open the files in their new location in your browser and try the links. They should not work if you have done everything correctly.

Now edit the files so that the links are relative like this:

```
<a href="./test.html">link text</a>
<a href="./test2.html">link text</a>
```

Try that in your browser. The links should now work again. Copy the two files back into your working directory and test them once more from this, their original location.

Colors and Images

1. The Web started out as a text-only medium. Now many sites are unusable if you cannot see their images. How has the increased use of images affected different groups of Web users?

2. Think about the colors that you see on Web sites. Which combinations of colors work well together, and which are unpleasant and make sites difficult to read?

3. Modify some of the pages that you have created so far, so that they have colored text and backgrounds. Play around with the colors until you get a set that looks good. (Appendix C should help.)

4. What are the most commonly encountered image types on the Web? How does the browser cope if it cannot handle an image type itself?

5. Use an image as the background to a Web page. If you do not have any suitable ones in the cache of your browser, then do a Web search. Many sites give away copyright-free images that anyone can use. Again, try a number of different combinations of image and text formatting. What combinations are generally successful?

6. Place some images on a page. There are a number of ways of getting a good layout but the easiest effects are achieved by using a table. Try to create a pleasing effect.

7. Once you have a page that looks good, use one of the images as the starting point for a hyperlink.

8. Rather than placing large images on a page, the preferred technique is to use thumbnails by setting the `height` and `width` parameters to something like 100 pixels by 100 pixels. Each thumbnail image is also a link to a full-sized version of the image. Create an image gallery using this technique.

9. What sorts of multimedia object can be hosted within a Web page? How does the HTML 4 standard support all multimedia types, even those not yet developed?

Lists

1. Create a simple HTML page which demonstrates the use of the three types of list. Try adding a definition list which uses unordered lists to define terms.

More HTML

3

Soon you will be ready to try your hands at system independent design and scripting. Not yet, though. Before you get to the complicated ideas, we are going to look at a few things which are not basic HTML and are not always needed, but which can be important on some sites. HTML ideas never get complicated enough to be called *advanced* so this chapter is more of a miscellany of topics which do not fit elsewhere.

After working through Chapter 2, you have enough material to put together a pretty interesting Web site. My personal opinion has always been that the content of a site matters most, followed by its usability, which leaves the overall design trailing at the back of the pack. Other people disagree, many professional Web *designers* place their emphasis on image and interactivity. In Chapter 15, I discuss a range of issues and ideas which are important when designing a site. This chapter looks at some things which can be used to introduce some elusive interactivity to your Web pages.

Interactive elements within Web pages range from fancy graphics, through animation created using Macromedia's Flash and Shockwave technologies, to streamed data, virtual worlds and JavaScript elements. A large section of this book looks at JavaScript which has many applications on the Web. In this chapter we will look at how you can use other types of multimedia data inside a Web page.

If you are building a complicated site, then you have to provide users with some form of navigation aid to help them find their way around. You do not want potential customers taking their business elsewhere simply because they cannot find what they want on your site. I am going to show you two ways of helping. The first uses a *frameset* to display more than one page at a time. Framesets are sometimes controversial, many Web designers and Web surfers really hate them, but they are also very useful. The alternative navigation aid uses simple hyperlinks to let users orient themselves within a site.

3.1 TABLES

The table is one of the most useful HTML constructs. You will find tables all over the Internet. Often you do not even know that the page which you are looking at is awash with tables; instead it just appears to be a very well structured site.

Tables have two uses: structuring pieces of information and structuring the whole Web page. If you want that professional look it is worth finding out how to use tables. Many of the best designed sites on the Internet are based around tables. Alternatively, you can structure a page using frames, images or stylesheets. I'll look at using frames in Section 3.3, stylesheets are covered in detail in Chapters 4 and 5. I will discuss the advantages and disadvantages of each approach in Section 15.2.

So tables are a good thing, but what are they? Well, a table is a grid of information such as you might have seen in a ledger or spreadsheet. Unlike a table from a spreadsheet, the data items in an HTML table do not need to have any kind of relationship. Unlike data in spreadsheets, you can put things in a table simply because you want to. If a table simplifies layout or formatting and you feel that you need one on your page, then you can use one.

The only consideration that you must think about is processing – most browsers struggle to process complex tables. The browsers are not optimized for tables and where tables are deeply nested on a page the browser may have difficulty a displaying the page. Web browsers have a *layout engine* which arranges the pieces before the Web page is displayed. Where the page is difficult to lay out there will be a noticeable delay before your content appears. This problem is made worse by the use of images within tables, especially where the size attributes of the image have not been set. Therefore, use tables freely but keep them as simple as possible.

Figure 3.1 shows how simple a table can be. The code which created it is pretty simple too:

```
1    <html>
        <head>
           <title>A Simple Table</title>
        </head>
5       <body>
           <h2>A Simple Table</h2>
           <table border="1">
           <tr>
              <th>Left Column</th>
10            <th>Right Column</th>
           </tr>
           <tr>
```

```
        <td>A little bit of data</td>
        <td>Rather more data in this cell which will
15      wrap around...</td>
      </tr>
      </table>
    </body>
  </html>
```

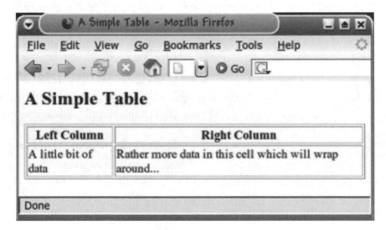

Figure 3.1 A simple table

```
<table [align="center"|"left"|"right"][border[="n"]]
[cellpadding="n"][width="nn%"][cellspacing="n"]> ... </table>
```

Everything between these two tags will be part of the table. These attributes control the formatting of the table as a whole, not that of the items in each cell. Tables can be aligned on the screen like most other items, usually they are centered for impact and clarity. A table can have a border, which includes a border between the cells. If the border attribute is not set, the table has no border. When the border attribute is set but a valid value is not given, a single, pixel-wide default border is drawn. For wider borders you must give a positive integer value.

Cellpadding, in pixels, determines how much space there is between the contents of a cell and its border; cellspacing sets the amount of white space between cells. The width attribute sets the amount of the screen that the table will use. This is best given as a percentage so that if the browser is resized the table will continue to make sense.

RULE OF THUMB

Tables can, if used carefully, provide the best way of structuring a Web page. If you are using a table to format the whole page it is best to avoid using a border and to play around with cellpadding and cellspacing to see what effects you can achieve.

```
<tr [align="left"|"center"|"right"]
[valign="top"|"center"|"bottom"]> ... </tr>
```

Each row of the table has to be delimited by these tags. The row can be aligned horizontally and vertically within the table if you want. Although the </tr> tag is strictly optional since it is obvious when rows end, you should always use it. If you are creating a complex table, which has other tables nested within it, these may be rendered incorrectly if all rows are not explicitly closed.

```
<th [align="left"|"center"|"right"]
[valign="top"|"center"|"bottom"]
[nowrap] [colspan="n"] [rowspan="n"]> ... </th>
```

These are table cells which are to be used for headings. Typically a table header will be rendered in emphasized text such as **<strong>**.

The contents of the cell can be aligned vertically and horizontally within their row; these attributes override any that were set for the row. If nowrap is set, the contents of the cell will not be automatically wrapped as the table is formatted for the screen. To prevent long lines ruining the look of your tables, use <br /> to force text wrapping.

The colspan and rowspan attributes allow individual cells to be larger than a one by one grid. It is often useful to have a heading which spans more than one column, for instance, if you are nesting headings, in which case you should use colspan. Similarly some data cells may need to be more than one cell deep and rowspan should be used.

```
<td [align="left"|"center"|"right"]
[valign="top"|"center"|"bottom"][nowrap][colspan=n]
[rowspan=n]> ... </td>
```

The basic data cells. For explanations of the options see <th>.

RULE OF THUMB

Be very careful when counting columns and rows for the colspan *and* rowspan *attributes. Get it wrong and your table will look a little weird. Spanning columns and rows gives your tables a very slick look and is very useful when the table is being used to format the page.*

3.1.1 A Table of Data – A Worked Example

```
1   <html>
        <head>
            <title>Bill Smiggins Inc - catalog</title>
        </head>
5       <body>
    <h3>Product Lists</h3>
        <table border="1" align="center">
        <tr>
            <th colspan="3" align="center"> Products</th>
10      </tr>
        <tr>
            <th><i>Name</i></th>
            <th><i>Description</i></th>
            <th><i>Cost</i></th>
15      </tr>
        <tr>
            <th>Widgets</th>
            <td>For families and the single person,<br/>
            available in three sizes: <i>small, medium, and
20          large, </i><br/> and a range of colors.</td>
            <td>12 dollars each, <br>delivery 50 dollars per
            mile.</td>
        </tr>
        <tr>
25          <th>ThingummyBobs</th>
            <td>Just what every home needs.<br/> Now available
            in teal and cerise stripes for the new season.<br/>In
            sizes 2 to 12.</td>
            <td>34 dollars per dozen.</td>
30      </tr>
```

```
    </table>
    </body>
</html>
```

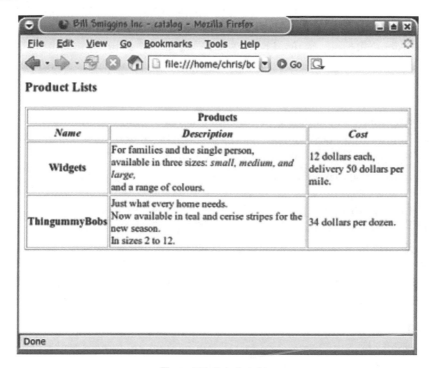

Figure 3.2 Data in tables

3.1.2 Advanced Table Elements

Tables are a very visual way of structuring data. Try reading the contents of a table to someone who cannot see it. Chances are that they will struggle to extract meaning from your words without a visual context. HTML tables can contain a number of additional elements which can help text browsers and screenreaders to make some sense from them.

<caption>string</caption>

> This element is used to provide a string which describes the contents of the table. If used it *must* immediately follow the table element.

<thead> ... **</thead>**
<tfoot> ... **<tfoot>**
<tbody> ... **<tbody>**

> The rows in a table *can* be grouped into one of three divisions. This grouping is optional. The idea is that browsers will be able to scroll the tbody section of the table without

moving either the thead or tfoot sections. When long tables extend over more than one page, the information in thead and tfoot can be automatically replicated on each page if you are printing the document. In my experience, different browsers use these elements in their own ways. Some place the thead element only at the start of the table whilst others repeat it on each page. The handling of tfoot seems to be more consistent: all browsers that I have tested place it only at the bottom of the last page of the table. Clearly relying on a correct or useful implementation of these particular elements is going to be a bad idea.

<colgroup [span="n"][width="n"]> ... </colgroup>

Columns within a table can be logically grouped together. Each group of columns can be assigned a default width which will apply to all columns which do not set one of their own. The span indicates the number of columns in the group.

col [span="n"][width="n"]> ... </col>

The attributes of individual columns are set using the col element. The span and width attributes work in the same way as for the colgroup element.

The following code shows a table which, whilst admittedly uninteresting in itself, shows how to use all of the table elements. The result is shown in Figure 3.3.

```
1   <html>
      <head>
        <title>A Comprehensive Table</title>
      </head>
5     <body>
        <h1>A Comprehensive Table</h1>
        <table align="center" width="75%" border="1">
          <caption>Comprehensive Table</caption>
          <colgroup width="30%" span="2">
10        </colgroup>
          <colgroup span="3">
          </colgroup>
          <thead>
            <tr><td colspan="5">The Table Header</td></tr>
15        </thead>
          <tbody>
            <tr>
              <td>First</td>
              <td>Second</td>
```

```
20            <td>Third</td>
              <td>Fourth</td>
              <td>Fifth</td>
            </tr>
            <tr>
25            <td>First</td>
              <td>Second</td>
              <td>Third</td>
              <td>Fourth</td>
              <td>Fifth</td>
30          </tr>
          </tbody>
          <tfoot>
            <tr><td colspan="5">The Table Footer</td></tr>
          </tfoot>
35      </table>
      </body>
    </html>
```

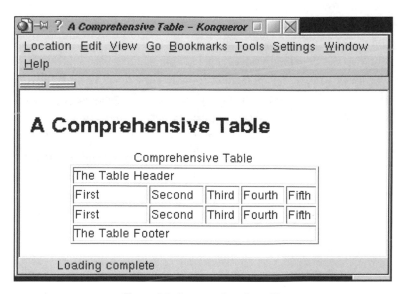

Figure 3.3 A comprehensive table

3.2 MULTIMEDIA OBJECTS

One of the biggest attractions of the Web must be the amount of multimedia data that can be presented from *within* simple text documents. You may have heard commentators over the years talking about the growing together of all types of media, well on the Web that has started to happen. This is not a universal truth, very many Web sites use only text and graphics, yet are still capable of providing effective and informative experiences to visitors. There was a trend in the late 1990s towards sites which were very interactive and heavily laden with graphics and sounds. These tended to be unpopular with visitors due to the long download times which they required and the lack of substance they provided after the wait. The trend now is towards judicious use of multimedia to *enhance* not replace textual content.

Multimedia is an all-encompassing term which can mean radically different things to different people. On the Web it is generally used to mean sound and image data, although it is probably best used to define any data which is not plain text or simple images. This can encompass everything from a JavaScript roll-over button to a fully populated three-dimensional world, taking in all types of Java applet along the way. There are good reasons for minimizing your use of multimedia data, which are covered in Chapter 15. For now let us ignore the negative and look at how you can include something a little more dynamic in your pages.

If you want to include external objects in your Web site you have a couple of choices. Images can simply be embedded in the text as shown in Section 2.8 and they will display normally because the browser understands how to process them itself. Of course I am assuming here that you are using an image type that your visitors can handle. Some data types, for instance MIDI sound or MPEG encoded movies, may be beyond the capabilities of some Web browsers.

Typically Web site developers have included complex data items as hyperlinks and left the browser to *spawn* an external application to handle the data. This may involve running an application outside the browser as happens with players for streamed data in Real audio and Real video formats. Other applications may be opened embedded inside the browser. Figure 3.4 shows Microsoft's PowerPoint presentation application opened inside Internet Explorer 5 and displaying one of my lectures. The differentiation between these approaches depends upon the configuration of the browser and the type of data. If you are listening to a radio broadcast over the Web using Real Player, you probably want to be able to continue surfing at the same time. Tying up a whole browser window would be a waste of screen space and system resources so you often get something like Figure 3.5 instead. However, sometimes the Real Player *can* be embedded inside a browser window. Figure 3.6 shows this being done.

3.2.1 Including Objects

HTML has an `object` element which is used to embed multimedia objects directly into the page. It is possible that in a future version of HTML the `img` tag will be fully replaced by `object` and, for sites that will be visited only by surfers using HTML compatible browsers, it may be safely replaced now.

Figure 3.4 Microsoft powerpoint inside internet explorer

```
<object classid="URL" data="URL" [codebase="URL"]
type="string" [standby="string"] height="n" width="n"
[title="string"]> ... </object>
```

Each object requires a classid which identifies the URL of the object. The codebase parameter is optional. It identifies the directory which contains the object but if it is not supplied, the full URL can be placed in the classid parameter. If classid has only a file name, the object is assumed to be in the same directory as the HTML page.

When an object needs command-line parameters these can be passed in through the param tag, which is defined below.

The type parameter is used to specify the MIME type of the object. This information can then be used by the browser to launch pre-set helper applications. For many data types no helper will have been established and in these cases the type tag is

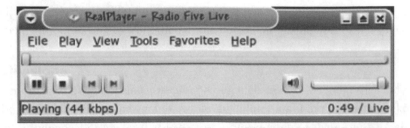

Figure 3.5 Separate real player

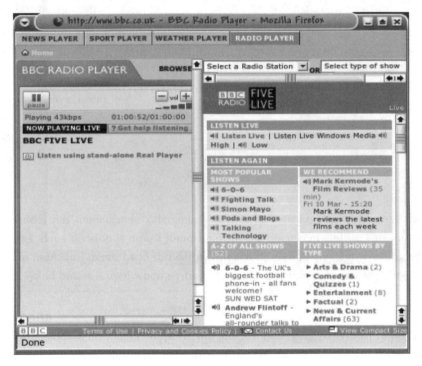

Figure 3.6 Embedded real player

redundant. Most objects must have their `height` and `width` defined so that the browser can allocate screen space to them. Finally, the `standby` parameter is used to display alternative text while the object itself is being downloaded from the server.

```
<param name="string" value="string" type="string"
valuetype=["ref"|"object"|"data"]>
```

Each parameter needs a `name` which corresponds to the name that the object expects to receive. The `value` parameter specifies the value that will be passed into the object. However, the value passed does not have to be numerical or textual. `valuetype` is used to tell the browser the format of each parameter, which can be an actual piece of data (data), the URL of a piece of data (ref) or another object (object). If the valuetype is set to ref then the browser needs the MIME type of the data. This is set through the type parameter.

Almost every Web page or online tutorial that you look at uses img elements to include graphics within a page. Using the object element provides a single consistent approach which you can use for many types of embedded data. The object element has many attributes as you have just seen, and choosing the correct ones can be difficult. The following code demonstrates those that you will need for a simple image. Notice that, although the element definition does not include an alt attribute, one is available. You should always use it.

```
1   <?xml version="1.0" encoding="UTF-8"?>
    <!DOCTYPE html
        PUBLIC "-//W3C//DTD XHTML 1.0 Strict//EN"
        "http://www.w3.org/TR/xhtml1/DTD/xhtml1-strict.dtd">
5
    <html xmlns="http://www.w3.org/1999/xhtml"
        xml:lang="en"
        lang="en">
         <head>
10            <title>Objects</title>
         </head>

         <body>
          <table border="1">
15          <tr>
             <th>Using <tt>img</tt></th>
             <th>Using <tt>object</tt></th>
            </tr>
            <tr>
20           <td>
                 <img src="./logo.png" height="80"
                     width="320" alt="Bill Smiggins Inc." />
              </td>
             <td>
25              <object data="logo.png" height="80"
                        width="320" type="image/png"
                        alt="Bill Smiggins Inc." />
              </td>
```

```
            </tr>
30      </table>

        </body>
    </html>
```

The following example shows how an arbitrary script object might be embedded within a page. Here a single parameter is being passed in to some embedded Python code.

```
 1  <html>
        <head>
            <title>An Embedded Object</title>
        </head>
 5      <body>
            <h1>An Embedded Object</h1>
            <p>The next paragraph contains an object and
            some parameters</p>
            <object height="50" width="250"
10                  classid="http://www.smiggins.com/objects/greet.py">
                <param name="greetee" value="Bill Smiggins"
                    valuetype="data">
            </object>
        </body>
15  </html>
```

3.2.2 Applets

Java applets are small applications written in the Java programming language. They have limited functionality and run under strict security conditions within HTML pages. HTML has a legacy applet element which is now deprecated. Its role has been subsumed into object. For backwards compatibility it may be necessary to retain use of applet in the short term. You will also see this tag used very widely if you ever use any Java programming texts and, hence, I will discuss it briefly here. Whilst applet was a Java-specific tag, object supports all non-native data and hence presents the possibility that in future applets themselves may be written in languages such as Visual Basic, JavaScript or even C++.

```
<applet code="classfile" [name="string"] width="n"
height="n" [codebase="URL"]>
```

The browser needs to understand a number of things about the Java applet before it can be run. Firstly it needs to know where to get the file from, this information is optionally supplied by the `codebase` parameter. If no `codebase` is given the applet is assumed to come from the same directory as the HTML page. Java applets are compiled into an interpretable form called classfiles. Each applet has a classfile from which it is initiated, the name of which *must* be given to the browser so that the applet can be executed. Applets can optionally be given unique names to identify them on the page through the `name` parameter. This means that the applet can be referred to by other objects, applets, and scripts executing on the same page.

Some, but not all, applets require command-line parameters. These are passed to it by the parameter object and work in exactly the same way as for the HTML 4 `object` tag.

Finally, the browser needs to know how much space it should allocate to the interface of the applet. This is done by the `height` and `width` parameters.

Here are two code samples showing the use of the `applet` tag to include some Java, and then the same thing rewritten to use `object`. Figure 3.7 demonstrates the running Java applet.

```
1   <html>
       <head>
          <title>A Simple Applet</title>
       </head>
5      <body>
          <p>Here is the SimpleAWTApplet</p>
          <p align="center">
             <applet code="SimpleAWTApplet.class"
                     width="200"
```

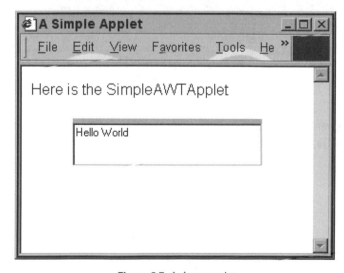

Figure 3.7 A Java applet

```
10                      height="50">
              </applet>
          </p>
      </body>
  </html>
```

```
1   <html>
      <head>
          <title>A Simple Applet</title>
      </head>
5     <body>
          <p>Here is the SimpleAWTApplet</p>
          <p align="center">
              <object code="SimpleAWTApplet.class"
                      width="200" height="50"
10                    alt="Simple Java Applet" />
          </p>
      </body>
  </html>
```

3.3 FRAMES

If you want a complex page structure but do not feel confident using a table to create it, your choices are a combination of divs and stylesheets or frames. You will discover in Chapter 4 that the first alternative requires complex code – and does not work terribly well across the complete range of browsers and devices. This leaves frames which can be annoying and unpleasant if you are not careful. Originally an extension of HTML from Netscape, frames are supported in most browsers and are part of the XHTML specification.

If you want to use frames within your site you will need to change the DTD to:

```
<!DOCTYPE html
    PUBLIC "-//W3C//DTD XHTML 1.0 Frameset//EN"
    "http://www.w3.org/TR/xhtml1/DTD/xhtml1-frameset.dtd">
```

Frames provide a pleasing interface which makes your Web site easy to navigate but there are a number of problems if you use them. These problems are covered in Section 15.2. If you're unsure about what frames actually *are* then skip ahead and look at Figure 3.8. When we talk about *frames*, what we are really referring to is a *frameset* which is a special type of Web page. The frameset page contains a set of references to HTML files, each of which is displayed inside a separate *frame*. All of the pages within a frameset are displayed inside the same browser window and can actually be made to appear to be a single page.

Because frame-based sites display more than one page at the same time, they can be complex to set up. Once the layout is established, frame-based sites can require less maintenance than alternative approaches. This is simply because the index is usually in one frame with page content displayed in another. If new pages are added to the site, their details are only added to the index. Non-frame sites tend to place an index on every page so that as new pages are added, or removed, all of the existing content needs editing.

A frame-based page is actually made from a set of documents, each displayed in its own frame. Each sub-document can have its own scrollbars and can be loaded, reloaded, and printed as if it were occupying the whole screen. Frames can be rather confusing and only really make sense when you see them in action. First I will define the tags that are needed, then present some examples.

`<frameset [cols="%,%"] [rows="%,%"]> ... </frameset>`

This tag determines how the screen will be divided between the various frames that you are using. You can have as many frames either vertically or horizontally as you want. Each has to be allocated a percentage of the screen. You can also nest framesets so that individual rows or columns can themselves be broken up into frames.

RULE OF THUMB

If you use several frames you will be occupying screen real-estate with information-free furniture such as scrollbars. Most people will be using a PC monitor set to 1024 by 768 pixels and will not be happy to see too much of that stuff when really it is your content they are after. Use frames sparingly.

`<frame [name="name"] src="filename"`
`[scrolling="yes"|"auto"|"no"] [frameborder="0"|"1"]>`

The `src` attribute works like an image source or a hyperlink address. It should point to a valid HTML file or image which can be displayed within the frame. It is a good idea to name your frames, as we shall see in the examples. If you know that you will not want a scrollbar on a frame, then you can force the browser not to use one, similarly you do not have to have borders on every frame – setting the `frameborder` attribute to 0 stops it being displayed.

`<a href="source" target="n">`

To ensure that pages display in the *correct* frame we need to extend the basic address tag. We need to add the target attribute, which takes the name of the frame that we are going to use, to display the information.

3.3.1 Frames – A Worked Example

You have already seen the two pages being displayed. The file company.html was used in Section 2.1 and the file orders.html in Section 2.3.1. Figure 3.8 shows what this frameset looks like in Netscape Navigator.

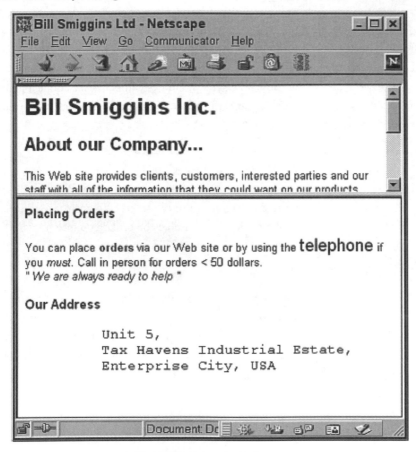

Figure 3.8 Using simple frames

```
1  <html>
     <head>
        <title>Bill Smiggins Ltd</title>
     </head>
5  <frameset rows="25%,50%">
        <frame name="A" src="./company.html" />
        <frame name="B" src="./orders.html" scrolling="no" />
     </frameset>
   </html>
```

3.3.2 Iframes – Frames Within Pages

Frames do not have to occupy large areas of the screen. A frame can be embedded within a document and used to include the content of other hyperlinked documents. One common way of structuring a large wordprocessed document is to break it into a number of small files which are brought together by including them in a single framework. Each file can be worked on separately without affecting the whole piece of work.

HTML pages can be constructed in exactly the same way. When we look at the programming languages Perl and PHP we will see technologies which can build a single HTML page from a set of scripts, each of which is itself a complete document. Those approaches use dynamic creation of documents by scripts which execute on the Web server. The HTML *iframe* element lets the browser client access documents which are addressable through URLs and then display those documents in a single page. URLs can be used to identify many types of resource from images to text pages. These resources may be content which is static and simply returned by a server or dynamically created on-the-fly before being sent to the browser.

The iframe element has a similar purpose to the object element. It permits the inclusion of resources within pages without changing the resources themselves. The most important difference between the two elements is that iframes can be used as the targets of address elements. This means that hyperlinks can be used for movement between pages, within pages and into included content.

```
<iframe [name="string"] src="URI" [scrolling="yes"|"auto"|"no"]
[frameborder="1"|"0"] [height="nn"] [width="nn"]
[marginwidth="nn"] [marginheight="nn"]></iframe>
```

The iframe element has many of the same attributes as the non-inlined frame. The most important is src which takes the URI of the page being included as its value. The name attribute gives an optional text string which can be used as the target of hyperlinks. The other attributes control the visual presentation of the iframe. The iframe may be presented in an area which is smaller than its content, in which case scrollbars can be added. By default, scrollbars are provided when needed but authors can specify that they are always used or that they are never used.

Most browsers will display the HTML page or other resource. If the browser does not support frames or has been set up so that frames are not displayed within it, the content of the iframe element will be displayed instead of the resource. If you are using iframes you should always provide some alternative information as element content for these occasions.

Iframes – An Example

We have already seen how frames are used. The inline frame is very similar except that it can be displayed anywhere in the page. This example is very simple. In Chapters 4 and 5 you will see how cascading stylesheets can be used to alter the appearance of the frame and its content.

 The text in this example is taken from the Project Gutenberg version of "Roman Farm Management" by Marcus Porcius Cato. Gutenberg provides electronic copies of over 16,000 out of copyright works and can be accessed at http://www.gutenberg.net.

```
1   <html>
      <head><title>Roman Farm Management</title></head>

    <body>
5       <iframe src="iframeLatin.html" width="40%">Latin salutation</iframe>

        <h2>Of the hands</h2>

        <p>LVI The following are the customary allowances for food: For the
10      hands, four pecks of meal for the winter, and four and one-half for the
        summer. For the overseer, the housekeeper, the waggoner, the shepherd,
        three pecks each. For the slaves, four pounds of bread for the winter,
        but when they begin to cultivate the vines this is increased to five
        pounds until the figs are ripe, then return to four pounds.</p>
15
    </body>
    </html>
```

The main page is a simple HTML document. In this example the iframe element has been placed at the top of the body. This will put the inline frame and its contents at the top of the displayed page. The content of the iframe is given here for completeness. Notice that it is a valid HTML document in its own right. The content is styled so that it can be easily distinguished in the accompanying screenshot, Figure 3.9. A version of the same documents with more styling applied is shown in Section 4.7.1.

```
1   <html>
      <head>
        <title>Roman Farm Management</title>
```

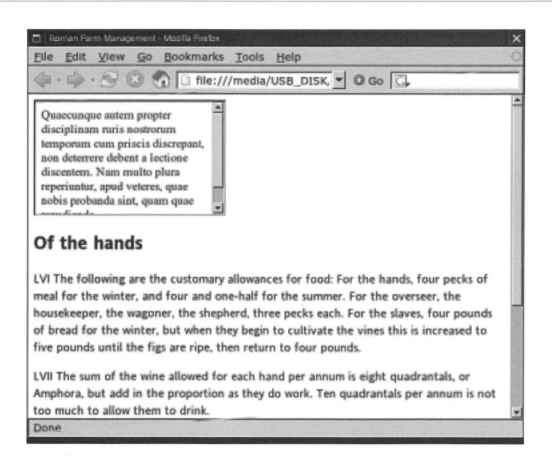

Figure 3.9 Using inline frames

```
    </head>

5

    <body style="font-family: serif">
        <p>Quaecunque autem propter disciplinam ruris nostrorum temporum
        cum priscis discrepant, non deterrere debent a lectione
        discentem. Nam multo plura reperiuntur, apud veteres, quae nobis
10      probanda sint, quam quae repudianda.</p>

    </body>
</html>
```

3.4 FORMS – TOWARD INTERACTIVITY

Forms are used to add an element of interactivity to a Web site. They are usually used to let the reader send information back to the server but can also be used to simplify navigation on complex Web sites. As with my discussion of frames I will outline the elements of the form first, describe how they work, and then give examples.

First a word of warning. If you use fill-out forms, then you will need to have programs running on the server which can process the information that you are sent. Web browsers can be configured to pass form data to an email program so *it* can be used to send the data elsewhere. I will be covering the Perl language later in this book before discussing CGI scripting. Forms can be written so that email is used to transfer data from the Web browser to the email account of the sites owner or administrator. Clearly this is unreliable since it only works if visitors to the site have their browser set up to handle email. If your site runs on a server which does not support CGI scripting then this alternative may be better than not collecting data from visitors.

If you want to use forms, check with the system administrator of your server that you are allowed to run CGI scripts, and if you are find out which languages they allow. CGI scripting raises issues of technical support and security which many Internet service providers (ISP) would rather not address. Clearly, forms and scripts are important for commercial Web sites so look around before selecting your ISP.

`<form action="URL" method="post"|"get"> ... </form>`

All forms are encapsulated like this. A form can contain virtually all other markup tags but cannot be nested within another form. The `action` attribute specifies the name, and location, of a CGI script that will be used to process the data.

Data can be sent in one of two ways: `post` or `get`. A fuller discussion of this can be found in Chapter 10. Basically, you should use `get` to retrieve information from a server and `post` to send information *to* a server. The choice of approach is made by the `method` attribute. When `get` is used, the data is included as part of the URL. The `post` method encodes the data within the body of the message. Post can be used to send far larger amounts of data, and is far more secure, than `get`. Post is also capable of sending a wide variety of character sets but `get` can only return ASCII data. If you expect to get data written in non-English languages then use `post`.

`<input type="text"|"password"|"checkbox"|"radio"|"password"|`
`"submit"|"reset"|"button"|"image"`
`name="string" [value="string"] [checked] [size="n"]`
`[maxlength="n"] [src="URL"]`
`[align="top"|"bottom"|"middle"|"left"|"right"]>`

The chances are that, if you want to get data from visitors, then you are going to use some variant of an input *widget* (the components in graphical toolkits which are to build the interfaces to programs). Several types of input widget such as text fields, radio buttons, and check boxes, exist. You will be used to these widgets from other applications which you have used such as word processors, Web browsers or email clients. I am going to give some more details of the widgets so that you are clear about their use in an HTML form:

- text creates an input device up to size characters long and is able to accept up to maxlength characters as input. If value is set, that string will be used as the default text. These fields support only a single line of text, if you need a to accept a larger amount of text then use a textarea.
- password works exactly like text but the input is not displayed to the screen. Instead each character is replaced by * (an asterisk). The password is not encoded but is sent to the server as plain text and hence provides very little real security but is a useful way of tracking your users.
- radio creates a radio button. These are always grouped: buttons within a group should have the same name but different values. The CGI script differentiates them by name + value.
- checkbox produces a simple checkbox. It will be returned to the server as name=on if checked at submission.
- submit creates a button which displays the value attribute as its text. It is used to send the data to the server.
- reset also creates a button but this one is used to clear the form.
- image can be used to place a picture on the page instead of a button. This is a simple way of brightening an otherwise dull form. Use the align attribute to control the positioning of the image.

<select name="string"> ... </select>

It is often very useful to have a list of items from which the user can choose. The tag encloses a set of options and, when sent to the server, the name of the particular select tag and the name of the chosen option are returned.

<option value="string" [selected]> ... </option>

The select statement will have several options from which the user can choose. The values will be displayed as the user moves through the list and the chosen one returned to the server. If an option has selected set it will be the value chosen initially when the form appears.

<textarea name="string" rows="n" cols="n"> ... </textarea>

creates a free format plain text area into which the user can enter anything they like. The area will be sized at rows by cols but will support automatic scrolling.

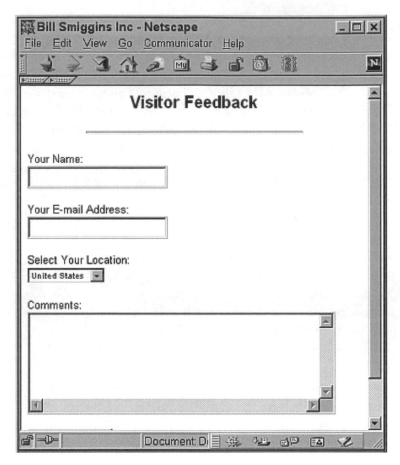

Figure 3.10 Getting information via a form

3.4.1 Forms – A Worked Example

This is a very simple form. It is shown in Figure 3.10. If you want to include a long list such as all countries or all US states, these are widely available to download on the Web. If you are going to provide a list of 200 or more countries then consider how it will be used. For example, is it reasonable to expect that a user from Kyrgyzstan, where the official languages are Kyrgyz and Russian and the alphabet is Cyrillic, to be able to scroll down your list and find their country using the English language and alphabet? There are no easy answers to this, which is why so many Websites assume that everyone is American.

```
1   <html>
      <head>
        <title>Bill Smiggins Inc</title>
      </head>
5     <body>
```

```
      <h2 align="center">Visitor Feedback</h2>
      <hr width="65%" />

      <form action="http://www.smiggins.com/cgi-bin/guest.cgi"
        method="post">
10      <p align="left">Your Name:
          <input type="text" maxlength="32" size="16" />
        </p>

        <p align="left">Your E-mail Address:
15        <input type="text" maxlength="32" size="16" />
        </p>
        <p align="left">Select Your Location:
          <select name="country" size="1">
            <option value="United States" selected>United
              States</option>
20          <option value="Mexico">Mexico</option>
            <option value="Canada">Canada</option>
            <option value="Brazil">Brazil</option>
          </select>
         </p>

25
        <p>Comments:<br/>
          <textarea name="comments" rows="5" cols="35" />
        </p>
        <p align="center">
30        <input type="submit" name="feedback" value="Submit Details" />
        </p>
      </form>
      <hr width="65%" />
    </body>
35 </html>
```

3.5 THE HTML DOCUMENT HEAD IN DETAIL

I introduced the document head in Section 2.1.3. The head is a very important part of any HTML page: it contains lots of control information that is needed by browsers and servers. Actually, having said that you *could*, and many people *do*, write HTML pages with nothing more complex than a title in the head section. If you want to use scripts or stylesheets, or provide information to search engines, then the simple head section is not appropriate: you need to use some of the tags that are discussed here.

We must begin our exploration of the advanced features of XHTML at the top of the document. Back in Section 2.1.3 we saw a very simple HTML page, which lacked a couple of important pieces of information. Every valid XML document has to begin with an XML declaration. This indicates the version of XML, you will always set this 1.0, and the encoding. The encoding indicates the set of characters which may be used in the document. Typically this is one of the Unicode variants. If you do not know which variant is used in your locale then it is likely that UTF-8 will be a good starting point.

```
1   <?xml version="1.0" encoding="UTF-8"?>
    <!DOCTYPE html
        PUBLIC "-//W3C//DTD XHTML 1.0 Strict//EN"
        "http://www.w3.org/TR/xhtml1/DTD/xhtml1-strict.dtd">
5       <html xmlns="http://www.w3.org/1999/xhtml"
            xml:lang="en"
            lang="en">
      <head>
          <title>A Minimal XHTML document</title>
10      </head>

        <body>
          <h1>The Largest Heading</h1>
          <p>A sample paragraph showing formatting and
15        followed by a line across the screen.</p>
          <hr>
        </body>
    </html>
```

After the XML declaration, the document type must be specified so that XML tools can understand and work with it. a validating XML parser will compare the structure of the document against the structure which is defined in the DTD. If it finds errors then your document needs repairing.

There are three possible DTDs for XHTML documents. The most common variant, XHTML transitional, is shown below.

```
1   <!DOCTYPE html
        PUBLIC "-//W3C//DTD XHTML 1.0 Transitional//EN"
        "http://www.w3.org/TR/xhtml1/DTD/xhtml1-transitional.dtd">
```

The transitional DTD is a halfway house between HTML 4 and full blown XHTML. If you are converting existing documents or working in environments which have a mix of old and new documents, then the transitional DTD is a good choice. When you are working on new sites which are going to be used in modern browsers or on devices such as PDAs or mobile phones then you should aim to create documents which conform to the strict XHTML standard. The three XHTML DTDs are:

1. strict
2. transitional
3. frameset.

You should only use `frameset` if your site uses frames. Many people frown on the use of frames on accessibility grounds and they are rarely used these days. You probably will not ever need to use the frameset DTD but it is useful to know that it exists.

DTDs list the rules which must be obeyed if a document is going to conform to the HTML recommendation. Each has a different use but generally you should try to create pages which are as compliant as possible. The easiest way of finding how compliant your pages are is to use a *validator*. W3C provide one at their Web site which is fast and fairly straightforward. Current Web browsers are tolerant of poorly written, and even severely broken, HTML, but that behavior cannot be guaranteed in future. Complying with the recommendations is arduous but not too difficult, you ought to get into the habit of including DTDs and checking your pages as soon as possible.

The final change that has been made to the simple HTML document is to alter the html element.

```
1  <html xmlns="http://www.w3.org/1999/xhtml"
         xml:lang="en"
         lang="en">
```

Three attributes have been added. XML documents can contain elements which are defined in a number of different document types, for example, there may be equations created using MathML or SVG images. These different document types may include elements which have the same name but different meanings. Namespaces are the way in which these elements are kept semantically separate from each other. The `lang` element tells Web browsers which language was used to define the elements and attributes in the document. The `xml:lang` element plays the same role where the processing application is an XML processor.

3.5.1 Control Information

The head of the document contains control information to be used by servers and browsers. It contains the title of the document which will be displayed at the top of the browser and, optionally, a list of keywords, a description of the document, any files to be linked into the document, and information about how the document was prepared.

```
1   <! doctype html public "-//w3c//dtd html 4.0//en"
        "http://www.w3.org/TR/PR-html4.0/loose.dtd">
    <html>
        <head>
5       <base href="http://www.smiggins.com">
        <link rel="Stylesheet"
            href="./test.css"
            type="text/css"
            media="screen">
10      <meta name="author" content="Chris Bates" >
        <meta http-equiv="expires"
            content="Wed, 05 Dec 2001 23:29:05 GMT">
        <meta name="description"
            content="On-Line Catalogue for Bill Smiggins Inc.">
15
        <title>Bill Smiggins Inc. On-line Catalogue</title>
        </head>
        <body>
        </body>
20  </html>
```

<title> ... **</title>**

> All HTML documents have just one title which is displayed at the top of the browser window. The title is also used as the name in bookmark files and on search engines. The HTML recommendation makes clear that valid HTML documents *must* have a title. This should provide meaningful information since you have no way of knowing how your page will actually be accessed. Something like *Bill Smiggins Inc. On-line Catalogue* has far more meaning and is far more useful than *Index* for instance. The title element has to be made available to users by whatever device they are using.

<base href="URI">

> This tag is used to enforce relative links. Linking between pages and documents will be explained in detail in the body section. This tag is optional.

<link rel="type" href="URI" type="string" media="string">

> The link tag is used to allow other documents to be linked to, or included in, the current document. This tag has not commonly been used but it is important and useful when using stylesheets. I will be discussing this in more detail in Chapter 4. This tag is optional.

```
<meta name|http-equiv="string" content="string">
```

Any information which describes the whole document should be included using one of these two alternatives. There are many possible meta tags, in fact you can create as many of your own as you need to adequately describe your document. You should use the name attribute for meta-data which you are defining. Meta tags can take a URI as a parameter, usually this will be inside the content attribute.

The http-equiv attribute is used to define meta-data which are intended to be part of an HTTP response message. Such messages are defined as part of the HTTP specification so you cannot simply invent your own.

The first two meta tags in the Bill Smiggins example indicate the author of the document, which is useful for version control, and an expiry date which tells the browser to reload from the server rather than using a cached version of the page after the specified date and time.

The third meta tag in the example gives a description of the document to be used by Web search and indexing engines. If it is not used they will include the first few lines of the actual document in their catalogue. It is possible to force a Web engine to see only the main page of your site in which case such descriptions become essential. This tag is optional. You can also define a set of keywords which will be used by indexing systems, robots and crawlers as they gather information.

3.6 XHTML – AN EVOLUTIONARY MARKUP

Most HTML authors, especially those using tools such as Dreamweaver, are currently writing HTML 4 which adheres more-or-less to the Recommendation. The W3C has moved the goalposts by introducing XHTML. They are now working on version 2 and authors must now play catch-up with a target that is getting further away. This section is meant to provide a quick guide to XHTML for authors who know some HTML 4.

It is important that you write pages which adhere to the standards and which are based around the latest standards that are available. Current Web browser technology is very forgiving. Major browsers such as Internet Explorer have been designed to display pages which contain invalid HTML. In fact you can get Explorer and Netscape Navigator to show pages which struggle to be identified as HTML at all. These pieces of software are a credit to their developers. Unfortunately, because they are so forgiving, Web developers have had little incentive to write compliant pages. That is all changing.

The big buzz in the on-line industry at the moment is not some new tag or a new scripting technology. Many of the big players are getting very excited indeed about the possibility of delivering on-line content to a range of new devices but predominantly to mobile telephones. A state-of-the-art Dynamic HTML page may look good on a PC screen, it may perform scripted miracles with a fast processor but it will not work on these next-generation devices.

Instead it is likely that we will see two parallel versions of the Web running side-by-side. The existing computer-based Web undoubtedly meets the needs of many users but it has severe limitations for Web surfers using mobile devices to access content.

When manufacturers create a new type of device, such as the Web-enabled phone, they can choose to make it compatible with existing practice or to push developers toward best-practice. A protocol called Wireless Application Protocol (WAP) has already been created to control content delivery to mobile browsers. These new systems will require compliant HTML. Devices with limited processing capabilities must be able to understand a document and ignore those parts which they cannot handle. Next generation developers cannot expect that the client-side software will cover up their limitations.

3.6.1 The XHTML Document

XHTML[1] is an application of XML. Therefore all XHTML documents must be capable of being generated by XML editors and of being parsed by XML parsers. You may be worried that your browser will be unable to support XHTML pages. In fact the more recent versions of both Explorer and Mozilla, including variants such as Firefox, should have few problems handling compliant XHTML.

The following discussion requires familiarity with XML terminology. If you are unfamiliar with XML ideas, please read Chapter 14 before this section.

Control Data

The actual tags that are used to mark up XHTML documents have not changed from HTML 4. What has changed is how those tags are used. I will examine the changes in the next section. First, though, I will look at the control information which you must place into your Web pages as you move toward XHTML.

Using An XML Declaration

Not all XML documents start with an XML declaration. The declaration tells applications that they are handling XML and which particular version of the standard has been used in the markup. The application is then able to make informed decisions about how it handles the markup. For instance it may choose to bypass tags which it does not understand, or it may choose to flag them as errors. In XML, parser applications which validate documents are supposed to stop when they encounter an erroneous tag and may display an error. Other

---

[1]The XHTML recommendation can be downloaded from:
http://www.w3c.org/TR/2000/REC-xhtml1-2000126

types of application are supposed to render all tags that they can and display the content of tags which they are unable to render. Where they encounter attributes which they do not understand, those attributes should be ignored. Clearly, knowing what your application is dealing with is important. Hence the use of the XML declaration. Start your XHTML documents with the following statement:

```
<?xml version="1.0" encoding="UTF-8">
```

This statement makes it clear to the application that it is handling XML and tells it how the characters within the document were encoded.

The New Document Type Definitions

XML documents must have Document Type Definitions (DTDs). These are used by validating parsers to check that the markup has been used correctly. DTDs are available for versions of HTML but have rarely been used by authors. Some of the HTML editing tools automatically include an appropriate DTD in the document but few authors pay much attention to their presence. XHTML documents have to have a DTD.

All XHTML DTDs take the same format:[2]

```
1  <!DOCTYPE html
      PUBLIC "-//W3C//DTD XHTML 1.0 Transitional//EN"
      "DTD/xhtml1-transitional.dtd">
```

There are three different DTDs to choose from. Replace transitional from the example with the one you want to use:

- transitional should be used in pages which include some presentational markup such as <font> tags. These documents will be accessible to browsers which do not understand stylesheets, for instance.
- strict is used when you want your document to be fully compliant with the standard. All presentational control is done through the use of cascading stylesheets.
- frameset lets you partition the screen into a number of separate frames.

The Expanded HTML Element

The top-level node of an XHTML document *must* be an <html> node. In previous versions of HTML this tag was used to carry control information about formatting and events such as onLoad. It now holds information about the page itself.

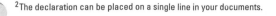

[2]The declaration can be placed on a single line in your documents.

```
1   <html xmlns="http://www.w3c.org/1999/xhtml"
           xml:lang="en"
           lang="en">
```

The `html` tag declares the namespace for the document through the `xmlns` attribute. The valid namespace for XHTML 1.0 is as shown above. The language of the document is also declared inside the `html` tag. The `xml:lang` attribute takes precedence over any other language declarations.

XHTML Elements

Although the elements remain the same as in HTML 4, the ways in which they may be used have been tightened up considerably.

- Nested tags must be terminated in the reverse of the order in which they were declared. You will no longer be able to have overlapping tags. The following example shows incorrect code followed by the correct version:

```
1   <tr><td>Some <b>Data</td></b></tr>
    <tr><td>Some <b>Data</b></td></tr>
```

- XML is case-sensitive. All XHTML tags and attributes *must* be in lower-case.
- All tags which have, or may have, content must have end tags. Again I will show some incorrect code and then the correct version:

```
1   <p>
    <p>Here's a paragraph of text


    <p></p>
5   <p>Here's a paragraph of text</p>
```

- Empty elements, tags which do not contain content, must either have end tags or be terminated properly. A space should be placed before the terminating slash. This example shows valid alternatives:

```
    <hr></hr> <hr />
```

- All attribute values must be placed inside quotes. This applies equally to numerical and textual arguments:

```
1   <hr width="50%"></hr>
    <p align="center">Content</p>
    <table rows="3">
```

- Scripts and styles must be *wrapped* so that they are not parsed as markup. Even inside <script> ... </script> tags the characters < and & will be treated as part of the XHTML markup. To avoid this, scripts and styles are declared as containing #PCDATA. The script element is included like this:

```
1   <script>
       <![CDATA[
          // your script goes here
       ]]>
5   </script>
```

- Some HTML elements have had a name attribute with which they could be uniquely identified by scripts. This has been particularly important for forms and for elements such as div which have been manipulated through scripting. In XHTML 1.0 the name attribute has been deprecated to be replaced by id. According to the recommendation document the name attribute will be removed from a future version of XHTML altogether. This is because XML has attributes only of type id.

3.6.2 An Example

The following document, which is admittedly trivial, demonstrates the structure of an XHTML document. Notice that all tags are closed including the *empty* ones. Because this document is also an XML document it starts with the XML version identifier. Whilst not all XML documents *require* this, it is advisable to use it in XHTML so that you can show which character encoding you are using. Typically you will use UTF-8, occasionally UTF-16. Apart from that, this document looks and feels like XHTML and should display nicely in your browser.

```
1   <?xml version="1.0" encoding="UTF-8">
    <!DOCTYPE html
       PUBLIC "-//W3C//DTD XHTML 1.0 Transitional//EN"
       "DTD/xhtml1-transitional.dtd">

5
    <html xmlns="http://www.w3c.org/1999/xhtml"
       xml:lang="en" lang="en">

       <head>
10        <title>Sample XHTML Document</title>
       </head>
       <body>
          <h1>Sample XHTML Document</h1>
          <hr/>
```

```
15      <p>This very basic document is an XHTML
        document</p>
        <ul>
            <li>It has an xml version identifier</li>
            <li>It has a valid DTD</li>
20          <li>All tags are closed</li>
        </ul>
        <hr/>
    </body>
</html>
```

 EXERCISES

Tables

1. What advantages do tables have over other methods of presenting data? Are there likely to be any difficulties if you use large tables and embed tables inside tables?
2. Add a table to your Web page. Try different formatting options – how does the table look if it does not have a border, for instance?
3. Nest a second table inside the first as one of the rows.

Framesets

1. Try using a simple frameset to display two pages at the same time. Split the screen first horizontally, then vertically. Which do you prefer?
2. Now try having a single screen with up to five frames, some horizontal and some vertical. Does that work from either a design or development perspective?

HTML Forms

1. What is the role of the HTML form?
2. Outline the relationship between HTML forms and CGI scripts. Can form data be processed if there is no related script?
3. Create an HTML form with all possible elements on board. That is a bit messy, so try a simple form such as might be used for a guestbook. Format the form so that it looks OK on the screen. Use a table to format the form.

The Document Head

1. What is a document type declaration and why is it needed?

2. What sorts of meta-information can be placed in the **head** of a document?

3. Add some meta information such as keyword lists to one of your pages. Does this have any effect upon the way that the browser handles the page?

XHTML

- Why has W3C developed the XHTML specification?
- Take an HTML 4 page that you have developed, possibly one of those from this book, and rewrite it so that it conforms to the XHTML recommendation.
- Search the Web for an XML validator. Does your XHTML page pass the validation process?

PART II

Stylesheets

Cascading Stylesheets

4.1 INTRODUCTION

One of the most important aspects of HTML is the capability of separating presentation and content. This is a sort of holy grail for anyone who is interested in publication. Often desktop publishing software, rather than a word processor, is used to lay out documents yet a word processor will have been used to create the content. The layout of documents includes positioning on the page and the choice of fonts, colors, borders, backgrounds and so on.

Formatting content for traditional publishing is a complicated procedure but is well understood and many aspects are now capable of complete automation. The Web presents a somewhat different proposition because the author or designer of a Web page has no way of knowing how it will be accessed. The page may be viewed on a television screen, a computer screen or a mobile phone, any of which may show images, text, tables or a mixture of them all. Straightforward HTML does not have the facilities that are needed to cope with this diversity, but stylesheets provide them.

A style is simply a set of formatting instructions that can be applied to a piece of text. There are three mechanisms by which we can apply styles to our HTML documents:

- the style can be defined within the basic HTML tag
- styles can be defined in the <head> section and applied to the whole document
- styles can be defined in external files called stylesheets which can then be used in any document by including the stylesheet via a URI.

In this book I will concentrate on the third technique as it seems to me that it is the most flexible. If you are interested in using the other techniques the simple examples I give should be enough to get you started. Comprehensive lists and definitions of the properties and values which you can use in creating styles are beyond the scope of this book. They can easily be found with a quick Web search, as can details of which browsers support which styles.

Not all browsers support stylesheets and many which do cannot yet process them fully. This does not matter too much as browsers are designed to ignore any HTML tags or attributes that they do not understand. When someone with an older browser views your pages the content will be formatted as if you had not used stylesheets. This means that you have to be careful about how you apply styles and how much you depend upon them. You may come up with a radical design, which looks excellent on your system, but when viewed without the styles it might look terribly mundane.

Styles can be *cascaded*. This means that formats override any which were defined or included earlier in the document. For instance, you may include an external stylesheet which redefines the h1 tag, then write an h1 style in the head of your page before finally redefining h1 in the body of your page. The browser will use the last of these definitions when showing the content. Furthermore, you can define a style which is applied to all instances of an HTML element, for instance, so that all h1 headings are changed, or you can alter the appearance of specific h1 elements, leaving the others unchanged.

RULE OF THUMB

More browsers are including support for style sheets. Styles can be used to provide complex formatting which previously had to be kludged using images. Therefore move to using styles now, but make sure that your pages are browser-friendly.

4.2 USING STYLES: SIMPLE EXAMPLES

Unfortunately you cannot really learn about stylesheets in a gradual or incremental fashion. You need to use a resource, such as the list of tags in this book, and then dive straight in. The following examples are just about as simple as the use of styles can get.

Changing h1

In this first example the <h1> tag is redefined. The text is colored in red, centered on the screen and has a thin border placed around it. Figure 4.1 shows the effect that this produces in the Konqueror browser.

```
1   <html>
      <head>
        <title>Simple Stylesheet</title>
        <style>
```

Figure 4.1 Changing h1

```
 5          <!--
            h1{
                color: red;
                border: thin groove;
                text-align: center;
10          }
            -->
            </style>
        </head>
        <body>
15          <h1>Simple Stylesheet</h1>
        </body>
    </html>
```

Notice that I am declaring the style in the head of the document using the style tag.
I place the actual style definition inside an HTML comment so that it will be ignored by
browsers which do not support styles. The declaration has the name of the element which
is being changed and then a definition which is placed inside braces. The attributes which
are being changed are placed in a list with each term separated by a semi-colon. I usually
place each attribute on a new line so that the definition is easier to read and maintain. Each
definition is made from the attribute and a list of values which are separated by a colon.
You might expect the values to be surrounded by double quotes in the same way that the

attributes of HTML tags are. Do not do this: it is not needed and, actually, the browser will not be able to handle the code if you include them. There are, as ever, exceptions to this. If you use a hexadecimal value to declare a color or if you use a font name which includes spaces then you can use either single quotes or quotation marks around it.

Changing More Styles

This example goes slightly further by altering both h1 and a paragraph. The paragraph is moved slightly to the right by giving it a left margin, has a colored background and a ridged border. The resulting Web page is shown in Figure 4.2.

```
1   <html>
      <head>
        <title>Simple Stylesheet</title>
        <style>
5       <!--
          h1{
            color: red;
            border: thin groove;
          }
10        -->
```

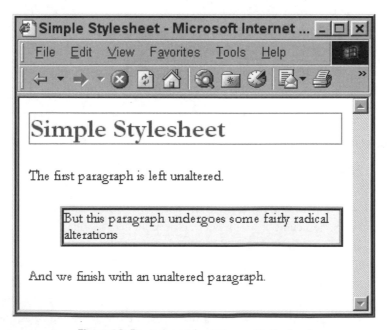

Figure 4.2 Declaring styles inline and in the head

```
        </style>
      </head>
      <body>
        <h1>Simple Stylesheet</h1>
15      <p>The first paragraph is left unaltered.</p>

        <p style="margin-left: 10%; border: ridge;  background: #ffffcc">
          But this paragraph undergoes some fairly radical alterations.</p>

20      <p>And we finish with an unaltered paragraph.</p>
      </body>
    </html>
```

The syntax of the style definition changes when it is done inside an HTML tag. The definition becomes an *attribute*, named style, of the tag. The description of the style is passed as the value of the attribute and so must follow an equals sign. The definition is placed inside quotation marks but otherwise uses the same syntax that we saw a moment ago.

Redefining elements as I have done with the paragraph in the example is unsatisfactory. There is no separation between the processing of an element and the definition of that element. Remember the markup should be logical; any physical changes (i.e., new formats) should appear outside of that markup.

A Slightly More Complex Example

This second example of styles builds upon the first. This time two classes are declared. There is much more on the use of classes in Section 4.3.3 and in Section 4.6.1. Notice this time that whole blocks of text can be moved around the screen. Here an entire paragraph is moved to the right of another, and hence acts as a sort of label. This code produces a page like that shown in Figure 4.3.

```
1   <html>
      <head>
        <title>Simple Stylesheet</title>
        <style>
5         h1 {
            color: red;
            border: thin groove;
          }
          h2 {
10          color: green;
```

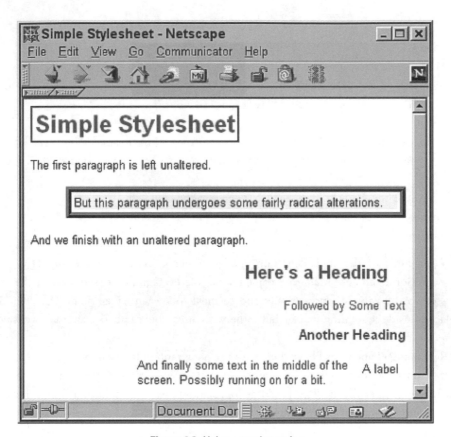

Figure 4.3 Using complex styles

```
      margin-left: 60%
    }
    .myid {
      text-align: right;
      color: purple;
    }
    .myid2 {
      align: right
    }
  </style>

</head>
<body>

  <h1>Simple Stylesheet</h1>
```

```
    <p>The first paragraph is left unaltered.</p>

    <p style="margin-left: 10%; border: ridge; background: #ffffcc">
        But this paragraph undergoes some fairly radical alterations.</p>

    <p>And we have an unaltered paragraph.</p>

    <h2>Here's a Heading</h2>

    <p class="myid">Followed by Some Text</p>
    <h3 class="myid">Another Heading</h3>

    <p class="myid2">A label</p>
    <p style="margin-left: 30%; color: blue">
        And finally some text in the middle of the screen. Possibly running
            on for a bit.</p>

    </body>
</html>
```

4.3 DEFINING YOUR OWN STYLES

Styles are defined by simple rules. A style can contain as many rules as you want and, as with processing HTML, if something does not make sense it will be ignored.

4.3.1 Cascading Styles

Conventionally, styles are cascaded. This means that you do not have to use just a single set of styles inside a document – you can import as many stylesheets as you like. This is useful if you define a set of organizational styles that can be modified by each department. The only difficulty with importing multiple stylesheets is that they cascade. This means that the first is overridden by the second, the second by the third, and so on. Of course the overriding only happens if a later stylesheet contains a definition of a style that is already defined. You can also override styles by defining styles within the body of the page as I showed in Section 4.2.

4.3.2 Rules

A style rule has two parts: a selector and a set of declarations. The selector is used to create a link between the rule and the HTML tag. The declaration has two parts: a property and a value. Selectors can be placed into classes so that a tag can be formatted in a variety of ways. Declarations must be separated using colons and terminated using semicolons.

```
selector {property: value; property: value ... }
```

> This form is used for all style declarations in stylesheets. The declaration has three items: the property, a colon, and the value. If you miss the colon or fail to put the semicolon between declarations, the style cannot be processed. Rules do not have to be formatted as I have shown – as with HTML you can lay the text out however you like. The rule will be more readable if you put each declaration on its own line. This is an example of a simple rule, followed by a more complex one:

```
1  body {
       background-color: #eebd2;
   }


5  h1 {
       color: #eeebd2;
       background-color: #d8a29b;
       font-family: "Book Antiqua", Times, serif;
       border: thin groove #9baab2;
10 }
```

> The detail of these style attributes will be discussed in Section 4.4.

4.3.3 Classes

The method shown above applies the same style to all examples of a given tag. That is fine if you want every paragraph equally indented or every level one heading in the same font. If you only want to apply a style to some paragraphs, for instance, you have to use classes:

```
selector.classname {property: value; property: value}
```

```
<selector class=classname>
```

> These examples show how classes should be used. In the stylesheet itself the rule is slightly modified by giving the style a unique name which is appended to the selector using a dot. In the HTML document when you want to use a named style the tag is extended by including class= and the unique name.

```
1  h1.fred {
       color: #eeebd2;
       background-color: #d8a29b;
       font-family: "Book Antiqua", Times, serif;
5      border: thin groove #9baab2;
   }


   <h1 class="fred">A Simple Heading</h1>
```

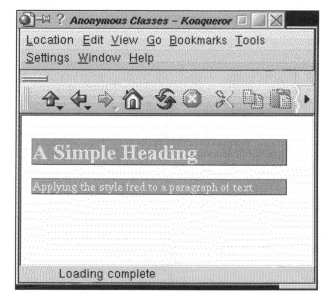

Figure 4.4 Using classes of style

The benefit of classes is that they can provide a lot of variety. They are especially good if you want to redefine the paragraph style so that your introductions look different from your content.

Anonymous Classes

Sometimes you want to apply a piece of formatting to many different elements within a page but not necessarily to the entire page. You could redefine every element in a stylesheet to make it use your formatting, and then redefine individual elements back to their defaults as you needed to. This is a rather awkward approach and would inevitably lead to a lot of duplication of effort. Cascading stylesheets provides a way of defining styles within reusable classes. The following code, and Figure 4.4, show how this works.

```
1  <html>
      <head>
         <title>Anonymous Classes</title>
         <style>
5        <!--
            .fred {
               color: #eeebd2;
               background-color: #d8a29b;
               font-family: "Book Antiqua", Times, serif;
```

```
10          border: thin groove #9baab2;
         }
      -->
      </style>
   </head>
15   <body>
      <h1 class="fred">A Simple Heading</h1>
      <p class="fred">Applying the style fred to a
         paragraph of text</p>
   </body>
20  </html>
```

4.3.4 Including Stylesheets

I have already mentioned how to include stylesheets, in Section 3.5. The following, adapted for your local needs, must be included in the <head> of your HTML page:

<link rel="StyleSheet" href="url" type="text/css" media="screen">

The href is a hyperlink to your stylesheet, rel tells the browser what type of link you are using. It is likely that in the future there will be many types of relationship available. You have to tell the browser what type of document you are including, the type statement gives the relevant MIME type. Finally it is useful, although not compulsory, to tell the browser how the document will be used. HTML specifies a variety of ways of using a document, including screen viewing, printing, and as presentations. Use the media attribute to describe the type of use.

This example shows how to include your organizational stylesheet:

```
1   <link rel="StyleSheet"
    href="http://www.smiggins.co.uk/mainstyles.css"
    type="text/css" media="screen">
```

[<style type="text/css">]
<!- @import url(url); - ></style>

These lines are both needed if you intend to use more than one stylesheet. The first sheet is included as if it were the only one; any further stylesheets have to be imported. Notice that the @import is enclosed within a comment so that it can be easily ignored by older browsers.

```
1   <link rel="StyleSheet"
    href="http://www.smiggins.co.uk/mainstyles.css"
```

```
     type="text/css" media="screen">
     <style type="text/css">
5      <! -- @import
          url("http://www.smiggins.com/style.css")
        -- >
     </style>
```

4.4 PROPERTIES AND VALUES IN STYLES

A number of properties of the text can be altered. These can be grouped together. I will list the properties in useful groups and give some of the options that you can alter. The best way of discovering how styles work is to play around with some of these properties. Try giving absurd values to elements and see what happens.

RULE OF THUMB

Do not change too many options. You are trying to present information, not give a lesson in typography and colors. Be careful, as ever, and make sure that your key changes are available to your target audience. Do not rely on styles to convey information. Although most browsers have decent support for CSS they often render the same element and style in radically different ways.

In the following descriptions of the properties I will not give examples; there is a large and fairly comprehensive example later in this section.

4.4.1 Formatting Elements

Styles cannot be haphazardly applied to elements, whether in XHTML or XML documents. If documents are going to be presented in a relatively uniform manner across processing agents, some rules are required which define how elements are styled. Cascading stylesheets use a box model to set out each element. Figure 4.5 shows this model.

For block-level elements, the size of the margin, padding and border can be set using CSS elements which are detailed later. Although the color of the border can be set and the padding uses the same background as the element content, the margin is always transparent.

display: none|block|inline|list-item

Many XHTML elements are defined as block or inline in the XHTML Recommendation. Headings and paragraphs, <h1> and <p>, for example, are always blocks. An element such as <em> will be inline. When defining styles for XML elements, it is

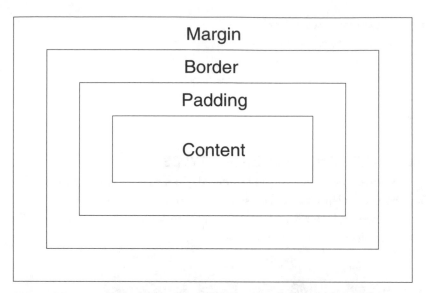

Figure 4.5 The box model for CSS elements

necessary to specify if the element is a block or an inline element so that the browser can format it correctly.

By default the width of a block is not set. When formatting XML, I have found that different browsers take radically different approaches to wrapping text. Mozilla appears *not* to wrap text, while other browsers wrap it at the width of the browser on screen. If the `width` property of the block is set, the text will be wrapped in all browsers.

4.4.2 Fonts

`font-family: <family name> [<generic family>]`

Fonts are identified by giving the name of a specific font. Many Microsoft Windows and Apple systems have similar sets of TrueType fonts. Unfortunately UNIX systems use Type 1 and PostScript fonts. Therefore it is unlikely that a reader on one of those computers will have access to the fonts from your PC. The TrueType fonts look better than Type 1 fonts and the user-base of Web surfers with access to True Type is far greater.

You should try to use TrueType fonts in your Web pages, but provide an option for users who do not have these fonts. This can be done in two ways. First, you may specify as many fonts as you like for each style in the hope that most people will have at least one of them. Second, you can specify a default generic font which all browsers on all systems can handle. Five generic fonts are specified: *serif (times)*, *sans-serif (arial)*, *cursive*, *fantasy*, *monospaced (courier)*. Font names which include whitespace should be placed in quotes. Generally a list of fonts is provided, the browser will try to use each in turn until it finds one that it recognises:[1]

```
1  p {
       font-family: "Bookman Old Style", "Times New Roman", Times,
           serif;
   }
```

font-style: normal|italic|oblique

Fairly straightforward. Oblique fonts are slanted, italic do not have to be.

font-weight: normal|bold|bolder|lighter|100|200|
300|400|500|600|700|800|900

The weight of any font can be altered. The first four options are relative while the numbered values give absolute weights. Not all fonts support all possible weights and you may want to be careful using absolute weights.

font-size: [small|medium|large]|[smaller|larger]|
<length>|<percentage>

As well as changing the weight you can alter the size. Again, a choice of relative sizes is possible. Font lengths should be given in appropriate units such as pt. A discussion of units is given in Section 4.4.6. Absolute sizes include small, large, and so on, while relative sizes are larger or smaller.

4.4.3 Backgrounds and Colors

color: <value>
background-color: <value>|transparent
background-image: URL|none

The color of any attribute can be changed. Values should be given as hexadecimal values. Backgrounds for the whole page or individual elements can have their color set from the stylesheet. Elements can also have transparent backgrounds. Instead of a color an image can be used, which is identified by its URL. If you set the background-color you should set the background-image to none.

---

[1] The line break here is simply so that the code fits onto the page.

4.4.4 Text

text-decoration: none|underline|overline|line-through

Any piece of text can be decorated. If you want to remove the underlining on links try this:

`A:link, A:visited, A:active{text-decoration: none}`

text-transformation: none|capitalize|uppercase|lowercase

allows you to set the case of text. This can be useful if you cannot be sure that text will be entered appropriately. For instance, if you are listing countries by their initials, create a capitalized style.

text-align: left|right|center|justify

One of the most useful text styles. Allows you to fully justify text in paragraphs, which many people like. By default HTML uses ragged right margins.

text-indentation: length|percentage

Before stylesheets were devised text could not be indented on the left side. Many people like their text indented, as this paragraph is, and would use small transparent GIFs to achieve it. Using the style is much better, as it downloads along with the text and it is flexible. Use a percentage and the amount of space will scale nicely if the browser window is resized.

4.4.5 Boxes

Many items can be encased in boxes. This can give some very good effects, although care needs to be taken. If the boxes become overwhelming or are used too much they can start to look rather odd.

margin: length|percentage|auto {1,4}
border-width: thin|thick|medium|length {1,4}
padding: length|percentage {1,4}

Any of the margins of a box can be changed. This time it may often be better to specify an absolute length – if you use a percentage the margins may become overly crowded when the window is resized. You can specify 1, 2, or 4 margin values. If you specify 4 they are applied in the order: top, right, bottom, and left. Specify just one value and it is applied to all four margins. Specify two values and the first will be applied to top and bottom, the second to left and right margins. As with margins you can specify the amount of white space within an element. Padding and border width are applied in the same way as margins.

```
border-color: value {1,4}
border-style: none|dotted|dashed|solid|double|groove|ridge {1,4}
```

This sets the color of the border around the element. Up to four different colors can be specified. They are applied to the borders in the same order as margins. Each edge of the border can have a different style.

```
width: length|percentage|auto
height: length|auto
```

Any block-level element can be given a specific width or height. As with so many items it is better to specify the width as percentages to allow for resizing of the browser window. The height must be specified as an absolute size.

4.4.6 Units and URLs

Lengths

These can be either absolute or relative. A relative length can be either positive or negative, which is indicated by preceding the value with an optional + or --.

Relative units that can be used are:

- em: the height of the font for this element
- ex: the height of the letter "x" in the current font
- px: pixels

Allowable absolute units are:

- in: size in inches
- cm. size in centimeters
- mm: size in millimeters
- pt: points where 1 pt equals 1/72 inch
- pc: picas where 1 pc = 12 pt.

URLs

URLs can be used in stylesheets just as they can in HTML documents. The format of the URL reference is:

```
url(location)
```

URLs can optionally be quoted and may be either absolute or relative. If a URL is partial it is considered to be relative to the location of the stylesheet source, not the HTML document source.

4.5 STYLESHEETS – A WORKED EXAMPLE
4.5.1 The stylesheet

```
1  body {
       background-color: "#eeebd2";
       margin: 5px 5px 5px 5px;
   }
5
   h1 {
       color: "#eeebd2";
       background-color: "#d8a29b";
       font-family: "Book Antiqua", Times, serif;
10     border: thin groove #9baab2;
   }

   h2 {
```

Figure 4.6 Formatting using stylesheets

```
         color: "#8b007c";
15       font-family: "Book Antiqua", Times, serif;
         border: thin groove "#8b007c";
    }

    h3 {
20       font-family: "Book Antiqua", Times, serif;
         color: "#8b007c";
    }

    em {
25       font-weight: bold;
         font-style: italic;
    }

    hr {
30       margin-right: 10%;
         margin-left: 10%;
    }

    p.link {
35       color: "#8b007c";
         text-align: center;
         font family: "Lucida Casual", Times, serif;
         font-weight: bold;
         font-size: 10pt;
40       margin-left: 0%;
    }

    p {
         font-family: "Bookman Old Style", Times, serif;
45       margin-left: 10%;
         text-align: justify;
    }

    strong {
50       font-family: Arial, sans-serif;
         font-size: 12pt;
```

```
        color: red
     }

55   th {
        background-color: "#b2a474";
        align: center;
        color: #8b007c
     }

60
     table {
           padding: 2pt 2pt 2pt 2pt;
     }

65   td.firstcol {
        background-color: "#00acac";
        font-weight: bold;
        text-align: center;
     }

70
     table.main {
        padding: 0px 0px 0px 0px;
     }
```

4.5.2 The HTML Page

```
1    <html>
        <head>
           <title>Bill Smiggins Inc</title>
           <link rel="StyleSheet" href="./test.css" type="text/css"
              media="screen">
5       </head>
        <body bgcolor="#ffffff" text="#362e00">
        <! -- start of the table -->

        <table class="main">
10         <tr>
              <! -- first of all the logo >
              <td colspan="2" align="center" bgcolor="#000000">
              <img src="./logo.gif"/> </td>
           </tr>
```

```
15          <tr>
               <td  bgcolor="#7cb98b" width="20%" valign="top">
               <! -- and then the links -->

               <h2 align="center">Links</h2>
20             <hr width="50%"/>

               <p class=link><img src="./bullet.gif"/> 
               <a href="./products.html">Products</a></p>

25             <p class=link><img src="./bullet.gif"/> 
               <a href="./products.html">Services</a></p>

               <p class=link><img src="./bullet.gif"/> 
               <a href="./products.html">Contacts</a></p>
30
               <p class=link><img src="./bullet.gif"/> 
               <a href="./products.html">Ordering</a></p>

               <br><hr width="50%"/><br>
35

               </td>
               <td width="70%">
               <! -- and finally the information -->
40
               <h2>About our Company...</h2>
               <p>This Web site provides clients, customers,
               interested parties and our staff with all of the
               information that they could want on our products,
45             services, success and failures.</p>

               <hr/>
               <h3>Products</h3>
               <p align="center"> We are probably the largest
50             supplier of custom widgets, thingummybobs and bits
               and pieces in North America.</p>
```

```
              <hr width="50%"/>
              </td>
55        </tr>
       </table>

       </body>
    </html>
```

4.6 FORMATTING BLOCKS OF INFORMATION

To conclude this discussion of stylesheets I am going to re-emphasize a couple of points and mention something new. It is important that you are clear about classes and how they work and that you understand two new ideas: divisions and spans. All of these affect the way that the page is laid out by the browser, but you also need to have a grasp of layers. I have not mentioned these before because they can be a little confusing. However, when I start to look at using JavaScript to create dynamic HTML pages I will be using layers (and divisions) quite a lot. In this section you will learn how to use layers to perform interesting textual effects as a prelude to using them to manipulate images and text together.

4.6.1 Classes

The discussion of stylesheets and the comprehensive example in Section 4.5.1 showed how to use classes. This is a reminder of why they are used, and what they are used for. Styles can be used to change the appearance of individual elements but often you will want to change the way that every instance of an element appears. This is easily done through the stylesheet, but what if you only want to alter *some* elements? In that case the most effective thing you can do is to use a class.

A class is a definition of a set of styles which can be applied as you choose: if you do not want the styles then you do not have to use them. Classes can be applied to a single type of element, or may be *anonymous* and hence applicable to any element. The following code shows the difference between the two types:

```
1   h1 {
        color: red;
        border: thin groove;
        }
5   h2.some {
        color: green;
        margin-left: 60%;
        }
    .anyelement {
10      text-align: right;
```

```
color: purple;
}
```

The style defined for h1 applies to all h1 elements in the document. The h2 style is only applied when it is explicitly called:

```
<h2 class="some">...</h2>
```

The .anyelement style can be applied wherever it is needed:

```
1   <h2 class="anyelement">...</h2>
    <p class="anyelement">...</p>
```

Notice that an h2 element is formatted using a class in that second example. Even though the h2 is already declared in predefined format *and* modified by an explicit h2 style, we can still apply a class of style to it.

It is probably a good idea to move to using stylesheets and classes as quickly as possible. Version 4 of HTML clearly and strongly requires a separation of formatting and content. If you want to make the background of your page red and use white text you might do this with:

```
<body bgcolor="red" text="white">
```

Doing this places formatting information about colors in with the text of the document. Browsers will continue to happily handle such statements but only for backwards compatibility. The preferred alternative would be to do this:

```
1    <html>
       <head>
         <title>Changing the body</title>
         <style>
5        <!--
            body {
              color: white;
              background-color: red;
            }
10       -->
         </style>
       </head>
       <body>
         <h1>A New Page</h1>
15     </body>
     </html>
```

And, of course, the benefit of this system is that you can change the formatting of parts of your text without having to work though the document making lots of small changes.

4.6.2 Divisions

An element in an HTML document is either a block element or an inline element. A block would be something like a paragraph, while an inline might be something like text, a figure or an individual character that is part of a block. Each of these can be manipulated separately.

First I will look at changing the appearance of block elements. This is really very simple. Rather than applying the formatting to the element itself, a `<div>...</div>` pair of tags are wrapped around the element. Any formatting that needs adding is placed inside the div tag thus:

```
1   <div class="anyelement">
        <p>...</p>
        <h2>...</h2>
        <p>...</p>
5       <hr>
    </div>
```

This does not immediately offer much that is not already available from the other HTML tags. But a division is now a logical part of the document and we can start to treat divisions as individual items. I will show how this can be used to create interesting effects in Section 4.7, and how it is used when writing Dynamic HTML in Chapter 8.

4.6.3 Spans

The HTML standard no longer supports the idea of modifying individual items in place. This is to remove problems that can arise with the indiscriminate use of colors and `<font>...</font>` tags. It is no longer regarded as acceptable to modify these items from within the body of the document. That does not mean that they *cannot* be altered; in fact, the reverse is true.

A simple and efficient model has been devised based around the span tag. Spans are used as follows:

```
<p><span class="anyelement">The</span> span tag
```

Whilst that is no easier to code than using font attributes directly, it will make sense when the page is accessed through any type of medium. Whether viewed on a browser such as Internet Explorer, accessed from a text-only browser like Lynx or though a browser devised for the visually handicapped, that span tag can be rendered in some meaningful way.

```
<div [id="..."] [class="..."|style="..."]>...</div>
<span [id="..."] [class="..."|style="..."]>...</span>
```

The div and span tags have identical parameters but the effects of those parameters are altered by the context in which they are used. Each can have an id so that it can be identified by other elements on the page. This is not generally useful on a static page of text, but it is useful in the context of Dynamic HTML as will be shown in Chapter 8. Styles are applied to span and div through either the class or style parameters. A set of styles can be defined within the tag and applied though style while a predefined class is applied through class. As with any use of styles these tags can, of course, be cascaded.

RULE OF THUMB

This cannot be overstated. Whenever possible use browser-independent tags. Make your site accessible to more browsers and you increase your potential revenue streams.

4.7 LAYERS

The page layout that a browser creates, results from layering text and images on top of each other. This lets Web designers use images as the backgrounds of their pages and then place further images and text over them. By extending the idea slightly we can place text items and images on top of each other in multiple layers. This is not especially impressive on a static Web page but, as I will show in Chapter 8, it lets the Dynamic HTML developer create some very interesting effects.

Netscape has extended the HTML standard by adding a layer tag which you may see discussed in books, magazines and on their Web site. The layer tag is browser-specific and its use leads to confusion with the more general idea of layers. Frankly, it would be better if everyone forgot[2] about that particular tag so I am not going to consider it in this book. Instead I will explain a platform-independent alternative that will work in the major browsers and should work in other browsers that comply with the standard.

When I discussed the div tag in Section 4.6.2 I deliberately ignored some of its most powerful attributes so that I could explain them in the context of layers.

z-index: n

The browser maintains a stack of layers of content. The background image is placed first, with text and images on top of it. For each div that you use you can determine where in that stack it will appear by setting the z-index parameter.

---

 [2]A number of ugly browser-specific "extensions" to HTML have appeared and died over the years. Netscape's blink and Microsoft's banner were particular abominations.

The lowest layer, appearing on top of the background, has a z-index of 1. There is not a functional upper limit to the value that you can assign to z-index. However, if you number your layers sequentially as you move up the stack you are unlikely to place more than about 20 layers before the screen becomes unmanageable.

Many layers can have the same z-index value if you want to place them at the same level. This is useful in many situations: for instance, you may have layers containing images placed around the screen which you want your text to appear over (or under!), or you may use some of the techniques I will demonstrate using Dynamic HTML to make content appear and disappear.

position: absolute|relative

Divisions have to be placed on the screen so that their top left corner starts at pixel 0,0. They can be given specific locations, but the placement of that layer may be either absolute (a fixed point on the screen) or relative to the placement of other content. This is optional and defaults to absolute.

left: n
top: n

The location of the division in pixels. You locate divisions around the screen by specifying the position of their top-left corner. Usually this is given relative to the origin of the screen, but it may also be relative to items that you've already placed.

These parameters are optional and both default to 0,0.

width: n
height: n

The size of the division in pixels. Defaults to the amount of space needed to display the content of the division.

4.7.1 Worked Examples of Divisions and Spans
Overlapping Layers

Now you know what layers *are* you probably want to know what they look like. The result is shown in Figure 4.7.

```
1   <html>
      <head>
        <title>Layering Text</title>
      </head>
5     <body>
      <h1>Layering Text</h1>
```

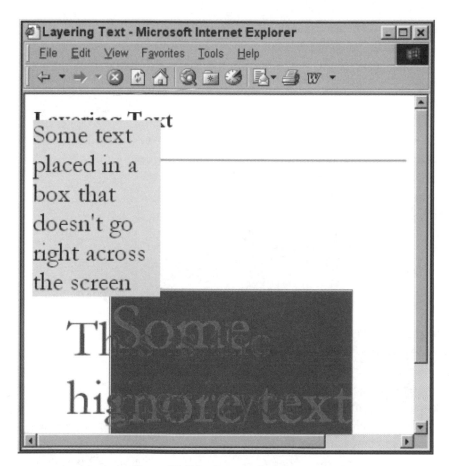

Figure 4.7 Using layers to format pages

```
      <div style="z-index: 2; left: 50px; top: 250px;
      position: absolute; color: red; text: white;
10    font-size: 36pt; border: thin-groove;">
          <p>This is the higher layer</p>
      </div>

      <div style="z-index: 1; left: 100px; top: 225px;
15    position: absolute; font-size: 46pt; color: magenta;
      background-color: green; border: thin groove">
          <p>Some more text</p>
      </div>

20    <div style="z-index: 4; left: 10; top: 30px; width: 150px;
```

```
            position: absolute; background-color: yellow;
            color: black; font-size: 18pt;">
                <p>Some text placed in a box that doesn't go right
                across the screen
25          </div>

            <div style="position: absolute; top: 300px; left: 500px;
            width: 25; background-color: #aeae00; color: blue;
            font-size: 16pt; font-style: italic; z-index: 2">
30              <p>And in the bottom right corner...
            </div>

            <hr/>
            </body>
35      </html>
```

Adjoining Layers

Creating layers which overlap each other is great for on-screen display. It has failings in a
couple of important situations: the page may not be easily navigated using a speech or text
browser; users may get unexpected results when they print your page – especially if they use
a black and white printer. Styles can be used to create relatively conventional layouts within
a Web browser which work in a number of different situations. A business will often provide
a nicely formatted invoice which users can print once they have completed a purchase, for
example. The example in this section takes a simple letter and formats it for printing.

```
1   <html>
    <head>
        <title>To: Mr B. Gates</title>
        <link rel="stylesheet" href="./letter.css"
5           type="text/css" />
    </head>

    <body style="width: 15cm">
    <div class="sender">
10      <p><span class="name">Mr. William James
            <span class="surname">Smiggins</span></span></p>
        <p>Bill Smiggins Incorporated<br />
        Unit 5<br />
        Tax Havens Industrial Park<br />
```

```
15      Enterprise City<br />
        California<br />
        CA 11223</p>
    </div>

20  <div class="recipient">
        <p><span class="name">Bill Gates</span><br />
        Microsoft Inc.<br />
        Seattle<br />
        United States<br />
25  </div>


    <div align="right">Thursday, 27<span class="sup">th</span>
                    May, 2005.</div>
```

Figure 4.8 Multiple styles

```
30    <p>Dear <span class="name">Bill Gates</span>,</p>
      <p class="content">
          Here at Bill Smiggins Inc. we're really proud of our
          ten-year reputation for the development of quality
          products. We're sorry to hear that you were unhappy with
35        the <span style="font-style: italic">Combined Trouser
          Press and Waffle Maker</span> that you recently purchased
          from us. I can only state that it was in full working
          order when we shipped, and the presence of fluff in your
          breakfast waffles was as much of a shock to us, as we're
40        sure it was to you.
      </p>

      <p class="content">
          If you return the Combined Trouser Press and Waffle Maker
45        in its original packaging, we'll arrange a full refund.
      </p>

      <p class="content">
          Bill Smiggins Inc. Giving you the quality of service you
50        deserve.
      </p>
      <p>Yours Faithfully,</p>
      <p><span class="name">Bill</span></p>

55    </body>
      </html>


1     .name {
          font-family: 'Times New Roman';
          font-size: 12pt;
          font-style: italic;
5         color: blue;
      }


      .surname {
          font-style: bold;
10        font-size: 16pt;
      }
```

```
     .sender {
         text-align: right;
15       font-family: fixed;
         font-size:12pt;
         font-variant: small-caps;
         color: green;
         width: 6cm;
20       left: 9cm;
         position: relative;
         background-color: wheat;
         padding-right: 10pt;
     }
25
     .recipient {
         text-align: left;
         font-family: fixed;
         font-size:10pt;
30       font-variant: small-caps;
         color: red;
         width: 6cm;
         background-color: wheat;
         padding-left: 10pt;
35   }

     p.content {
         font-family: 'Arial';
         font-size: 10pt;
40       margin-left: 20pt;
         margin-bottom: 10pt;
     }

     .sup {
45       vertical-align: super;
         font-style: italic;
         text-decoration: underline;
         font-size: 8pt;
     }
```

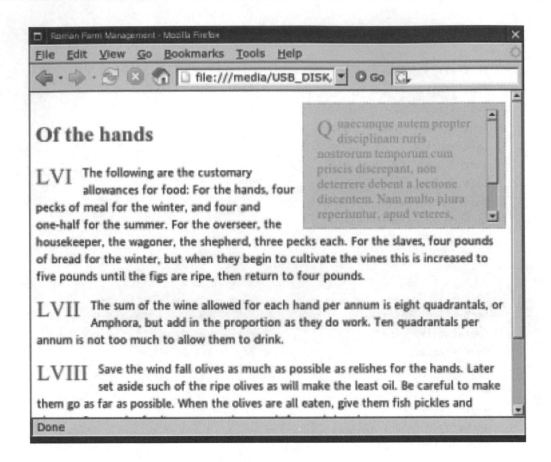

Figure 4.9 Styling inline frames

Styling Inline Frames

Section 3.3.2 introduced inline frames which are used to include one HTML document inside another. The example was very plain but inline frames can be used to create many interesting effects as Figure 4.9 shows.

Documents which are placed inside inline frames are rendered as if they were being displayed in a browser of their own. The only constraint which is placed is that the size of the displayed document is restricted to those defined by the `height` and `width` attributes of the `iframe` element. When the included document is larger than that area, scrollbars can appear around the content of the `iframe`.

```
1  <html>
     <head>
       <title>Roman Farm Management</title>
       <style type="text/css">
```

```
5          .salute {
               font-family: serif;
               color: blue;
               background-color: lightgrey;
               font-size: 12pt;
10         }
           .firstCap {
               float: left;
               font-size: 20pt;
               padding-right: 4pt;
15         }
       </style>
   </head>

   <body>
20     <p class="salute"><span class="firstCap">Q</span>uaecunque
       autem propter disciplinam ruris nostrorum temporum cum priscis
       discrepant, non deterrere debent a lectione discentem. Nam
       multo plura reperiuntur, apud veteres, quae nobis probanda
       sint, quam quae repudianda.</p>
25 </body>
   </html>
```

The Latin salutation has two styles. The majority of the text has a fairly standard format with color and font changed. The initial capital letter is formatted more dramatically. Many traditional printing layouts used a large initial capital with following text wrapped around it. The only way to make text wrap is to float the capital letter to the top left of the available space and add some padding so that it does not butt directly up against the rest of the text.

float: left|right

Using the float property lets the browser render elements outside of the normal flow. Instead of elements following one after the other, floated elements can be moved to the left or right margins of the page. Content which remains in the normal flow of the page will be wrapped around the floated elements. Additionally, floated elements are placed as far *up* the containing block as possible. The container may be a page, a div or another block-level element.

clear: left|right|both|none

The clear property indicates whether an an element allows floated elements alongside it. This property defaults to none which means that floated elements can appear on

any side. When set to left, for example, floated elements are not allowed on the left
of the styled element.

```
1    <html>
       <head>
         <title>Roman Farm Management</title>
         <style type="text/css">
5            .id {
                 float: left;
                 font-family: serif;
                 font-size: 20pt;
                 color: purple;
10               padding-right: 10pt;
             }
             .salute {
                 float: right;
                 padding: 5pt;
15               padding-left: 10px;
                 border: 1pt blue dotted;
                 background-color: lightgrey;
             }
         </style>
20     </head>

       <body>
         <iframe src="iframeLatinCSS.html" width="40%" frameborder="0"
         class="salute">Latin salutation</iframe>
25
         <h2 class="id">Of the hands</h2>

         <p style="clear: left"><span class="id">LVI</span> The following
         are the customary allowances for food: For the hands, four pecks
30       of meal for the winter, and four and one-half for the summer. For
         the overseer, the housekeeper, the wagoner, the shepherd, three
         pecks each. For the slaves, four pounds of bread for the winter,
         but when they begin to cultivate the vines this is increased to
         five pounds until the figs are ripe, then return to four
35       pounds.</p>
```

```
     <p><span class="id">LVII</span> The sum of the wine allowed for
     each hand per annum is eight quadrantals, or Amphora, but add in
     the proportion as they do work.  Ten quadrantals per annum is not
40   too much to allow them to drink.</p>
   </body>
</html>
```

The Latin quotation is placed inside an iframe which is floated to the right of the page. The remainder of the page content is floated to the left. This could be done by placing it all inside a div which then floats. Here a different approach is taken. The h2 heading is floated to the left of the iframe. The first paragraph is styled with the clear property so that it is placed beneath the heading. If that was not done the paragraph would be placed next to the floated heading. The Roman numerals which identify each stanza are styled in a similar way to the initial capital of the Latin quotation.

A simple use of styles and floats has created a complex document which works in plain text and spoken word browsers and which is usable even when frames are not supported. It is difficult to see how this mix of formatting, usability and simplicity could have been achieved in any other way.

 # EXERCISES

Styles

1. What do Web designers mean when they talk about a *style*?
2. Although stylesheets have been a W3C recommendation for a while now, many browsers do not yet support them fully. How should a browser behave if it encounters formatting that it cannot handle?
3. Describe the different ways that styles can be added to a page.
4. What are the benefits of using styles compared with placing formatting directly into the text of the Web page?
5. What is a stylesheet class?
6. Create a stylesheet for your Web site. You will probably make a few mistakes, even if only in typing. How does *your* browser react to these errors?
7. What happens if you specify a font that is unavailable?

Formatting Blocks of Content

1. HTML has two commands which are used to apply formatting to elements within the page. Compare and contrast the use of <div> and <span>.

2. In one of your pages, include a number of div elements. How does the browser handle these? If you have access to more than one type of browser, compare the effects that the same commands can create.

3. What is a layer? How are they described within HTML code?

4. Alter the page that you created using <div> so that each division acts as a layer and is moved vertically relative to other layers.

5. Try using *absolute* and *relative* positioning. What effect do they give both with and without the use of layers?

Cascading Style Sheets Two

ascading stylesheets have proven themselves as a robust, developer-friendly technology. They are applicable to both XHTML and XML data files, they are lightweight and they work well. As defined in the Cascading Stylesheets Recommendation of 1996, and its later update in 1999, CSS is intended purely for display of data on screen. Although the Recommendation uses the term *user-agent* throughout, the fact that this means Web browser is implicit in the document. The Web has changed in any number of ways since 1996:

- Millions more people now use the Web every day.
- The technologies that underpin it, such as HTTP, are being put to a changing set of uses in areas like intranets and messaging systems.
- Web data has changed from simple HTML to XHTML and XML.
- Whole new types of application such as Web Services are being developed.
- The Web is now truly world-wide, accessed continually from every continent.
- Many pages contain a mixture of fonts and character sets.

One of the most intriguing things, from a developer's point of view, is that Web data is no longer just viewed on a computer screen. Data originating in XHTML or XML may be accessed through mobile phones or television screens, used in presentations, printed in paper documents or presented aurally. The original CSS technology does not allow for these myriad uses. It focused solely upon the presentation of data in a Web browser.

The Cascading Stylesheets Two, CSS2, Recommendation of May 1998 addressed the limitations of the original Cascading Stylesheets Recommendations. In particular, properties were added to:

- format printed documents

- support the aural presentation of data
- include formatting specifically of tables
- aid the presentation of data to disabled users
- allow the scripting of stylesheet properties using languages such as JavaScript.

Although the primary developer community using CSS2 is going to be Web authors working in XHTML, many aspects of CSS2 are important for other XML applications. In particular, enhancements have been made to the way that stylesheets work while remaining totally backwards compatible and usable in a variety of media. CSS2 is another one of those technologies where the specification has a significant lead over the software. At the time of writing, few, if any, applications have been developed that support more than a relatively tiny subset of CSS2. Perhaps this is not surprising since an application that uses the aural stylesheets may never need to format XML for display. It is worth remembering that CSS-compatible applications will come in a number of different types. Unfortunately, many applications do not, as yet, implement all of the properties that they could use. Most Web browsers do not even include all of the visual properties, partly due to the complexity of implementing them all, and partly due to lack of demand.

5.1 THE DESIGN OF CSS2

Cascading Stylesheets Two, follows many of the same design principles that underpin the original CSS. Most importantly for developers who want to start using CSS2, the standard is totally backwards compatible with CSS. This means that browsers that only support CSS can load CSS2 stylesheets and ignore those elements that they do not understand. Since CSS2 is a super-set of CSS, any CSS2-compliant browser is also able to load CSS styles pages and render them as intended. Any user-agent such as a browser that is unable to manipulate stylesheets should be able to display the content of the file without styling it. This is more of an issue for XHTML developers than it is for XML developers. Any of the current browsers that can parse XML can also handle cascading stylesheets.

Separating the style and display information from the content brings several benefits. Different stylesheets can be created for different uses. This makes systems more maintainable, provides better utilization of network resources, since browsers only download stylesheets that they can handle, and it works without affecting the structure of the markup in the XML file.

CSS2 has been designed to be simple to use. Since more properties have been added to those which are available in CSS, there has been a necessary increase in complexity. The syntax of the CSS language remains both clear and simple. Because properties have been added, the CSS2 model is extremely feature-rich. Many features that Web designers had been asking for were added to CSS2. It is just a little unfortunate that the richness of the Recommendation is not equaled by the richness of use of CSS2 on the Web.

CSS2 adds many properties which are specifically designed to make content more accessible to those with disabilities. Specifically:

- the appearance of fonts can be controlled so that bitmaps which are difficult to read are eliminated
- layout is controlled through CSS2 properties rather than through the use of tricks such as invisible images
- using !important rules means that users can override aspects of stylesheets
- media support is now provided for braille, embossed and tty terminals
- voice and audio output can be styled using aural properties
- attribute selectors provide alternative content within stylesheets
- counters and numbering can be used to make document navigation easier on braille terminals.

5.1.1 Media Types

Cascading Stylesheets Two defines a number of different media types on which content might be displayed. These are given as attribute values in the <xml-stylesheet> element when the relationship between the XML file and stylesheet is established. The list of devices that is given in the Recommendation, and reproduced below, is not comprehensive. New devices will always appear so this list will inevitably grow as technologies change.

all
> The content is suitable for all applications.

aural
> The content is designed for speech synthesis software.

braille
> The data will be formatted for tactile braille readers.

embossed
> The data will be formatted for paged braille readers.

handheld
> Formatting for handheld devices, such as PDAs and mobile phones, which have extremely small screens.

print
> The document will be printed conventionally on paper.

projection
> The output will be displayed on a projection device or printed onto transparencies for display on a large screen.

screen

> The output will appear on a typical computer monitor capable of displaying colored output.

tty

> The output will be shown on a terminal or other device which can only display fixed fonts.

tv

> The output which will be used on a television screen.

5.2 STYLING FOR PAGED MEDIA

When information is displayed on a computer screen, it is usually available as a single long document. On modern systems, the document may be split into a series of files which are connected by hyperlinks or embedded within each other (for instance, using OLE or COM on Windows). The computer provides a scrolling window onto the data within which the content is moved up or down to access different areas. Computer systems do not have the concept of paging, chunking data into screen-sized pieces and displaying a screenful at a time. That is the way that printed media works, though. Whether a newspaper, bound report, book or set of slides for a presentation, the content is split into page-sized chunks. When styling an XML file using CSS2, we do not necessarily know if the data will always be viewed on a computer screen or if it will be printed out. Fortunately, CSS2 includes properties which are designed to provide some, admittedly rather primitive, paging facilities.

CSS2 extends the box model, shown in Figure 4.5, and introduces a page box model. The page box is an abstract rendition of a page of the document in which page size, margins and layout can be specified. It does not necessarily map directly onto a physical piece of paper. Instead, once the author has defined the page layout and specified the page breaks, the processing software should be able to transfer the page boxes onto sheets of paper. CSS2 does not get involved in the details of the transfer process but the Recommendation does list the following possibilities:

- One page box is transferred to each sheet of paper. This is sometimes called *simplex* printing.
- Two page boxes are transferred to each sheet of paper. One is printed on each side of the paper. This is sometimes called *duplex* printing.
- A number of page boxes are transferred to the same side of a sheet of paper. This may be called *n-up* printing.
- A single page box is transferred across a number of sheets of paper.
- Pages may be printed on a single sheet in such order that, when the sheet is folded and cut, a book of correctly ordered pages is produced.

- A single page box or document may be printed simultaneously on a number of output devices.
- The formatted document may be written to a file in printable form.

Defining a page box involves defining the page and specifying its margins. Unlike the CSS box model, the padding and border properties do not apply to page boxes.

5.2.1 Page Rules

Page boxes are defined using the @page rule. This is then applied to pseudo-elements which represent the first page, all left pages, all right pages, named pages or, by default, all pages in the document. The following code defines a page box equivalent to an A4 sheet, with a 20mm margin on all four sides:

```
@page { size: 210mm 294mm; margin: 20mm; }
```

The printed area of the page is equal to the area of the page box minus the margins. The margin can be broken down and specified differently for each side of the page as shown here:

```
1  @page {
       size: 210mm 294mm;
       margin-left: 30mm;
       margin-right: 20mm;
5      margin-top: 20mm;
       margin-bottom: 25mm,
   }
```

The page size does not have to be defined using exact measurements. Instead it can be set to:

auto

> which sets the size and orientation of the page box to the same as the target sheet.

portrait

> The page box will be in portrait format, regardless of the format of the target.

landscape

> The page box will be in landscape format, regardless of the format of the target.

When printing in book format, the left and right margins change between the left and right pages. The outer margin is always set to be wider than the inner one. The CSS2 page box allows for this by letting the designer create left and right pseudo-elements which are configured differently:

```
1   @page {
        size: 210mm 294mm;
        margin-top: 20mm;
        margin-bottom: 20mm;
5   }

    @page:left {
        size: 210mm 294mm;
        margin-left: 30mm;
10      margin-right: 20mm;
    }

    @page:right {
        margin-left: 20mm;
15      margin-right: 30mm;
    }
```

This code sets the page size and the margins at the top and bottom of the page, for *all* pages in the document. It then sets different left and right margins for left and right pages. Managing the pagination so as to decide which pages are left and which are right is left to the processing application. Setting a different page box for the first page is done through the :first pseudo-element.

5.2.2 Page Breaks

Although the processor will manage pagination throughout the document, there will be times when you need to force a page break. For example, if you are styling your XML so that it can be printed as a book, you will probably want to start each chapter on the right-hand page.

```
page-break-before: always|left|right|avoid|auto|inherit
page-break-after: always|left|right|avoid|auto|inherit
page-break-inside: avoid|auto|inherit
```

The values shown for these properties mean:

- auto – page breaks are neither forced nor inhibited
- always – a page break is *always* forced either before, or after, this element
- avoid – a page break is *never* allowed either before, or after, this element
- left – page breaks are forced so that the next page will be a left-hand page
- right – page breaks are forced so that the next page will be a right-hand page.

`page: <name>|inherit`

   Use this property to give a unique identifying name to a page.

`orphans: integer|inherit`
`widows: integer|inherit`

   These properties specify the minimum number of lines that must be present in a paragraph. Orphans are lines at the bottom of a page, widows are lines at the top. It is generally regarded as a *bad thing* to have one or two lines of a paragraph dangling in isolation from the rest of it. Formatting text so that widows and orphans are avoided is extremely difficult. Even well-established typesetting systems such as TEX get it wrong. Using these two properties will, at least, give your software a start on the problem.

5.3 USING AURAL PRESENTATION

Presenting computer documents in aural form is a relatively immature technology, but one that has developed rapidly. In particular, applications intended for use by the blind or visually impaired, or others who have difficulty with text and printed material, are now widely available. Such software usually relies upon a speech synthesizer *reading* the content of the document to the user. The conversion of text into a form that a speech synthesizer can use often involves the removal of all formatting instructions so that the synthesizer receives plain text.

   Clearly this is not a desirable situation, although it is preferable to having no access to the document. Structuring information conveys important meaning about the document and its content. Documents may be structured using such features as titles, sectional headers, lists or emphasized passages. Structuring a document in XML, which is basically text, and using stylesheets to format it means that both the structure and meaning of the document are preserved and can be used to aid the aural presentation of the material. Changing tone, adding sound effects and other *aural icons* can massively improve the listener's range of responses to the material.

Data may need to be presented aurally in a number of situations. Although the primary motivation is access for the disabled, access to data in situations in which reading is not possible is also of benefit. These may include access while driving, at work where access is restricted, or in some educational situations.

5.3.1 Properties

The CSS2 properties that deal with the aural presentation of data include the ability to change sounds, volume or pitch. Sounds can be presented in three-dimensional space or spread out temporally so that one sound follows another.

`volume: <number>|<percentage>|silent|x-soft|soft|medium|loud|x-loud|inherit`

The relative volume of the output is set using the `volume` property. The volume referred to is the median value of the waveforms, at some points it may be far louder or far quieter than this median value. Its absolute volume will be determined by the settings of the output device. The dynamic range of output devices will vary greatly. Auditory output in an office environment will need to be relatively quiet, while a device such as a television will have to produce louder sounds. Therefore the CSS2 Recommendation states that the user should be able to control the setting for the `volume` from their output device. The parameters of the `volume` property have the following meanings:

- `<number>` An integer between 0 and 100. At first sight you might expect 0 to mean that the sound was off and 100 was as loud as the output device could manage. In fact, 0 means the minimum audible volume, which will be approximately as loud as whispered speech. 100 means the loudest comfortable volume – quieter than shouted speech or a rock concert.
- `<percentage>` The volume setting, which may be inherited from the containing element, is moderated by this percentage which is then converted to an integer in the 0 to 100 range.
- `silent` No sound is transmitted at all. Obviously this is not the same as setting the volume to 0.
- `x-soft` The same as 0.
- `soft` The same as a value of 25.
- `medium` The same as 50.
- `loud` As for 75.
- `x-loud` Equivalent to a volume of 100.

`speak: normal|none|spell-out|inherit`

specifies how the text will be rendered aurally. The `normal` setting uses language-dependent rules to read the text; `none` means that the content is not rendered aurally. Finally, `spell-out` spells the text one letter at a time.

When the `volume` is set to `silent`, the content is still rendered but no sound is generated. Doing so takes the same length of time as outputting the text at an audible volume. The time taken includes any breaks or pauses set before or after the text. Setting the `speak` property to `none` means that the text is not rendered and, therefore, no time elapses.

```
pause-before: <time>|<percentage>|inherit
pause-after: <time>|<percentage>|inherit
pause: [<time>|<percentage>]{1,2}|inherit
```

A delay can be introduced before or after the content of the element is read. The `time` attribute sets the absolute delay in milliseconds or seconds. The `percentage` sets a delay which is relative to the `speech-rate` property. If the `speech-rate` is 60 words per minute, a delay of 100% will give a pause of one second. Generally, using relative pauses is preferred since it makes the stylesheet more transferable.

The `pause` property is a form of shorthand for `pause-before` and `pause-after`. It can receive either one or two values. If one is given, it will be applied to `pause-before`; if two are given, the second will be applied as `pause-after`.

```
cue-before: <uri>|none|inherit
cue-after: <uri>|none|inherit
cue: [<cue-before><cue-after]|inherit
```

These properties determine which, if any, *auditory icons* will be played. Auditory icons are sounds which are used to distinguish or emphasize pieces of speech. The URI must point to a valid sound file. If it points to something that cannot be handled by the application, it should be treated as if the property had the value `none`. The cue property works in the same way as `pause`. If it gets one URI, that is used for `cue-before`; if it gets two, the second is used for `cue-after`.

```
play-during: [uri [mix] [repeat]]|auto|none|inherit
```

A sound may be played in the background as text is being read. The `uri` must be a valid sound file. The optional `mix` value mixes sounds inherited from the parent element with the sound from the `uri`. The optional `repeat` value indicates that if the sound is shorter than the content of the element, it will be repeated for as long as required. The `auto` property indicates that the sound from the parent element continues.

```
azimuth: <angle>|[left-side|far-left|left|center-left|
center|center-right|right|far-right|right-side]behind|
leftwards|rightwards|inherit
```

Many systems that can give the illusion of playing sound in three dimensions are now available. Some systems, such as those for home-cinema or multi-speaker computer game systems, really do play sounds from all around the listener. The `azimuth` property is used to move sound through the horizontal plane around the listener.

- `<angle>` Indicates the position of the sound in the range −360 deg to 360 deg. A value of 0 indicates that the sound plays from directly in front of the listener.
- `left-side` Equivalent to a value of 270 deg. The directional properties can be combined with `behind` to change their value. If `behind left-side` is used, the sound plays from an angle of 270 deg.
- `far-left` An angle of 300 deg. With `behind` this is 240 deg.
- `left` An angle of 320 deg. With `behind` this is 220 deg.
- `center-left` An angle of 340 deg. With `behind` this is 200 deg.
- `center` An angle of 0 deg. With `behind` this is 180 deg.
- `center-right` An angle of 20 deg. With `behind` this is 160 deg.
- `right` An angle of 40 deg. With `behind` this is 140 deg.
- `far-right` An angle of 60 deg. With `behind` this is 120 deg.
- `right-side` An angle of 90 deg. With `behind` this is 90 deg.
- `leftwards` Moves the sound to the left of the current angle by 20 deg.
- `rightwards` Moves the sound to the right of the current angle by 20 deg.

elevation: <angle>|below|level|above|higher|lower|inherit

moves the sound in a vertical plane. Combining this with `azimuth` gives three-dimensional movement. The value of `<angle>` specifies the angle relative to the horizontal. A value of 0 deg is horizontal with movement in the range −90 deg to 90 deg. Using `below` is equivalent to −90 deg, `above` is equal to 90 deg and `level` is 0 deg. `higher` adds 10 deg to the current elevation, while `lower` subtracts 10 deg from it.

speech-rate: <number>|x-slow|slow|medium|fast|x-fast| faster|slower|inherit

The speaking rate can be set for individual elements. Think of this rather as you might think of font size. Both relative and absolute values can be set:

- `<number>` The rate in words per minute. This may be language and application dependent. For example, software to help language learners may need to use both extremely slow and more normal speeds.
- `x-slow` 80 words per minute.
- `slow` 120 words per minute.
- `medium` In the range 180 to 200 words per minute.
- `fast` 300 words per minute.
- `x-fast` 500 words per minute.
- `faster` Adds 40 words per minute to the current rate.
- `slower` Subtracts 40 words per minute from the current rate.

voice-family: [<specific>|<generic>]|inherit

This is a comma-separated list of voices that might be used to speak the text. These are analogous to font-families. Whilst the exact meanings are likely to be application dependent, possible values for generic include male, female or child.

pitch: <frequency>|x-low|low|medium|high|x-high|inherit

Specify the *average* pitch of the speaking voice. The relative values are application dependent.

pitch-range: <number>|inherit

specifies the variation in the average pitch of the speaking voice. This will help to add inflection and meaning to the spoken text. Values between 0 and 100 are allowed. A value of 0 gives a monotonic voice, 50 gives a normal voice.

stress: <number>|inherit

Spoken languages use stressed words to emphasize meaning. This property, in the range 0 to 100, specifies how much stress should be put into the voice.

richness: <number>|inherit

Adding richness to the voice will make it penetrate and carry better. Values in the range 0 to 100 are permitted.

speak-punctuation: code|none|inherit

When set to code, punctuation marks are spoken. When set to none, they are rendered as natural pauses.

speak-numeral: digits|continuous|inherit

If set to digits, the individual digits within a number are read as separate words. When set to continuous, the entire number is read as a single unit.

5.4 COUNTERS AND NUMBERING

It is sometimes necessary to generate additional content as a document is being rendered. The most obvious example of this is probably the creation of a table of contents and associated sectional numbering, or creating lists of numbered items. The XML document cannot, by its very nature, include such information. XML has structure, it is all about structure, but its structure is to do with the nature of the data. Numbering sections or lists is a presentational matter. This sort of content is as distinct from the raw XML as the color in which it is printed.

`:before`

`:after`

These are pseudo-elements, not properties. They are applied to existing elements to modify their behavior before styling is applied. They control the way in which generated content is added to the element as it is displayed.

Here is a quick example. I am going to modify the example shown in Figure 4.8 so that the word NAME appears in red, small capitals before any name fields. This is done by adding a new element to the stylesheet specifying the text that must be added:

```
1   name:before{
        content: "Name";
        color: red;
        font-style: normal;
5       font-variant: small-caps;
    }
```

The result as displayed by Mozilla is shown in Figure 5.1.

content: [<string>|<uri>|<counter>|attr()|open-quote|
close-quote|no-open-quote|no-close-quote]+|inherit

The content property is used with the :before and :after pseudo-elements to add material into the displayed version of a document. The optional values shown in the description can be mixed and repeated as needed to create the desired effect. For instance, putting quotes around the NAME string could be done with:

content: open-quote "Name" close-quote;

- <string> Adds text content in string format.
- <uri> The URI points to an external resource. If the processing application cannot handle the content there, it is ignored. Otherwise it is added to the document. This is especially useful for adding *boiler-plate* text to the content of an XML document.
- <counter> Adds a counter. Counters are described in detail in Section 5.4.1.
- open-quote and close-quote are replaced with the appropriate characters. These characters are likely to be application and locale specific.
- no-open-quote and no-close-quote Nothing is inserted; levels of indentation appropriate to the use of quotes are applied.

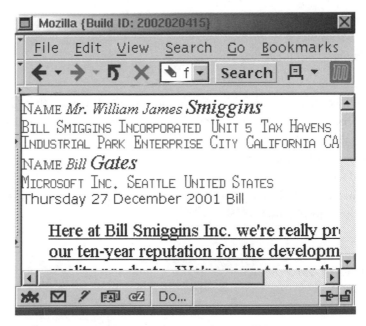

Figure 5.1 Adding content with CSS2

- `attr()` An attribute is given as the parameter to this function. Its content is used as the content of `content` (if you see what I mean).

5.4.1 Counters

Cascading Stylesheets Two supports the automatic generation of counter values as part of the generation of content. Developers can define the counter, the elements with which it is associated and when it should be incremented. Counters have two properties:

counter-increment [identifier [integer]]|none|inherit

The counter whose name is given as the `identifier` property is incremented by one. To increment by other amounts, including negative values, an optional `integer` parameter can be supplied.

counter-reset [identifier [integer]]|none|inherit

The value of the counter can be reset to 0, or to any other value which is given in the optional `integer` parameter.

```
1  name:before{
       counter-increment: name;
       content: open-quote "Name  "  counter(name) close-quote;
```

```
      color: red;
5     font-style: normal;
      font-variant: small-caps;
    }
```

In this code sample, a counter value now appears after the word NAME. The result, as displayed by Opera, is shown in Figure 5.2. Counters can be nested and modified. Nesting counters is trivial. The only thing to remember is that nested sectional counters need resetting when the outer section increments. Counters can be modified using the same properties as for bullets used with list elements. The style of counter you are using can be altered. To get a style other than the default, use `counter(name, <style>)` where the `<style>` parameter is taken from the following list:

- decimal
- decimal-leading-zero
- lower-roman
- upper-roman
- hebrew
- georgian
- armenian
- cjk-ideographic
- hiragana
- katakana
- hiragana-iroha

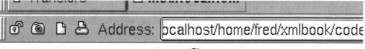

'NAME 1" *Mr. William James* **Smiggins**

BILL SMIGGINS INCORPORATED UNIT 5 TAX HAVENS
INDUSTRIAL PARK ENTERPRISE CITY CALIFORNIA CA 11223

'NAME 2" *Bill* **Gates**

MICROSOFT INC. SEATTLE UNITED STATES
Thursday 27 December 2001 Bill

Here at Bill Smiggins Inc. we're really proud of
ten-year reputation for the development of quali

Figure 5.2 Dynamic counters

- katakana-iroha
- lower-latin
- lower-alpha
- upper-latin
- upper-alpha
- lower-greek

EXERCISES

1. What shortcomings of Cascading Stylesheets does CSS2 address?
2. When might you need to present data in non-textual forms such as might be found in an auditory application?
3. What are pseudo-elements? Give examples of how you might use them in preparing a document.

PART III

JavaScript

An Introduction to JavaScript

Static Web pages are fine: they are useful and can be entertaining or informative. What they are not is part of a truly interactive multimedia experience. Nothing moves about, pages do not respond to the reader's actions and they cannot be dynamically tailored to suit a user's needs. The static Web page is essentially just a different way of presenting information that could equally easily have been published in a book.

From a developer's point of view, a Web page can be equally frustrating. As an example, consider the humble Web form. Users enter data and submit it to the server, where a CGI script is used to verify and validate that data. The whole process of passing data across the network before it can be checked is slow. How much more interactive could a site be if data were checked by the browser and any error messages originated locally? Users are always more likely to return to a fast site than a slow one, and of course return visitors are important to all businesses. The interactive Web site becomes more like an application than a book, which changes the whole Web experience.

A number of technologies have been developed that enable the creation of Web applications rather than static Web pages. The Java programming language is probably the best known such technology. It is a fully-fledged development language, which is much nearer to C++ than it is to HTML. It is complex and requires a good deal of skill when building even simple applications. The benefit of Java is that developers can place Java applets (small programs) inside HTML pages. Java is slow and such applets can take a long time to download and initiate. In fact many Web surfers switch the Java functionality off in their browser because of the overhead of using it.

Few programming languages other than Java have been adapted for use in client-side Web applications. Visual Basic from Microsoft is probably the best known but is not widely used for general browser applications. In fact, most programming on the client side is done in a language called ECMA Script. You may never have heard of ECMA Script but you will almost certainly have heard of JavaScript (from Netscape) and JScript (from Microsoft).

ECMA Script is an international standard which was developed retrospectively and based around version 1.1 of JavaScript. The language was specified by the European Computer Manufacturers Association in a document called ECMA-262 and later ratified by the International Organisation for Standards (ISO). Further versions of the standard have been released and these are supported by most browser developers. The language is well implemented and supported by Mozilla and Microsoft in their browsers.

JavaScript is used to manipulate parts of the browser and the pages which it displays. Those items which can be used in scripts are defined in a W3C standard called the Document Object Model, DOM. The DOM was developed by the World Wide Web Consortium (W3C) but is not implemented in the same way in every browser. Code which complies with the standard and which works in one browser may not work in others. Different versions of browsers from the same development team are not even guaranteed to support the same pieces of code. Problems with DOM implementations mean that most scripts work in some browsers but rarely in all of them. In the end most developers take a pragmatic approach and code for either Mozilla or Internet Explorer but the best solution is to use as little client-side code as possible. I will try to show some code that will work with both, but I will also demonstrate the differences between the two environments and show how to code for each of them. Section 14.4 examines the standard DOM.

6.1 WHAT IS DYNAMIC HTML?

Dynamic HTML is a combination of content formatted using HTML, cascading stylesheets, a scripting language, and the DOM. Usually the scripting language is ECMA Script compliant although it does not have to be. By combining all of the technologies from W3C, developers can create interesting and interactive Web sites which continue to download quickly and which have relatively low hardware requirements. Many multimedia plug-ins need modern high-specification PCs and are unusable by the disabled or through non-traditional hardware. For instance, a page based around a fancy plug-in cannot be used via a mobile telephone but a DHTML page can.

RULE OF THUMB

The DHTML aspects of the page should be the icing on the cake rather than the cake itself.

You may have been left wondering what ECMA Script is. It is really a standard rather than a real thing: it is the standard for languages which manipulate the document object model and is actually based upon Netscape's JavaScript version 1.1. Given that JScript from Microsoft is equivalent to JavaScript, and that both of them are ECMA Script compliant in many ways, either can be used to develop standard Dynamic HTML pages.

6.2 JAVASCRIPT

I am going to refer to JavaScript throughout the next few sections. Much of what I will have to say is appropriate to programmers who are working with JScript because the two languages are meant to be implementations of the same thing.

JavaScript originates from a language called LiveScript. The idea was to find a language which could be used to provide client-side in-browser applications, but which was not as complicated as Java. Although in the original concept there was a certain overlap between the roles of Java and JavaScript, the actual implementations are radically divergent. The only similarity between the two languages is in their names. Having good programming skills in Java will make the learning of JavaScript relatively simple. Having good JavaScript skills will not help you to learn Java.

JavaScript is a fairly simple language which is only suitable for fairly simple tasks. The language is best suited to tasks which run for a short time and is most commonly used to manipulate the pieces of the document object model. Many developers experience problems when they try to build Web pages which have embedded JavaScript and which must run on both of the major browsers. Often these problems are more closely related to the implementations of the DOM than to the implementations of the language.

The version of JavaScript that was used as the basis of the ECMA Script standard was 1.1. Therefore everything that is written using JavaScript 1.1 should comply with the standard.

6.2.1 How Simple is JavaScript?

Many companies which supply HTML editors have added JavaScript capabilities to their tools. They supply a library of common code that you can adapt and use in your own pages. Most people who use the language will not have access to such a tool, and most of those who *do* will eventually find the tool quite limited. That is because the tool can only ever do what its designer envisaged.

A language is far more flexible than any tool and hence it is likely that sooner or later you will want to write code that your tool does not support. In addition, and as I said when I introduced HTML, if you do not understand the detail of how your code works then you cannot fix it when it goes wrong. It is inevitable that at some point your code will fail. Hopefully that happens during the development process, but not always and the Web is full of seriously broken code. You will want to debug and repair your code, and as browsers change and requirements get more sophisticated you will also want to upgrade and add new code. To do that you need to be able to program.

So how easy is programming in JavaScript? Well most experienced software developers will tell you that writing scripts is not really like programming. Programs tend to be large pieces of code, possibly a number of modules which combine together to make a full application. Scripts are small pieces of code which accomplish a single, relatively simple, task. I do not agree with this view. If you are a novice but can write some JavaScript to control a roll-over effect on a Web page, then you should be as pleased with your efforts as a programmer with thirty years' experience, who writes part of a word processor. Programming is simply making a computer do what you want, when you want it to.

Of course there are differences between full-scale programs and small pieces of JavaScript. Programs tend to be compiled while scripts are interpreted. That simply means that if you have written a script, another program called an interpreter takes that script code and works through it, carrying out the instructions that are contained in the script. When a program is compiled it is converted into *binary code*, a series of 0s and 1s. These can be run directly by the operating system of the computer.

Compiled programs are hardware and operating system specific and have to be compiled separately for every platform on which they will execute. Because it is the text of the script which will be run by the interpreter, any script can be run on any system that contains a suitable interpreter. I can write JavaScript code on a PC that is running Linux then place it on my Web site. Users on any system, whether Linux, Windows 2000, Apple MacOS or anything else – can use that script if their browser contains a suitable JavaScript interpreter.

So JavaScript is nicely platform independent and can be run everywhere. And using it is not like writing a program in, say, C or Pascal or C++. In fact, JavaScript has been designed to run through browsers and can actually do very little. If you have never programmed, then learning it may initially seem a bit daunting, but very quickly you will feel comfortable.

6.2.2 Borrowing Code

One of the many good things about the Web is that there is an awful lot of code out there. All the JavaScript that your browser encounters is freely available to you. It all gets stored in the cache of your machine and you can look at it at your leisure. That does not mean that you can steal that code. Far from it. Everything you download has a copyright, even when it does not have an explicit copyright notice. Most Web developers will not mind you taking a look at their code to see how they implement things. In fact, most programmers, whatever the type of system they build, started like that – most of us still use other people's code samples when we learn a new language. Those samples might come from a Web site or a textbook but they are an invaluable learning aid wherever they are from.

Any book can only give a few ideas. Hopefully the code samples that I will show you will cover a wide range and yet are generic enough to be used in many applications. If they are not suitable for you, then look around for anything that will help.

WARNING

*Borrowing ideas is fine. Borrowing code is **NOT**. It is copyright theft unless the original author specifically states otherwise.*

6.2.3 Benefits of JavaScript

JavaScript has a number of big benefits to anyone who wants to make their Web site dynamic:

- it is widely supported in Web browsers
- it gives easy access to the document objects and can manipulate most of them
- it can give interesting animations without the long download times associated with many multimedia data types
- it is relatively secure – JavaScript can neither read from your local hard drive nor write to it, and you cannot get a virus infection directly from JavaScript.
- Web surfers do not need a special plug-in to use your scripts

6.2.4 Problems with JavaScript

Although JavaScript looks like it should be a win-win for both developers and users, this is not always the case:

- Most scripts rely upon manipulating the elements of the DOM. Support for a standard set of objects currently does not exist and access to objects differs from browser to browser.
- If your script does not work then your page is useless.
- Because of the problems of broken scripts, many Web surfers disable JavaScript support in their browser.
- Scripts can run slowly and complex scripts can take a long time to start up.

6.2.5 Do I Have to Use JavaScript?

There are many alternative solutions to the problem of making Web sites interactive and dynamic. Some of these rely upon complex multimedia data, while others are script based. Some of the scripting solutions which might be considered as competitors to JavaScript are listed below along with some comments.

Always remember that your Web pages do not *have* to provide a total interactive experience. If you want to provide content and information rather than entertainment then you are probably best advised to keep it simple and stick mostly to text and static images.

Perl

A complex language that is commonly used for server-side CGI scripting. Perl is available for client-side work through a subset called Perlscript which can also be used when writing Active Server Pages. It is not widely used in client-side applications, although that situation may change. Due to its text manipulating nature, it is probably better fitted to remaining on the server.

VBScript

Widely used but, unfortunately, platform specific. This language is only available under the Microsoft Windows operating system. It can be used to develop browser applications, but they will only run inside Internet Explorer.

Python

A little known language that is making inroads into the CGI writing area. A Web browser has been written in Python which can run Python applets. It is likely that Python will also move more towards client-side scripting.

Tcl

This has been a popular choice for systems programming. The language itself has been widely criticized by proponents of other scripting languages, but it is clearly effective in its own niche. A Tcl plug-in can be downloaded from the Internet and the demonstration programs show that this is in fact a worthy contender in many of the same application areas as Java.

Java

This is not a scripting language,[1] but it is used for many of the same things as JavaScript. It is very good at menus and data validation on the client but can be very slow. It is probably a better language for the development of proper networked applications than simple browser applets.

In summary, if you want to embed some interactivity within a Web page then you can use any combination of a number of scripting languages and multimedia packages. If you want to make the basic HTML of your page both dynamic and interactive then you currently have no choice but to use JavaScript.

6.3 JAVASCRIPT – THE BASICS

In many respects JavaScript code resembles C. I do not mean that programming in JavaScript is in any way like programming in C, but if you look at a page of code in each language then the two will look fairly similar. The semantics (i.e., the meaning of the code) of the

---

 [1]Although it is *interpreted*. Actually it is compiled *and* interpreted.

two languages are very different but the syntax (i.e., the symbols and construction) of a JavaScript program and of a simple C program are quite close. The syntax of a language is the set of tokens that comprise it. Many languages borrow from the set of tokens used in C simply because most programmers can read C and hence most programmers can read code written in other languages.

JavaScript can be run on some file and Web servers but the vast majority of users are developing front-ends for Web pages. That is the use that I am going to demonstrate. I am not going to explain the whole language in intricate detail. Plenty of books and on-line resources are available which will do that. A list of keywords does not really help you to learn the language – a basic explanation of how it all works and some simple examples is a much more useful educational tool.

6.3.1 A Simple Script

The script that follows could hardly be easier. It is almost the JavaScript version of "Hello World!". It is a program that everyone can use to convince themselves that they really *could* learn to program. Read through the code first then I will explain what is going on.

```
1    <html>
       <head>
         <script language="javascript">
         <!--
3        function describe(){
             var major = parseInt(navigator.appVersion);
             var minor = parseFloat(navigator.appVersion);
             var agent = navigator.userAgent.toLowerCase();
             document.write("<h1>Details in Popup</h1>");
10           document.close();
             window.alert(agent + " " + major);
         }

         function farewell(){
15           window.alert("Farewell and thanks for visiting");
         }
         //-->
         </script>
       </head>
20     <body onLoad="describe()" onUnload="farewell()">
       </body>
     </html>
```

JavaScript programs contain variables, objects, and functions. These will all be covered in detail soon. For now it is enough to know that JavaScript code can interact directly with the Web browser, window in the example, can write into the page which is being displayed, document and can query the browser about itself using navigator.

The key points about JavaScript that you need to apply in all scripts are listed below.

- Each line of code is terminated by a semicolon.
- Blocks of code must be surrounded by a pair of curly brackets. A block of code is a set of instructions that are to be executed together as a unit. This might be because they are optional and dependent upon a Boolean condition or because they are to be executed repeatedly.
- Functions have parameters which are passed inside parentheses.
- Variables are declared using the keyword var.
- Scripts require neither a main function nor an exit condition. These are major differences between scripts and *proper* programs. Execution of a script starts with the first line of code and runs until there is no more code.

Many people set their browsers so that JavaScript and other programming languages are barred from opening new windows. This is a perfectly sensible thing to do as it prevents Websites opening lots of popup windows and polluting the Web experience. The code you have just seen writes to an alert box which is a standard component of Web browsers rather than a new window. The code could be modified to write to a new Window as you will see in Section 8.2. If you want to see how to write into the existing document window try this alternative version of the describe() function.

```
1  function describe() {
       var major = parseInt(navigator.appVersion);
       var minor = parseFloat(navigator.appVersion);
       var agent = navigator.userAgent.toLowerCase();
5      document.write("<h1>Your Browser</h1>");
       document.write("<p>" + agent + " " + major + "</p>");
       document.close();
   }
```

6.3.2 JavaScript and the HTML Page

Having written some JavaScript, you need to include it in an HTML page. You cannot execute these scripts from a command line as the interpreter is part of the browser. The script is included in the Web page and run by the browser, usually as soon as the page has been loaded. The browser is able to debug the script and can display errors.

> **NOTE** *To get Mozilla to show errors, type* javascript: *in the location box. A console will appear which will display the errors, although they may not be stunningly useful. Mozilla does not display errors by default. Internet Explorer uses a different scheme. When it encounters a script error it opens a popup window with details of the error. A debugger for scripting language can be downloaded free of charge from the Microsoft Web site.*

If you are only writing small scripts, or only use your scripts in a few pages, then the easiest scheme is to include the script code in the HTML file. The following example shows how this is done. It is important that you remember to use the HTML comments around the script code. If you do not do this then some browsers may try to display your JavaScript code as part of the page.

```
 1   <html>
         <head>
             <title>A Sample JavaScript</title>
             <script language="javascript">
 5           <!--
                 // the JavaScript code goes here...
             // -->
             </script>
         </head>
10       <body>
             ...
         </body>
     </html>
```

If you use a lot of scripts or your scripts are complex then including the code inside the Web page will make your source files difficult to read and debug. A better idea is to put your JavaScript code in a separate file and include that code in the head of the page as shown below. By convention, JavaScript programs are stored in files with the .js extension. In the following example, notice that the script element must be terminated by an end tag, </script>.

```
 1   <html>
         <head>
             <title>A Sample JavaScript</title>
             <script language="javascript" src="sample.js"></script>
```

```
5        </head>
         <body>
            . . .
         </body>
     </html>
```

Finally, small pieces of code can be included inside the body of the Web page. Doing this may have side effects, that is it can cause things to happen which you did not intend. Let us look at how the script is included first, then I will consider possible side effects.

```
1    <html>
         <head>
            <title>A Sample JavaScript</title>
         </head>
5        <body>
            <script language="javascript">
            <!--
               alert("The page has loaded");
            //-->
10          </script>
         </body>
     </html>
```

Side Effects

Sometimes a piece of code is intended to do one thing but, when run, it does another. I am sure that most of you will, at some time or another, have used a program which occasionally displays erratic behaviour. Often these problems are caused by *side effects*. A piece of code may appear to be perfect in isolation but, when used, it has effects on programs which are already executing. Some programs even have unforeseen effects upon *themselves* as they run. Often these problems are caused because the programmer has made a trivial mistake, such as incorrectly setting a value.

HTML pages with embedded JavaScript rarely exhibit serious flaws, but they can have side effects. This is especially true if you place your scripts inside the body of the page. If you have a script at the top of the page, then some HTML, the script may be executed before the body of the page has loaded. Similarly, having the script at the foot of the page causes the reverse to be true: the script only executes after the text of the page has been loaded. These differences in when a script is run are caused because the browser is loading the page in order from the top and executing the scripts as it loads them. If your page relies upon a combination of scripts, text and images you might not be getting the result that you expect:

the images will be downloaded a long time after the text and will be processed last by the browser. If the script and images rely upon each other then the page will not run properly.

Scripts which are loaded from separate files or placed in the head of the page do not exhibit this behavior because they need to be triggered by *events* which are controlled externally. The relationship between JavaScript and events is discussed in Section 7.6.

6.3.3 The Output

Take the code from Section 6.3.1 and save it in a file called `SimpleScript.html`. The script writes some text into the Web browser window and opens up an alert window which contains a message. The result of all of which is shown in Figure 6.1. It is easy and useful and, in fact, we are going to use the same idea in several of the scripts in Chapter 8.

6.3.4 The Code Samples

I am going to spend the rest of this chapter describing the features of the JavaScript language. You cannot do a lot with this code in isolation or in small snippets but it is important that you understand the language before I introduce more complicated ideas and full programs.

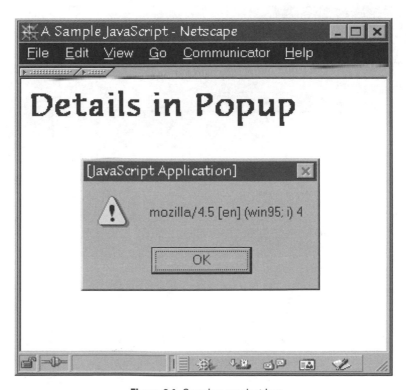

Figure 6.1 Opening an alert box

Wherever possible I have attempted to place code samples into simple Web pages to illustrate the text. If you really want to learn this language, type these code samples into your favorite text editor, save them as HTML files and view them in your Web browser.

Do not worry if you make mistakes and the scripts do not work straight out of the box. Debugging simple code is good practice for what comes later. Never believe anyone who tells you that they can program without making mistakes: we all have to track bugs through our work.

 NOTE *If you use Netscape, typing* `javascript:` *in the location bar brings up a console which displays error messages. Figure 6.2 shows this in action.*

The scripts in this chapter are really very simple, in fact I guess you could almost call them *scriptlets*. Despite their simplicity, they all use a couple of the really neat features of

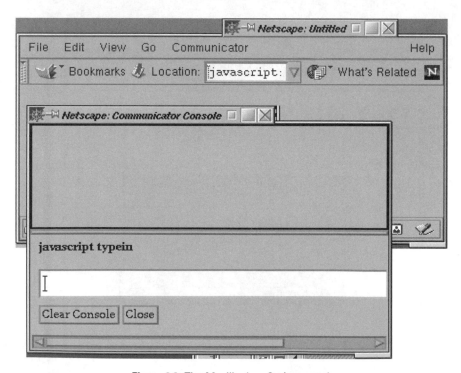

Figure 6.2 The Mozilla JavaScript console

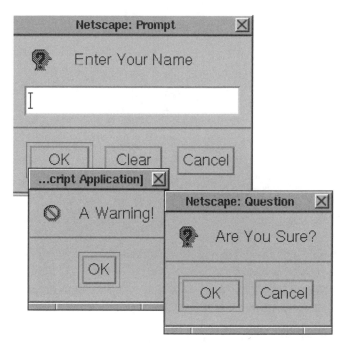

Figure 6.3 The dialog boxes

the DOM. Browsers are able to open dialog boxes to display messages to the user and to get data from them. These dialogs are really easy to use from within JavaScript so rather than trying any fancy programming tricks or writing non-interactive scripts, I am going to use them. Figure 6.3 shows the dialog boxes in action from within Netscape. Section 8.3 describes these dialogs.

6.4 VARIABLES

Like any programming language, JavaScript has variables. These are data items that you can manipulate as the program runs. If you have never programmed before then you need to know a little something about variables. If you *have* done some programming then skim over this bit as I bring the beginners up to speed.

A variable is a named value that you use in your programs. Most people will have used variables without realizing it. If you remember something that looked like x = 5 being written at school, then you remember seeing a variable. That example is of a variable named x which is set to the value 5. In computing we call giving a value to a variable *assignment*. Variables in programs do not have fixed values, just as they did not in basic algebra. Instead the variable name is used to track changing values as the program runs. If you are unsure about what I mean, try finding the values of x and y after the following set of mathematical statements:

```
1   x = 0
    y = 3
    x = y + 4
    y = x times x
```

At the end x equals 7 and y equals 49. If you did not follow that, spend some time thinking about what was happening before you read on.

6.4.1 Variable Names

There are strict rules governing how you name your variables in JavaScript:

- Names must begin with a letter, digit, or the underscore (_).
- You cannot use spaces in names.
- Names are case-sensitive, so that fred, FRED and frEd all refer to different variables.
- You cannot use a reserved word as a variable name. Reserved words are those words which are part of the JavaScript language.

Provided you obey the rules, then anything goes when choosing variable names. It is always better to make them meaningful. It is more than likely that once your code is running you will want to start making improvements and changes. All programmers do that all of the time but we usually call it maintenance. You can call it tinkering if you like. Imagine tracking two variables through a program, one called visitor_name, the other called vn, both of which are the user name of a visitor to your Web site. Many simple and potentially disastrous mistakes are possible with the variable named vn. For instance, you would be unlikely to write:

```
visitor_name = visitor_name + 45.32
```

but might accidentally write:

```
vn = vn + 45.32
```

which would be equally illogical within the context of your script.

6.4.2 Data Types

Programming languages usually have several different types of data. Commonly, programmers may use characters, integers (whole numbers), Booleans (logical values of true and false), strings (ordered sets of characters), reals (complex numbers), and many others besides. In keeping with its restricted ambitions, JavaScript has only four types of data:

numeric

> These are basic numbers. They can be integers such as 2, 22, and 2,222,000 or floating point values like 23.42, − 56.01, and 2E45. You do not need to differentiate between them as you declare and use them – in fact, you can merrily change the type of data which a variable holds as the program runs. Ideally, of course, doing so will make sense in your program.

strings

> These are collections of characters that are not numbers. The value of a string can even contain spaces and may be totally made from digits. All of the following are strings: "Chris", "Chris Bates", and "2345.432". How can the last one possibly be a string? Well why not? If it is never used in a mathematical expression, the system has no way of knowing that it is a number. In JavaScript anything which is not used in a mathematical expression is not a number, even if it looks like one.

> When a value is assigned as a string to a variable name you must tell the JavaScript system what type of data it is now handling. To do this you put quotes around the value:

```
visitor_name = "Chris Bates"
visitor_name = 'Chris Bates'
visitor_name = "34.45"
```

> If you are nesting strings one inside another you have to be careful about how you use quotes. The best approach is to use double quotes for the outer string and single quotes for all inner strings. Do not try to do more than one layer of nesting in this way because it will not work:

```
visitor_quote = "A quote inside 'a quote' needs different marks.";
```

> If you simply have to use nested quotes, then you can force the interpreter to do your bidding by placing a \ before the inner quotes. This momentarily switches off the default behavior:

```
visitor_quote = "A quote inside \"a quote\" with the same mark.";
```

Boolean

Boolean variables hold the values `true` and `false`. These are used a lot in programming to hold the result of conditional tests. You might want to know if a particular event has happened yet or if a value has been assigned. You will be seeing lots of Boolean values throughout the rest of this book.

null

This is used when you do not yet know something. A `null` value is one that has not yet been given a value. It *does not* mean nil or zero and should not be used in that way – ever.

6.4.3 Creating Variables

Creating a variable could not be easier. You do not need to decide upon the type of data that the variable is going to hold when you declare it. That is completely different to languages such as Pascal and C++ . All that you need to do is use the keyword **var** before the variable name. You do not even have to give the variable a value – that can be done later. Finally, you can easily copy the value of one variable directly into another as you create it. Look at the following examples:

```
var first = 23;
var second = "Some words";
var third = second;
var first_boolean = true;
```

If you were to examine the value in `third` you would see that it contains the string Some words. That is not the exact same string as in the variable `second`, but is a copy of it.

When you have finished with a variable you do not have to delete it or set it to `null`. Just leave it there and the browser will automatically delete it for you when a different Web page is loaded.

One more thing about variables is that the use of the JavaScript keyword `var` is often optional. The interpreter knows just enough about scripts to understand that if it sees an unquoted string inside a script, it is dealing with a variable. Unfortunately the behavior that the variable displays may vary depending upon the way it is being used. Since we want our scripts to be consistent and to work as we intended when we wrote them, it is best to always use `var` before variable declarations.

Using Variables in JavaScript

The simplest way of finding how variables work is, perhaps not surprisingly, to actually use them. The following code prompts the user for their name and then writes that information into the browser window.

```
1   <html>
        <head>
            <title>A Sample JavaScript</title>
        </head>
5       <body >
            <script language="javascript">
            <!--
                var visitor_name;
                visitor_name = prompt("Enter Your Name", "");
10              document.writeln("<h1>Your name is</h1>");
                document.writeln("<h2>" + visitor_name + "</h2>");
                document.close();
            //-->
            </script>
15      </body>
    </html>
```

The input from the user is stored in a variable called visitor_name. Writing the text out to the browser window uses a method called writeln which is actually part of the document. The document is a special type of JavaScript object and is covered in some detail in Chapter 7. All that you need to know about it for the moment is that it enables you to write HTML formatted text into a browser window. Notice that I have placed that script into the body of the page. This simplifies the process of writing to the document. If the script had been placed inside the page head, an entire HTML page would have had to be written out. In the simple case, the script is run as soon as the page is loaded, if the code is in the head then the page must force execution of the script. The following code shows how this is done:

```
1   <html>
        <head>
            <title>A Sample JavaScript</title>
            <script language="javascript">
5           <!--
                function test() {
                    var visitor_name;
                    visitor_name = prompt("Enter Your Name", "");
                    alert("Your name is " + visitor_name);
10                  document.writeln("<html><head>");
                    document.writeln("<title>Sample</title>");
                    document.writeln("</head><body>");
```

```
          document.writeln("<h1>Your name is</h1>");
          document.writeln("<h2>" + visitor_name + "</h2>");
15        document.writeln("</body></html>");
          document.close();
       }
     //-->
     </script>
20   </head>
     <body onLoad="test()">
     </body>
</html>
```

I will show you how to create and use functions in Section 6.10, but for now I will stick to the simple model. In both of those examples the variable held string data, which the user had entered, and then displayed that data. In JavaScript you can do an awful lot more with your data. The language has many builtin functions which you can use to simplify your coding tasks.

RULE OF THUMB

One of the most important lessons that a programmer can learn is to stand on the shoulders of giants. Many simple and repetitious tasks have been programmed by others and are available for your use. JavaScript has a copious library of routines, so instead of writing your own data manipulation routines, use the ones which are supplied. They are likely to be faster and more efficient than yours anyway.

I am not going to describe all of the operations, functions and capabilities which JavaScript provides. Netscape have a reference guide which does just that and which is available in HTML and PDF formats. It is long; very long and I do not have the space to cover all of that material here. Instead I have picked selected highlights, those parts of the language which you will use most often, and described them. In most cases I will demonstrate some partial code which shows how the functions are used. Some functions are so interesting or useful that I will devote more time and space to them and give complete examples. I would advise taking the smaller pieces of code and building them into your own test pages, and where I have not provided an example, try writing your own. This is good practice and it will give you a real feel for the language.

Converting data types

Always assume that a value in JavaScript is a string unless you have explicitly converted it to a number. The interpreter will try to best-guess your intentions if they are not clear. Here is an example of the confusion which can arise.

```
1    <html>
         <head>
             <title>The Math Object</title>
         </head>
5        <body>
             <script language="javascript">
             <!--
                 document.writeln("<h1>Confusion</h1>");
                 var valueOne = "12";
10               var valueTwo = "34";

                 var vo = vt = 0;
                 vo = parseInt(valueOne);
                 vt = parseInt(valueTwo);

15
                 document.writeln("<p>The first number is " + vo + ", the second
                     is " + vt + ".</p>");

                 var result = valueOne + valueTwo;
                 document.writeln("<p>Adding the two inputs gives " + result +
                     "</p>");
20
                 result = vo + vt;
                 document.writeln("<p>Adding the converted values gives " +
                     result + "</p>");

                 document.writeln("<p>Adding the converted values inside a
                     writeln " + vo + vt + "</p>");
25
                 document.close();
             //-->
             </script>
         </body>
30   </html>
```

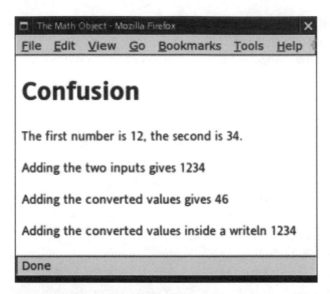

Figure 6.4 Converting between data types

Two numerical values are stored as strings. The two values are then converted to Integers and stored in two more variables. This gives us two copies of each variable. These are printed individually to the document and display as expected, see Figure 6.4. The initial values are joined together and displayed once more. Because the values are held as strings, JavaScript concatenates one onto the end of the other when it processes the + operator. The Integer values created in the conversion are now added together and the result stored in the variable `result`. This is displayed and gives the answer we might expect.

Finally, the confusing part. The two integers are added together within a call to the `document.writeln` method. This places the integer values in a context which expects strings as its values. The values held in `vo` and `vt` are automatically converted into strings when they are passed into the method. This does not affect the variables in `vo` and `vt` since copies of the data which they hold are passed. Technically, programmers say this is *call by value*. The data in the variable is not affected – that only happens during a *call by reference*.

6.5 STRING MANIPULATION

Most of the data that you will handle in your JavaScript are going to be text strings. Some of the most useful text manipulations involve *regular expressions*. These are an advanced topic which you will need quite a lot of knowledge to really tackle. Consequently I have left a discussion of regular expressions until Section 7.2, by when you will have seen, and hopefully written, quite a lot of JavaScript.

Even if we only think about relatively simple operations using strings, JavaScript has many which are very useful. Broadly speaking, string manipulation involves either joining strings together, splitting them apart or searching through them. JavaScript has functions which perform all of those operations and much more.

length

A value which holds the number of characters in the string. Note that this is *not* a function and so you do not have to place parentheses when using it.

```
1   var agent = navigator.userAgent.toLowerCase();
    var ll = agent.length;
```

charAt(index)

This function returns the character which is at position index in the string. By repeatedly calling the function you can parse a whole string, which is quite useful if, for instance, you want to perform crude validation of data input. Here is an example:

```
1   <html>
      <head>
        <title>A Sample JavaScript</title>
      </head>
5     <body>
      <script language="javascript">
      <!--
        var you = prompt("Enter your name", "");
        var num = prompt("Enter a whole number", "");
10      document.writeln("<h1>charAt</h1>");
        document.write("<p>The character at position ");
        document.writeln(num + " in your name is</p>");
        document.writeln("<h2>" + you.charAt(num) + "</h2>");
        document.close();
15    //-->
      </script>
      </body>
    </html>
```

Do you remember that I said that JavaScript does not have formal data types? You can change the type of data which a variable is holding as the program executes. This example gives you the opportunity to play around with that idea. Try entering a number as your name or a string as the position indicator. Rather than crash with some terrible error, the program simply prints what it can into the browser and ignores data it cannot handle. The same thing happens if you enter a number that is higher than the number of characters in your name – and also if you enter a negative number.

The result of the prompt is always returned as a string, if you need it to be a number then you must check the data type and convert it yourself using a combination of isNaN() and either parseInt() or parseFloat().

concat("string"[, "string"[, ... "string"]])

JavaScript has two ways that you can join strings together. The simplest is to use the + operator as I did in the last example. If you want to create a new string by joining two existing strings then + is slightly unsatisfactory. As an operation it is not *explicit* about what it is doing. Remember, JavaScript variables can have their data type changed during the run of a script. A prompt will return a string but that could be converted into a number elsewhere in your program. By the time that your code reaches the + operator, the two values may both be numbers, so whilst the following code may leave the result holding a sensible value in some circumstances, in others it may not:

```
1   var you = prompt("Enter your name", "");
    var yourAge = prompt("Enter your age in months", "");
    you = parseInt(you);
    yourAge = parseInt(yourAge);
5   var result = you + yourAge;
```

The solution is to use the concat() operator. This method is part of the string object and takes another string, or comma separated list of strings, as its argument.

```
1   var you = prompt("Enter your name", "");
    var yourAge = prompt("Enter your age in months", "");

    var msg = "Thank You ";
5   document.writeln(msg.concat(you));

    you = you + " ";
    var result = you.concat(yourAge);
    var result = you.concat(yourAge, "Thanks");
10  document.writeln(result);
```

Every string that you have in a piece of JavaScript is implemented internally as a software object. Objects are one of the most powerful and important ideas in the field of software engineering. They are constructs which contain data and the code which manipulates that data. When you create a string it contains a set of characters and a whole slew of bits of code. The concat() method is just one such method. To use a method you give the name of the variable which holds the string followed by a ., the name of the method and a set of parentheses. Any values which you need to pass into the method's parameters are placed inside the parentheses.

In the example a variable called you is created. This holds the string which is returned from the prompt. To concatenate another string onto the value held in you we call its concat() method with the second string given as a parameter:

```
1  var result = you.concat(yourAge);
```

That might seem like a lot of effort compared to using +. It is, in this trivial example, but if you want to join lots of strings together concat() starts to make more sense. This example shows what happens if we want to create a string holding a number of values that the user has entered elsewhere. The first line uses +, the second uses concat():

```
1  var result = name +" "+ addressLine1 +" "+ addressLine2 +" "+ state +"
       "+ zip);
   var result = "".concat(name, " ", addressLine1, " ", addressLine2, " ",
       state, " ", zip);
```

Notice that in both cases I have had to be explicit about where I want spaces placed between values to give a readable result. Other programming languages have variants of concat() which do that automatically.

indexOf("search"[, offset])

The string is searched for the string or quoted character in the first parameter. If the search is successful, the index of the start of the target string is returned. The indices in the original string, number from 0 to string.length - 1. If the search is unsuccessful the operation returns -1. By default the indexOf() function starts at index 0, however, an optional offset may be specified so that the search starts part way along the string.

The following example shows how this works:

```
1  <html>
     <head>
       <title>Browser Agent</title>
     </head>
5    <body>
       <script language="javascript">
       <!--
       // find the maker of the browser
       var agent = navigator.userAgent.toLowerCase();
```

```
10        var result = agent.indexOf("msie");

          document.writeln("<h1>Your Browser is</h1>");
          document.writeln("<p>" + agent + "</p>");

15        if(result == -1){
              document.write("<p>It was not made by ");
              document.writeln("Microsoft</p>");
          }
          else
20            document.writeln("<p>It was made by Microsoft</p>");

          document.close();
          //-->
          </script>
25    </body>
    </html>
```

lastIndexOf("search"[, offset])

This function does exactly the same thing as `indexOf()` but works its way backwards along the string. The offset works in exactly the same way as for `indexOf()`, but the default value is `string.length - 1`.

split(separator[, limit])

Often we need to split a string apart into its constituent elements. The `split()` function breaks the string apart whenever it encounters the character passed in as the first parameter. The pieces of the string are stored in an *array*. `split()` has an optional second parameter which is an integer value indicating how many of the pieces are to be stored in the array.

Add the following code into the earlier example just before `document.close();` and see what happens.

```
1   var words = agent.split(" ");
    for(var i = 0; i < words.length; i++) {
        document.writeln("<p>" + words[i] + "</p>");
    }
```

substr(index[, length])

This function returns a substring which starts at the character indicated by the index parameter. The substring continues either to the end of the string or for the number of characters indicated by the length parameter.

If the index is greater than the length of the string then nothing is returned. If it is negative then it is taken as the offset from the *end* of the string working backwards along its length. If a length of 0, or a negative number, is provided then no characters are returned.

```
1   piece = agent.substring(3, 17);
    document.writeln("<p>" + piece + "</p>");
```

substring(index1[, index2])

returns the set of characters which starts at *index1* and continues up to, but does not include, the character at *index2*. The following rules apply:

1. If *index1* is less than 0, it will be treated as 0.
2. If *index2* is greater than the length of the string, it is treated as the length of the string.
3. If the two index values are equal, an empty string is returned.
4. If *index2* is missing, all characters up to the end of the string are taken.
5. If *index1* is greater than *index2*, a runtime error occurs.

toLowerCase()

Converts all characters in the string to lower case.

toUpperCase()

Converts all characters in the string to upper case.

6.6 MATHEMATICAL FUNCTIONS

Mathematical functions and values are part of a built-in JavaScript object called Math. All functions and attributes used in complex mathematics must be accessed via this object. This is usually done by preceding the function name with the object name:

```
1   var area = Math.PI * (r * r);
    var next = Math.ceil(area);
```

If a section of your code includes a lot of math operations, the repetition of Math can become tedious. It can be replaced using the keyword with like this:

```
1  with(Math){
       var area = PI * (r * r);
       var next = ceil(area);
   }
```

The choice of construct is yours. Sometimes using Math. will add clarity to your code. At other times it will lead to confusion as the code will be needlessly crowded with the same construct.

NaN

> This is a value which represents something which is not a number. That might sound slightly peculiar: why should a programming language need to indicate whether values are numbers? Because variables can hold different types of data in JavaScript, you need a way of knowing if a value is currently numeric so that your script can decide how to process it.
>
> Many functions return numbers if they have completed successfully. Checking the return value against NaN gives a way of deciding if the function operated properly.

In all versions of JavaScript before 1.3 NaN was not a top-level object. This meant that it could not be accessed directly. Instead it had to be used through the Number object. If you want your code to work in browsers running older versions of JavaScript be sure to use Number.Nan.

6.6.1 Global Methods

There are some methods which are always available to your scripts. Amongst these are three methods which you will often use when working with numerical input. You will have seen these methods used in some of the earlier examples in this chapter.

isNaN(value)

> This function returns true if its argument is not a number and false if it is numeric.

parseFloat(string)

> This function parses a string, passed in as an argument, and returns it as a floating point number. The string is parsed from the start with the parser looking for the numbers 0 through 9, the signs + and −, decimal points and exponents (the characters e and E) only. When any other character is encountered the parser stops and returns what it has already found. If the first character of the string does not belong to the valid set, NaN is returned.

parseInt(string[, radix])

> The string is parsed and its value as an integer returned. Once an invalid character is encountered the parsing stops and the function returns what it has already found. If the first character of the string is invalid, NaN is returned.

> The function optionally takes a radix as its second argument, defaulting to base 10 if an alternative is not supplied. The set of valid characters depends upon the supplied radix:

> - in base 2 only the characters 0 and 1 are permitted
> - in base 10 the digits 0 through 9 are permitted
> - in base 16 the characters 0 through 9 and the letters a, b, c, d, e and f, in lower or upper case, are allowed
> - if the string starts with 0x the number is assumed to be hexadecimal (base 16).

> During parsing the number is converted to decimal. If a user enters 0xa that will be available as 10.

NOTE *Both* parseInt() *and* parseFloat() *extract as much of a number from the input string as they can. If a user types* 123qwe *these functions will return* 123.

6.6.2 The Math Library

All of the specialized mathematical operations are available in the Math library. To use these simply put the name of the operation after Math. and include any parameters inside the parentheses.

abs(value)

> returns the absolute value of the number passed into it.

acos(value), asin(value), atan(value)

> These functions return the arccosine, arcsine and arctangent, respectively, of the value passed into them. All return values are in radians.

atan2(value1, value2)

> returns the arctangent, in radians, of the quotient [2] of the values passed into it.

ceil(value)

> returns the smallest integer which is greater than, or equal to, the value passed in.

cos(value), sin(value), tan(value)

> return the cosine, sin and tangent, respectively, of the value passed in as an argument.

[2]The result of dividing one by the other.

floor(value)

returns the largest integer which is smaller than, or equal to, the number passed in.

log(value)

returns the natural logarithm of its argument. If the argument is not a number or is a negative number then NaN will be returned.

max(value1, value2)

returns the larger of its arguments.

min(value1, value2)

returns the smaller of its arguments.

pow(value, power)

returns the result of raising *value* to *power*.

random()

returns a pseudorandom number between 0 and 1. The random number generator is seeded from the current time.

Creating a truly random number computationally is impossible. All random number generators create sequences of numbers which will eventually repeat themselves. The trick in writing such code is to create such a long sequence that it will not repeat during the expected runtime of the program. That way the sequence, and its effects, will appear random to the user.

round(value)

returns the result of rounding its argument to the nearest integer.

sqrt(value)

returns the square root of the value.

The code which follows is a template which you can use to try out the Math object and its functions. Replace the call to Math.floor() with calls to any of the other Math methods and see what happens.

```
1   <html>
        <head>
            <title>The Math Library</title>
        </head>
5       <body>
            <script language="javascript">
            <!--
```

```
         document.writeln("<h1>The Math Library</h1>");
         do {
             var valueOne = prompt("Enter a number", "");
         } while (isNaN(valueOne));

         do {
             var valueTwo = prompt("Enter another number", "");
         } while (isNaN(valueTwo));

         var vo = vt = result = 0;
         vo = parseFloat(valueOne);
         vt = parseFloat(valueTwo, 16);

         document.writeln("<p>The first number is " + vo
+ ", the second is " + vt + ".</p>");

         // Change the next line to test other functions
         result = Math.floor(vo);
         document.writeln("<p>The floor of the first number is "
+ result + "</p>");

         document.close();
         //-->
         </script>
    </body>
</html>
```

Notice how I handle input from the user. There is no point in proceeding with the script until we have two valid numbers entered and stored. I prompt for input inside a do... while loop. This will keep iterating until the call to isNaN() returns false which will indicate that a number has been extracted from the input.

6.7 STATEMENTS

Programs are composed of two things: data and code which manipulates that data. I have already shown how to define data items. Now I am going to show you how to create usable code. Program instructions are grouped into units called statements. A statement is a fairly low-level thing: as you will see, one statement will not do anything worthwhile on its own. We create programs from lots of statements.

Constant	Description
Math.E	Approximately 2.718. Euler's Constant, base of natural logarithms.
Math.LN2	Log of 2.
Math.LN10	Log of 10.
Math.PI	3.14159. The ratio of the circumference of a circle to its diameter.
Math.SQRT1_2	The square root of 1/2.
Math.SQRT_2	The square root of 2.

Table 6.1 JavaScript numerical constants

if ... else

Whenever you want to test the truth of a condition before executing any more of your program, use this construct. This statement means that if some condition is true then do one thing, if the condition is false do another. Easy – and useful even in the simplest of scripts. You will be using this one a lot. Here is a typical example:

```
1  <html>
     <head>
       <title>Browser Sniffing</title>
     </head>
5    <body>
       <script language="javascript">
       <!--
         var agent = navigator.userAgent.toLowerCase();
         document.writeln("<h1>Browser Sniffer</h1>");
10       document.write("<p>");

         if (agent.indexOf("mozilla") != -1){
           document.write("Your browser is Netscape");
         } else {
15         document.write("Your browser is Not Netscape");
         }
         document.writeln("</p>");
         document.close();
       //-->
20     </script>
     </body>
   </html>
```

Sometimes you might want to test for more than one possible condition at the same time. In that case you must *nest* your if ... else statements like this:

```
1  if (agent.indexOf("mozilla") != -1){
     if (major <= 4){
       document.write("Your browser is Netscape");
     } else {
5      document.write("Your browser is Mozilla");
     }
   }
```

Notice how the brackets are placed to help make the nesting of the code a bit clearer. There are many ways of setting out your code; whichever you end up using, try to ensure that it clarifies the code for reading rather than making it easier to write.

The code shown there is not suitable for browser sniffing. So many different browsers are available that writing robust code which can detect them all with any degree of reliability is almost a full-time occupation. If you need a good quality browser sniffer, many examples are freely available on the Web.

for (counter = 0; counter <= n; counter++)

Many operations need to be repeated a number of times. These go inside a for loop. By convention these start counting at 0 and terminate when the desired number of iterations (i.e., Passes through the loop.) has been reached. The variable which holds the counter can be given any name you like. Often counters are called i or j. Those names are meaningless but traditional. If you are just starting to program I would encourage you to use names like count instead. They may take longer to type but at least they make sense.

```
1  <html>
     <head>
       <title>For Loops</title>
     </head>
5    <body>
       <script language="javascript">
       <!--
         document.writeln("<h1>A For Loop</h1>");
         for (var count = 0; count < 12; count++) {
10         // repeated statements go here
           document.write("<p>The counter is " + count);
           document.writeln("</p>");
```

```
          }
          document.close();
15      //-->
        </script>
      </body>
    </html>
```

The syntax of the for loop can worry some people. The parentheses contain three statements which are separated by semicolons. The first one initializes the counter when the loop is first encountered. The second statement tells the program when the loop has finished. The third statement contains an operation that is performed to the counter at the end of each loop. In the example the counter is incremented by one.

while (Boolean condition)

Sometimes you do not know how many iterations are going to be needed. The loop may continue forever if an external event does not act upon it. Or you may be processing data and not know how much data you are going to get. In cases like these use the while loop:

```
1   <html>
      <head>
        <title>While Loops</title>
      </head>
5     <body>
        <script language="javascript">
        <!--
          document.writeln("<h1>While Loop</h1>");
          var done = false;
10        var msg;

          while (done == false) {
            // Get a string from the user then display it
            msg = prompt("Enter a String");
15          document.writeln("<p>" + msg + "</p>");

            // If the input was quit, QUIT, Quit
            // or any other variant then finish
            if (msg.toLowerCase() == "quit") {
20            document.writeln("<p>Thanks, Goodbye</p>");
              done = true;
```

```
            } // if
          } // while
25
            document.close();
          //-->
          </script>
        </body>
30    </html>
```

Again, testing for logical conditions inside loops is something you will need to do quite often in your scripts. Notice that I put a comment at the end of each selection statement or loop. This is done so that I can follow the structure of my code. It is not so important in a small example but large programs with complicated nested structures are difficult to read. Ending loops at the wrong point is a common and irritating mistake. These comments effectively eradicate that problem before it even arises.

break

What happens if you want to be able to leap out of the middle of a loop? You can either create a construct based around a while loop with if statements embedded in it or use the break statement. Use break with care. Your loops should always be designed to run smoothly. If you break out of the middle of them you may put variables into unknown states. Compare these two loops and decide which you prefer.

```
1     var answer = 0;
      var correct = 49;
      var done = false;
      var counter = 0;

5
      while ((done == false) && (counter < 3)) {
        // note that && means a logical 'and'
        answer = prompt("What is 7 times 7?", "0");
        if (answer = correct) {
10          done = true;
        } else {
          counter++;
        }
      }

15
      for (counter = 0; counter < 3; counter++) {
```

```
      answer = prompt("What is 7 times 7?", "0");
      if (answer == correct) {
          break;
20    }
    }
```

eval()

This is a very useful JavaScript builtin function. String versions of mathematical expressions can be passed into the function where they are evaluated and the result returned as an integer – great for bringing simple interactivity to a page. For instance:

```
eval("32 * 75674.21");
```

switch

Choosing between a number of alternatives can lead to awkward code if you only use if ... else statements. Where you need to make a choice between more than two items you will find the switch statement much easier to write and maintain. The complete switch looks like:

```
1  switch(expression) {
     case label:
         statement;
         [statement;]
5        break;
     [case label:
         statement;
         [statement;]
         break;]
10   [default:
         statement;]
   }
```

A switch selects between a number of choices depending upon the value of the expression. The choices are identified by case statements, each has a label which equals one of the potential values of the expression. If none of the cases matches the expression, the optional default may be used instead.

Each case includes one or more statements and is terminated by a break. If you omit the break you will get random, potentially harmful, behavior.

Here is an example of the switch:

```
1   <html>
      <head>
        <title>Using Switches</title>
      </head>
5     <body onLoad="Switcher()">
      <script language="javascript">
      <!--
          function Switcher() {
            var inp = prompt("Enter a number from 1 to 4", "");
10          var val = 0;
            switch(Math.floor(eval(inp))){
              case 1:
                val = inp;
                break;
15            case 2:
                val = inp;
                alert("Case 2");
                break;
              case 3:
20              val = inp * inp;
                break;
              case 4:
                val = Math.sin(inp);
                break;
25            default:
                alert("Only values from 1 to 4 are allowed");
            }

            document.writeln("<h1>Using Switches</h1>");
30          document.writeln("<h3>val is now " + val + "</h3>");
            document.close();


          }
      //-->
35    </script>
      </body>
    </html>
```

The script prompts for an input, and stores it in a variable. To perform the selection, the script converts the input to an integer using a combination of `Math.floor()` and `eval()`. If an invalid input is encountered, the default behavior is triggered and an alert box is shown.

6.8 OPERATORS

JavaScript has two types of operator: those used in tests of logic and those used to affect variables. All should be fairly easy to understand and are shown in Table 6.2. If you look

Operator	Meaning
+	If the arguments are numbers then they are added together. If the arguments are strings then they are concatenated[3] and the result returned.
−	If supplied with two operands this subtracts one from the other. If supplied with a single operand it reverses its sign.
*	Multiplies two numbers together.
/	Divides the first number by the second.
%	Modulus Division returns the integer remainder from a division.
!	Logical NOT returns false if the operand evaluates to true. Otherwise it returns true.
>	Greater than returns true if the left operand is greater than the right.
>=	Returns true if the left operand is greater than or equal to the right.
<	Returns true if the left operand is less than the right.
==	Returns true if the two operands are equal.
<=	Returns true if the left operand is less than or equal to the right.
!=	Returns true if the two operands are not equal.
&&	Logical AND returns true if both operands are true. Otherwise returns false.
||	Logical OR returns true if one or both operands are true, otherwise returns false.
=	Assigns a value to a variable
+=	Adds two numbers then assigns the result to the one on the left of the expression.
−=	Subtracts the term on the right from the term on the left, then assigns the result to the one on the left of the expression.
*=	Multiplies two values then assigns the result to the one on the left of the expression.
/=	Divides the term on the left by the term on the right and then assigns the result to the one on the left of the expression.
%=	Performs modulus division then assigns the result to the one on the left of the expression.
++	Auto-increment, increases the value of its (integer) argument by one.
--	Auto-decrement, decreases the value of an integer by one.

Table 6.2 JavaScript operators

[3] One is joined to the end of the other.

through the code in this book you will see these operators used by both JavaScript and Perl. In fact most programming languages use these same constructs. Instead of giving lots of examples of the use of these operators here, I am going to rely on your finding them as you work through the book and then referring back to this table when you need more information. Generally, though, you will be able to work out from the code what each operator is used for.

Although you cannot subtract strings, you *can* add them. The process is called concatenation and joins the second string onto the end of the first:

```
1  var first = "A string is ";
   var second = "added to the end";

   // a new string which is the others added to each other
5  var third = first + second;

   // change the value of first to be itself + second...
   first += second; // honestly!
```

6.9 ARRAYS

An array is an ordered set of data elements which can be accessed through a single variable name. Conceptually, an array is made up of a set of slots with each slot assigned to a single data element. You access the data elements either sequentially, by reading from the start of the array, or by their *index*. The index is the position of the element in the array (with the first element being at position 0 and the last at (array length − 1)). Figure 6.5 shows what an array looks like.

In many programming languages arrays are contiguous areas of memory which means that the first array element is physically located next to the second, and so on. In JavaScript an array is slightly different because it is a special type of object and has functionality, which is not normally available in other languages. Generally I have left discussion of JavaScript objects until Chapter 7, but arrays are so fundamental to programming that I am making an exception in this case.

An array is a data store. Its sole function is to hold data until the script requires it. The data inside an array is *ordered*, because elements are added and accessed in a particular order, but is not *sorted*. There is no relationship between the way the data is held and any external meaning it has. For instance, if words are being added to the array they are not necessarily going to

Figure 6.5 The structure of an array

be stored in alphabetical order. The contents of the array may have a particular ordering as an artifact of the way that they were presented to the array but not as a result of being in an array. This point needs emphasizing simply because many beginning programmers assume that the system can order data for them. Fortunately, as we will see in Section 6.9.2, JavaScript has some rather neat features which overcome the limitations of the array format.

6.9.1 Basic Array Functions

Before I look at JavaScript arrays as objects, I am going to show how they can be used as more *traditional* arrays. The basic operations that are performed on arrays are: creation, addition of elements, accessing individual elements, removing elements. I will look at each of these in turn.

Creating Arrays

JavaScript arrays can be constructed in no fewer than three different ways. The easiest way is simply to declare a variable and pass it some elements in array format:

```
var days = ["Monday", "Tuesday", "Wednesday", "Thursday"];
```

That creates an array of four elements, each holding a text string. Notice that the array of elements is surrounded by *square* brackets. In most programming languages square brackets denote arrays and array operations. The second approach is to create an array object using the keyword new and a set of elements to store:

```
var days = new Array("Monday", "Tuesday", "Wednesday", "Thursday");
```

Using this construct, the contents of the array are surrounded by parentheses because they are parameters to the constructor of the `Array` object. Finally an empty array object which has space for a number of elements can be created:

```
var days = new Array(4);
```

JavaScript arrays can hold mixed data types as the following examples show:

```
var data = ["Monday", "Tuesday", 34, 76.34, "Wednesday"];
var data = new Array("Monday", 34, 76.34, "Wednesday");
```

Adding Elements to an Array

Array elements are accessed by their index. The index denotes the position of the element in the array and, as in for loops, these start from 0. Adding an element uses the square bracket syntax we saw a moment ago:

```
var days[3] = "Monday";
```

What happens if you want, or need, to add an item to an array which is already full? Many languages struggle with this problem but JavaScript has a really good solution: the interpreter simply extends the array and inserts the new item:

```
1. var data = ["Monday", "Tuesday", 34, 76.34, "Wednesday"];
2. data[5] = "Thursday";
3. data[23] = 48;
```

The code creates an array of four elements in line one. A new element is added at position 5 in line two. At line three an element is added to position 23. To do this the array is first expanded so that it is long enough and then the new element is added.

Accessing Array Members

The elements in the array are accessed through their index. The same access method is used to find elements and to change their value.

length

When accessing array elements you do not want to read beyond its end. Therefore you need to know how many elements have been stored. This is done through the length attribute. Remember that index numbers run from 0 to length - 1.

The following code shows how to read through all elements of an array:

```
<html>
    <head>
        <title>Looping Through an Array</title>
    </head>
    <body>
        <script language="javascript">
        <!--
            document.writeln("<h1>Looping Through an Array</h1>");
            document.write("<p>");

            var data = ["Monday", "Tuesday", 34, 76.34, "Wednesday"];
            var len = data.length;

            for(var count = 0; count < len; count++) {
                document.write(data[count] + ", ");
            }
            document.writeln("</p>");
            document.close();
```

```
        //-->
20      </script>
    </body>
</html>
```

The result of running that code inside Konqueror is shown in Figure 6.6.

Searching an Array

To search an array, simply read each element in turn and compare it with the value that you are looking for. Try the following code in the script you have just seen. This loops through the array and compares each element with a string, if the two elements are equal a message is printed out. To stop the search, I use the built in `break` function which terminates the current loop. You can use `break` with `for` and `while` loops.

```
1   for(var count = 0; count < len; count++) {
        if(data[count] == "Tuesday"){
            document.write(data[count] + ", ");
            break;
5       }
    }
```

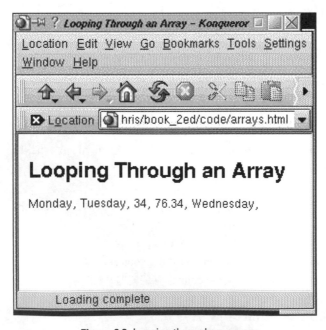

Figure 6.6 Looping through an array

Removing Array Members

Removing elements from an array is quite straightforward. JavaScript does not provide a built-in function to do this for you. Given the rich set of facilities the language *has*, this is quite a surprising omission. To remove an element for yourself use the following procedure:

- read each element in the array
- if the element is *not* the one you want to delete, copy it into a temporary array
- if you want to delete the element then do nothing
- increment the loop counter
- repeat the process.

The next piece of code loops through an array and deletes a single item. The output it gives in Firefox is shown in Figure 6.7. I tried this code in Konqueror but the original array was not written to the screen until all of the script had executed. This is the sort of nasty feature which can easily bite JavaScript developers. Simply because your code works in one browser on one platform you have no guarantee that it will execute as you intend on every platform.

```
1   <html>
      <head>
        <title>Removing an Array Element</title>
```

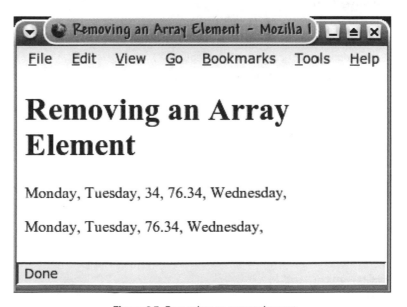

Figure 6.7 Removing an array element

```
       </head>
5      <body>
          <script language="javascript">
          <!--
          document.writeln("<h1>Removing an Array Element</h1>");


10        var data = ["Monday", "Tuesday", 34, 76.34, "Wednesday"];


          // Show the original array
          document.write("<p>");
          var len = data.length;
15        for(var count = 0; count < len; count++) {
             document.write(data[count] + ", ");
          }


          document.writeln("</p>");
20

          // Ask the user what to remove
          var rem = prompt("Which item shall I remove?", "");
          rem = parseInt(rem);
          var tmp = new Array(data.length - 1);
25        var count2 = 0;


          // This loop searches for, and removes a single item
          for(var count = 0; count < len; count++) {
             if(data[count] == rem) {
30              // do nothing
             } else {
                tmp[count2] = data[count];
                count2++;
             }
35        }


          data = tmp;


          // Show the new Array
40        document.write("<p>");
          var len = data.length;
```

```
        for(var count = 0; count < len; count++) {
          document.write(data[count] + ", ");
        }
45
        document.writeln("</p>");
        document.close();

        //-->
50      </script>
      </body>
    </html>
```

Some of the code there is quite cryptic so I will briefly explain the key features. The script includes a loop which writes out the contents of the array as an HTML paragraph. If you have done a bit of programming then you may think that this code should have been removed and placed in a *function* which could have been called twice. This is certainly the best way of writing a program but since I have not covered functions yet, I have used a more straightforward brute-force approach. The display code is basically the loop which you have now seen used a couple of times:

```
1   document.write("<p>");
    var len = data.length;
    for(var count - 0; count < len; count++) {
        document.write(data[count] + ", ");
5   }
    document.writeln("</p>");
```

Removing an element from the array is slightly more complicated, although it is still based around a loop. The basic algorithm for the removal of an array element is:

- create an empty, temporary array
- initialize separate counters for each array
- read the next array element
- compare the element with the target for removal
- if the two elements do not match, copy the element from the original array into the temporary array
- if the elements *do* match
  - increment the counter on the original array
  - copy all remaining elements from the original array into the temporary one
- otherwise, if the original array has any remaining elements, return to the third step.

What is happening in the algorithm is that we are copying all of the data from our array into a temporary data structure *except* for the element which we want to remove. Each array needs its own counter because once an item has been removed the two arrays will be working on different items. Look at the following code and try to understand how it works:

```
1   var remove = prompt("Which item shall I remove?", "");
    var tmp = new Array(data.length - 1);
    var count2 = 0;


5   // This loop searches for, and removes a single item
    for(var count = 0; count < len; count++) {
        if(data[count] == remove){
            // do nothing
        } else {
10          tmp[count2] = data[count];
            count2++;
        }
    }


15  data = tmp;
```

If the code is confusing you, simply insert some statements to print the values held by array counters and in the array elements as the loop progresses:

```
1   for(var count = 0; count < len; count++) {
        if(data[count] == rem){
            // do nothing
            document.write("Target found. data[count] = " + count);
5           document.write(": " + data[count] + "<br>");
        } else {
            tmp[count2] = data[count];
            document.write("Copying. data[count] = " + count);
            document.write(": " + data[count] + "<br>");
10
            document.write("  tmp[count2] = " + count2);
            document.write(": " + tmp[count2] + "<br>");

            count2++;
15      }
    }
```

6.9.2 Object-based Array Functions

In JavaScript an array can act like an object (this is actually because it *is* one). Do not worry about the details of what objects are, or how they work, for now you do not need to know. What you *do* need to do is spend some time familiarizing yourself with the useful functions which follow. Each of the array functions is used in the same way. You must specify the name of the array which you want to operate on, followed by a dot, then the name of the function. Finally, in parentheses, you must specify any parameters in a comma separated list:

```
arrayname.function(parameter1, parameter2);
```

I will give a few examples which should help ease you through the notation as I describe the functions.

Array([item0[, itemN]])

Array objects are created with calls to this *constructor*. It builds an array which contains all of the items which are passed in as parameters in a comma-separated list. If no parameters are given the array will be empty. In scripts, the call to the constructor must be preceded by the keyword new which tells the JavaScript interpreter to build a new object. Array objects can also be created using the square brackets as we saw earlier.

concat(array2[, array3[, arrayN]])

A list of arrays is concatenated onto the end of the array and a new array returned. The original arrays are all unaltered by this process. Do not be worried about the idea of a list of arrays. I simply mean that some arrays are specified in a particular order. If you are joining just two arrays, that is fine because in computing a list can, and often does, have just one item. Here is some code which concatenates three arrays:

```
1   <html>
       <head>
          <title>Concatenating Arrays</title>
       </head>
5      <body>
          <script language="javascript">
          <!--
          document.writeln("<h1>Concatenating Arrays</h1>");

10         var first = ["Monday", "Tuesday", 34, 76.34, "Wednesday"];
           var second = ["one", "two", "three", 76.9];
           var third = new Array("an", "object", "array");
```

```
     var result = first.concat(second, third);
15
     // Show the resulting array
     document.write("<p>");
     var len = result.length;
     for(var count = 0; count < len; count++) {
20        document.write(result[count] + ", ");
     }
     document.writeln("</p>");
     document.close();
     //-->
25   </script>
   </body>
</html>
```

The resulting output from the concatenation is shown in Figure 6.8.

join(string)

Sometimes it is useful to have all of the elements in an array joined together as a string. For instance, in earlier examples I have been using a loop to display an array, if that process could be wrapped into a single function it would be cleaner and simpler. That is exactly what the join function does. It passes through the array creating a string of

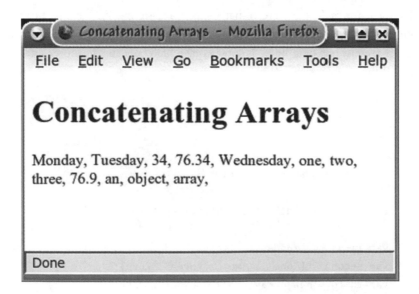

Figure 6.8 Concatenating arrays

all elements. In the resulting string the elements are separated using the optional string parameter. If this is omitted the elements will be separated using a comma but if you want anything more complex, such as "， "，then you will have to specify it explicitly.

pop()

This function removes the last element from the array and in doing so reduces the number of elements in the array by one.

push(element1[, element2[, elementN]])

This adds a list of items onto the end of the array. The items are separated using commas in the parameter list.

reverse()

As the name suggests, this function swaps all of the elements in the array so that which was first is last, and vice versa.

shift()

This removes the first element of the array and in so doing shortens its length by one.

The following code and Figure 6.9 show those five functions in action:

```
1   <html>
      <head>
        <title>Array Operations</title>
```

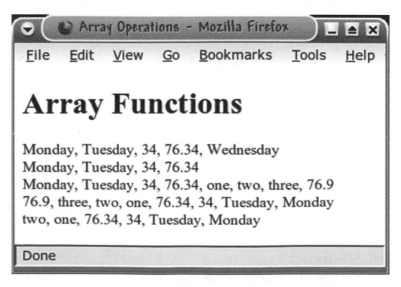

Figure 6.9 Array operations

```
      </head>
5     <body>
      <script language="javascript">
      <!--
        document.writeln("<h1>Array Functions</h1>");

10      var first = ["Monday", "Tuesday", 34, 76.34, "Wednesday"];
        document.write("<p>");

        document.write(first.join(", "));
        document.write("<br>");
15
        first.pop();
        document.write(first.join(", "));
        document.write("<br>");

20      first.push("one", "two", "three", 76.9);
        document.write(first.join(", "));
        document.write("<br>");

        first.reverse();
25      document.write(first.join(", "));
        document.write("<br>");

        first.shift();
        first.shift();
30      document.write(first.join(", "));

        document.writeln("</p>");
        document.close();
        //-->
35      </script>
      </body>
    </html>
```

slice(start[, finish])

Sometimes you need to extract a range of elements from an array. The slice() function does exactly this. Two parameters are possible: the first element which you want to remove is specified in the first parameter, the last element you want is specified in the second one. If you only give a single parameter, all elements from the specified one to the end of the array are selected. Once the elements have been sliced they are returned as a new array. The original array is unaltered by this function.

sort()

The array is sorted into lexicographic, *dictionary*, order. Elements in the array which are not text are first converted to strings before the sort operation is performed. This means that, for instance, 732 will be placed before 80 in the sorted array.

You can optionally create a function which will control how the sort is performed. This function can be called as a parameter to the **sort** function. I am not going to describe how this can be done, look in an advanced JavaScript book for details.

splice(index, number[, element1[, element2[, elementN]]])

If you need to alter an array by removing some elements and at the same time adding in new ones, then you will need the **splice** function. This function is somewhat peculiar, read through the following explanation, then look at the example. Finally re-read the explanation which *should* be a bit clearer.

The **splice** function has two compulsory parameters and an unlimited number of optional ones. The first parameter indicates the position in the array at which the new elements will start. The second parameter indicates how many elements will be deleted from the original array. If you do not want to delete elements, then set this to 0. Finally there is a list of elements which are to be inserted into the array. If you insert more elements than you remove then the array will grow longer. Figure 6.10 shows this in action.

```
1   document.writeln("<p>");
    data.splice(2, 0, "element one", "element two");
    document.writeln(data.join(", ") + "<br>");
    data.splice(3, 3, "element three", "element four");
5   document.writeln(data.join(", "));
    document.writeln("</p>");
```

unshift(element1[, element2[,elementN]])

inserts a list of elements onto the front of the array. The list of new elements can have just one item.

Although this discussion of arrays has been long and rather involved, they are an important structure in JavaScript. When I start to show some dynamic HTML you will see that everything revolves around the manipulation of arrays so it is important that you have a good understanding of how they work.

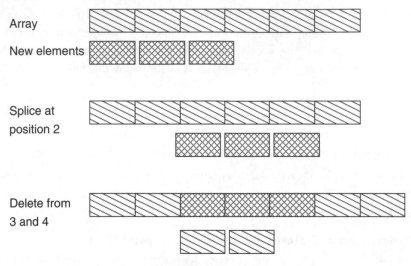

Array

New elements

Splice at
position 2

Delete from
3 and 4

Figure 6.10 Splicing arrays

6.10 FUNCTIONS

A function is a piece of code that performs a specific task. These tasks are larger than those of a statement – almost every function is made up of a number of statements. By creating a function the same piece of code can be used repeatedly throughout the time that the program runs yet it only needs to be developed in one place. JavaScript has a lot of functions built into the language. You have already seen some of these and you will meet more as we go along.

Once you have created some functions you need to know how to use them. This is done by *calling* the function. When programmers talk about a function call they are talking about using the code in the function at another point in the program. Until the program *calls* a function, that code will not do anything. This can be useful as it means that you can partially develop your functions without affecting the rest of your program *provided you do not call them*.

6.10.1 Defining Functions

`function name(parameters)`

Functions are (not surprisingly) defined using the `function` keyword. The function name can be any combination of digits, letters, and underscore but cannot contain a space. That is the same rule as for variable naming. With function names it is even more important that you make them meaningful because you will use them so often. The name of the function has to be followed by parentheses which will contain any values that you want to pass into the function code.

A function is a block of code which is surrounded by curly brackets:

```
1  function the_name_of_your_function( ) {
       // the code goes here
   }
```

6.10.2 Parameter Passing

Not every function accepts parameters. Not all values have to be passed as parameters. Remember global variables? Well they can be used by any function without having been passed in as parameters, which looks like a good idea but can get very messy when you are writing complex programs.

When a function receives a value as a parameter, that value is given a name and can be accessed, using that name, by the function. The names of parameters are taken from the function definition and are applied in the order in which parameters are passed in. Let us look at a simple function and see what all of that means. The function takes in three parameters – name, age, and shoe size – and displays them in a Web page:

```
1  function about_you(name, age, shoesize) {
       document.write("<h1>All About You</h1>");
       document.write("<p><strong>Your Name is:</strong>" + name);
       document.write("<p><strong>You Are</strong>" + age + "Years Old"),
5      document.writeln("<p><strong>Your Shoe Size is:</strong>" + shoesize);
       document.close();
   }
```

That might be called like this as the page is loaded:

```
1  <html>
     <head>
        <title>About You</title>
     </head>
5    <body onLoad="about_you('Chris', 34, 8)">

        <script language="javascript">
        <!--
        function about_you(name, age, shoesize) {
10          document.write("<h1>All About You</h1>");
            document.write("<p><strong>Your Name is:</strong> " + name);
            document.write("<p><strong>You Are</strong> " + age + " Years
               Old");
```

```
        document.writeln("<p><strong>Your Shoe Size is:</strong> " +
            shoesize);
        document.close();
15  }
    //-->
    </script>
  </body>
</html>
```

or simply like this from within a more complex script:

```
1  about_you('Chris', 34, 9);
```

which would print out exactly as you might expect (it is shown in Figure 6.11). But what if the order of the parameters was messed up in the call? Well then you end up with strange output. That is not too important here but would be if you were going to use the numbers in some later mathematical function. Here is that error (shown in Figure 6.12):

```
1  about_you(9, "Chris", 34);
```

It is also OK not to pass any parameters in. You can also miss out a parameter altogether – but only the last one. If you want to miss out any other parameter then pass in an empty string (""). Here is an example with a missing parameter (see Figure 6.13):

```
1  about_you("Chris", "", 9);
```

Figure 6.11 Function call 1

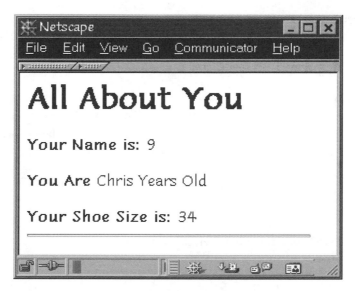

Figure 6.12 Function call 2

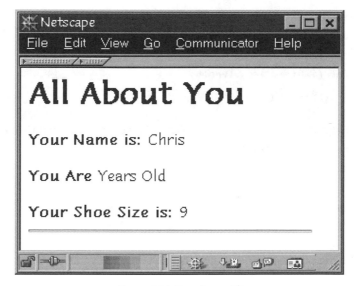

Figure 6.13 Function call 3

6.10.3 Examining the Function Call

In JavaScript parameters are passed as arrays. Every function has two properties that can be used to find information about the parameters:

`function.arguments`

This is the array of parameters that have been passed.

function.arguments.length

This is the number of parameters that have been passed into the function. You could easily use this to check that all parameters have been sent and to issue a warning if they have not.

You might also write a function that can accept a variable list of parameters and use these two functions to control its operation. The example which follows shows a function which takes a variable number of arguments which it then concatenates into a single string. Each argument in the new string is separated from the preceding one by a single space character.

```
1   <html>
      <head>
        <title>Examining the function call</title>
      </head>
5     <body>
      <script language="javascript">
      <!--
          function concatenator() {
              var args = concatenator.arguments
10            var returnThis = "";
              for (i=0; i< args.length; i++) {
                  returnThis = returnThis.concat(args[i], " ");
              }
              returnThis = returnThis.substr(0, returnThis.length-1);
15            return returnThis;
          }


          var result = concatenator("oh", "blah", "di");
          document.write("<p>The result is " + result + " "
20                           + result.length);
          document.close();
      //-->
      </script>
      </body>
25  </html>
```

6.10.4 Comments

JavaScript code, like code written in most programming languages, can be difficult to read. If you need to look back at your code to alter it, you may struggle to remember what it is doing and how. This has always been a problem in software development. The solution is to find a way of adding *documentation* to your programs which describes them. This is done by placing comments throughout the program.

Comments are pieces of text which can be used by programmers as they read through the source but which are ignored by the interpreter or compiler. In JavaScript each line of comment is preceded by two slashes and continues from that point to the end of the line.

```
// this is a JavaScript comment
```

Unlike some other languages JavaScript does not have a way of commenting large blocks of text as a block. If you want a block comment then you have to comment each and every line.

6.10.5 Parsing

Why does the JavaScript interpreter not raise an error when strange parameters are being passed around? Well because JavaScript does not spend a lot of effort telling numbers from strings, the interpreter does not need to bother. If you tried to pass a string into a Math function such as `Math.sin()` you would get an error. Ordinarily though, the difference is not important *to the interpreter*. Of course the difference matters to the application so it is up to you as the developer to check that you are handling the correct data.

When a Web page is loaded, the browser will check through it looking for mistakes in the code. Most browsers do not mind errors in HTML code – in fact the browser manufacturers almost seem to encourage poor code. Browsers do care about errors in JavaScript programs but only certain types of error.

Any JavaScript in the `head` section is parsed (i.e., read through and checked) by the browser. If it finds any errors in your coding such as missing semicolons or inverted commas, or even mistyped built-in function names, then you will get an error. However, the parser does not check the logic of your code. It checks that your code *could* run correctly but it does not check that it *will*. That is a job for you.

6.10.6 Returning Values

Hopefully you remember that any variables that you declare in a function are local to that function. You cannot get at their value outside the function unless you pass them around as parameters. Well that is not always convenient, so a mechanism is needed to return a value from a function. That mechanism is provided by the `return` statement.

Although you can only pass a single value with `return` that value can be a JavaScript object which, as you will see in Chapter 7, can be a complex data set.

```
1   var reset = getSine(32);

    function getSine(number){
```

```
        var answer = Math.sin(number);
5       return answer;
     }
```

That simple example should be quite clear. A variable is set based upon the return value of a function. The sin() function is, of course, yet another of JavaScript's useful built-in functions.

6.10.7 Scoping Rules

Scoping is an important concept in programming. When you declare a variable you might naively expect that it can be used anywhere in your program, but that is not actually the case. If every variable were available to every function then your code would get messy, you would make mistakes and find that your programs were actually quite inefficient. Programming languages usually impose rules, called *scoping*, which determine how a variable can be accessed. JavaScript is no exception. In JavaScript variables can be either *local* or *global*.

global

Global scoping means that a variable is available to all parts of the program. Such variables are declared outside of any function and are usually used to hold static data that you will not alter once it has been created. A good use of a global variable might be to find the type of browser so that you can tailor your code to suit.

local

Local variables are declared inside a function. They can only be used by that function. If you want the value associated with a local variable to be available to other functions then you must pass it as a *parameter*. How this is achieved was shown in Section 6.10.2.

The following code shows the difference between global and local variables:

```
1    <html>
       <head>
         <title>Variables, Functions and Scope</title>
       </head>
5      <body>
         <script language="javascript">
         <!--
            var the_var = 32;
            var tmp = the_var;
10          var tmp2 = setLocal(17);
```

```
        document.writeln("<h1>Scope</h1>");
        document.writeln("<p>The global is " + the_var);
        document.writeln("<br>tmp is " + tmp);
15      document.writeln("<br>tmp2 is " + tmp2);
        document.writeln("</p>");
        document.close();

        function setLocal(num) {
20          the_var = num;
            alert("tmp is: " + tmp);
            return(the_var);
        }
    //-->
25  </script>
  </body>
</html>
```

In the script I declare three global variables. These are accessible from anywhere in the rest of the script. When a script is written in the body of the page it is parsed as it is loaded and global variable declarations are possible. If you want to declare your script in the head of the page then global variable declarations will not work. You will have to create some sort of object to hold the values and initialize them when the script is loaded. I will show you how to do that in Chapter 7.

In my example, the first line of the script assigns a value to the_var. This is copied into tmp in line 2 for storage. I am going to attempt to manipulate the original and I want a copy so that I can display its starting value later. In line 3 I call a function, setLocal() with the value 17 as an argument and set the variable tmp2 based upon the return value from this function.

The setLocal() function has its own variable called the_var which it sets to be equal to the argument it receives. In this case the_var is going to be set to 17. It might, therefore seem reasonable that since we declared a variable earlier called the_var, it now has a value of 17. After all the two variables have the same name so they must be the same thing, mustn't they? Well, no, they are not. Although the names are the same in our script, each name actually refers to a different data item. The first one is global, the second is local. The local variable has precedence inside its own function. That means the system will use the local variable whenever it can.

Another question you might ask is "Why bother with global variables?" The answer to that is also demonstrated in setLocal(). I have added an alert box which I use to display the value held by one of the global variables. Global variables are used to hold values which need to be accessed by more than one function. Generally, such values are not going to change during the runtime of the program and passing them as variables is an unnecessary additional overhead.

Finally, notice that the HTML page is only written out after all of the function calls have been completed. If you try to call a function before you have called `document.close()` you will get a runtime error in Netscape.

 # EXERCISES

Scripting Technologies

1. What are the differences between a set of Web pages and a Web application? What technologies are currently available for the creation of such applications?
2. List the technologies that are used to create DHTML pages.
3. Describe the Document Object Model.
4. The DOM is at the heart of the incompatibilities between the main browsers. How might these problems be resolved?
5. How do ECMA Script, JScript and JavaScript relate to each other?
6. JavaScript is an interpreted language. What advantages does interpretation have over compilation when prototyping applications?
7. How does JavaScript compare with other technologies that are available for use on client browsers?

JavaScript

1. Why do you think JavaScript code closely resembles code in languages such as C?
2. Outline the structure of a JavaScript program.
3. How is JavaScript included in HTML documents?
4. Can JavaScript be executed without using a Web browser?
5. What is the difference between a variable and a value? How should variables be named?
6. What data types does JavaScript use?
7. What are scoping rules – why are they so important in all programming languages?
8. Describe each of the loop constructs that JavaScript provides. Why do languages typically have more than one type of loop?
9. What are functions used for? How are functions defined in JavaScript?
10. How does parameter passing work?

11. Why do some functions return values to the calling statement?

12. How does JavaScript create HTML pages *on the fly*?

Using JavaScript

1. Write a simple JavaScript that adds some numbers together, concatenates a couple of strings, and then shows the result in an `alert()` dialog and on the page.

2. Create a Web page which uses `prompt()` dialogs to ask a user for their name, age and shoe size. Display the information they enter on the page formatted as a small table.

3. Write a Web page which contain the code from page 171.

4. Try removing the JavaScript code from the HTML page show in Section 7.6. Place the code in a file called `testscript.js`. See if you can link this into the HTML page. Does the page act as you expected?

5. In the discussion of arrays in Section 6.9 I demonstrate some, but not all, of the functions. Write a Web page which prompts the user for six items of input, stores this in an array and displays it using `join()`. Display the data in sorted order. Use `splice()` to add some more elements into the array and display the result.

Objects in JavaScript

7.1 DATA AND OBJECTS IN JAVASCRIPT

The previous section introduced the ideas of variables and control structures in JavaScript. If you worked through it and played around with the exercises then you should by now be comfortable with using functions and returning values. JavaScript has one more concept left that you need to understand before diving into DHTML. JavaScript tries to be an *object-oriented* (OO) language. It is not actually a true OO language like Smalltalk or Eiffel, but it tries, the primitive objects that JavaScript does provide are very useful. Because the built-in functions all use these ideas, you will need to get a grasp of them before going any further, so next up we have JavaScript objects for beginners.

7.1.1 Objects – A Brief Introduction

Object orientation is one of the most powerful concepts yet developed by computer scientists. Objects are widely applicable and object-based systems can be developed using many languages. Experienced programmers who are used to developing in traditional languages such as COBOL or FORTRAN, which have historically not supported objects, often find the OO paradigm confusing. Beginning programmers tend to be able to think in object terms right from the start.

As you will see in a while, JavaScript objects are easy to understand and use, but the language does not support all of the features found in most object systems. Before I discuss JavaScript objects I will just spin rapidly through the general idea of objects.

Objects

An object is a *thing*. It can be anything that you like from some data through a set of methods (which is the name for functions in OO.) to an entire system. The reason that object-orientation is such a powerful idea is that, quite simply, it lets software designers and developers mimic the real world in their designs. This idea might be so obvious as to be not worth mentioning, after all software is usually meant to solve real-world problems. The benefit of OO is the tight linkage between the description of a problem and the ways in which it can be solved.

Real objects are more than just data or processing: data often describe something but the thing being described also has the ability to act. For instance, a student has a name and address and is, usually, enrolled on one or more courses. A piece of software written using any language and any development technique can model the data which describes the student. But students are more than simple data: they each have unique behaviors. Some students attend regularly, others hand all work in early, others change course frequently. Any software which manages data about students needs to track some, or all, of those behaviors. The big win for a software engineer from using OO is that the data and the dynamic aspects of a system can all be included in the finished product.

Objects are described in software and design constructs called classes. A class usually contains some data items and some methods. Each class provides services to other classes in the system. Often programs are composed of a set of class hierarchies in which generic classes are declared which then have their functionality refined and specialized into usable form. This is where more of the power of OO comes from. A single generic class can be specialized in many ways and each of the specialized versions *inherits* some of the properties and behavior of the generic class. That means that common parts of the program can be developed just once and easily reused.

Think about the typical students again. The data describing them and some behavior such as attendance at lectures can be described in a student *base class*. More specialized behavior can be described in *subclasses*. A biochemistry student who attends laboratory sessions would be an example of a different subclass to a literature major who goes to seminars but not labs.

When a program runs, objects are created. An object is a run-time *instance* of a class. The object has all of the behavior that was defined in the class and is able to perform processing. The dynamic aspects of an object are captured through pieces of code written inside methods. When an object needs to do something, the appropriate method is executed. Generally objects do not act independently. Instead, their actions are triggered by events throughout the system, in particular the program that they belong to. Usually actions occur because an object somewhere in the system requests a service from another object. In our student example, a record management system might need to know the name of a particular student. It finds this by asking the object, which represents that student, for its name.

There is one more thing that you ought to know about objects. Very often an object is formed by aggregating together lots of simpler objects. Again this is simply a way of mirroring the world around us. We are made from a set of complicated components such as our brains, cardio-vascular system and gastro-intestinal system. If we were modelling an object-oriented human we would start by modelling each of those systems. We would then combine those systems to make more complex pieces, finally we would join all of the pieces together to make a person.

 NOTE *A class is a description of something; an object is an instance of a class. It is the object that exists in the computer's memory and which does the work.*

In summary:

- an object is described by a class
- a class can be specialized through inheritance
- a class usually contains both data items and processing capability.

JavaScript Objects

So does JavaScript implement all of that object stuff? Well it would be true to say that it does and then again it does not. The built-in JavaScript objects such as document and window act, and are used, like standard OO objects. I will be showing how to use these in Section 7.4.

Where JavaScript diverges from *traditional* OO is in its treatment of user-defined objects. An object is really a data structure that has been associated with some functions. It does not have inheritance and the structure of the code can look a little peculiar. The easiest way of understanding how to combine your data and functions into objects is to work through an example. Code first, then explanation:

```
1   <html>
      <head>
      <script language=javascript>
      <!--

5
      function ObjDemo(){
         popup("Hello");
         myhouse = new house("Dun Hacking", 2, 4);
         alert(myhouse.name + " Has " + myhouse.floors + " Floors And " +
            myhouse.rooms() + " Rooms");
10       myhouse.leave("Farewell");
      }

      function house(name, floors, beds) {
         this.name = name;
```

```
15        this.floors = floors;
          this.bedrooms = beds;
          this.rooms = frooms;
          this.leave = popup;
      }

20
      function frooms(){
          var groundfloor = 3;
          var utilities = 2;
          var total = 0;

25
          if(this.floors <= 0){
             total = 0;
          } else {
             if(this.floors == 1) {
30               total = this.bedrooms + utilities;
             } else{
                total = (this.floors * utilities);
                total += groundfloor;
                total += this.bedrooms;
35           }
          }
          return total;
      }

40    function popup(msg){
          alert(msg);
      }


      //-->
45    </script>
      </head>
      <body onLoad="ObjDemo()">
      </body>
  </html>
```

Before reading this explanation, try to work out what is happening there yourself.

The script is initiated as soon as the **onLoad** event happens during page loading:

```
1   <body onLoad="ObjDemo()">
```

The `ObjDemo()` function performs four tasks. First it calls the **popup** function which displays an alert box with the string `Hello` displayed. That is simply using functions as I have done before. The next bit of code does something different and new[1].

```
1  popup("Hello");
   myhouse = new house("Dun Hacking", 2, 4);
```

new

> The keyword **new** is used to create objects. It allocates memory and storage for them and sets all variables that can be set at this stage. Whenever you define an object you should make sure that all variables are set: strings to "" and numbers to 0. **new** calls a function which has the same name as the type of object that is being created. This function is called the *constructor*.
>
> After the call to **new** in this program, the object `myhouse` exists and can be used. If you try rewriting the script so that `myhouse` is used *before* it is created you will get a JavaScript error.

The object-oriented aspects of the script all revolve around the `myhouse` object which is an *instance* of **house**. The constructor takes a number of parameters and assigns them to variables.

Objects can have functions as well as variables. These object functions, or *methods*, are *aliased* by giving them a unique name within the object. By doing this aliasing, a function can be accessed either as a top-level part of the script or as part of an object. The local object functions are aliases of, or pointers to, if you prefer, the actual functions rather than copies of those functions. This code shows the **house** constructor:

```
1  function house(name, floors, beds) {
       this.name = name;
       this.floors = floors;
       this.bedrooms = beds;
5      this.rooms = frooms;
       this.leave = popup;
   }
```

The `name`, `floors` and `beds` values are copied from the parameters of the function into variables which are part of the object. The other two values in the constructor do not hold data values. If you look back at the full program you will see that `frooms` and `popup` are functions. These are assigned to variables within the `house` object.

---

[1]No pun intended!

this

> To differentiate between global variables and those which are part of an object but *may* have the same name, JavaScript uses this. Whenever you refer to a variable which is part of an object you *must* precede the variable name by this. Separate the variable name from this with a dot.

.(dot)

> When referring to a property of an object, whether a method or a variable, a dot is placed between the object name and the property.

Sometimes it would be useful if you could write information to the screen from within an object and carry on with the processing. Unfortunately, JavaScript does not allow you to mix screen output and processing. Instead you need to use your scripts to prepare a complete page and write that before performing more processing. Once you use a statement such as document.write(), the interpreter expects to encounter a document.close() statement before it will handle any JavaScript functions you have written. I mention this because, when you use JavaScript objects, you often need to write to the screen from those objects. Doing so is *not* easy.

7.2 REGULAR EXPRESSIONS

One common task in software development is the parsing of a string looking for a particular pattern. For instance, a script might take name data from a user and have to search through it, checking that no digits have been entered. This type of problem can be solved by reading through the string, one character at a time, looking for the target pattern. Although that might seem like a straightforward thing to do, actually it turns out that it is not. Efficiency and speed matter, and any code which performs these tasks needs to be constructed very carefully. The usual approach in scripting languages is to create a pattern called a *regular expression* which describes a set of characters that may be present in a string.

JavaScript versions after 1.1 include a set of routines to manipulate strings and search patterns. These are wrapped up as regular expression objects. JavaScript regular expressions are more than patterns: they include functions which you call from your scripts when you need a pattern finding. You might expect that you would use search patterns by applying a pattern to a string. JavaScript allows this way of working:

```
1   var pattern = "target";
    var string = "Can you find the target?";
    string.match(pattern);
```

but you can also work the other way. A string can be passed into a regular expression as a parameter:

```
1   var pattern = new RegExp("target");
    var string = "Can you find the target?";
    pattern.exec(string);
```

JavaScript regular expressions are based on those found in Perl. In fact, from the programmers point of view, they work in just the same way. Rather than describe them in detail twice, I am going to point you to the Perl description in Section 9.9. Regular expressions are a fundamental part of Perl, discussion of their complexities sits more naturally in a discussion of *that* language.

7.2.1 Creating Regular Expressions

A regular expression is a JavaScript object. As with any other type of object there are multiple ways of creating them. They can be created *statically* when the script is first parsed, or dynamically at run-time. If performance is an issue for your script then you should try to use static expressions whenever possible. If you do not know what you are going to be searching for until run-time, for instance if the search pattern depends on user input, then you will need to create dynamic patterns. Let us look at an example of each. A static regular expression is created as follows:

```
regex = /fish|fowl/;
```

Dynamic patterns are created using the new keyword to create an instance of the RegExp class:

```
regex = new RegExp("fish|fowl");
```

7.2.2 Writing Patterns

Search patterns can be very simple or incredibly complicated. The most difficult thing about them is, probably, working out what you want to search for. Once you have worked that out you need to be able to express the search pattern in a format which can be used by a computer program. Describing a pattern in natural language is relatively easy. Unfortunately few computer programs are able to successfully handle natural language instruction. On the other hand, computers are very good at repetitive symbolic manipulation. If your search pattern can be expressed as a set of symbols, a computer can use it, some search rules and a target string, very effectively. This is exactly the approach taken by regular expression systems.

Patterns are expressed in a cryptic, but powerful, grammar which uses symbols to replace complex statements. As I mentioned earlier, the JavaScript regular expression grammar is identical to that used in Perl. I am leaving a discussion of the grammar until Section 9.9, but Table 7.1 lists a few highlights. One complication is that some of the characters in the JavaScript grammar are preceded by a backslash character. This is an escape character which is used to tell the browser that the character signifies an operation not a letter. Browsers (or

Token	Description
^	Match at the start of the input string.
$	Match at the end of the input string.
*	Match 0 or more times.
+	Match 1 or more times.
?	Match 0 or 1 time.
a|b	Match a or b.
{n}	Match the string n times.
\d	Match a digit.
\D	Match anything except for digits.
\w	Match any alphanumeric character or the underscore.
\W	Match anything except alphanumeric characters or under-scores.
\s	Match a whitespace character.
\S	Match anything except for whitespace characters.
[...]	Creates a set of characters, one of which must match if the operation is to be successful. If you need to specify a range of characters then separate the first and last with a hyphen: [0-9] or [D-G].
[^ ...]	Creates a set of characters which must not match. If any character in the set matches then the operation has failed. This fails if any lowercase letter from d to q is matched: [^d-q].

Table 7.1 JavaScript regular expression grammar

at least all those that I have used) have a tendency to remove the backslash, thus breaking your neatly created expression. The solution is to escape the backslash by preceding it with another one. If you use \\d, for instance, in JavaScript, the browser will actually use \d.

7.2.3 Remembering the Result

You may be simply looking through a string to see if it matches some particular pattern. At other times, though, you will be looking for a pattern that you are going to use elsewhere.

This means that you will need to remember the result of your search. The RegExp object holds the result of its operations in an array which it returns to the calling script.

Any part of a pattern which you need to remember is placed inside parentheses. You can match, and remember, as many substrings as you want to. These are returned in an array and can be recalled very easily. The order of storage matches the order in which the sets of parentheses appear in the pattern. The first match, therefore, is stored in array[0]. If you wanted to find and use the pattern "fred" in a string and use it later, you would do something like:

```
1   <html>
        <head>
            <title>Remembering Patterns</title>
        </head>
5       <body>
        <script language="javascript">
        <!--
            var re = new RegExp("[F|f]red");
            var msg = "Have you met Fred recently?";
10          var results = re.exec(msg);
            if(results) {
                document.writeln("<p>I found " + results[0] + "</p>");
            } else {
                document.writeln("<p>I didn't find the search string </p>");
15          }

            document.close();

        //-->
20      </script>
        </body>
    </html>
```

The regular expression is designed to search for either f or F followed by the string red. If the string is found, it is stored as the first element of the results array. If the search fails, nothing is written into results. We can test for the success of the search by testing whether the array has any sort of value. Depending upon the result of that test, a message is displayed.

7.2.4 Functions
Regular expressions are manipulated using functions which belong to either the RegExp or String classes.

Class `String` Functions

`match(pattern)`

searches for a matching pattern. Returns an array holding the results, or `null` if no match is found.

`replace(pattern1, pattern2)`

searches for `pattern1`. If the search is successful `pattern1` is replaced with `pattern2`.

`search(pattern)`

searches for a pattern in the string. If the match is successful, the index, offset, of the start of the match is returned. If the search fails, the function returns − 1.

`split(pattern)`

splits the string into parts based upon the pattern, or regular expression, which is supplied as a parameter.

`escape(string)`
`unescape(string)`

Web browsers convert certain characters into escape sequences. Some of these sequences may be for characters such as < which have meaning within HTML. Others may be for Unicode characters. Regardless of this, your scripts need to be able to convert into and out of escape sequences. URLs and cookies are just two places where you will need to use escape sequences rather than characters.

The escape() function takes a string as its parameter and returns a new string with characters converted to escape sequences. The unescape() function does the reverse, converting escape sequences into characters. This code shows both.

```
1   <html>
    <head><title>Escape</title></head>
    <body>
        <script language="javascript">
5           var initial = "A small string with < > one or two & characters
    which need escaping";
            var converted = escape(initial);

            document.writeln("<p>" + initial + "</p>");
10          document.writeln("<p>" + converted + "</p>");
            document.writeln("<p>" + unescape(converted) + "</p>");
```

```
            </script>
        </body>
    </html>
```

Class RegExp Functions

exec(string)

> executes a search for a matching pattern in its parameter string. It returns an array holding the result(s) of the operation.

test(string)

> searches for a match in its parameter string. It returns true if a match is found, otherwise returns false.

7.2.5 Flags

The default behavior for regular expressions is to work only on single lines of data, to stop as soon as a match is successful and to use the pattern exactly as written. The behavior of RegExp objects can be modified using three *flags*.

i

> performs searches which ignore the case of the pattern and the input string.

m

> allows searching of data which spans several input lines.

g

> Rather than stopping when the match is successful, this forces global matching across all of the input.

The flags are applied either directly into the regular expression:

```
regex = /fish|fowl/ig;
```

or as an additional parameter to the object constructor:

```
regex = new RegExp("fish|fowl", "ig");
```

7.2.6 Examples

The best way of seeing how regular expressions work is to actually use them. The following set of scripts should give you some insight into how this powerful tool can be used.

Finding a Pattern Match

The following script prompts you for a string and then a pattern. The pattern is converted into a RegExp object which is then used to search the string looking for the pattern. Depending upon the success of the search, a message is written into the browser.

```
1   <html>
        <head>
            <title>Pattern Matching</title>
        </head>
5       <body>
        <script language="javascript">
        <!--
            var msg = prompt("Enter a test string", "");
            var hunt = prompt("Enter a regular expression", "");
10          var re = new RegExp(hunt);

            var results = re.exec(msg);
            document.writeln("<h1>Search Results</h1><p>");
            if(results) {
15              document.write("I found " + results[0]);
            } else {
                document.write("I didn't find it");
            }
            document.writeln("</p>");
20          document.close();
        //-->
        </script>
        </body>
    </html>
```

Splitting a String

String splitting is incredibly useful. If you are getting input data from users then it is likely to come into your script as a string. The following sample shows how you can take a string and split it into pieces. The script uses a character which the user enters to perform the split. If you run this script you will notice that the character which you are splitting on is discarded.

```
1   <html>
        <head>
            <title>String Splitting</title>
        </head>
```

```
5    <body>
     <script language="javascript">
     <!--
         var msg = prompt("Enter a test string", "");
         var hunt = prompt("Enter a split character", "");
10       var results = msg.split(hunt);
         document.writeln("<h1>Split Results</h1><p>");
         for(var i = 0; i < results.length; i++) {
            document.write("results[" + i + "} " + results[i]);
            document.writeln("<br />");
15       }
         document.writeln("</p>");
         document.close();
     //-->
     </script>
20   </body>
     </html>
```

Replacing a Matched String

This time the user enters the string and any regular expression pattern. If the pattern is matched then it is replaced with a simple string. You could try modifying this script so that it replaces all instances of the search string.

```
1    <html>
        <head>
           <title>Replacing a Matched String</title>
        </head>
5       <body>
        <script language="javascript">
        <!--
            var msg = prompt("Enter a test string", "");
            var hunt = prompt("Enter a   regular expression", "");
10
            msg = msg.replace(hunt, " REPLACED ");

            document.writeln("<h1>Replacement Results</h1><p>");
            document.write(msg);
15          document.writeln("</p>");
            document.close();
```

```
     //-->
     </script>
     </body>
20   </html>
```

Swapping Two Words

Swapping two words is a very common requirement. It is not too difficult to do either. The regular expression is composed of the words we are looking for and the set of characters which separate them. Each of the target words is placed inside parentheses. If it is matched then the result, the word, is stored in a variable. The replace function takes the regular expression as its first parameter and a string made of the two words in reversed order, as its second. In the following example I identify the words in the replacement string using the names of hidden JavaScript variables in which they are stored. Do not worry about the strange syntax there, once you have worked through the Perl sections of this book $1 will look positively normal.

```
1    <html>
       <head>
         <title>Swapping Words</title>
       </head>
5      <body>
       <script language="javascript">
       <!--
         initial = "this is a test string";
         re = "(test) *(string)"
10       finished = initial.replace(re, "$2 $1");
         document.writeln("<h1>Swapping Words</h1><p>");
         document.write(finished);
         document.writeln("</p>");
         document.close();
15     //-->
       </script>
       </body>
     </html>
```

7.3 EXCEPTION HANDLING

Runtime error handling is vitally important in all programs. Your programs should never simply fall over or stop just because a user enters invalid data or does something unexpected. Many object-oriented programming languages provide a mechanism for dealing with general classes of error. This mechanism is called *exception handling*. JavaScript 1.4 was the first version of the language to include exception handling.

> **NOTE**
> *The following discussion and example assumes that you're working with a browser which implements at least JavaScript 1.4. If users are likely to be viewing your site on an older browser then do not use exceptions.*

An exception is an error which you have designed your program to cope with. Well that pretty much describes all errors does it not? If you write robust code then your programs will be able to handle them. After all, a user has a finite number of choices at any point in a program so if you know what all the choices are then you can cope with any errors that the user, data or program cause, can't you? In a small piece of JavaScript the answer is probably *yes*, you ought to be able to cope with any errors. In more complex scripts or large programs, that may not always be the case. This is where exceptions come into the picture.

An exception in object-based programming is an object, created dynamically at run-time, which encapsulates[2] an error and some information about it. The great thing about exceptions is that you can define your own exception classes to include exactly what you need in order to handle the problem successfully. But more than that, if you are using exceptions, you no longer need to think about every single mistake that a user might make. Instead you can wrap whole groups of mistakes up inside a single class. For instance, all incorrect input might be described by UserInputException objects. This is a real *win-win* situation. Because you have exceptions, your code is more robust *and* it is simpler too. Using exceptions needs two new pieces of the JavaScript language.

throw

An exception is an object. It is created using the standard new method. Once the exception object exists, you need to do something with it. What you do is throw the exception, that is you pass it back up the call stack until there is a piece of code which can handle it. The syntax of the throw is:

```
do something
  if an error happens {
    create a new exception object
    throw the exception
  }
```

---

[2]A term which comes from object-orientation and which really just means "wraps up".

try ... catch

Where you have a block of code which *might* cause the creation of an exception, you need to program some code to handle the exception if it should happen. The `try ...` `catch` mechanism is found in many programming languages not just JavaScript. The idea here is that your program is going to try to execute a block of statements. If an exception is thrown by any of those statements, execution of the whole block ceases and the program looks for a `catch` statement to handle the exception. `try ... catch` blocks take this form:

```
try {
    statement one
    statement two
    statement three
} catch exception {
    handle the exception
}
```

If `statement one` throws an exception, `statement two` and `statement three` will not be executed. Instead the program will move straight to the `catch`.

7.3.1 An Exceptional Example

Exception handling is best demonstrated through an example.

```
1   <html>
      <head>
        <title>Using Exceptions</title>
      </head>
5     <body onLoad="RunTest()">
      <script language="javascript">
      <!--
          function InputException(msg) {
            this.val = msg;
10          this.toString = function () {
                return "Input Exception in " + this.val
            };
          }

15          function AreLetters(msg) {
            var input = msg;
```

```
                      var re = new RegExp("[^a-zA-Z]");
                      if(input.match(re)) {
                          Oops = new InputException(input);
20                        throw Oops;
                      }
                  }


                  function RunTest(){
25                    document.writeln("<h1>Using Exceptions</h1>");
                      var input = prompt("Type Something", "");

                      try {
                          AreLetters(input);
30                    } catch (e) {
                          document.writeln("<p>" + e.toString() + "</p>");
                          document.close();
                      }

35                    document.writeln("<p>You only see this if the exception is not
                          thrown</p>");
                      document.close();
                  }
              //-->
              </script>
40        </body>
      </html>
```

Let us look at that example in a little more detail. The first thing to notice is the code to create the exception object:

```
1    function InputException(msg) {
         this.val = msg;
         this.toString = function () {
             return "Input Exception in " + this.val
5        };
     }
```

This has a variable which we are going to use to hold an error message, and a function which will be used to display the message. The toString() function is declared *inline*, that is it is declared inside another function. Although you have not seen code created like this before, it is *used* exactly like any other function which is part of an object.

```
1   if(input.match(re)) {
        Oops = new InputException(input);
        throw Oops;
    }
```

The script executes a regular expression match. If the input string matches the regular expression, an object of type `InputException` is created. The script then `throws` the new exception and control transfers back to the calling block.

```
1   try {
        AreLetters(input);
    } catch (e if e == "InputException") {
        alert(e.toString());
5   }
```

The block of code which handles the exception is a simple `try ... catch` statement. This encloses just a single function call to the input function. If an exception is thrown during the execution of `AreLetters` it will be handled by the `catch` which closes the `try` statement. In this example the `catch` only operates if the `InputException` is thrown. I could have written the catch statement to handle all exceptions:

```
catch(e)
```

The catch block encloses a set of statements inside braces. In this case the error message inside the exception object is written into the document. If no exception is thrown, the program continues execution after the closing brace of the `catch`.

7.4 BUILT-IN OBJECTS

Most of the objects that you will use in your scripting will be pre-built ones that came with the browser. In this section I will describe a few of these. These objects mirror aspects of the Document Object Model, DOM. The vast majority of incompatibilities which exist between browsers are caused by the way that they implement the DOM. This is a difficult problem which, as developers of client-side code, we just have to live with. The available solutions include using as little JavaScript as possible, using only elements which form part of the DOM, coding just for one browser or putting up with JavaScript errors on at least some clients. The choice that you make depends upon the constraints within which you are working and your own views about the way that the world is.

7.4.1 The Document Object

A document is a Web page that is being either displayed or created. The document has a number of properties that can be accessed by JavaScript programs and used to manipulate the content of the page. Some of these properties can be used to create HTML pages from within JavaScript while others may be used to change the operation of the current page.

write

writeln

As you have already seen, HTML pages can be created *on the fly* using JavaScript. This is done by using the `write` or `writeln` methods of the document object:

```
1  document.write("<body>");
   document.write("<h1>A test</h1>");
   document.write("<form>");
```

bgcolor

fgcolor

These are the same properties that can be set in the <BODY> tag. The difference here is that the values can be set from within a JavaScript. The methods accept either hexadecimal values or common names for colors:

```
1  document.bgcolor = "#e302334";
   document.fgcolor = "coral";
```

Those values can be used in dynamically created documents like this:

```
1  document.write("<body bgcolor=" + cols[counter] + ">");
   document.write("<h1>A Test </h1>");
```

anchors

Any named point inside an HTML document is an anchor. Anchors are created using <a name = ... >. These will commonly be used for moving around inside a large page as shown in Section 2.4.3. The `anchors` property is an array of these names in the order in which they appear in the HTML document. Anchors can be accessed like this:

```
1  document.anchors[0];
```

links

Another array holding potentially useful information about the page. All links are stored in an array in the same order as they appear on the Web page.

forms

Again this is an array in the order of the document. This one contains all of the HTML forms. By combining this array with the individual `form` objects each form item can be accessed.

layers

> A document can be made from a number of layers of content. This array contains the layer objects. Layers have many methods and properties of their own and will be discussed in detail in Section 4.7.

close()

> The document is not completely written until the close() method has been called. If you do not use this method then the browser will keep waiting for more data even if there is none.

7.4.2 The Window Object

The browser window is a mutable object that can be addressed by JavaScript code. In Chapter 8 I will show how new windows can be used to give a controlled Web experience or to break your site out from the mundane. All that I want to do here is to show some of the properties and methods that are available from Window objects.

open("URL", "name")

> This opens a new window which contains the document specified by URL. The window is given an identifying name so that it can be manipulated individually.

close()

> This shuts the current window.

toolbar=[1|0]
location=[1|0]
directories=[1|0]
status=[1|0]
menubar=[1|0]
scrollbars=[1|0]
resizable=[1|0]

> Many of the attributes of a browser are undesirable in a pop-up window. They can be switched on and off individually.

width=pixels
height=pixels

> When positioning content, especially on dynamic pages, it is useful to be able to locate it whatever the resolution of the screen or size of window being used. These values are easily available.

> When a new window is being opened then you may choose to open it at a set size, for instance, if you are displaying an image there. These properties can be used to set the window size. The following code shows how this might work:

```
1   newWin = open(address, "newWin", status=0, width="100", height="100",
        resizable=0);
```

scroll(coordinate, coordinate)

The content of the window can be automatically scrolled using this command. As with HTML layers the screen coordinates start from 0, 0, which is the top left corner, and increment as you move across and down. The coordinates are given in pixels.

Later I will show how to scroll individual layers – which is a more satisfying effect than scrolling the entire screen.

7.4.3 The Form Object

Two aspects of the form can be manipulated though JavaScript. First, most commonly and probably most usefully, the data that is entered onto your form can be checked at submission. Second you can actually build forms through JavaScript.

The elements of the form are held in an array (you might have guessed there would be an array in there somewhere!). This rather neatly means that any of the properties of those elements that you can set using HTML code can be accessed though your JavaScript. This example shows a form and a function which reads the properties of the form elements:

```
1   <html>
    <head>
    <script language="javascript">
    function validate() {
5       var method = document.forms[0].method;
        var action = document.forms[0].action;
        var value = document.forms[0].elements[0].value;
        if(value != "Mary"){
           document.forms[0].reset();
10      } else {
           alert("Hi Mary!!");
        }
    }
    </script>
15  </head><body>
    <form method="post">
        <input type="text" id="user" size="32" />
        <input type="submit" value="Press Me!" onClick="validate()" />
    </form>
20  </body>
    </html>
```

That code is not really very good. I do not use the variables `method` and `action` once I have created them. Creating variables which you never need is a waste of system resources and makes your code cluttered and complex. I have done it here simply to demonstrate the way that arrays can be used to access form data.

The worst aspect of the code is that it directly accesses the internal arrays within the form. That was the established and correct technique until quite recently. Modern browsers support a standard interface called the Document Object Model. The DOM lets you access any HTML elements which have a valid `id` attribute using a method called `getElementById`. You will see examples of its use throughout the rest of this chapter. The big advantage of the DOM is that it is used by all of the latest browsers. Older techniques, such as array access, varied between browsers. This meant that code had to include lots of conditional statements and browser sniffing to select the appropriate sections for each piece of software. In the last listing the DOM-compliant code would have looked like:

```
1  var value = document.getElementById("user").value;
```

I will look at a data validation in more detail in Section 8.1, for now you just need to know which events can be used to trigger validation routines:

onClick="method"
> This can be applied to all form elements. The event is triggered when the user clicks on that element. It is not triggered if you try to force events through the `click()` method.

onSubmit="method"
> This event can only be triggered by the form itself and occurs when a form is submitted.

onReset="method"
> Like the previous one this is a form-only event and is (obviously) triggered when a form is reset by the user.

7.4.4 The Browser Object

No two browser models will process your JavaScript in the same way. It is important that you try to find out which browser is being used to view your page. You can then make a choice for your visitors:

- exclude browsers that are unable to use your code
- redirect them to a non-scripted version of your site
- present scripts that are tailored to suit each browser. You will be glad to know that this can be done from within your code and does not involve rewriting the entire site.

The browser is a JavaScript object and can be queried from within your code. For historical reasons the browser object is actually called the `navigator` object. The following properties are just some that can be gathered:

navigator.appCodeName

> This is the internal name for the browser. For both major products this is *Mozilla*, which was the name of the original Netscape code source.

navigator.appName

> This is the public name of the browser – Navigator or Internet Explorer for the big two.

navigator.appVersion

> The version number, platform on which the browser is running, and (for Internet Explorer) the version of Navigator with which it is compatible.

navigator.userAgent

> The strings `appCodeName` and `appVersion` concatenated together.

navigator.plugins

> An array containing details of all installed plug-ins.

navigator.mimeTypes

> An array of all supported MIME types – useful if you need to make sure that the browser can handle your data.

Browser Sniffing

JavaScript implementations are based on the ECMAscript standard and most manufacturers do a pretty good job of implementing the language. You might, therefore, expect that your code will work in the same way in most browsers and on most platforms. As with so many Web technologies the reality is rather different to hype and expectation. The language might be the same, but each browser uses a different Document Object Model, and it is the elements of the DOM which JavaScript manipulates. Code which works in one browser cannot always be guaranteed to work in another simply because the objects that you are trying to manipulate might not exist there.

Some people, probably the majority of JavaScript developers, ignore incompatibilities by creating sites which will only work in a few browsers. Commonly, Web sites include a warning that aspects of the site only work in Internet Explorer or, less often, Netscape Navigator. There are lots of browsers out there, and making code which is compatible with all of them can be very complicated. If you write code which tests for the browser type then selects appropriate processing based on that type you will have an unmaintainable mess.

Your code will be full of *forks*, many of which will become obsolete as browsers fall out of use, but which will remain *in situ* because the difficulty of finding and removing them outweighs the inconvenience of keeping them.

Over the years a lot of effort has gone into writing robust code which identifies browsers. If you look around the Web you will find many examples. These tend to be large pieces of JavaScript which you can embed in your own pages. These days there is a better alternative. Simply write pages which adhere to the W3C HTML document object model. This DOM is supported across browsers which are used by the vast majority of Web surfers. DOM-compliant code will reduce your development and maintenance efforts and keep your costs down.

Because you may continue to come across situations in which browser sniffing is used I have included a primitive example. This code creates a JavaScript object containing data about the browser and then displays that data in a new window:

```
1   <html>
      <head>
      <script language="javascript">
      <!--
5
      function Sniff() {
          browser = new Is();
          browser.display(),
          }
10
      function Is() {
          this.app = navigator.appName.toLowerCase();
          this.version = navigator.appVersion;
          this.major = parseInt(navigator.appVersion);
15        this.minor = parseFloat(navigator.appVersion);
          this.codename = navigator.appCodeName.toLowerCase();
          this.agent = navigator.userAgent.toLowerCase();
          this.display = showData;
          }
20
      function showData() {
          win = open("", "newWin");
          win.document.write("<body>");
          win.document.writeln("<h1>About Your Browser</h1>");
25        win.document.writeln("<p><em>Application</em> " + this.app);
```

```
        win.document.writeln("<p><em>Agent</em> " + this.agent);
        win.document.writeln("<p><em>Codename</em> " + this.codename);
        win.document.writeln("<p><em>Version</em> " + this.version);
        win.document.writeln("<p><em>Version (major)</em> " + this.major);
30      win.document.writeln("<p><em>Version (minor)</em> " + this.minor);
        win.document.writeln("</body>");
        win.document.close();
    }


35  //-->
    </script>


    </head>
    <body onLoad="Sniff()">
40  </body>
</html>
```

7.4.5 The Date Object

Manipulating dates and times is a complicated business. There is plenty of difficulty whether handling leap years or formatting output for different regions. JavaScript includes a well-developed Date class which provides functions to perform many different date manipulations.

In JavaScript, dates and times represent the number of milliseconds since 1st January 1970 UTC. JavaScript, like most programming systems, has two separate notions of time: UTC and local. UTC is universal time, also known as Greenwich Mean Time, which is the standard time throughout the World. Local time is the time on the machine which is executing the script. A JavaScript Date object can represents dates from − 100,000,000 to +100,000,000 days relative to 01/01/1970. Since this range of dates clearly covers several millennia it is important that you always specify years fully. If you mean 2001, use 2001 not 01.

Table 7.2 lists some of the more useful functions for setting and retrieving values from Date objects. I have not included those which manipulate UTC dates since the table would become unwieldy.

Date()

Construct an empty date object.

Date(milliseconds)

Construct a new Date object based upon the number of milliseconds which have elapsed since 00:00:00 hours on 01/01/1970.

Function	Description
getDate	Return the day of the month.
getDay	Return an integer representing the day of the week, Sunday is 0 and Saturday is 6.
getFullYear	Return the year as a four digit number.
getHours	Return the hour field of the Date object.
getMilliseconds	Return the milliseconds field of the Date object as a number from 0 to 999.
getMinutes	Return the minutes field of the Date object, from 0 to 59.
getMonth	Return the month field of the Date object. The month is represented by an integer: 0 for January through 11 for December.
getSeconds	Return the seconds field of the Date object.
getTime	Returns the number of milliseconds since midnight on 01/01/1970 which the Date object represents.
setDate(day)	Set the day value of the object. Accepts values in the range 1 to 31.
setFullYear(year[, month, day])	Sets the year value of the object. Optionally also sets month and day values. All are passed as integers. Year as a four digit date, month in the range 0 to 11, day in the range 1 to 31.
setHours(hours[, mins, secs, ms])	Set the hours v<html> <head> <script language="javascript"> function validate() var value = document.getElementById("user").value; if(value != "Mary") document.getElementById("user").reset(); else alert("Hi Mary!!"); </script> </head><body> <form method="post"> <input type="text" size="32" id="user" /> <input type="submit" value="Press Me!" onClick="validate()" /> </form> </body> </html>alue of the object to an integer in the range 0 through 23. Optionally set minutes, seconds and milliseconds values.
setMilliseconds(ms)	Set the milliseconds value of the object in the range 0 through 999.
setMinutes(min[, secs, ms])	Set the minutes value using an integer in the range 0 though 59.
setMonth(month[, day])	Set the month value to an integer in the range 0 through 11.
setSeconds(secs[, ms])	Set the seconds value of the object to an integer in the range 0 to 59.
setTime(time)	Set the value of the Date object. The parameter is a string representing the number of milliseconds since midnight, 01/01/1970.
toGMTString	Returns the Date formatted as a string in GMT format.
toLocaleString	Returns the Date formatted in local format.
toString	Returns the Date as a string.

Table 7.2 JavaScript date functions

Date(string)

Create a Date object based upon the contents of a text string. The string must be in the format which is created by the Date.parse() function.

Date(year, month, day[, hour, minute, second])

Create a new Date object based upon numerical values for the year, month and day. Optional time values may also be supplied. January is represented by the integer value 0, December by 11.

Parse(String)

This returns the number of milliseconds since midnight on 01/01/1970 which the string represents. The string must be in the following format:

```
Mon, 9 April 2001 14:02:35
```

The timezone can be specified at the end of the string. If no timezone is specified then the local timezone of the machine executing the script is assumed. Timezones may be one of the U.S. continental zones or a numerical offset relative to GMT:

- Mon, 9 April 2001 14:02:35 GMT
- Mon, 9 April 2001 14:02:35 EST
- Mon, 9 April 2001 14:02:35 GMT+2

Here is a simple piece of code which demonstrates how easily dates can be manipulated:

```
1   <html>
      <head>
        <title>Handling Dates</title>
      </head>
5   <body onLoad="Dater()">
    <script language="javascript">
    <!--
      function Dater() {
        var today = new Date();
10      var yesterday = new Date();
        var diff = today.getDate() - 1;

        yesterday.setDate(diff);

15      document.write("<h3>The date is " + today  + "</h3>");
        document.write("<h3>The date yesterday was ");
```

```
            document.writeln(yesterday  +  "</h3>");
            document.close();
        }
20    //-->
      </script>
      </body>
</html>
```

7.5 COOKIES

Cookies are strings which browsers can store within their cache. They are widely used for tracking users, sessions and controlling access to parts of a site. The creation and manipulation of cookies is often associated with server-side programming languages such as Perl or PHP but they can be worked with from the client too. The Document Object Model exposes cookies as a property of the document but JavaScript does not have any built-in code to work with them. The code in this section shows how to work with the lifecycle of a cookie: creation, retrieval and deletion.

7.5.1 Setting a Cookie

Cookies are not just random strings. Their structure was first defined in RFC 2109 from 1997, has been refined since then and is adhered to by all browsers. If you want your cookie code to work you will need to stick to the standard too. Fortunately this is very easy to do. We will start by creating a cookie. Because a cookie is a string we will simply build the string then assign it to document.cookie.

The cookie has six properties which you might want to set in your scripts. Cookie properties are set as key-value pairs with the key and the value separated by an equals sign. The properties are separated using semi-colons.

All cookies must have a name and some content. The name is used to identify the cookie – you can set several for the same site. The content is the information which you wish to store in the cookie. These two items make up a key value pair and are the only mandatory part of a cookie.

By default, cookies remain in the cache only until a session ends – when the browser is closed. Generally you will want to use them either to regulate sessions or to store data between sessions. In the former case you may, for example, be building a shopping cart and impose a limit of 30 minutes during which products can be added to the cart. After that time the cart is automatically deleted. A cookie can easily be used as the cart. To set a time when the cookie must be deleted you use the expiry property. This takes a time in UTF format as its value. If you want to save information between sessions the expiry time is set at some suitable point in the future. To delete a cookie simply set the expiry time at a point in the past.

Cookies are only returned to the server which created them. This server may host a number of domains. If your cookie is used for a subset of those domains you use the domain property. The value assigned must start with a dot and be a valid domain name. Domain is optional.

Path indicates the set of valid URLs within a domain or site which the cookie is used for. This is an optional attribute.

If the cookie can only be transferred back to the server over a secure connection then set the secure property. This is a Boolean which does not take a value.

```
1   function setCookie(name, value, expires, path, domain, secure) {
        cookie = name + "=" + escape(value);
        if (expires)
            if (expires.toString().indexOf("GMT") == -1)
5               expires = expires.toGMTString();
            cookie += "; expires=" + expires;
        if (path)
            cookie += "; path=" + path;
        if (domain)
10          cookie += "; domain=" + domain;
        if (secure)
            cookie += "; secure";

        document.cookie = cookie;
15  }
```

The example code should be treated as a starting point from which you can further develop your cookie generating script. If you then want to set only the secure property you must pass in empty strings for expires, path and domain. You could easily modify this code to accept an object which would act as a data structure.

Because the expiry time has to be in UTF format it is examined for the string GMT. If that is not present the time is converted to UTF using the toGMTString() function. For the purposes of JavaScript and cookies GMT and UTF are identical.

7.5.2 Retrieving a Cookie

A document can possess more than one cookie but all of them are held in the document.cookie property. The process of extracting a cookie is simple: first retrieve all the cookies; then split the cookies apart into an array; finally extract the name of each until the cookie you want is found and return it.

The following function takes the name of the cookie as a parameter. A regular expression is used to find that name. name + "=.+;*" builds a string with the name followed by an equals sign and one or more characters optionally terminated with a semi-colon. The array of cookies is examined in the `for` loop and when a match is found the loop is terminated. The regular expression returns the key=value pair. The value is extracted by splitting this pair at the equals sign. Any escape sequences are converted to characters using `unescape()` and the string returned to the calling code. If the cookie is not found an empty string is returned. The calling code must check for this and handle it appropriately.

```
1   function getCookie(name) {
        var documentCookies = document.cookie;
        var eachCookie = documentCookies.split(";");
        // search for the name followed by =
5       var name_re = new RegExp(name + "=.+;*");
        var res = "";

        for (var i=0; i<eachCookie.length; i++) {
            var results = name_re.exec(eachCookie[i]);
10          if (results) {
                var parts = results[0].split("=");
                res = unescape(parts[1]);
                break;
            }
15      }
        return res;
    }
```

7.5.3 Deleting a Cookie

Cookies are deleted when an attempt is made to access them after their expiry time has passed. This code retrieves the cookie using the method shown above and resets the expiry time. Since the cookie is being deleted its value is not needed so it is discarded once the cookie has been found. If the path and domain properties were set when the cookie was created these must also be set when deleting it.

```
1   function deleteCookie(name, path, domain) {
        if (getCookie(name)) {
            cookie = name + "=";
            if (path)
5               cookie += "; path=" + path;
            if (domain)
                cookie += "; domain=" + domain;
```

```
         cookie += "; expires=Thu, 01-Jan-70 00:00:01 GMT";
         document.cookie = cookie;
10     }
   }
```

7.5.4 Using Cookies

This example is a page with a form which has two drop-down lists. One is for cookie names, the other is used to select content for the cookie. Three buttons let users create, delete or view cookies. The values which are selected in the drop-down lists are accessed using document.getElementById() with the ID of the list as parameter. Cookies expire two minutes after they are created so that they are not lying around for a long time if you forget to delete them.

The cookie handling code is generic stuff which can be used in any Web page. I have put it in a file called cookies.js.

Finally when a cookie is retrieved its contents are written into a special div using the document.getElementById("debug").innerHTML property.

If you try this code you will find that your browser will let you view cookies which it has cached. See the help documentation for you particular browser to find out how this is done. Try creating a few cookies and then seeing what is stored.

```
1    <html>
     <head>
         <title>Using Cookies in JavaScript</title>
         <script language="javascript" src="cookies.js"></script>
5        <script language="javascript">

         function bakeCookie() {
             var name = document.getElementById("cookieNames").value;
             var value = document.getElementById("cookieValues").value;
10
             var today = new Date();
             var minutes = today.getMinutes() + 2;
             today.setMinutes(minutes);

15           setCookie(name, value, today);
         }

         function showCookie() {
             var name = document.getElementById("cookieNames").value;
```

```
20          var biccie = getCookie(name);<html>
        <head>
        <script language="javascript">
        function validate() {
            var method = document.forms[0].method;
25          var action = document.forms[0].action;
            var value = document.forms[0].elements[0].value;
            if(value != "Mary"){
                document.forms[0].reset();
            } else {
30              alert("Hi Mary!!");
            }
        }
        </script>
        </head><body>
35      <form method="post">
            <input type="text" name="user" size="32">
            <input type="submit" value="Press Me!" onClick="validate()">
        </form>
        </body>
40  </html>
            document.getElementById("debug").innerHTML =
                document.getElementById("debug").innerHTML + "<p>Returned: " +
                biccie + "</p>";
        }

        function breakCookie() {
45          var name = document.getElementById("cookieNames").value ;
            deleteCookie(name);
        }
        </script>
    </head>
50  <body>

    <h1>Using Cookies in JavaScript</h1>

    <form action="#">
55      <table border="0">
```

```
        <tr>
            <td><select id="cookieNames">
                <option id="test1" value="test1">test1</option>
                <option id="test2" value="test2">test2</option>
60              <option id="test3" value="test3">test3</option>
                <option id="test4" value="test4">test4</option>
            </select></td>
            <td colspan="2"><select id="cookieValues">
                <option id="val1" value="val1">This cookie is 1</option>
65              <option id="val2" value="val2">This cookie is 2</option>
                <option id="val3" value="val3">This cookie is 3</option>
                <option id="val4" value="val4">This cookie is 4</option>
                <option id="val5" value="val5">This cookie is 5</option>
            </select></td>
70      </tr>
        <tr>
            <td><button id="bake" onclick="bakeCookie()">Bake a
                cookie</button></td>
            <td><button id="show" onclick="showCookie()">Show a
                cookie</button></td>
            <td><button id="delete" onclick="breakCookie()">Delete a
                cookie</button></td>
75      </tr>
    </table>
</form>

<div id="debug" style="top: 200; left: 10; width: 80%; position: relative;
80  background: pink"> </div>
</body>
</html>
```

7.6 EVENTS

JavaScript is an *event-driven* system. Nothing happens unless it is initiated by an event outside the script. JavaScript is always reactive rather than proactive, with event triggers coming via the browser. An event is any change that the user makes to the state of the browser. You are used to using a lot of event-driven software, although you may not always recognize it as such. For instance, a word processor simply responds to your actions.

Most software you ever use is controlled by you. That is not always true about Web applications. Animations created using Macromedia's Flash software play when the page is

Event	Handler	Description
blur	onBlur	The input focus is moved from the object, usually when moving from a field of a form or from the form itself.
change	onChange	The value of a field in a form has been changed by the user entering or deleting data.
click	onClick	The mouse is clicked over an element of a page.
dblclick	onDblClick	A form element or a link is clicked twice in rapid succession.
dragdrop	onDragDrop	A system file is dragged with a mouse and dropped onto the browser.
focus	onFocus	Input focus is given to an element. The reverse of blur.
keydown	onKeyDown	A key is depressed but not released.
keypress	onKeyPress	A key is pressed.
keyup	onKeyUp	A depressed key is released.
load	onLoad	The page is loaded by the browser.
mousedown	onMouseDown	A mouse button is pressed.
mousemove	onMouseMove	The mouse, and hence cursor, is moved.
mouseout	onMouseOut	The mouse pointer moves off an element.
mouseover	onMouseOver	The mouse pointer is moved over an element.
mouseup	onMouseUp	The mouse button is released.
move	onMove	A window is moved, maximized or restored either by the user or by a script.
resize	onResize	A Window is resized by the user or by a script.
select	onSelect	A field on a form is selected by clicking the mouse or tabbing from the keyboard.
submit	onSubmit	A form is submitted (the submit button is clicked).
unload	onUnload	The user leaves the Web page.

Table 7.3 JavaScript events

loaded provided the browser has the correct plug-in installed. Often users simply have to put up with Flash because they are unable to control it except by disabling the plug-in. JavaScript can work in the same way. Your script can be initiated when the page loads and then run automatically. This is one of the most annoying things about scripted Web pages and is the main reason that many people switch off JavaScript when they configure their browser. Generally you are adding a script to a page to improve its functionality or appearance. Hence the script is an integral part of the page but its operation should always be controlled by the user.

JavaScript event handling can be quite a complex issue. Different manufacturers have implemented their own ways of capturing and handling events. Internet Explorer has a large set of complicated, but useful, event routines which can be used to extend its functionality beyond the Web and onto the Windows desktop. Unfortunately, despite being useful and well-designed, these lack platform independence. I want to show you some ideas that you can actually use and which most visitors to your page can use too. Therefore I am going to concentrate upon a lowest common denominator set of event handlers.

The original set of event handlers appeared in Netscape 2 and was broadly replicated in Internet Explorer 3. These still work today, even in version 6 browsers, and are available in all browsers which support JavaScript. Despite the limited number of events which can be handled using these techniques, they provide most events that you are likely to need on a Web page. Table 7.3 shows some of the more common JavaScript events. The names of simple event handlers are not case-sensitive; `onload`, `onLoad` and `ONLOAD` all represent exactly the same thing.

Not all objects can create all events. Some HTML objects such as paragraphs and headings cannot create any events although this may change in a future version. When an event happens, your script may want to do something with it. Not all events need handling; some can be ignored if they are not relevant. Where you want an action from the user to lead to some action from a script you will need to implement an *event handler*. Event handlers are JavaScript functions which you associate with an HTML element as part of its definition in the HTML source code:

```
<element attributes event="handler">
```

The handler will be a JavaScript function that you have defined elsewhere and which is available to the element.

Plenty of examples of event handling are given in Chapter 8. For now, the following code demonstrates a few different events being created and handled.

```
1  <html>
      <head>
         <title>Handling Events</title>
      </head>
```

```
5    <body onLoad="ShowLoaded()" onUnload="SayGoodbye()">
        <h1>Handling Events</h1>
        <p>
          <a href="#" onMouseOver="Mouse()">A Hyperlink</a>
        </p>
10      <form>
          <input type="button"
            value="Click Me!"
            onClick="Clicked()"
            onMouseOver="Mouse()">
15      </form>
     <script language="javascript">
     <!--
        function ShowLoaded(){
           alert("The page has loaded");
20         }


        function SayGoodbye() {
           alert("Goodbye, thanks for visiting");
25         }


        function Clicked() {
           alert("You clicked the button");
30         }


        function Mouse() {
           alert("The mouse is over the link");
           }
35
     //-->
     </script>
     </body>
  </html>
```

Each of the event handlers performs an identical task. When they are called, an `alert` dialog is used to display a message. The messages differ so that we can track which event has just occurred and which object caused it. The relationship between events, event handlers

Object	Event Handlers
window	onload onunload onblur onfocus
link	onclick onmouseout onmouseover
area	onmouseout onmouseover
image	onabort onerror onload
form	onreset onsubmit
text	onblur onchange onfocus onselect
textarea	onblur onchange onfocus onselect
password	onblur onchange onfocus onselect
button	onclick
reset	onclick
submit	onclick
radio	onclick
checkbox	onclick
select	onblur onchange onfocus
fileupload	onblur onselect onfocus

Table 7.4 JavaScript 1 objects and event handlers

and page elements should be obvious from the code. Notice, though, that the button has two event handlers. One is for an onClick, the other for onMouseOver. If you run the code you will find that the button never creates the onMouseOver event. You might think that a button would need to somehow *know* that the mouse was over it before it was clicked. In fact it does not. Table 7.4 lists the objects and event handlers which are supported by JavaScript 1.1. These provide a sort of minimal functionality which almost every browser supports. If you work from this list then your scripts will work for almost all visitors to your site (or at least those with JavaScript enabled!).

EXERCISES

Object-oriented JavaScript

1. Briefly detail the main features of the theory of object-orientation.
2. How does JavaScript fare as an object-oriented language? Would it be correct to say that JavaScript is *object-based* rather than object-oriented?
3. Try the code from Section 7.1.1 "JavaScript Objects" Does it do what you expected?
4. The new keyword is very special. What does it do?
5. Detail the functioning of the JavaScript keyword this and the dot operator.

Using JavaScript Objects

1. Write a script to create a new browser window and display some text in that window. Put your script inside a suitable HTML page and test it.
2. Modify your window creating script so that it has less *furniture* such as scrollbars.
3. Create an HTML page which includes a simple form. Write a script to extract the data from the form when the submit button is clicked. Display the extracted data in a new document.
4. Add the browser sniffer from Section 7.4.4 "Browser Sniffing" to an HTML page. Modify the script to display more information about the browser being used.

JavaScript Events

1. JavaScript is *event driven*. What are events? What events can JavaScript handle?
2. Create a Web page containing a form which has a single button and a text input field. When the button is clicked a dialog box should open which displays the contents of the text field.
3. Put an image on a page. Write some JavaScript which displays a message when the mouse is over the image. Try to display the co-ordinates of the mouse if it is clicked on the image.

Dates

1. Write a script which accepts a date as input from the user, adds 70 years to it and displays the result. The date will come into your script as a string.
2. Display the current date and time in both GMT and locale forms.

Regular Expressions

1. Write a regular expression which searches strings for non-alphabetic characters. Test your script in a Web page.
2. Write and test a regular expression which swaps the first two words of a string.
3. Write an expression which replaces every occurrence of the letter 'a' in a string with the letter 'q'.

Dynamic HTML with JavaScript

Much of the JavaScript code that I have shown so far has created new documents and written directly to them. The commonest unit that your JavaScript will have to interact with is the document. Remember that the structure of data and the way that the browser manipulates that data depend upon the document object model (DOM). Almost all of the objects that can be manipulated by a script are part of a document. In the previous chapter you saw how to manipulate some of the elements of the DOM. In this chapter I will show you how to manipulate the actual browser window. The examples in this chapter demonstrate some of the most popular uses of JavaScript that you will find on the Internet today.

Dynamic HTML (DHTML) is the combined result of everything that I have discussed so far. It is well structured HTML code which adheres to the standards, it is stylesheets used to present neutral formatting control, and finally it is the use of scripts to make the text, images, and style elements active. In this chapter I am going to show how to build some of the most common and useful DHTML applications, and how to build applications that are more often associated with Java than DHTML.

I will show you how to make that popular perennial, the rollover image. You will have seen these on a lot of Web sites: as your mouse moves over some text or an image, the element changes in some way. Second I will show a very simple way of moving images around the screen. Third up is the use of layers to reduce downloads. Basically you can put a collection of pages into a single HTML file and use JavaScript to let surfers navigate through them. The great thing about this technique is that your site *looks* like it is a normal download-every-page kind of site but it will run far more quickly. Although it will take longer to load in the first place. The usual caveats that *some you win, some you lose*, apply.

Finally, I present two big, complex applications which are developed for the bleeding edge of today's Web design. Having all of your navigation support provided by menus is a sensible way of structuring a site. You *can* use Java applications to give drop-down menus, but I will show a clean and easy way of doing the same with text, stylesheets, and JavaScript. Second, many companies now offer free Web site hosting supported by revenue from advertising. Some of these sites use a neat technique to *brand* all of the pages that they host. This branding is usually an image that floats in the bottom right-hand corner of the screen. The last DHTML application that I will give you shows how to do the same by floating a layer. In the example I will use a piece of text rather than an image but, because the technique uses floating layers, you can place any content inside it that you choose.

8.1 DATA VALIDATION

Before doing anything dynamic, I am going to discuss the validation of data. It would be nice to validate data that is entered into your forms at the client. Existing techniques rely upon the use of server scripting and are very robust. There is a delay between the user entering data, the script performing validation, and an error (or confirmation) being returned to the user. Many potential errors such as entering a space or character other than a digit or a letter into a user name should be spotted at the client and dealt with.

A common technique for restricting access to a site is to check user IDs against a file of valid users. For security reasons it turns out to be a bad idea to do this sort of data validation at the client. Any code or data that you send to the client gets cached there. If you send a long list of items to validate against, then that list is available to the user. If they are trying to hack your system then you have given them the key to the door.

Generally the RegExp class discussed in Section 7.2 provides everything that you need to start validating data. Before getting too deeply involved in the *how*, you have to understand *what* validation is and what it is not. Validation is simply the process of ensuring that some data *might* be correct data for a particular application. Broadly speaking data validation is the process of ensuring that users submit only the set of characters which you require. It is *not* the process of ensuring that the data is in any way accurate.

Why can we not test for accuracy? Well under some circumstances we can. If a program accepts data from a remote data logger and that input is always going to be in a particular range, then the program knows that data outside the range is invalid and should not be accepted. What it does with the incorrect data depends upon the way that the application was specified, of course. A Web form is rather different. Most of the data that your scripts get from users will be textual and almost impossible to verify. Consider a form which accepts names. Generally, names contain a limited set of characters: the letters a to z in upper and lower case and a few punctuation marks. They do not tend to include digits, exclamation marks or equals signs.

This means that you can write a regular expression which checks that any name entered by users only has allowable characters in it. What you cannot do is check if they have entered a real name. The string Abcde Fghij-Klmno has all of the characteristics of a real name, but you are unlikely ever to meet anyone who answers to it.

One common request is for a way of validating email addresses. Many Web sites use email addresses to track users, and their developers would like to be sure that the email addresses they use are correct. Email addresses follow regular patterns and come in a limited number of types so they would appear to be an ideal candidate for automatic validation. The same problem applies to email addresses as to people's names: you can only ever test the validity of the characters and combinations. You cannot tell from an email address if there is a real user on a real system anywhere behind it. So what about testing for valid characters and combinations? Again this is *not* an easy problem to solve. Simple regular expressions can be created which will work on many Internet addresses but a fully featured version is very long and complicated. If you want to see one of these monstrosities, take a look at *Mastering Regular Expressions* by Jeffrey Friedl.

8.1.1 Validation: An Example

Now that you know what validation is, it is time to see some code. The following Web page has two text fields. One accepts names, the other accepts ages. Both fields are validated using regular expressions and, if the data is valid the contents of the form are transmitted in an email message. Look at the code, then I will, show you some of the important pieces in a little more detail.

```
1   <html>
      <head>
        <title>Data Validation</title>
      </head>
5     <body>
        <form method="post"
          action="addUser.php"
          onSubmit="return Validate()">
          <table border="0">
10          <tr>
              <th>Your Name</th>
              <td><input type="text" length="24" id="name" /></td>
            </tr>
            <tr>
15            <th>Your Age</th>
              <td>
```

```
              <input type="text" size="3" maxlength="3" id="age"/>
            </td>
          </tr>
20        <tr>
            <td><input type="submit" value="Submit" /></td>
            <td><input type="reset" value="Reset" /></td>
          </tr>
        </table>
25    </form>

      <script language="javascript">
      <!--
        function Validate() {
30          var valid = false;
            var name = document.getElementById("name").value;
            var age = document.getElementById("age").value;

            name_re = new RegExp("^[A-Z][a-zA-Z '-.]+$", "g");
35          age_re = new RegExp("^[\\d]+ $", "g");

            if(name.match(name_re)){
              // only validate the age if the name is OK
              if(age.match(age_re)){
40              // name and age are both valid
                valid = true;
              } else {
                alert("Age does not match " + age_re);
              }
45          } else {
              alert("Name does not match " + name_re);
            }
            return valid;
          }
50      //-->
        </script>
      </body>
    </html>
```

Very often novice JavaScript programmers find they can write simple validation routines but they cannot find a way of calling the routine before the data is submitted. Or, if they do call the routine, the form is submitted regardless of the validity of the data. The solution is definitely non-intuitive because it relies upon a little-documented property of the form tag. forms have an onSubmit event which is generated when the submit button is clicked. Data validation is performed by the event handler which you create for the onSubmit event. So far, so normal. The trick is to make your event handler function return true if the data in the form is valid or false if it is not. The onSubmit event is then assigned the return value from the handler. The form will only be submitted if the event gets set to true. This example shows what I mean:

```
1  <form method="post"
      action="addUser.php"
      onSubmit="return Validate()">
```

You can mimic this process from an onClick event. Do not use a submit button on your form, use a plain button, and create an event handler for its onClick event:

```
<input type="button" value="Submit" onClick="Validate()">
```

then use the boolean value in the validation function instead of returning it. If the function evaluates to true, force the submission of the form:

```
1  if(valid == true) {
     document.forms[0].submit();
   }
```

Back to the example. The value from the name field is copied into a local variable and then compared against a regular expression:

```
1  var name = document.getElementById("name").value;
   name_re = new RegExp("^[A-Z][a-zA-Z '-.]+$", "g");
```

The regular expression there checks for a capital letter at the start of the line followed by one or more characters until the end of line is reached. The valid character set I have used includes upper and lower case letters, spaces, hyphens and apostrophes. Your set will differ depending upon your location and requirements. If any invalid character is encountered, the regular expression will return false. Notice that I use $ to search all the way to the end of the string. If you leave that out, the regular expression will stop quite happily after the second character and return true even if the third character entered is a digit.

Checking the age field is a similar process:

```
1  var age = document.getElementById("age").value;
   age_re = new RegExp("^[\\d]+$", "g");
```

This time the regular expression only accepts digits 0 through 9 between the start and end of the string. Again, if you leave out the start and end specifiers, the regular expression engine will be quite happy with the expression, provided, of course, any of the three characters is a digit.

8.2 OPENING A NEW WINDOW

Perhaps the majority of the JavaScript coding that you will do will be based around the use of windows. The typical piece of Microsoft Windows software uses the multiple document interface (MDI) structure. The application has a single *global* frame and when new windows are opened they appear inside that frame. The application frame is said to be the *parent* of all of the internal frames. Web browsers are based around a different model in which each new window is independent of the application from which it was launched. This model is more akin to that typically used in the UNIX world when programming applications for the X Window System.

The Web/X model has some interesting side effects that we can use to our benefit when programming in JavaScript. The main benefit is that, because windows are independent of each other, any windows spawned from our code can be made to look and act totally differently from the rest of the application.

Here are the main points from the window object definition given in Section 7.4.2:

```
open("URL", "name")
close()
toolbar=[1|0]
location=[1|0]
directories=[1|0]
status=[1|0]
menubar=[1|0]
scrollbars=[1|0]
resizable=[1|0]
width=pixels
height=pixels
```

A new window can be opened which contains a URL identified resource and the attributes of that window can be tailored to suit the application. Imagine developing a Web site to show off artwork or photographs. You may want to display thumbnail images which, when clicked, open a larger version of the image for better viewing. However, if for reasons such as copyright protection, you do not want the image to be printed or its location revealed, the options to the window object declaration give you that power. Here is some code that should demonstrate what I mean:

```
1   <html>
      <head>
        <script language="javascript">
        <!--
5       function Load(url){
          var next = url;
          newwin = open("url", "newwin",
              'status=0,toolbar=0,resizable=0,width=258,height=137');
        }
        //-->
10      </script>
      </head>
      <body>
        <p>
          <a href="" onClick="Load('./pic1.gif')"> Show the next page </a>
15      </p>
      </body>
    </html>
```

This code loads an image into a new window. Care has to be taken with this though: I have found that not all browsers open the new window at the specified size. Some open child windows at the same size as the parent window. This may well be due to a problem they have parsing the JavaScript – the only parameters that appear to present random behavior are height and width. To reduce the chances of seeing random behavior, follow these rules:

RULES

- *The parameter list must be inside a single set of single quotes.*
- *There cannot be line breaks or spaces in the parameter string. In this book I use line breaks so that the code will print properly in book format. Unfortunately much of the code in my JavaScript examples needs reformatting before a browser will handle it successfully.*
- *Do not have any spaces between the parameters.*
- *Do not forget the commas between parameters.*

These rules assume that the parameter string under discussion contains all optional parts of the open() command. The URL and window name are **not** optional, although the URL can be replaced with empty quotes if you need to open a blank window.

8.3 MESSAGES AND CONFIRMATIONS

JavaScript provides three built-in window types that can be used from application code. These are useful when you need information from visitors to your site. For instance, you may need them to click a confirmation button before submitting information to your database.

prompt("string", "string")

> This command displays a simple window that contains a prompt and a textfield in which the user can enter data. The method has two parameters: a text string to be used as the prompt and a string to use as the default value. If you do not want to display a default, then simply use an empty string.

confirm("string")

> This shows a window containing a message and two buttons: OK and Cancel. Selecting Cancel will abort any pending action, while OK will let the action proceed. This is useful when submitting form data, or possibly as the user tries to follow a link that leaves your site for another.

alert("string")

> This displays the text string and an OK button. This may be used as a warning or to provide a farewell message as visitors leave your site.

Figure 8.1 The popup dialog boxes

The next code sample shows how the popup windows can be used. The results of these statements are demonstrated in Figure 8.1.

```
1  prompt("Enter Your Name", "");
   confirm("Are You Sure?");
   alert("A Warning");
```

8.4 THE STATUS BAR

Some Web developers like to use the browsers status bar as part of the site. Text strings can be displayed in the status bar but should be used with care. The status bar usually displays helpful information about the operation of the browser. It cannot do that if it is displaying *your* message. Few people ever look at the status bar, so if it is showing your message they may well not notice. Finally anything that can be done in the status bar can be done more interestingly using DHTML techniques. If you want to use the idea, the following code, and Figure 8.2, show how:

```
1   <html>
      <head>
        <script language="javascript">
        <!--
5         function Init(){
            self.status = "Chris's Message";
          }
        //-->
        </script>
10    </head>
```

Figure 8.2 Writing to the status line

```
<body onLoad="Init()">
   <h1>And the Status Bar Says...</h1>
</body>
</html>
```

self

The previous script used the keyword `self` which I have not introduced you to before. Sometimes the script needs to act upon the browser window in which it is running. Other times objects need to change their own parameters. In both cases `self` is used so that the object can identify itself or its browser.

8.5 WRITING TO A DIFFERENT FRAME

In Section 3.3 I introduced the use of frames as a site layout device. Once frames and JavaScript are combined on the same page, a site can begin to develop some interesting interactive aspects. Often developing a site with links in one frame and output in another provides easy movement through complex data. That is pretty straightforward if you are using static HTML pages, but what if you are using a combination of HTML, JavaScript and, for instance, CGI scripting to build pages on the fly? Though certainly more difficult, it is not *that* difficult. One popular use of frames and JavaScript is a color picker.

The simple color picker that I am going to build here is shown in Figure 8.3. It has two frames. The upper one contains a form which is used for data gathering. The lower frame shows the result of the color selections but has been created directly by JavaScript code. This application is run totally on the client side. Once you know how to use CGI scripts to handle form data you may want to try adapting it to use both client- and server-side processing.

I will describe each of the components, although they ought to be fairly self-explanatory if you have read everything up to this point.

8.5.1 The Frameset

The whole page is built around a simple frameset. When the page is initially loaded I display the form in the upper window and an empty HTML page in the lower window. Some browsers will cope if the bottom frame is left empty, others will not. It is better to use a simple empty page in the bottom frame to be totally browser-friendly. The code for the frameset is:

```
1   <html>
       <head>
          <title>Color Picker</title>
       </head>
```

Figure 8.3 The color picker

```
5
    <frameset rows="40%,*">
      <frame name="topone" src="./cols.html">
      <frame name="botone" src="./blank.html">
    </frameset>
10  </html>
```

Here's the code for the empty frame:

```
1   <html>
      <head>
        <title></title>
      </head>
5     <body>
      </body>
    </html>
```

8.5.2 The Upper Frame

The top frame (from the file cols.html) is simple enough. The only part that has not been introduced already is the use of an external file to hold the JavaScript code. In this case it is in a file called picker.js and is called from the script tag. The JavaScript is loaded by the browser but is not run until the onClick() action of the button is triggered.

```
1   <html>
        <head>
            <script language="javascript" src="./picker.js">
            </script>
5       </head>
        <body bgcolor="white" text="red">
        <h1 align=center>Chris's HomeBrew Color Picker</h1>

        <form>
10          <table align="center" border="0" cellpadding="5">
            <tr>
                <td colspan="4" align="center">
                <h2>Enter Color Values in the Boxes</h2>
                </td>
15          </tr>
            <tr>
                <td>
                <h3>Background Color</h3>
                </td>
20              <td>
                    <input type="textfield" size="16" name="bgcol" value="white" />
                </td>
                <td>
                <h3>Text Color</h3>
25              </td>
                <td>
                    <input type="textfield" size="16" name="fgcol" value="black" />
                </td>
            </tr>
30          <tr>
                <td>
                <h3>Table Headings</h3>
                </td>
```

```
             <td>
35               <input type="textfield" size="16" name="thcol" value="black" />
             </td>
             <td>
             <h3>Table Data</h3>
             </td>
40           <td>
                 <input type="textfield" size="16" name="tdcol" value="black" />
             </td>
         </tr>
         <tr>
45           <td colspan="2" align="center">
                 <input type="button" value="Show It!!" onClick="ShowIt()" />
             </td>
             <td colspan="2" align="center">
                 <input type="reset" value="Reset It" />
50           </td>
         </tr>
         </table>
     </form>
     </body>
55 </html>
```

I have placed the JavaScript in a separate file which I am including in the head section of the document. Each `textfield` is given a unique name when it is created so that it can be easily identified in later code. The `textfields` could have been anonymous, not given names, and accessed through the `forms` and `elements` arrays. This would increase the size of the code and potentially lead to more bugs.

8.5.3 The JavaScript Code

The HTML part of the page is simple. The JavaScript is actually not much more complex but because I have not shown anything quite like it before I will go into it in some detail. First the code which is stored in a file called `picker.js`. This code has been formatted so that it prints correctly in a book. You will need to make sure that each JavaScript statement is placed on a single line.

```
1 function ShowIt( ){
     var topbox = document.forms[0].elements;
     var bottombox = parent.frames['botone'].document;
```

```
5      // first extract the values from the form
       var bg = topbox.bgcol.value;
       var fg = topbox.fgcol.value;
       var thc = topbox.thcol.value;
       var tdc = topbox.tdcol.value;
10
       // now build the new page
       bottombox.open();
       bottombox.write("<body bgcolor=" + bg
    + " text=" + fg + ">\n");
15     bottombox.write("<h1 align=center>The Result Is:</h1>");
       bottombox.write("<table align=center border=2"
                       + "cellpadding=4 cellspacing=4>\n<tr>"
                       + "<th>Plain Heading</th>"
                       + "<th bgcolor="
20                     + thc
                       + ">Colored Heading</th>"
                       + "</tr>"
                       + "<th>Plain Data</th>"
                       + "<th bgcolor="
25                     + tdc
                       + ">Colored Data</th>"
                       + "</tr>"
                       + "</tr>\n</table>");
       bottombox.write("</body>");
30     bottombox.close();
       }
```

The page uses just a single JavaScript function called ShowIt which accepts no parameters. The color values that were entered into the form do not need to be passed as parameters. They are available to the script through the frameset itself. When the frames were created they were given the names topone and botone. The script is part of the document that is being displayed in frame topone and is going to create a document to be displayed in frame botone. This structure is shown in Figure 8.4.

Ithough the structure sounds complex it really is not. Each frame is a part of the main window and contains a single document. Each frame has a unique name and we can use that name to write to, or read from, those documents.

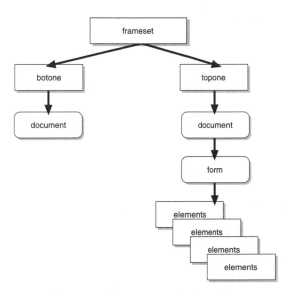

Figure 8.4 The structure of color picker

The first thing that I do is create two local variables:

```
1  var topbox = document.forms[0].elements;
   var bottombox = parent.frames['botone'].document;
```

These variables are used to reduce the amount of typing that is necessary. Let us look at them a little more closely. The first variable, **topbox**, is going to be used to refer to all items in the upper frame. This is the frame with the HTML form and which holds the HTML document containing the JavaScript code. The document only has one form, which is therefore at the start of the forms array on position zero. The values that are entered into the form will be stored in the elements array.

The second variable, **bottombox**, refers to all items in the lower frame. If a method in one frame is going to refer to another frame it must do so via the parent window. The main, or *parent*, window has an array of all frames which can be referred to either by their position in the array or, as in this example, by name. Each window includes a single HTML page. Having referenced the correct frame, the document and elements can be referred to easily.

The alias for the upper frame is able to refer directly to the **document** property because it is referring to the document in which it is contained. The alias for the lower frame first has to reference the frame because that is a separate HTML document in another window.

Once the documents have been correctly aliased, the values can be extracted from the form. The aliasing is not necessary but is desirable. Compare these two:

```
1  var bg = topbox.bgcol.value;
   var bg = documents.forms[0].elements.bgcol.value;
```

Having extracted the parameters, the colored sample page can now be created. First the document has to be opened. If this is not done then the document is unavailable to be written into:

```
1  bottombox.open();
```

The HTML page can now be created. Notice that you need to make the <body> </body> pair of tags as well as the visible content. The JavaScript interpreter performs string substitution and concatenation on the fly. The values from the local variables are substituted directly into the strings as they are written:

```
1  bottombox.write("<body bgcolor="
                  + bg
                  + " text="
                  + fg
5                 + ">\n");


   bottombox.write("</body>");
```

Finally we can close the document. This is the point at which the HTML gets sent to the frame and the page gets displayed.

```
1  bottombox.close();
```

Most JavaScript tasks are more straightforward than even the color picker. The arrival of browsers which can support complex scripting and which use layers to arrange content has given rise to Dynamic HTML.

8.6 ROLLOVER BUTTONS

The most common usage of dynamic HTML, and one that you are bound to have seen, is the image rollover. The technique is used to give visual feedback about the location of the mouse cursor by changing the images on the page as the mouse moves over them. This is a highly effective technique, especially where images are used as the hyperlinks in a menu, or where an image map is being used.

The JavaScript code does not directly manipulate the image. If you need to change the actual image then you ought to investigate ActiveX, Flash or Java programming. The JavaScript rollover is far simpler because it uses *two* image files which it swaps between as the mouse is moved. One image is created for the inactive state when the mouse is *not* over it. A second image is created for the active state when the mouse cursor is placed over it. Usually the images are identical apart from some highlighting for the *active* image.

Study the following code[1] then I will explain what is happening:

```
1   var browser_is, topon, topoff;

    function Init() {
        browser_is = new Is();
5       if(browser_is.major >= 4) {
            if( (browser_is.browser.indexOf("netscape"))
                || (browser_is.browser.indexOf("explorer")) )
                PreLoad();
            } else {
10              // don't break strings in "real" code
                alert("This Dynamic HTML Page Only Works in Netscape
    Navigator v4 or Internet Explorer 4 (or later)");
            } // suitable browser

15  } // Init

    function Is() {
        // convert characters to lowercase
        // to simplify testing
20      var agt = navigator.userAgent.toLowerCase();

        // *** BROWSER VERSION ***
        this.major = parseInt(navigator.appVersion);
        this.minor = parseFloat(navigator.appVersion);
25      this.browser = navigator.appName.toLowerCase();

    } // Is

    function PreLoad() {
30      // mouseOn
        topon = new Image(256, 64);
        topon.src = "./top_on.jpg";

        // mouseOff
35      topoff = new Image(256, 64);
```

---

[1] Don't forget that you cannot use line breaks in JavaScript parameter strings. I have done so here to get the code formatted for a book.

```
        topoff.src = "./top_off.jpg";

    } // PreLoad

40  function myMouseOn(n) {
        imageON = eval(n + "on.src");
        document.images[n].src = imageON;

    } // myMouseOn
45
    function myMouseOff(n) {
        imageOFF = eval(n + "off.src");
        document.images[n].src = imageOFF;

50  } // myMouseOff
```

This is the HTML page for the rollover:

```
1   <html>
        <head>
            <title>Rollover Buttons</title>
            <link rel="stylesheet" href="./styles.css" />
5           <script language="javascript" src="./rollo.js" />
        </head>

        <body onLoad="Init()">
        <h1>Demonstrating the Mouse-over Effect</h1>
10      <a href="#"
            onMouseOut="myMouseOff('top')";
            onMouseOver="myMouseOn('top')";
            return true>
          <img src="./top_off.jpg" alt="Show Next"
15            width=60 height=37 name="top" />
        </a>

        </body>
    </html>
```

8.6.1 The Explanation

The obvious place to start the explanation is the HTML page. The JavaScript for the example is stored in a separate file but it does not *have* to be. Like any JavaScript the rollover code can be embedded in the HTML page. Including it from a separate file is simpler as it lets you debug the HTML source and the JavaScript independently. The key parts of the HTML revolve around event handling. Three events concern us here:

- The onLoad event happens when the page is first loaded into the browser. As you will see shortly, handling this event is used to set up the page and script by acquiring all necessary resources.
- onMouseOver calls a JavaScript function when the cursor passes over the image.
- onMouseOut calls a function when the cursor moves away from the image.

The address tag includes this construct:

```
a href="#"
```

In this and subsequent examples, I need to use a hyperlink in my code. The rollover is usually applied to links but I do not actually want my code linked to another page. Instead I want the image to change while the content remains the same if the hyperlink is clicked. JavaScript provides a *dummy* target. If you use # as the address of a link, the browser will simply reload the current page. This dummy link has many uses when you are developing complex sites or scripts, or if you have incomplete links on your production site. It is certainly better than the alternative. Leaving the address empty may make the browser load index.html, if it exists, or return a directory listing.

The JavaScript

When the onLoad event happens, the Init() function runs. This starts by creating an object called browser_is which holds the results of the browser sniffing routine. This object is an instance of the Is() function. Being able to use a piece of code as both a function and as an object is potentially very confusing. If you are going to use JavaScript as an object-oriented language you will need to be really careful. Using a function when you mean to use an object, or vice versa, will lead to runtime errors which are not easy to debug. You will spend time expecting an object of type A, seeing a call which appears to be to a function called A, then wondering why your code does not work.

If browser_is holds values which indicate that the browser is of a suitable type then the PreLoad() function runs. If the browser is *not* suitable then a warning message is displayed. Because no further JavaScript runs after the warning, early versions of some browsers will not try to run the code and hence will not give run-time error messages.

The browser_is object contains the browser name which has been converted to lower-case letters, version number, and the version of JavaScript which it supports. When I check the browser type I do so by using the builtin method indexOf. This method is part of the JavaScript string object. It searches along the string looking for another string which is supplied as a parameter to the method. If the search is unsuccessful the method returns 0. This 0 can be used as a Boolean value in tests. This is the approach I adopt in this particular browser sniffing routine.

RULE OF THUMB

Always use browser sniffing and provide an alternative for those who cannot run your code. The rollover is a nice visual effect which does not affect the functionality of the page. The links still work even if the images do not change.

PreLoad() makes a new object for each image. These are all instances of the JavaScript Image object and you will need two for each location: one for when the mouse is over the image and one for when it is not. Each image object holds the size of the image and the location of the actual image file in the src parameter. By creating these images early in the loading process, in this case from the onLoad event, the objects are available for use even before the image files have been downloaded.

Two functions remain: myMouseOn and myMouseOff. Both work in the same way so I will just examine myMouseOn. The function is called when the onMouseOver event is triggered. The function receives the name of the image as a parameter:

```
onMouseOver="myMouseOn('top')";
```

Notice that it is not the full name. I have deliberately used variable names for the objects created in PreLoad() so as to simplify the calling routines. I created two objects called topon and topoff, each of which contains a link to a different image file. I can choose between the objects by appending the value on or off to the first part of the name. The following line of code chooses the object and then passes its src value (the file name) into a temporary variable:

```
imageON = eval(n + "on.src");
```

If you want to be sure this is really happening, put an alert message at the end of the PreLoad() function and see what effect it has:

```
1  alert("topon " + topon + " src " + topon.src +
   "topoff " + topoff + " src " + topoff.src);
```

eval

JavaScript can build expressions dynamically as it interprets scripts. This slightly odd feature is available to you through eval. When your scripts need to process information which will not be available until runtime, you can place that information into an expression as it becomes available. You subsequently execute the expression as if all of the code had been created at the same time.

The document object holds an array of images. Each object in that array can be identified either by its name, its ID or by its position within the array. The image in our link was named top (check the code for the HTML page) so to change the image we simply change the file associated with the src value of the document image object named top:

```
document.images[n].src = imageON;
```

That is quite a complex procedure. To clarify what is happening you should run the code from my example. Use any old images that you might have lying around (your browser cache would be a good place to start looking). Once you have the code working with just one image on the page try adding another image and making them *both* work as rollovers. Here is a hint: the only JavaScript that will need changing will be in the PreLoad() function.

Hopefully you will see that almost all of our rollover code could go into a library and be included in any of your pages. If each page uses different images then simply put the PreLoad() routine into the HTML file (between <script> ... </script> tags) and modify it to suit your needs.

Some HTML authoring packages will create rollover code for you. Some of that code is simple and efficient but much of it is bloated and inflexible. It may take you a while to understand the code I have just outlined, but because it can be placed into a library and re-used, that effort will be worthwhile. Once you understand the code you can start to modify it. For instance, why not move the image slightly as the mouse is clicked to give the impression of a button being pressed in? Or try using three images: one for onMouseOut, one for onMouseOver, and one for onClick?

8.7 MOVING IMAGES

Unlike the rollover which takes some understanding, moving images around the screen is pretty simple. I am not going to show the full code here, just the function that moves the image. In fact this is not a moving image at all, that is just the effect. What is actually moving is a layer of content. The example flies a logo in from the left of the screen five times before positioning it in the center of the screen. Images (layers) can move around repeatedly but doing so takes up processor cycles. It is more user-friendly if your images only move for a restricted amount of time, such as when the page is first loaded or when the user specifically triggers the event.

You might remember from Section 4.7 that content can be created in layers which are stacked vertically by assigning a z-index to them. Each layer can be positioned on the screen by changing the offset of the top left corner of the layer. If you look at the body of the following HTML page you will see that it contains two divisions which are located within the page by fixing their top left corners.

```
1   <html>
      <head>
        <title>Moving an image</title>
        <script language="javascript">
5   var count;
    var pos;
    var obj;

    function Init() {
10          count = 0;
            obj = document.getElementById("logo").style;
            pos = parseInt(obj.left);

            FlyLogo();
15  }

    function FlyLogo(){
            document.getElementById("debug").innerHTML = "<p>The image is now at
                " + pos + "</p>";

20          if(count < 5) {
                if(pos <= 100) {
                    count++;
                    pos = 1000;
                }
25              pos -= 50;
                setTimeout('FlyLogo()', 500);
                obj.left = pos;
            } else
                obj.left = 200;
30  }
        </script>
      </head>
```

```
      <body onLoad="Init()">
35      <h1>Moving an image</h1>

        <div id="logo" style="top: 60; z-index: 4; left: 600; visibility:
          visible; position: absolute;">
          <img src="./logo.png" /
        </div>

40
        <div id="debug" style="top: 100; left: 10; width: 80%; position:
          relative; background: pink"></div>

      </body>
    </html>
```

The first layer contains an image which is positioned off to the right at 1000 pixels. For many users this will mean that when the page loads the image is not visible, it is off their screen to the right. This is the effect that we want to achieve with the image gradually appearing and moving toward the left. Browsers will display their horizontal scrollbar.

```
1  <div id="logo" style="top: 5; z-index: 4; left: 1000; visibility: visible;
     position: absolute;">
     <img src="./title.jpg" /
   </div>
```

The second division is initially empty. It stretches across most of the screen and is going to be used to display debug messages. When the page loads the Init() function is called.

```
1  function Init() {
       count = 0;
       obj = document.getElementById("logo").style;
       pos = parseInt(obj.left);

5
       FlyLogo();
   }
```

Init() is used to initialize the global variables which the rest of the script is using. So far so straightforward. Look at the content of obj. This is a pointer to the style property of the logo div. Using DOM-compliant code means that document elements are accessed using their IDs. Each element is found with a call to the getElementById() method of the current document. Method calls are computationally quite expensive and time consuming. Your code will be more efficient if you reduce the number of such calls that you make. JavaScript presents an easy technique: pointers. At several places in the code we will need to access the `style` property of the `div`. We make a single call to `getElementById()` and store the result in `obj`. Whenever we access `obj` we are now going to be accessing `document."logo".style` making `obj` an alias.

The image is moved by the `FlyLogo()` function.

```
1   function FlyLogo(){
        document.getElementById("debug").innerHTML = "<p>The image is now at
            " + pos + "</p>";
        if(count < 5) {
            if(pos <= 100) {
5               count++;
                pos = 1000;
            }
            pos -= 50;
            setTimeout('FlyLogo()', 500);
10          obj.left = pos;
        } else
            obj.left = 200;
}
```

Whenever the function is called, it starts by printing the position of the image in the second `div` element of the document. Because so much is happening in the page we cannot update its content using `document.write()`. That method would overwrite the entire content of the document. Here we want to add content without altering anything that we already have. This is done by altering the value of the `innerHTML` property of the `debug` division. Whenever you need to debug JavaScript this technique is useful. Create a `div` at the bottom of the screen then write to it. If you have a very long page you can float the `div` above the other content, as shown in Section 8.10, so that it is always visible.

Having printed the location of the image, the function checks the counter to make sure that it should run. If the counter is equal to 5 then the left edge of the logo is placed at pixel 200 and no more processing is performed by this routine.

If the counter is less than 5, the layer containing the logo will be moved. If the left-hand side of the layer is at pixel 200 then the image has finished moving across the screen. The counter is incremented and the layer repositioned to pixel 1000. However, if the left edge of the logo is not at position 200 it is repositioned 10 pixels to the left of its current location. The `FlyLogo()` routine then calls itself[2] using the builtin `setTimeout()` call. This takes the name of the function and a delay in milliseconds. It will not run the routine until after the delay has elapsed. In this case our image moves 10 pixels left every 200 ms.

---

[2]This is called *recursion*. Do it too often in JavaScript and the browser will fall over as it runs out of memory.

If the delay were too short, say 50 ms, then the image would whip across the screen so rapidly that it would not be visible. If the delay were too long, say a second, then the image would crawl across the screen in a really disappointing way.

Some of you will be wondering why I am bothering to code this rather than use an animated GIF. Writing the JavaScript is easier than creating a GIF, the download is far smaller and this version is very flexible. I might, for instance, decide to move the image vertically instead of horizontally. If I had used a GIF then I would need to recreate the entire thing. Here I simply alter the code to move from bottom to top instead of right to left.

As an aside, if you want to move an image along a diagonal then move the top left corner horizontally and vertically at the same time. Easy!

8.8 MULTIPLE PAGES IN A SINGLE DOWNLOAD

DHTML opens up some interesting possibilities. One that is fairly obvious, but rarely used, is having several pages in a single download. Instead of using a separate file for each page, why not place each page of content in a separate layer and switch between those layers? This technique will not work if the layers have too much content or too many images, simply because the overhead of downloading the page will be too great. It also will not work well if visitors to your site are unlikely to want to see all of the pages. However, where most of your data is text-based and where users are going to want to see all of that information, this is a good trick. It will also work well as a way of splitting a single large document into several screens of data so that users do not have to scroll up and down.

On the other hand, if you base a site around this technique then you will find that many people cannot use it. This is true of any new idea and as more people use version 4 or later browsers, so more and more people will be able to view your pages.

8.8.1 The Stylesheet

This stylesheet is going to be used in this section and the next two. I have included it here for convenience and completeness. Notice the style for address elements. Normally browsers change the presentation of address elements when the mouse is over them and once they have been selected. In this example I want these to remain the same. They are not links to other documents but are links to hidden parts of the same document, which means that the usual visual clues given to users are less important.

```
1   .SWITCH {
        font-size: 20pt;
        font-family: Arial, helvetica, "sans serif";
        color: ultramarine;
5       background: wheat;
    }
```

```
    a:link, a:visited, a:active {
       text-decoration:none;
10  }


    p {
       font-family: "Times New Roman", times, serif;
       font-size: 12pt;
15     color: purple;
       text-align: justify;
       margin-left: 10%;
    }


20  h1 {
       font-size: 16pt;
       color: teal;
       text-decoration: underline;
       text-align: center;
25  }
```

8.8.2 The HTML Page

The HTML page is rather more interesting than the stylesheet. As usual, take a look at the
code before I explain some of what it is doing:

```
1   <html>
      <head>
        <link rel="stylesheet" href="./multi.css" />
        <script language="javascript">
5   var active = 0;


    function ChangeLayer(now) {
      document.getElementById("content" + active).style.visibility = "hidden";
      document.getElementById("content" + now).style.visibility = "visible";
10    active = now;
    }
        </script>
      </head>
      <body>
15
```

```
      <div id="menua" style="top: 5; left: 5; visibility: visible;
      position: absolute; z-index: 5; width:90%">

        <p class="SWITCH">
20      <a href="#" onClick="ChangeLayer(0)">One</a>
        <a href="#" onClick="ChangeLayer(1)">Two</a>
        <a href="#" onClick="ChangeLayer(2)">Three</a></p>
      </div>

25    <div id="content0" style="top: 60; left: 20; visibility: visible;
      position: absolute;">
        <h1>A test header</h1>
         <p>here's some text</p>
         <hr>
30    </div>

      <div id="content1" style="top: 60; left: 20; visibility: hidden;
      position: absolute;">
        <h1>Another test header</h1>
35      <p>here's some more text</p>
        <hr>
      </div>

      <div id="content2" style="top: 60; left: 20; visibility: hidden;
40    position: absolute;">
        <h1>Yet another test header</h1>
        <p>here's yet more text</p>
        <hr>
      </div>

45
      </body>
    </html>
```

The page contains four divisions or layers. The first is a menu layer which holds three hyperlinks. Each hyperlink points to the dummy page # so that the browser does not attempt an unwanted page load. We are going to move around totally within this one page so do not need to go back to the server. The links all use the same event handler. When onClick occurs they call the ChangeLayer() routine using the number of the layer that is to be displayed as a parameter.

Division menua is formatted using the SWITCH style from the stylesheet. It is placed 5 pixels in from the left and top edges of the screen. I have also given the layer a z-index of 5 to ensure that it is always at the top of the stack. The layer has to be positioned using absolute and visible.

The other layers are all content holders. These are all positioned in the same place at 40 pixels from the top of the screen. That value was selected so that the layers appear below the menu on the screen. Only one content layer is visible, the other two are hidden. If more than one of these layers is visible then the content of both will display at the same time, which is obviously not ideal.

8.8.3 The JavaScript

```
1  var active = 0;

   function ChangeLayer(now) {
     document.getElementById("content" + active).style.visibility = "hidden";
5    document.getElementById("content" + now).style.visibility = "visible";
     active = now;
   }
```

Divisions have a visibility property as part of their style which accepts the values visible and hidden. These can be set either directly in HTML or through JavaScript code. The layers are named in the form content0. The integer which distinguishes each layer is passed into the function as a parameter.

Always hide the current layer first. This method lets the user select the current layer for re-display. Users will sometimes select the current layer by accident. If you display the new layer *then* hide the current one and both have the same value you will end up with no content showing.

Having displayed the new page, the variable active needs to be set to the value of the page that is now showing so that it is stored ready for the next call to the function.

Swapping between layers is yet another simple technique. The most difficult part of this is writing the HTML page. It is probably done most easily if you use an iframe for each page level. You will need to place the iframe inside a div and watch out for formatting – some browsers need you to set a width for the div otherwise they will not display the iframes properly.

8.9 A TEXT-ONLY MENU SYSTEM

Clearly the rollover and layer swapping are powerful techniques. They can make any site look interesting and if used properly they make even relatively mundane sites into bleeding-edge multimedia experiences. They do not seem to satisfy many site builders. In fact, many sites use Java programs towards the same ends. Java is not an ideal solution on today's Web. It is slow, difficult, and less popular with users than an e-mail virus.

The most common use of Java is the site menu. There are many ways of providing navigation but allying a global menu to hyperlinks is one of the most popular. How do you build a global menu? There are many ways, some of which I have outlined earlier. Java is another option. What about JavaScript? Can we use JavaScript to build an interesting menu? The answer is emphatically, yes. By combining the techniques from rollovers and layer swapping we get a simple, fast, and effective menu system.

The menu system that I will show here is actually incomplete. What I am trying to do is demonstrate the principles so that you can take and use them in your own pages. This code will demonstrate how to use layers in a rollover, changing the formatting of the page as the mouse moves about. This is yet another example in which the HTML is more complex than the JavaScript. In fact the HTML is *so* complex that you will be rewarded by spending some time studying it in detail.

8.9.1 The HTML Page

As usual, look through the code then I will explain some of the highlights:

```
1   <html>
      <head>
        <link rel="stylesheet" href="./styles.css">
        <script language="javascript">
5   var active = 0;

    function Highlight(id) {
      document.getElementById("menua").style.visibility = "hidden";
      document.getElementById("menu" + id + "b").style.visibility = "visible";
10  }

    function UnHighlight(id) {
      document.getElementById("menu" + id + "b").style.visibility = "hidden";
      document.getElementById("menua").style.visibility = "visible";
15  }
        </script>
      </head>
      <body>
        <div id="menua" style="top: 5; left: 5;
20      visibility: visible; position: absolute; z-index: 5;">

        <p class="SWITCH">
          <a href="#"
             onMouseOver="Highlight(0)"
```

```
25              onMouseOut="UnHighlight(0)">One</a>
          <a href="#"
             onMouseOver="Highlight(1)"
             onMouseOut="UnHighlight(1)">Two</a>
          <a href="#"
30           onMouseOver="Highlight(2)"
             onMouseOut="UnHighlight(2)">Three</a>
        </div>

        <div id="menu0b" style="top: 5; left: 5;
35      visibility: hidden; position: absolute; z-index: 5;">

        <p class="SWITCH">
           <span class="OVER"><a href="#">One</a></span>
           <a href="#">Two</a>
40         <a href="#">Three</a>
        </div>

        <div id="menu1b" style="top: 5; left: 5;
        visibility: hidden; position: absolute; z-index: 5;">

45

        <p class="SWITCH">
           <a href="#">One</a>
           <span class="OVER"><a href="#">Two</a></span>
           <a href="#">Three</a>
50      </div>

        <div id="menu2b" style="top: 5; left: 5;
        visibility: hidden; position: absolute; z-index: 5">

55      <p class=SWITCH>
           <a href="#">One</a>
           <a href="#">Two</a>
           <span class="OVER"><a href="#">Three</a></span>
        </div>

60
      </body>
    </html>
```

The HTML page has four divisions. The main one is menua which will be displayed when the menu is inactive. This layer is positioned at pixel 5, 5. It contains a single paragraph which is styled by assigning a class from the stylesheet. Inside the paragraph there are three hyperlinks which, in this example, go nowhere. In an actual site these would point to the linked pages.

Each hyperlink is a piece of text but because they are links the onMouseOver and onMouseOff events still work. These events are tied to the link rather than to an image. The event handling will be shown when I discuss the JavaScript.

The remaining three layers are all hidden. As the mouse moves over the menu these layers will be made visible and hidden. Each sub-menu is basically identical to the main one. Each has one item that is formatted differently. A different class of formatting is applied to the items through the use of <span> ... </span>.

8.9.2 The JavaScript

```
1   var active = 0;

    function Highlight(id) {
      document.getElementById("menua").style.visibility = "hidden";
5     document.getElementById("menu" + id + "b").style.visibility = "visible";
    }

    function UnHighlight(id) {
      document.getElementById("menu" + id + "b").style.visibility = "hidden";
10    document.getElementById("menua").style.visibility = "visible";
    }
```

This script should not need any explanation. It is very similar to the code from the layer switching example. The Highlight() function hides the default menu and makes one of the other layers visible. The UnHighlight() function reverses this by hiding the visible layer and making the default menu visible.

8.10 FLOATING LOGOS

The final JavaScript example is by far the most complex and took the most time and effort to develop. You may have seen Web sites like Geocities which displayed floating logo in the bottom right-hand corner of the screen. As you resized the browser or scrolled the window, the logo remained fast in the corner. Depending upon your point of view this is either an affront to all Web surfers or, in my view, a great way of providing relatively unobtrusive branding. The easiest way of doing this is to use a background image.

Floating content on a page using JavaScript is a well-established technique. Sites like Geocities used to float an image (usually a small GIF) to brand their page. The W3C uses floating menus on some of their specification pages. In this example I am going to float a layer which only holds some text. If you want to float a picture then change the text to the appropriate URL.

If you use this technique be aware that the floating brand should always have a z-index which puts it on top of the display stack. If the brand is too big or garish it will either hide site content or attract attention away from it. That is why Geocities, for instance, used a mostly transparent image.

8.10.1 The HTML Page

The HTML page is nice and simple. It only has two layers. If you are copying these code samples you will have to put more content into the main layer so that you can see what happens during scrolling.

```
1   <html>
      <head>
        <script language=javascript src="logo.js">
        </script>
5     </head>
      <body onLoad=Init()>
        <div id="lay0" style="visibility: visible;
        position: absolute; width: 95%">
          <!--Your Content Here -->
10      </div>

        <div id="lay10"
          style="visibility: visible;
            position: absolute;
15          font-size: 20pt;
            background: aquamarine;
            color: purple;
            text-align: center;
            left: 5px;
20          top: 5px;
            width: 256px;
            height: 64px;">
          <p>LOGO</p>
        </div>
25
      </body>
    </html>
```

8.10.2 The JavaScript

The JavaScript is pretty complex. I have shown the browser-sniffing functions a number of times before so I will ignore them here. There are three other functions and I will go through them all in detail. As you read this code be aware that it works for both main browsers.

```
1   var obj;
    var orig_width = orig_height = 0;
    var px = py = 40;
    var logoWidth = logoHeight = 0;
5


    function Init(){
        Setup();
        PositionLogo();
10
    } // Init



    function PositionLogo() {
15      var height = window.innerHeight - py;
        var width = window.innerWidth - px
        var top = height - logoHeight;
        var left = width - logoWidth;

20      obj.left = left;
        obj.top = top;


    } // PositionLogo


25
    function Setup() {
        obj = document.getElementById("lay10").style;

        logoWidth = parseInt(obj.width);
30      logoHeight = parseInt(obj.height);
        window.onresize = new Function("PositionLogo()");
        window.onscroll = new Function("PositionLogo()");


    } // SetupEvents
```

Once again we are going to be manipulating the `style` property of the layer. Floating the layer is going to work in a similar way to the moving image. The important difference is that the image will only be repositioned when the parent window is either re-sized or scrolled. In the moving image example the layer was frequently re-positioned to give the illusion of seamless movement. The `Setup()` function is used to assign a method to the `onresize` and `onscroll` events. This is done by creating a new object which encapsulates the function and then simply performing an assignment.

To position the image in the bottom right corner we start by finding the height and width of the window using its `innerHeight` and `innerWidth` properties of the window. To create some whitespace as a small border around the floated image we subtract 40 pixels from each of these values. Next we subtract the size of the image from the values which we got in the previous step. The top left corner of the image style is placed at this position.

EXERCISES

Basic Dynamic HTML

1. Find a large image and modify the script in Section 8.2 to display it in a window of its own.
2. Write a page which demonstrates the use of the different types of popup window that are available in JavaScript.
3. What are the benefits of using the browser status bar to pass messages to the user?
4. Implement the Color Picker from Section 8.5. Modify it to color more page elements.
5. List the difficulties that you might experience if you use JavaScript to perform data validation.
6. Create a simple form and write a script that performs primitive checking of data.

Advanced DHTML Applications

1. Why is it better to use the `div` tag rather than the `layer` tag to create movable layers of content?
2. Why are rollover images *so* popular among Web developers?
3. Implement a site menu system based around rollover images. Try to write the main code so that it can be placed in a library of useful JavaScript routines.
4. What are the main benefits of creating a library of code rather than rewriting everything each time that you create a site?

5. Will your rollover images still work as hyperlinks if someone fails to download the images?

6. Is it generally better to write your own code for something like a rollover image or to use the code that some authoring tools can generate for you?

7. Create a library of routines to move images around the screen in the following ways:
   - vertically up
   - vertically down
   - horizontally right to left
   - horizontally left to right
   - diagonally from top left to bottom right corners
   - diagonally from top right to bottom left corners
   - diagonally from bottom right to top left corners
   - diagonally from bottom left to top right corners.

8. Try moving a number of images around the screen at the same time.

9. Look at your site and see where you might be able to download a number of pages at the same time. Try implementing the site to work in this way. Is this an improvement over the original version?

10. Can you make the site work in both Netscape Navigator and Internet Explorer?

11. What are the advantages of using JavaScript rather than Java for a site menu?

12. Put the flying logo code from Section 8.7 into a page and see if you can get it to work. Try using as many browser as possible to see how platform-independent JavaScript is.

13. JavaScript has some disadvantages when used for menus. List three of them.

14. Expand the code in Section 8.9 to work as a full-text menu system.

15. Implement a floating logo on your site. Try floating the logo in each corner of the browser in turn. Again, try to make this work in both major browsers.

16. Why do many people object to having floating logos placed on their pages by companies such as Geocities?

PART IV

Perl

Programming in Perl 5

So far I have shown you the basics of creating Web pages using HTML, JavaScript, and Cascading Stylesheets. These are enough to create most of the pages that you find on the Internet. In fact, if you combine the ideas we have seen already alongside a few well-chosen plug-ins, sound effects and moving images, *and* a sense of good design, you could soon be writing award winning Web pages. Add in some Dynamic HTML, possibly using JavaScript, and you have got a really exciting Web experience.

Design, layout, and the look and feel of a Web site are only part of the story once a business decides to use the Internet. Businesses need enhanced revenue, or new revenue streams, from their sites. This means that, not only does the Web site provide a leading edge advertising tool, which is particularly useful if the company wants to be seen as go-ahead, youthful or thrusting, it must generate sales. Sales do not *have* to come through the familiar e-commerce route where product selection, purchase and payment all happen on-line. Web sites may be used simply to raise brand awareness or to increase customer loyalty. Many organizations already have well established sales routes through catalogs. A Web site can be used to enhance this type of business, for instance by giving customers more information on products which they can order through conventional paths.

For the developers of commercial sites anything which is robust and powerful enough to be used for revenue generation has to go beyond simple HTML. When data has to be gathered about customers and their needs the Website has to become part of a comprehensive business application. The incorporation of forms which are used to enter data into the system, business rules to govern how that data is processed and database systems to store it, mean that significant amounts of processing must be performed on the server.

Getting a Web server to perform application processing is not difficult: most support the Common Gateway Interface, CGI, protocol which allows a degree of interaction between the client browser and the server. Assuming that your Web server is set up to allow CGI then all that you have to do is write some programs which can process data from the client and place them on your server. The difficult part of the whole process is writing the server-side applications. These have a few common characteristics:

- processing of textual data
- output of text, images, sound etc.
- errors must be returned to the client browser
- fatal exceptions (run-time errors, which mean the program cannot safely continue) should be logged for the system administrator
- short residency – generally a CGI program executes then quits and is restarted each time it is needed
- each Web site requires a unique solution – off-the-shelf CGI programs are always inadequate
- the ability to port programs to new servers and operating systems is desirable: you do not want to have to rewrite your whole Web site if you change ISP
- short development times and rapid prototyping are used to encourage flexible, readily updated Web sites
- no concept of state. Each time a user accesses a new page or uses a new service, the server considers it to be a new interaction. Some applications such as shopping carts require that a set of interactions be created for each user. We shall examine ways of maintaining state between transactions.

CGI applications can be written in any language – the set of requirements given above does not dictate any particular solution. However, we can make some general observations about the suitability of certain languages. The standard languages today for most solutions are C and C++. These are powerful and general-purpose, but compiled code is not platform-independent. They provide poor text handling facilities and may be overkill for programs with such short residency. Java is platform-independent and has some very good text-handling classes, an excellent exception handling mechanism, and inherently supports the common Web data types such as GIFs and WAVs. However, Java is also too powerful for simple CGI unless you choose to write a multi-threaded Java program to handle all of your needs. This would be an excellent solution but the development time would be comparable to building any other large application.

The favored solution is to use a scripting language. Scripting languages have been around in the UNIX world for many years and are used to develop many complex, site-specific system administration tools. Programming support applications such as makefiles, source-code control systems, and configuration utilities are extensions of sophisticated scripts. The UNIX world also provides many powerful text and file management tools such as sed, grep, awk, and find. These tools have few direct equivalents in the world of the PC desktop where graphical tools are more commonly used.

Increasingly, scripting languages are being made available under Windows. The commonest language for that platform is Visual Basic which comes in a number of variations, including a command-line version called VBScript. In the ideal world a common scripting language would be available across all platforms. A number of such languages exist, including established favorites such as Tcl/Tk, Scheme, Python, and Perl. Of these I would argue that Perl is the best established, especially in the CGI scripting arena.

Although this book concentrates on using CGI scripts on the server, Microsoft provides a powerful technology called Active Server Pages which is designed to achieve much the same ends. ASP scripts are usually written in VBScript and less often in JScript. This is simply because those are the languages which Microsoft pushes as being best suited to ASP scripting. ASP is an example of a *templating* system which embeds scripting commands inside Web pages for processing by the Server before the pages are sent to the user. Templating is a widely used alternative to CGI scripting and, in Chapter 12, I will examine an open-source language called PHP4 which is starting to rival Perl in popularity.

9.1 WHY PERL?

Having been told that you are going to have to learn yet another programming language it would be understandable if you simply asked, *why*? A number of answers leap to mind. First, I have shown that the languages that you may already know are not suitable for the task. Second, each programming language carries a certain intellectual stance around with it. C++, for instance, in its design encourages the building of complex systems and monolithic applications, Java makes it easy to network and distribute an application, Visual Basic naturally leads to solutions that concentrate on the user interface. Perl has its own approach and culture which is best summed up in the peculiar acronym TMTOWTDI, There's More Than One Way To Do It.

Perl gives programmers freedom: freedom to develop their own solutions in their own way. It can be an interpreted scripting language, it can produce compiled code, you can write monolithic scripts or use structured procedures, if you want to use objects then that is fine, Perl can do that too. Variables can be declared and initialized before use or can pop up inline, non-fatal errors can be caught or ignored. Perl solutions can be quick and dirty or highly sophisticated; rapid prototypes or fully-fledged applications. One of the more interesting aspects of Perl is that you do not need to know much of the language to develop real applications. Given just a few simple commands you can be writing CGI scripts that are sufficiently powerful for most needs. As you learn more of the language your solutions become more complex, as do the types of problem that you can tackle. Learning Perl is supposed to be like learning a natural language: a gradual and evolutionary approach.

9.1.1 A Brief History Lesson

Perl is a growing and evolving language which continues to change, and for which major new versions are released every few years. Its originator, and the man who remains its creative and driving force is Larry Wall. Larry Wall currently works for the leading publisher of UNIX books O'Reilly and Associates where he is one of the associates. At some point in the mid-80s Larry needed a text manipulation tool and quickly realized that sed, awk, and related tools would not get the job done so he wrote his own. That tool evolved over time and was released as version one of Perl in early 1988.

That first version of Perl, plus all subsequent ones and thousands of extensions supplied by users and developers, was given away, released onto the Internet so that people could freely use and adapt it. Prior to releasing Perl, Larry had already written, and given away, `metaconfig`, `rn`, and `patch`, all of which turned out to be useful and successful UNIX utilities. Like many people who have been around the Internet community for a long time, Larry Wall has always been committed to the idea of free software and free support. Free software does not mean software which is given away by its developers without charge. Instead it is a term which encapsulates a whole slew of philosophical ideas about the best way to produce software.

The free software idea lets developers release not only compiled and executable programs, but also the source for their programs under a legally binding licence. Wherever the code goes, the licence goes too. Anyone can modify the source of such programs provided that they make their changes freely available and use the original licence for their modified code. This does not mean that you cannot charge for free software but it does give the end-user the right to further modify and distribute what they have bought provided the original licence accompanies it. You may have heard of open-source software. This is a variation of the free software concept which is said to be more *business friendly*. Open source software has the source code freely available but, generally, if you modify the code you cannot distribute your changes.

The dominant free software licence is the GNU Public Licence, GPL, developed by Richard Stallman and the Free Software Foundation. It is exceptionally restrictive in the way that it enforces the free software concept. If you modify code which is licensed with the GPL then your work is licensed with GPL too. You have no choice. Because the GPL is so restrictive, many alternative licences are available. Perl is developed and distributed using two licences: GPL and the Artistic Licence. The latter gives users more freedom about how they manage source code.

9.2 ON-LINE DOCUMENTATION

The Perl distribution is exceptionally well documented but many beginners seem to have difficulties finding or using the documentation. Three types of help system are available: all provide the same content but deliver it in different ways. The major Perl files contain inline comments which describe how they should be used, structured in a special way which can be interpreted by Perl scripts and translated into a variety of formats. This documentation is called *POD*, which is short for plain old documentation. POD can be viewed using a utility called perldoc which comes with all of the Perl distributions. If you do not like the way that the documentation viewer works, POD can be converted into standard UNIX manual pages or HTML Web pages. The manual pages can be viewed using the man utility, the HTML pages with any Web browser.

To access POD directly from a UNIX command-line you use a utility called perldoc. The name of the documentation file which you want to read is given as a parameter:

```
perldoc <file>
```

This launches the POD viewer. To page down press the spacebar, to move down by one line press the down arrow, to move up by one line use the up arrow. You can also move in page sized steps by using the Page Up and Page Dn keys. To leave the viewer press q.

Table 9.1 lists some of the key commands which you should investigate. Perl comes with a *very* comprehensive on-line manual. In fact over 100,000 lines of documentation are

perldoc command	Description
perldoc	Displays a brief version and help message.
perldoc -h	Verbose help, including listing all command-line parameters.
perldoc -q *expression*	Searches questions (not answers) in parts 1 to 9 of the Perl FAQ for the string contained in *expression*. For instance perldoc -q CGI lists all items which directly discuss CGI scripting.
perldoc perldoc	Displays the POD for the perldoc program.
perldoc perl	Displays the top-level of the Perl manual which includes a comprehensive index of the included documentation.
perldoc *manual section*	Displays the POD for a particular section of the manual.
perldoc *module name*	Displays the POD for the named module. For instance perldoc CGI displays the POD from the CGI.pm module and perldoc perlwin32 shows information relating to building and using Perl on Microsoft systems.

Table 9.1 perldoc commands

said to be provided as part of the standard distribution. The manual is broken into a number of sections, an index for these is available by typing:

```
perldoc perl
```

One of the best pieces of advice I can give to someone learning Perl is to consult this documentation whenever they get stuck. Using it can be difficult as material is often not where you expect it to be, but the sheer scale and depth of knowledge you are being given here is breathtaking. Personally I prefer the HTML version of the material. If you struggle to use `perldoc` or find it too unfriendly, see if the HTML files are available for your particular installation.

If you are using Perl on a Windows machine and have installed a recent version from ActiveState[1] then you already have all of the documentation that you will need to get going. This distribution has documentation as both HTML and POD. Briefly this is how to use them.

- **HTML** Viewing the HTML documentation could not be easier. When you install Perl a new tree of directories is created:
  - `bin` which includes executable programs such as the Perl interpreter
  - `lib` includes all of the standard libraries that come with the distribution
  - `site` holds any additional modules which you choose to install to modify the distribution to meet your personal needs
  - `html` has all of the documentation in HTML format.
  To access the HTML documentation open the file `index.html` in the `html` directory in a Web browser. In the frame on the left of the screen you will see all of the help files listed. Choose one and the file is displayed in the right-hand frame. As you scroll down the list of contents you will see that the distribution includes many modules which are especially created for programming Microsoft systems (listed under Win32). These are obviously not available on the UNIX distributions of Perl.
- **POD** Viewing the POD directly under Windows works just like it does under UNIX. You need to open up a DOS command box. At the prompt, type `perldoc` which will give you a brief help message. Again, Table 9.1 lists some of the more useful things that you can try with perldoc and POD.

9.3 THE BASIC PERL PROGRAM

The simplest Perl script is a one-line print statement run from the command-line. If you are using UNIX it is a relatively easy thing to do; if you are using Windows then the process is slightly more complex. If you have a Macintosh you will need to consult the documentation for your version of Perl to find out how to compensate for the lack of a command shell[2].

First the easier situation from UNIX. From a command prompt enter this:

```
perl -e 'print "Hello World\n"'
```

---

[1]http://www.activestate.com
[2]In MacOS X use the UNIX versions in the built-in shell.

Make sure that you get all of those quotes correct – the script uses three different types. Press Enter to execute the script.

Under Windows you must first start a DOS shell. The quotes need to be *escaped* so that DOS does not try to interpret them as commands meant for it, but instead passes them to the Perl interpreter. This can be done in one of two ways. Try each of these in turn:

```
1  perl -e "print \"Hello World\n\""
   perl -e "print qq(Hello World\n)"
```

In the second example you'll see a command called qq being used. Often in scripts you will need to put quotes around strings or words but doing so may be impossible due to the structure of the code. In JavaScript it was important to use single quotes inside double quotes. Well, it is just the same with Perl. The commands qq and qw provide a safe way of quoting. The former puts a single pair of quotes around its entire parameter. The latter takes a list of words as its parameter and places quotes around each one:

qq(Hello World) produces "Hello World" while qw(Hello World) gives "Hello" "World".

Before moving on to writing complex programs it is useful to test your Perl installation. Find out exactly what version you have available by typing perl -v at a command prompt. This should display version information. If it does not you will need to check your installation and environment variables.

Create a file using your favorite editor and enter:

```
print "Hello World!\n";
```

Save the file as hello.pl. Notice that the line is terminated by a semicolon: all statements in Perl have to be terminated in this way. Missing the semicolon is one of the easiest mistakes for a beginner. To run your Perl scripts you will need to change to the directory in which you are editing the file[3] in a command shell and type:

perl -w hello.pl

Hopefully that ran the "Hello World" program which you saved a moment ago. If there are any problems with your code, the -wflag makes the interpreter print lots of useful information to the command shell. Using this is so useful that it is usually considered to be an essential part of good Perl programming style.

Let us try a slightly more complicated example. Modify hello.pl so that it contains *just* the following code:

```
1  #!/usr/bin/perl -w
   print "Hello World!\n";
   exit(0);
```

---

[3]I will assume that you know how to do this for the particular operating system that you are using.

The first line of that short script is the magic *shebang* line. This is made from the characters #! and the full path to an application. In that simple script the path points to the Perl interpreter and includes a *flag* which I am passing to the interpreter to change its behavior. The shebang line *must* be the first line of the file since the #! character pair are an instruction to the shell telling it to pass the rest of the file to another application. In your particular situation the Perl interpreter may be stored in a different directory to mine. You will need to find out where it is and change the line to suit your local conditions. The following lines show possible alternatives:

```
1   #!/usr/local/bin/perl
    #!/bin/perl
```

Microsoft Windows does not use the same mechanism. It generally associates a type of file with a particular application which it uses to process the file. If you have installed ActiveState Perl this association will have been automatically set-up for you so that all files which end .pl are passed to the Perl interpreter. If you need to set flags when the script is run you have a problem with this mechanism. This particular distribution lets you use the shebang mechanism to execute the script and control its behavior. This means that you can run these from the prompt in exactly the same way that you would under UNIX by just typing the file name. Use the following line:

```
#! perl -w
```

Now it is time to execute the script we created and saved earlier. Open a command shell and change to the directory in which you saved the file. At the prompt type:

```
hello.pl
```

On a Windows machine, that should run the script which displays a simple message. On a UNIX machine you should get a message telling you something like:

```
bash: ./hello.pl: Permission denied
```

UNIX uses a system of permissions to control access to files. Each Perl script that you write, whether saved as .pl or as .cgi, needs to be made executable with the chmod utility. This is done by entering the following at a command prompt:

```
chmod 755 <scriptname>.pl}
```

This gives the owner of the file, usually its creator, permission to read, write, and execute the file as a program. Other users on the system can read the file or execute it but cannot edit its source. To run a Perl script you simply type the file name at the command prompt, there is no need to place the perl command before it. The operating system uses the shebang line to find out how to run the program, in this case it will pass it to the Perl binary.

Perl does not use normal data types such as integers, floats or chars. Instead data items are simply things which are accessed through a variety of structures. Control over the operations which you perform on a data item is pretty much left up to you. If you want to try adding a string of characters to a floating point number then the Perl interpreter is not going to stop you.

In this book I will use the primitive data types: scalar, array and associative array. Because they are rather different to data types in other languages there should be plenty to keep us all busy. Perl can be used for object-based programming, just as JavaScript can, but generally it is used to develop simpler, procedural programs.

9.4 SCALARS

The basic data type is called the *scalar*. Scalar items are identified by having a $ at the front of their name.

 NOTE *In Perl, the data type of a variable is identified by a character symbol which precedes its name.*

So what is a singular piece of data? Well, single data items might be numbers or characters, strings or individual data items inside a structure such as an array. Table 9.2 shows some examples of this.

Because the type of a scalar is not predetermined they can be used rather creatively. Try saving the following script in a file called `scalar.pl`.

```
1  #!/usr/bin/perl -w

   $item = 0;
   $item = 34 * 54.364762;
5  $item .= " fred";
   print $item."\n";
   print "$item\n";

   exit(0);
```

Make the script executable if you are using UNIX with the `chmod` command:

```
chmod 755 scalar.pl
```

Run the script by entering the following command at a prompt, then pressing Enter:

```
scalar.pl
```

Assignment	Explanation
`$item = 0;`	Scalars can be simple integers.
`$item = 0.32536;`	A scalar can also hold a float.
`$item = " ";`	This scalar is initialized as an empty string.
`$item = "fred";`	Here we assign a string to the scalar.
`$item = 23.03e4;`	Scalars can use scientific format.
`$item = 34 * 56.78;`	The result of any operation can be assigned to a scalar. It will be typed correctly for the context.
`$item = "A whole sentence";`	Scalars can hold strings with spaces – which will turn out to be very useful.
`$new = $item;`	Scalars can be assigned the value of other scalars.
`$item = $array[3];`	A scalar can be assigned a value from an array.

Table 9.2 Scalar data assignments

In the script, `$item` undergoes the following set of operations:

- It is initialized as a number with the value 0.
- It then takes the result of the multiplication operation.
- A string is then joined onto the end of the numerical value. Notice the `.=` construct which is used for certain string concatenation operations. See Section 9.8 for more details on this and similar operators. What is important for now is that the scalar was able to act as a number and then become a string when it needed to.
- The scalar is then displayed, using the `print` function, with a newline character joined to its end.
- Finally the scalar is displayed from within a string.

Perl has a rich set of printing operations which are borrowed directly from C. Most of the examples in this chapter use the most primitive `print` operation. Detailed descriptions of the printing and display operations can be found in Section 9.8.5.

Within the script, whenever it was necessary, `$item` was automatically converted into a string so that `fred` could be concatenated onto it. But what happens if we insert the following code:

```
$item = $item * 3;
```

just before the print statements?

```
1   #!/usr/bin/perl -w

    $item = 0;
    $item = 34 * 54.364762;
5   $item .= "fred";
    print $item."\n";
    print "$item\n";

    # new things below here...
10  $item = $item * 3;
    print $item."\n";
    print "$item\n";

    exit(0);
```

The interpreter throws out an error message saying that `$item`, or rather the argument to the operation on line 10 (`1848.401908fred`), is not numeric. Once you have non-numerals in a string you cannot convert it into a number. But ... notice what the final two print statements output:

```
5545.205724
```

That is the result of the multiplication the script performed before `fred` was concatenated onto `$item`. Strings which could represent valid numbers such as "`54.123`" or "`54.3e02`" can be used in either string or numerical operations as the following example shows:

```
1   #!/usr/bin/perl -w

    $item = "3245.02e4";
    $item2 = $item;

5
    $item .= "12";
    $item2 = $item2 + "12";

    print $item."\n";
10  print $item2."\n";
    exit(0);
```

Initially both variables are set to string values. The first, `$item`, then has a string concatenated on. When displayed, this scalar holds the value

```
3245.02e412
```

The second scalar is used in an arithmetical operation although both of the operands (the values used in the operation) are strings. Since both operands contain only digits, the operation can be performed legally and the result displayed:

```
32450212
```

If the line were changed to:

```
$item2 = $item2 + "q";
```

the addition operation would no longer be legal. The interpreter would display this message instead:

```
Argument "q" isn't numeric in add at ./test.pl line 7.
```

NOTE *I cannot stress the importance of thorough testing and debugging, when developing in Perl, strongly enough. Even a very simple script can contain hidden errors and potential side-effects.*

9.4.1 Functions Which Operate On Scalars

A number of Perl functions operate on scalar data. I have defined some of the more useful ones in this section.

chomp[(variable)]

This is usually used to remove the newline character from the end of the scalar. If no scalar variable is specified chomp will operate on data coming from the standard input. Standard input is usually the keyboard.

chop[(variable)]

This works exactly like chomp but returns the character which was removed.

lc[(parameter)]

This returns its parameter with all characters converted to lower case. If the parameter is omitted lc will operate on standard input.

length[(parameter)]

This returns the length in characters of its parameter. It operates on standard input if no parameter is specified.

q/string/

places single quotes around the string.

qq/string/

>   places double quotes around the string.

substr(string, offset[, length])

>   extracts and returns a substring from the string, starting at the supplied offset. The first character of the expression is at position 0. An optional length may be supplied to indicate how many characters are returned. If this is omitted the substring continues to the end of the string.

uc[(parameter)]

>   returns its parameter with all characters converted to upper case. If the parameter is omitted uc will operate on standard input.

9.5 ARRAYS

The first of the plural data types is the array. These have an @ before their name and are, broadly, like those which you may have met in JavaScript. Although you have already used arrays, it is probably worth giving a quick refresher on arrays in general before I write about how they are used in Perl. If you know your array from your linked list, your stack from your queue, feel free to skip the next bit and leap to the discussion of arrays in Perl. A couple of warnings: in Perl an array can be used as a stack so you need to keep your wits about you; and Perl arrays are not type sensitive – we can mix and match numbers, strings, arrays, and hashes as items in an array.

The array is a common, popular, and useful data structure which is found in most programming languages. An array is an ordered list of scalar variables. To access an item in an array you use its position in the list. This is called its index. If we take some simple items: "dog", "cat", 234, "Uncle Bill", we can put them into an array. The following code creates an array and displays its contents:

```
1   #!/usr/bin/perl -w

    @firstarr = ("dog", "cat", 234, "Uncle Bill");
    print "@firstarr\n";
5
    exit(0);
```

Having put our strange list into an array, it is now ordered and we can access items based upon that order. The first item in the array is at index 0 (zero), not index 1, many programming languages count from 0 and Perl is no exception. This is not simply a convention designed to trap the unwary novice, but is very useful in counting through loops. In Perl, as in JavaScript, you need to get used to counting the first instance of anything as instance zero. The index of the last item in our array is not the same as the number of items in the array. In the example I have 6 things in the array, yet if the first is at index 0 the last must be at index 5. That is, the last item is at index "number of items in the array" − 1.

Let us now consider the matter of ordering. I said that the items in an array are ordered. That ordering is due to their being in the array and is not an artifact of any property of the array items themselves. If I swap "cat" and "my uncle Bill" the array remains ordered. This is one way in which an array differs from a list. Another is that deleting an item from an array does not affect the other items in the array. If I delete cat, which was at index 1, the array still has 6 items, the only difference is that the item at index 1 is empty. If this data structure worked like a list then deleting cat would reduce it to 5 items. I could easily write a function which would delete an item from an array and shuffle the other items along one place so that there is no gap. Similarly I could write a function to insert items into an array but these are add-ons to the array rather than inherent within the data structure.

Arrays in Perl are nice and straightforward with a couple of useful enhancements over the traditional array. You create an array by assigning it a list of values:

```
@myarray = ("dog", "cat", "mouse", 234, "my uncle Bill");
```

You can also set the value of an individual array item:

```
$myarray[5] = "horse";
```

Perl supplies two operations which allow you to manipulate the last item in the array. These are called push and pop. The following code shows these functions in action:

```
1   #!/usr/bin/perl -w

    @myarray = ("dog", "cat", "mouse", 234, "my uncle Bill");
    $string = "foobar was my uncle";
5   print "@myarray\n";

    push(@myarray, $string);
    print "@myarray\n";

10  $item = pop(@myarray);
    print "$item\n";

    exit(0);
```

Using push then pop can leave the array in its initial state:

```
1   #!/usr/bin/perl -w
```

```
     @myarray = ("dog", "cat", "mouse", 234, "my uncle Bill");
     $string = "foobar was my uncle";
 5   print "@myarray\n";

     push(@myarray, $string);
     print "@myarray\n";

10   pop(@myarray);
     print "@myarray\n";

     exit(0);
```

You will not find these operations in a traditional array implementation, rather they are usually reserved for use with stacks. However, they are very useful if you want to swap things. If you push items into one array and pop them off into another you have quickly reversed their order.

The following script shows most of the array syntax in operation. Try it out:

```
 1   #!/usr/bin/perl -w

     $array = "";
     $discard = "";
 5   for($i = 0; $i < 12; $i++) {
        $array[$i] = $i*1000;
     }

     $i = 0;
10   foreach $t (@array) {
        print("$i    $t\n");
        $i++;
     }

15   $discard = pop(@array);
     push(@array, "uncle Jack");
     $i = 0;
     foreach $t (@array) {
        print("$i    $t\n");
20      $i++;
     }
```

```
($fred, $jack, $mary) = @array;
printf("$fred, $jack, $mary");
25   exit(0);
```

Let us look at the interesting behavior that we see there. I will go through each loop in turn. First we initialize two scalars then iterate through the first simple loop writing a value into an array on each loop. You should notice that the array is declared and referenced as a scalar. This works because Perl is fairly flexible about data management, once the Perl interpreter sees something like $var[$count] it knows that it is dealing with an array. In writing to an individual array cell we are addressing part of the array not all of it, therefore we cannot use @array as this means the whole array. The loop writes a number to each cell of the array but, of course, later we may treat this number as a string if we have to.

RULE OF THUMB

If we want to perform an operation on the whole array we use @arrayname; if we want to perform an operation on an individual item in the array we use $arrayname[$index].

The second loop iterates through the array, copies the value at each index, and displays it on the screen. This time a foreach loop is used as the size of the array is fixed. Once the end of the array is reached the loop will terminate. The notation:

```
foreach $t (@array)
```

is used to set the value of $t on each loop. After displaying the array we remove the last item using pop, the array now has only 11 items. We then replace the popped item with a string and once more print the array.

Finally three new scalars are declared and assigned values. This type of assignment starts from the beginning of the array (index 0) and assigns to as many variables as are declared. If you try to assign to more variables than you have items in your array you will get a run-time error. The assignment statement will work perfectly but once you try to use the variables which did not get a value from the array you will be warned that you are trying to use an uninitialized value. This can lead to undefined behavior so care needs to be taken when using arrays.

RULE OF THUMB

Although Perl is more flexible than C about arrays, using variables with an indeterminate value will still give problems. The safest approach is usually to track the length of the array manually so that you can never fall off the end.

Here is a final useless but amusing thing that you can do with arrays and pop. You can pop items off the end of your array whilst manipulating it in a loop:

```
1  #! /usr/bin/perl -w

   $array = "";
   $discard = "";
5  for($i = 0; $i < 12; $i++) {
     $array[$i] = $i*1000;
   }

   $i = 0;
10 foreach $t (@array) {
     $discard = pop(@array);
     print("$i    $t\n");
     $i++;
   }
```

I honestly cannot think why anyone would want to do this, and it could be really dangerous. It does, though, demonstrate just how flexible Perl is.

9.5.1 Functions Which Operate on Arrays

A number of Perl functions operate on arrays of data. I have defined some of the more useful ones in this section.

join(separator, item[, item[, item]]]

joins the items specified in the comma separated list into a single string. The items in the new string are separated by the character passed in as the first parameter:

```
1  #! /usr/bin/perl -w
   print join("!", "Jack", "Mary", "Fred", 32),"\n";
   exit(0);
```

which displays

```
Jack!Mary!Fred!32
```

push(array, scalar)

adds a scalar item to the *end* of the array.

pop(array)

removes one item from the end of an array, returning it so that it can be used.

qw/string/

places quotes around the scalar values in the array.

reverse(item[, item[, item]]])

returns the list of items in reversed order:

```
1   #! /usr/bin/perl -w
    print reverse("Jack", "Mary", "Fred", 32,),"\n";
    exit(0);
```

which displays

```
32FredMaryJack
```

shift

takes the first item off the array and returns. After this operation the array is shortened by one item.

sort

sorts the elements of the array and returns them in sorted order.

splice(array, offset, length, item[, item[, item]]])

works in the same way as the JavaScript `splice` function which was described in Section 6.9.2. Items from `offset` to `length` are removed from the array and replaced by the items in the comma separated list. The following example shows how this works:

```
1   #! /usr/bin/perl -w

    @orig = ("first", "second", "third", "fourth", "fifth", "six");
    print "@orig\n";
5
    splice(@orig, 2, 3, "new 1", "new 2");
```

```
    print "@orig\n";

    exit(0);
```

which displays

```
1   first second third fourth fifth six
    first second new 1 new 2 six
```

9.6 HASHES

The second, and last, of the plural data types is the hash. Identifiable by the **%** before their unique name, hashes consist of a series of pairs of items with each pair comprising a **key** and an associated **value**. Hashes are formally called *associative arrays* but that is rather long-winded so I prefer to stick to the simpler name. The clearest way of getting a grasp on the hash concept is to see some examples. Hashes can be declared in one of two ways:

```
1   %myhash = ("key", "value",
        "Mon", "Monday",
        "Tue", "Tuesday",
        "Dog", "Rover",
5       "Cat", "Fluffy");
```

or:

```
1   %myhash = ("key" => "value",
        "Mon" => "Monday",
        "Tue" => "Tuesday",
        "Dog" => "Rover",
5       "Cat" => "Fluffy");
```

In my opinion, the second version makes the relationship between the key and its value obvious while the first could be a mislabeled array. In the first example I am going to write some values into a hash and then read them back and display them. Code first, then some explanation:

```
1   #! /usr/bin/perl -w

    %myhash = ("key" => "value",
        "Mon" => "Monday",
5       "Tue" => "Tuesday",
        "Dog" => "Rover",
        "Cat" => "Fluffy");
```

```
     foreach $key (keys %myhash) {
10       $value = $myhash{$key};
         printf("Key: %s\tValue: %s\n", $key, $value);
     }

     exit(0);
```

Save that code in a file called hash.pl then run it. The output should look like this:

```
1   Key: Cat        Value: Fluffy
    Key: key        Value: value
    Key: Dog        Value: Rover
    Key: Mon        Value: Monday
5   Key: Tue        Value: Tuesday
```

When you run this script you will find that the key/value pairs are printed in a different order to the one in which you entered them. You have not made a mistake and this is not a bug but a powerful feature. Clearly something more than simple storage is going on.

RULE OF THUMB

What happens when you add something to an array is that Perl applies a hashing algorithm to the key. This is then assigned to one of eight buckets depending upon the result of the hash. A hash array is called that because it uses a hashing algorithm to optimize storage.

That seems a lot of effort. Why bother? Imagine that you have a large database to manipulate and that you are using Perl, which is free, rather than Oracle which is immensely expensive. You would not want all of your data items placed into the same data structure: searching for a specific item would take an eternity. By creating eight data structures Perl is able to radically reduce search times. The reduction is by at least 7/8 as Perl applies the hashing algorithm to your search request and will only ever search one bucket. If you want to know how many buckets have been used to store your data, try this which will tell you:

```
print %myhash."\n";
```

It is important that you realize that every key must be unique. If you add something to your hash and later re-use the same key, the second value will overwrite the first which will be irretrievably lost.

Let us look at the script to see how it works. The first thing to notice is the line which reads the *keys* out of the hash.

```
foreach $key (keys %myhash) {
```

Before we can operate on the data values we need to get them out of the hash. We cannot access them directly (I will show you how to do that in a moment), instead we will get at the values through the indexed keys. To get all of the keys from the hash we use the keys function.

The keys come out of the hash in an array. I want to iterate across this list of keys and extract and display each associated value. The easiest way of moving across a structure like an array is to use a foreach loop. Once we have a key we can apply this to the hash to access its associated value. In this program I am going to copy the value into a scalar so that I can display it. As with the array if we only want to work on a single item, we treat the hash like a scalar by calling it using the $ notation. Notice that the key is surrounded by curly brackets not parentheses:

```
1  $value = $myhash{$key};
```

 NOTE *This is an opportunity for errors which are difficult to spot when debugging your code: if you are reading from a hash by applying a key, use curly brackets.*

Sometimes you will not be interested in the keys but will want to look at all of the values. As well as the keys function, Perl has a function to return a list of values from a hash. Not surprisingly it is called values.

```
1  foreach $value (values %myhash) {
     printf("Value: %s\n", $value);
   }
```

You cannot reverse engineer the hash to get the keys from their associated values but there should never be any reason to do that unless you got the key/value pair the wrong way round.

RULE OF THUMB

Try to think in hashes. Although you will use arrays and scalars more often, much of the real power and flexibility of Perl lie in the murky recesses of the hash.

You put ordered data into your hash, you get unordered data out. This does not seem to be a very useful solution does it? Fortunately you can sort your data as it comes back using the, rather appropriately named, sort function.

Try this in the earlier hash example:

```
1   foreach $key (sort keys %myhash) {
      $value = $myhash{$key};
      printf("Key: %s\tValue: %s\n", $key, $value);
    }
```

There is a lot more that you can do with sort but I have not shown you enough Perl yet to use it. One thing to note is that sort puts the data into ascending alpha-numerical order. It has no understanding of context so although Monday comes before Wednesday in sorted data that is simply a result of "M" being before "W" in the ASCII table. If you want context sensitive sorts then you have to craft them for yourself.

Here is a complicated way of displaying data in reverse sorted order. It is a slow and dirty approach which involves reading and sorting from the hash, putting the keys and values into a pair of arrays and then popping the arrays. To use this program, enter pairs of keys and values separated by colons at the command line until you are finished or fed up. Then type quit and the sorting will start:

```
1   #! /usr/bin/perl -w

    $in = "";
    print "Enter a key/value pair separated by a colon
5   (quit to finish)\t";
    $in = <STDIN>;
    chomp $in;

    while($in ne "quit") {
10    ($key, $val) = split(/:/, $in);
      $myhash{$key} = $val;
      print "Enter a key/value pair separated by a colon
```

```
      (quit to finish)\t";
      $in = <STDIN>;
15    chomp $in;
   }


   $count = 0;
   foreach $temp (sort keys %myhash) {
20    $keyarray[$count] = $temp;
      $valarray[$count++] = $myhash{$temp};
   }


   while($count > 0) {
25    $t = pop(@keyarray);
      $tt = pop(@valarray);
      print("Key: $t    Value: $tt\n");
      $count--;
   }
30
   exit(0);
```

The only unfamiliar thing left in that script should be:

```
($key, $val) = split(/:/, $in);
```

Which will split the input into pieces each time it finds a colon. The pieces are then stored into two scalar variables. String manipulations like this will be explained in Section 9.8. For those of you who like quick solutions to your problems, here is how to print out an array in reverse order using the reverse function:

```
1  #! /usr/bin/perl -w


   $in = "";
   print "Enter a key/value pair separated by a colon (quit to finish)\t";
5  $in = <STDIN>;
   chomp $in;


   while($in ne "quit") {
      ($key, $val) = split(/:/, $in);
10    $myhash{$key} = $val;
      print "Enter a key/value pair separated by a colon (quit to finish)\t";
      $in = <STDIN>;
```

```
    chomp $in;
}
```

15

```
@revkeys = sort keys %myhash;
print "@revkeys\n";

foreach $key (reverse @revkeys) {
    $value = $myhash{$key};
    print("Key: $key  Value: $value\n");
}

exit(0);
```

20

Notice how that looks just like the earlier sorted array but uses a different function? This is a good example of reusing your knowledge to good effect.

9.6.1 Functions Which Operate on Hashes

A number of Perl functions operate on associative arrays, hashes, of data. I have defined some of the more useful ones in this section.

delete $hash{$key}

>deletes the specified key and its associated value from the hash

each %hash

>returns a list of pairs of keys and values. This function is used to iterate over the contents of the hash:

```
#! /usr/bin/perl -w

%myhash = ("key", "value",
    "Mon", "Monday",
    "Tue", "Tuesday",
    "Dog", "Rover",
    "Cat", "Fluffy");

while(@pair = each %myhash) {
    print "@pair\n";
}

exit(0);
```

1

5

10

exists %hashvalue

returns TRUE if the value exists as a *key* in the hash. Try adding this to the previous example:

```perl
if(exists $myhash{"Dog"}){
    print "It's there\n";
}
```

keys %hash

returns all of the keys from the hash as an array.

values %hash

returns all of the values from the hash as an array.

9.7 CONTROL STRUCTURES

Perl is a block structured language like JavaScript. This means simply that operations can be grouped into blocks so that they can be performed repeatedly, or not at all. Blocks have to be delimited by curly brackets, { ... }.

In JavaScript you can leave the brackets out if the block consists of only one line. Not so in Perl: you must use the brackets.

Perl coders also tend to be fussy about the way that brackets are used and how the program is laid out. This is partly because Larry Wall has made his own somewhat idiosyncratic views known, and partly because so many Perl loops do have just a single line. If you are not careful you can end up with lots of white space in your scripts, which can be as unreadable as not having enough space.

The *approved* approach looks like this:

```perl
condition() {
    rest of block;
}
```

A common alternative which uses an extra line is:

```perl
condition()
  {
    rest of block;
  }
```

I tend to use the approved style for Perl, although I use the alternative for languages such as C, C++, and Java. For some reason I cannot read my programs if I get the indentation wrong. More important than whether you can read your own code, is the fact that other people may need to read it. If you are writing code for yourself, that code may never be read again, most developers work in teams and share code. Many organizations use the same code for years. Over time this code will need regular maintenance and updates. The person who originally wrote the code is unlikely to be the one who modifies it five or ten years later. All code needs to be neatly structured with liberal use of comments throughout. Perl is an especially messy language because it uses *lots* of characters which have special meanings. One of the easiest ways of making Perl code more legible is to use consistent blocks. As you read some of the larger pieces of code in this book, you will see that consistent layout really *does* make the code more readable.

There are three basic types of block in Perl: subroutines which I will consider later, repetition, and conditional loops. Conditional loops form `if ... elsif ... else` structures; repetition is achieved by `while`, `for`, and `foreach` loops. Looping is terminated when a controlling condition is true. In Perl almost everything is true, in fact generally speaking only two conditions are considered false:

- the integer 0
- the strings " " and "0"

9.7.1 Loops

for

for loops in Perl work exactly as they do in languages like C and JavaScript. They repeat the same operation, or set of operations, until the looping condition becomes false. The counter is a scalar value.

```
1  for($i = 0; $i < 10; $i++) {
     print "The Counter is $i\n";
   }
```

This simple loop will repeatedly print its message to the screen and terminate once the value of $i is no longer less than 10. The $ declaration of variables will be explained later, as will the syntax of the `print` statement.

foreach

Sometimes you want to perform the same operation on each item of an array. It is perfectly possible to use the `for` statement but `foreach` makes for neater code. In the following example I use a `for` loop to set the value of each element of an array and then use a `foreach` loop to print those values to the screen. Notice the strange

@ symbol which is used to indicate an array, and the different ways that an array can be referenced. Section 9.8 will cover this in detail.

```perl
1   for($i = 0; $i < 10; $i++) {
        $array[$i] = $i;
    }
    $j = 0;
5   foreach(@array) {
        print "value: ".$array[$j++]."\n";
    }
    exit(0);
```

while

while loops are best used if you do not know in advance when the loop will terminate. In this example I print a message to the screen prompting for some input, receive the input, and display it back to the user. When the string quit is entered, without the inverted commas, the program terminates:

```perl
1   #!/usr/bin/perl -w

    $in = "";
    while($in ne "quit") {
5       print "Enter a String (\"quit\" to terminate): ";
        $in = <STDIN>;
        chomp $in;
        print "You Entered $in\n";
    }
10  exit(0);
```

The next example is the same program but manipulating numbers. Try running them both, and in the second example enter a mix of integers and floats. What happens if you enter a string?

```perl
1   #!/usr/bin/perl -w

    $in = 0;
    while($in != -99) {
5       print "Enter a Number (\"-99\" to terminate): ";
        $in = <STDIN>;
        chomp $in;
        print "You Entered $in\n";
```

```
      }
10    exit(0);
```

Finally, a simple program that reads parameter values from the command-line and displays them back.

```
1     #!/usr/bin/perl -w
      $i = 0;
      while($array[$i] = shift @ARGV) {
          print "Item $i: $array[$i]\n";
5         $i++;
      }
      exit(0);
```

Save that code in a file called param.pl. Run it like this:

```
param.pl Mary, Jane, Susan
```

There is quite a lot to consider in these simple programs. I will give a full treatment of data types later, for now some basic information will suffice.

Just like JavaScript, Perl is not a strongly typed language; which means that you do not have to declare the type of a variable when you create it. The context in which the variable is used will give the interpreter sufficient information to process it correctly. Data values occupy a different namespace to Perl keywords; in Perl it is not possible to declare a variable which has the same name as a keyword. This is achieved by preceding the name of the variable with a special symbol: $ for scalars, @ for arrays and % for hashes. Notice that in the final example I refer to two arrays: array and ARGV but that I use $array and @ARGV.

In the first while example I read values from the keyboard and assign them to a scalar using:

```
$i = <STDIN>
```

Like most languages, Perl uses three standard streams, STDIN for input, STDOUT for output, and STDERR for error messages. You can use these streams as if they were files. We shall look at input and output in more detail in Section 9.8. I then removed the return character from the end of the input using chomp $i. There are two ways of chopping the last character from a scalar: chop removes the last character, chomp is more friendly and removes the last character only if it is a new line. The sample programs demonstrate a number of Boolean checks. The use of the Boolean operators eq, ne, ==, !=, etc. is considered in Section 9.7.2. Postfix incrementing of scalars works just as in JavaScript ($i++).

exit()

Ultimately even simple programs have to work with the operating system. It is always a good idea to use:

```
exit(0);
```

to terminate your programs as this ensures that all processes finish safely.

last <label>

Although teachers of structured programming sometimes tell students that loops should have a single entry point and a single exit point, they should not. Any loop must have a single entry point otherwise your code can have all sorts of side-effects and will be impossible to maintain. Having a single exit from a loop leads to contrived and often inefficient code.

Consider the problem of reading through a text file looking for a specific line. Ideally when (or if) you find the line you want, the reading of the file should end so that you can get on with processing the text. The following pseudocode examples show differing approaches to this problem. Example one, reads the whole of the file regardless of how quickly the line is found; example two uses a Boolean test to control the reading of the file.

Example one

```
1  while(not end_of_file) {
     read next line;
     if(next line equal test){
       process line;
5    }
   }
```

Example Two

```
1  done = false;
   while(done equals false) {
     read next line;
     if(next line equals test){
5      process line;
       done = true;
     }
   }
```

Both of these examples are common approaches to this type of problem. It makes much more sense to break out of the loop either when the end of file is reached or when the required line is found. In C this might be done by adding a break statement into the first example:

```
1   while(not end_of_file) {
       read next line;
       if(next line equals test){
         process line;
5        break;
       }
    }
```

Perl has a similar mechanism. The start of the loop is given a label and the last operation is provided. This is used to jump out of the loop:

```
1   TEST: while($in = <INPUT_FILE>) {
       chomp $in;
       if($in eq "quit"){
        last TEST;
5      }
    }
```

This example reads from INPUT_FILE until the line entered, and chomped, equals the test. The program then jumps out of the loop.

Here is the script which reads numbers from the command-line rewritten to use LAST:

```
1   #! /usr/bin/perl -w

    $in = 1;
    $total = 0;
5
    CHANCE: while( ) {
       print qq(Enter a Number ("0" to terminate): );
       $in = <STDIN>;
       chomp $in;
10     $total = $total + $in;

       print "You Entered $in\n";
       print "The running total is now $total\n\n";
```

```
15      if ($in == 0) {
            last CHANCE;
        }
    }
    exit(0);
```

Iteration is one of the most common things that you will be doing in your Perl programs. Many simple CGI scripts contain no iteration but simply return a series of strings; I will be looking at how we develop more complex CGI applications. The scripts that we look at later in this book perform real processing; they use the excellent string-handling capabilities of Perl and are required to iterate through files, strings, and values returned by the user. If you want to do any serious work with Perl you must be comfortable with its loop constructs and the way that it checks for truth.

9.7.2 Boolean Conditions

The status of operations, return values from subroutines, and the existence, or not, of data values can be checked in Perl, just as in other languages using Boolean conditions. A Boolean condition is a logical operation which evaluates to either true or false. Perl has two Boolean operators that are specifically used for operations on strings and four which are used for operations on numbers.

The string operators are eq and ne. The first test will return true if the two strings are equal; the second will return true if they are not equal. When comparing strings it is important that you consider exactly what the values are that you want to compare. In the following example I want to read input from the keyboard and compare it to the string quit. If the user types in quit the program will terminate. Consider what the user actually enters: they type quit followed by the <ENTER> key which appends a newline character onto the string. If I simply compare the input with quit, the program will never terminate:

```
1   if($input eq "quit")
```

The test will always be false because I am not testing for the newline at the end of the input. Therefore I must remove that newline character before I perform the test. To do this I use the built-in chomp function. Here is the code:

```
1   #!/usr/bin/perl -w
```

```
DONE: while( ){
    print qq(Enter a string ("quit" to finish)\t);
    $in = <STDIN>;
    chomp $in;
    if($in eq "quit"){
      last DONE;
    }
}
```

```
exit(0);
```

That code can be rewritten to use a Boolean condition to control looping:

```
#!/usr/bin/perl -w

$done = 0;
while($done != 1 ){
    print qq(Enter a string ("quit" to finish)\t);
    $in = <STDIN>;
    chomp $in;
    if($in eq "quit"){
      $done = 1;
    }
}
```

```
exit(0);
```

When evaluating numerical conditions we have four Boolean operations available. These should be familiar from JavaScript:

- == is used to test if the two values are equal
- != evaluates to true if the two numbers are not equal
- <= is true if the value on the left is less than or equal to the value on the right
- >= is true if the value on the left is greater than or equal to the value on the right.

These operations work exactly as they would in JavaScript or the vast majority of conventional programming languages. In the following example the program repeatedly executes a loop, and at the end of each iteration a variable is incremented. When the value of the variable equals 13 the program terminates. Notice that, rather than testing for $i ==

13 I test for $i <= 12. This gives me no performance benefits and, in fact, makes the code slightly less readable, but does demonstrate the use of a different operator. Without running the program, work out how many messages are displayed on the screen.

```perl
1   #!/usr/bin/perl -w

    $i = 0;
    $done = 0;
5   while($done == 0) {
        if($i <= 12){
          print "$i\tIt's a boy!\n";
        }
        else {
10        print "$i\tIt's a girl!\n";
          $done = 1;
        }
        $i++;
    }
15
    exit(0);
```

If ... elsif ... else

Not all conditions have only two correct answers. Often you will want to test a condition against a range of values and perform different operations for each possible value returned. In JavaScript we might use a switch statement:

```javascript
1   switch(fred) {
        case(0):
            do something;
            break;
5       case(1):
            do something else;
            break;
        default:
            do another thing;
10      }
```

Perl does not have a switch but does provide a simple construct to perform almost the same operation. Subtle differences exist because of the need for a break statement in JavaScript, and the fact that you can only switch on an integer value. In Perl that statement would be written as:

```
1  if($fred == 0) {
      do something;
   }
   elsif($fred == 1) {
5     do something else;
   }
   else {
      do another thing;
   }
```

The Perl version is more difficult to write and maintain and less efficient at run-time. If you have 20 options instead of three, the JavaScript switch statement needs to make only a single check on the conditional value to switch to the correct next operation. In Perl if you wanted the last of the 20 options you would be making 19 conditional checks.

RULE OF THUMB

Structure your Boolean operations carefully to minimize the run-time overhead. When writing if ... elsif ... else *take care that you type* elsif *rather than* elseif: *it is an awkward one to spot when debugging!*

9.8 PROCESSING TEXT

Perl is a text processing language. Its facilities and optimizations are there to make the manipulation of text strings and plain text files fast, and relatively easy. UNIX systems generally have far richer text manipulation tools than Apple or Microsoft systems. These tools tend to be command-line based and work very well in automated applications such as batch processing. If you wanted to search for an individual sentence among all of the files in a directory on a PC you might open each file into a text editor and perform an individual search. Alternatively you could use the graphical Find utility which Windows provides. To perform the same operation on a UNIX box you would write a one-line grep script and run it. The advantage of the graphical approach is that novice users can perform relatively complex operations without needing to acquire too much knowledge. The command-line approach provides more flexible tools which can be embedded within scripts and called programmatically, that is clearly better if you need to repeat an operation in the future.

Here we see just one of the benefits of Perl: it brings programmatic access to a range of utilities to all platforms. Perl is available on many different systems and it always works in the same way on each of them. Perl can therefore be used to bring the power of UNIX text manipulation to every desktop.

Perl is much more than an extended grep, sed, and awk clone. Because it is a proper programming language you can use it to perform all manner of complex text transformations. Many computer-based operations need databases of information which are usually too small to need the services of fully fledged database management software. For example, system administrators need to know things such as which system log-on codes have been assigned, which workgroup a user belongs to, which printers they have permission to use, and how often systems are accessed. Webmasters may want to know where most accesses to their Web site are from, which pages are accessed most often, how accesses map throughout the day, and where the peaks are. All of this information is available to them but hidden in system log files. They could read through the logs and extract the information for themselves but many sys-admins now choose to write Perl scripts which extract and process their data. They can then present themselves with pre-digested summary information which they can usefully use.

Perl provides at least the following facilities:

- searching files for strings
- searching strings for substrings
- extraction of substrings into summary files
- copying of data from one file to another
- replacement of one substring with another
- manipulation of individual characters
- displaying strings
- formatted report generation.[4]

9.8.1 Splitting Strings

The two operations that you will encounter frequently, especially once we start to look at CGI programming, are splitting strings into lists and building strings from lists. To take a string apart we use the `split` function which is defined as:

split /pattern/, [expression], [limit]

The function takes a string and searches it for a specified pattern of characters; each time it finds that pattern it returns a substring. This operation is repeated either until the end of the string is reached or the number of substrings is equal to the optional limit. Where multiple strings are being returned they are usually made available in an array.

---

[4]I am not going to look at this as the facilities are rather limited and the output looks a little old-fashioned.

The string itself may optionally be specified in the expression field. If no string is specified the default input, called $_ is used. The default input is usually the standard input but may also be any arguments to the function. The substrings run from the start of the string's previously found delimiter to the most recently found delimiter, but do not include the delimiters, which are discarded.

That definition might be quite confusing so here is a simple example that shows most of what you can do. Try running the code before you read the explanation:

```
1   #! /usr/bin/perl -w

    # create a text string
    $test_string = "cake::cookies::candies::chocolate";
5
    # split the strings into the elements of an array
    @nice = split(/::/, $test_string);
    foreach $t (@nice) {
        print("Item: $t\n");
10  }

    # split the items into a list of scalars
    ($first, $second, $rest) = split(/::/, $test_string);
    print("Items: $first, $second, $rest\n");
15
    ($first, $second, $rest) = split(/::/, $test_string, 3);
    print("Items: $first, $second, $rest\n");

    exit(0);
```

I start by creating a string in which the data items are separated by pairs of colons. If you are using strings to store data it is important that your separators are characters, or combinations, which are not going to appear in the data items. If they do appear in the data you will get unforeseen side-effects – incorrect substrings. This might seem obvious, but when you write the script you may have little idea about the content of the data your users will enter. This can make the selection of a delimiter fraught. Popular choices for delimiters include pairs of colons (::) and the pipe character (|) which almost never appear in English text.

In the first split I put all of the items into an array called @nice. I always put the operands of split inside parentheses as this makes them more readable, but this is optional. The pattern that we are going to split on can be written in one of two ways: /pattern/ or "pattern". The former is usually preferred as it matches the notation used in regular expressions, see Section 9.9, but the latter may be more legible: especially for beginners.

If you return the result of split to an array it will push each item onto the end of the array as it is split off. If you give it a list of scalars, each will, in turn, be assigned a substring as these are split off. The second split assigns the substrings into three scalars, the fourth substring is discarded as there is nowhere to put it. This is somewhat corrected in the third split. This time I give split a limit of three substrings. The first two scalars get the values you would expect of cake and cookies respectively. The third scalar is set to candies::chocolates. Everything remaining goes into the final substring once the limit is reached. Specifying the number of output values ensures that split does not lose any data. The final type of split can be very useful in searching text databases on key fields:

```
1  #! /usr/bin/perl -w

   $test_string = "cookies::multipack::chocolate::brownies";

5  ($first, $rest) = split(/::/, $test_string, 2);
   if($first eq "cookies") {
     ($pack, $flavor, $type) = split(/::/, $rest);
     if($type eq "graham") {
       print "found it\n";
10   }
     else {
       print "not this one\n";
     }
   }
15
   exit(0);
```

If $test_string were being read from a file of product descriptions I could easily search for all relevant items and then further refine my search on that subset of the original database. If I only wanted to find information on graham crackers I would split all strings into two parts and a few strings into three parts instead of having to split all the strings into four pieces:

```
1  #! /usr/bin/perl -w

   $test_string = "cookies::multipack::chocolate::brownies";

5  ($prod, $pack, $flav, $type) = split(/::/, $test_string);
   if($type eq "graham") {
     print "found it\n";
   }
   else {
```

```
10    print "not this one\n";
   }

   exit(0);
```

If you know that the key values in your database are unique you can write the result of the first split into a hash which will speed up data retrieval. However, in this example there is likely to be more than one type of cookie and so hashing would not work.

```
1  #! /usr/bin/perl -w

   $test_string = "cookies::multipack::chocolate::brownies";
   ($product, $rest) = split(/::/, $test_string, 2);
5  $foodhash{$product} = $rest;

   foreach $t (keys %foodhash) {
     if($t eq "cookies") {
       print "found it\n";
10   }
     else {
       print "not this one\n";
     }
   }
15 exit(0);
```

I will be examining pattern matching in more detail in Section 9.9 but a few comments are worth making here.

- If you want to split on white space, use either split(/ /) or split(" ").
- To split every character out of the string use split(//). Notice that no space is left between the slashes.
- Some characters must be *escaped* before being used in pattern matching. If Perl is going to interpret the character as a control string you need to make clear that it should not be expanded. Such characters have a backslash placed in front of them in the pattern:

  \", \n, \t,\$

- The pattern can become quite complex. Items can be grouped together using [ ], options can be separated using pipe |:
  - split(/[0-9]/, string) splits on any digit,
  - split($/::|\|/$, string)
    splits on either paired colons or pipe. Notice that the pipe character has to be escaped.

9.8.2 Building Strings

Building strings is easier than splitting them apart. You have already seen a lot of string concatenation in my sample code although you may not have recognized it as such. Many of the print statements that I have used have a newline character appended onto the string. To concatenate (join) substrings into a string, use the dot operator:

```
1   $next = "world";
    $fred = "hello ".$next."\n";
```

It is also possible to put scalar values directly into the middle of strings:

```
$fred = "hello $next\n";
```

If you want to append something onto the end of a string, use the .= operator:

```
1   $fred = "hello ";
    $fred .= "world\n";
```

Finally to concatenate lots of items use the join function rather than the dot operator.

join(separator, item[, item[, item]]])

> Joins the items specified in the comma separated list into a single string. The items in the new string are separated by the character passed in as the first parameter.

9.8.3 Formatting Date and Time

This sample program uses two built-in Perl functions to get the current system time and date, formats that information and prints it to the screen. Look for the various ways that strings are concatenated:

```
1   #!/usr/bin/perl -w

    print &GetTime();
    exit(0);

5
    sub GetTime {
      ($sec, $min, $hour, $mday, $month, $year, $wday,
       $yday, $isdst) = localtime(time);

10    @dotw = qw(Sunday Monday Tuesday Wednesday Thursday Friday
    Saturday);
      @moty = qw(January February March April May June July August
    September October November December);
```

```perl
15      $day = $dotw[$wday];
        $month = $moty[$month];


        # correct the year for time travellers heading back to 20th Century
        # time returns years from 1900 so 2000 is 100 in Perl
20      $year = 1900 + $year;


        # add the correct *ending* onto the day
        # e.g. to make 21->21st or 13->13th
        if( ($mday == 1) || ($mday == 21) || ($mday == 31) ) {
25          $mday = $mday."st";
        } elsif ( ($mday == 2) || ($mday == 22) ){
            $mday = $mday."nd";
        } elsif ( ($mday == 3) || ($mday == 23) ) {
            $mday = $mday."rd";
30      } else {
            $mday = $mday."th";
        }


        $today = join ' ', $day, $mday, $month, $year;

35
        # put in the leading 0 if it's less than 10 minutes
        # past the hour
        if($min < 10) {
            $min = "0".$min;
40      }


        $time = join ':', $hour, $min;

        return "It is ". $time ." on ". $today ."\n";
45  }
```

This script is based around the output from the localtime function. This function takes the time as returned by the time function and converts it into an array of 9 elements. The elements are formatted for the locale of the particular Perl implementation. When this array is assigned to a list of variables, one array element is stored in each variable.

The function needs lists of days and months as strings. These are created as arrays, @dotw and @moty. The data is placed in the array using the qw() function which takes raw strings and places appropriate quotes around them. This saves me the effort of building arrays and typing the quotes. The localtime() function has placed numeric values for the day of the week and the month into $wday and $month – both starting with zero for Sunday and January, respectively. These integers are used to extract string representations from @dotw and @moty.

The time and date need to be tidied up before being returned. In Perl years are returned incorrectly. They are given as offset from 1900 so that 2005 is returned as 105. We must allow for this by adding 1900 to the year. When expressed as strings English dates are given suffixes such as "nd" for second or twenty second. A simple if statement is used to select and append the correct suffix.

Finally concatenation creates the string which the function returns.

9.8.4 Character Manipulation

Sometimes it can be useful to have all characters in a string in the same form. For instance, if you want to perform a comparison it might be useful if all the letters were in the same case. To convert an expression to lower-case through brute force you could use the tr function which works like the one in sed. tr takes two arguments separated by forward slashes; the first is the set of characters to be altered, the second is the set of characters to which they will be altered:

```
1   #!/usr/bin/perl -w

    $fred = "SOme sTrinG";
    $fred =~ tr/[A-Z]/[a-z]/;
5   print $fred."\n";
    exit(0);
```

The =~ operator takes the string on the left, applies the function on the right, and returns the result as the scalar on the left. You can have some, not especially useful, fun with this. The following script uses the tr and uc functions:

```
1   #!/usr/bin/perl -w

    $fred = "SOme sTrinG";

5   $fred =~ tr/[A-Z]/[a-z]/;
    print $fred."\n";

    $fred =~ tr/[a-i]/[0-9]/;
    print $fred."\n";
10
    $fred = uc $fred;
```

```
print $fred."\n";
```

```
exit(0);
```

9.8.5 Printing Strings

There are two functions which can be used to `print` strings. The `print` function performs no additional formatting on the string before printing it; `printf` is used to format a string before it is displayed. You can also print large blocks of pre-formatted text using what is called the "here" syntax of the shell.

`print [filehandle] list`

> This is the simpler print routine. It takes a string, or a comma-separated list of strings and prints them. If a filehandle (see Section 9.10) is given, the string will be written to the file that it references. If no filehandle is given, the strings will usually be written to the screen. When using `print` in CGI scripts on a Web server the data will automatically be returned back to the client browser because the default filehandle for `print` is actually STDOUT. If your printing requirements are simple you should use `print` rather than `printf`: it is quicker because it does less processing, and you are likely to make fewer errors with it.[5]

`printf [filehandle] format, list`

> This is the more complex, and more flexible printing routine. Again, a string, or comma-separated list of strings, is printed to either STDOUT or a named filehandle. The big difference here is that the output must be formatted before it is printed. The formatting operators are listed in Table 9.3. First look at an example, then I will describe the formatting:

```
1   #! /usr/bin/perl -w

    $string = "Some Examples:";
    $number = 76523;
5   $decimal = 34.5612;
    $float = 23.08e35;
    $hex = 0x23a7;

    print("$string, $number, $decimal, $float, $hex \n");

10
    printf("%s\t%d\n\t\t%f\n\t\t%e\n\t\t%x \n", $string, $number, $decimal,
        $float, $hex);
```

---

[5] C coders may prefer to regard this advice with the sniffy disdain it probably deserves!

Code	Meaning	Code	Meaning
c	Character.	lo	Long octal integer (base 8).
d	Decimal integer.	lu	Long unsigned decimal integer.
e	Floating point number in exponential format.	lx	Long hexadecimal integer (base 16).
f	Floating point number in fixed point format.	o	Octal integer (base 8).
g	Floating point number in compact format.	u	Unsigned decimal integer.
s	String.	x	Hexadecimal number with lowercase letters (base 16).
ld	Long decimal integer.	X	Hexadecimal number with uppercase letters (base 16).

Table 9.3 printf formatting controls

```
printf("%s\t%d\n\t\t%3.3f\n\t\t%1.3e\n\t\t0x%X \n", $string, $number,
    $decimal, $float, ($hex + 0xa));
```

15 `exit(0);`

Which produces the following on my system:

```
1   Some Examples:, 76523, 34.5612, 2.308e+36, 9127
    Some Examples: 76523
                   34.561200
                   2.308000e+36
5                  23a7
    Some Examples: 76523
                   34.561
                   2.308e+36
                   0x23B1
```

Formatting information is embedded in the format string, but you can also put *raw text* in there. The formatting commands take the form:

`%m.nx`

where % is used to tell the interpreter that there are formatting commands next. m and n are optional integer values which indicate how many characters should be displayed.

In the example script I display some numbers without formatting before redisplaying them using formatting to restrict the sizes of fields. Notice also that, in the second example, I perform hexadecimal arithmetic from within the printf statement.

special characters

When printing you will want to use tab characters to easily format messages and, of course, you will need to use newlines in your print statements. The correct way of specifying a tab is by using backslash-t and to specify a newline use backslash-n. If you want to display any character which Perl interprets as a command you will need to first escape that character with a backslash:

```
1   #!/usr/bin/perl -w

    printf("Printing Special Characters:
    \tbackslash \\
5   \tinverted commas \"
    \ttab.\t.
    \tdollar \$
    \tnewline \n
    \texclamation mark \!\n");
10
    exit(0);
```

which looks messy but shows what is going on. If your printf statements are not working as you expect, check for the presence of special characters.

sprintf format, list

This works exactly like printf but instead of displaying a string it returns it to be used by the program:

```
1   #!/usr/bin/perl -w

    $msg = sprintf("Printing Special Characters:
    \tbackslash \\
5   \tinverted commas \"
    \ttab.\t.
    \tdollar \$
    \tnewline \n
    \texclamation mark \!");
```

```
10    print $msg."\n";

      exit(0);
```

print <<identifier;

This function is used to print here documents. Perl provides a line-oriented form of printing. The delimiters used in formatting strings for printing are end-of-line markers rather than display characters. The syntax for using this printing style is:

```
1   print <<END_OF_TEXT;
        Print this line
        and this one!
    Here's another with a scalar $value.
5   END_OF_TEXT
```

Printing starts on the line following the function call. The call must be written as shown, although the identifier can obviously be changed. The string is printed until the terminating identifier is reached. This identifier must be on a line of its own with no characters before it and only a newline character after it. It is also useful to put a blank line after the terminating identifier. This is not strictly necessary, although some ports of Perl will throw out error messages without it. The blank line will not do any harm, so use it to be safe. The text will print exactly as you have formatted it in the script code.

9.9 REGULAR EXPRESSIONS

Now you have tried a bit of Perl, hopefully you like it. It probably meets some of your needs, it is not as rigorous as C, or as mind-numbingly vast as C++ and is sufficiently different to give you an edge in the jobs marketplace. How do you go from hacking a few Web pages to developing serious applications? Just what does it take to move from acolyte to guru, from sweaty-palmed novice to sneering, disdainful expert? Regular expressions, that's what. Learn a little of using regexes and you will be able to perform complex text manipulations easily and rapidly; learn a lot and you will be able to solve apparently insoluble problems automatically. Regular expressions cannot meet all of your text manipulation needs but they can meet many of them.

Of course other languages have regular expression facilities. They are now an integral part of JavaScript, for instance. The reason that regular expression facilities are so widespread is quite simple: they are extremely useful when you are processing text. So why do they matter so much in Perl? Basically Perl is designed and optimized for text manipulation. It is generally used for that purpose and, realistically, the sort of processing that you do on the Web is just handling large quantities of text. Therefore anything which simplifies that whole process is important to Perl programmers.

A regular expression is a meta-description of a piece of text, it is a grammar for a mini language. A regular expression is a method of describing patterns so that software can match text against them. Perl uses pattern matching in these places:

- we have already seen and used `split` which takes a pattern as its first argument, and a string as its second, and returns a list of substrings which match the pattern
- we have used `tr///` to change individual characters within a string
- the match operator `m//` in Perl is used to find matching substrings
- the `s///` operator is used to replace substrings matching the pattern with a replacement string
- checking if a particular combination of characters exists inside a string. This use is the one that is most commonly associated with the idea of regular expressions.

When the pattern matching routine runs, a number of things can happen. You might simply want to know that your pattern, or part of it, matches something in the search string, for instance to test a Boolean condition. You might want to know where in the string the match is. You might choose to delete matching substrings or to replace them with another string.

9.9.1 Using Regular Expressions

Before looking at what makes a regular expression, I will show you how to use them. They are generally used in just two ways. The expression is applied to a string and the result of the expression is used to replace the value of the string:

```
1   $string =~ s/foobar/fred/
```

Alternatively a string is tested against the expression and a Boolean value returned. This is useful when, for instance, you want to see if a string contains a particular substring before performing any more processing upon it:

```
1   $value = ($string =~ m/foobar/)
```

Before trying to use regular expressions I will list all of the components which combine to make them. It is important to know how they are constructed before seeing too many examples as they can become very complicated very quickly.

9.9.2 Pattern Matching Operators

Each of the operators which use regexes can be modified to work slightly differently. Before I describe the regex grammar that Perl uses I will get the operator modifiers out of the way.

m/pattern/gimosx

Pattern matching returns either 1, if the pattern matches, or 0, if it does not. You must either specify a string through =~ or allow m// to search $_ which is the default input. The six available modifiers are shown in Table 9.4.

s/pattern/replacement/egimosx

Replaces pattern with replacement. If the pattern is found the function returns the number of matches made (will only be > 1 if you specify /g) or 0 if the pattern does not match. The flags which modify the behavior of s// are listed in Table 9.5.

tr/searchlist/replacements/cds

replaces occurrences of the search list with the corresponding value from the replacement list. The modifiers which can be applied to tr are shown in Table 9.6.

9.9.3 Components of Regular Expressions

A regex is made up of a number of different types of component. If you want to read and understand them you need to know what the components are.

	Meaning			Meaning
g	Find all occurrences of the pattern.		o	Only compile pattern once.
i	Case insensitive matching.		s	Treat string as single line.
m	Strings are treated as multiple lines.		x	Use extended regular expressions.

Table 9.4 Modifiers for pattern matching

	Meaning			Meaning
g	Find all occurrences of the pattern.		o	Only compile pattern once.
i	Case insensitive matching.		s	Treat string as single line.
m	Strings are treated as multiple lines.		x	Use extended regular expressions.
e	The replacement is treated as an expression and evaluated.			

Table 9.5 Modifiers for pattern replacement

	Meaning
c	The search list is complemented (logically NOTted).
s	Duplicate replaceable characters are given a single character.
d	Any characters which are not replaced will be deleted.

Table 9.6 Modifiers for list replacement

Alphanumeric Characters

A regex can contain literal strings and ordinary ASCII characters. These can be composed of any character which is not a metacharacter (see next). Characters can become special characters by putting a backslash in front of them. In regular expressions this is called quoting (in printf it was called escaping.)

The following script matches all instances of the patterns "grommit", "Grommit", and "grOmmiT" including the inverted commas. It also includes a match which will find those strings *without* the inverted commas:

```
1  #!/usr/bin/perl -w

   push(@strings, "Wallace and Grommit");
   push(@strings, qw(Wallace and "Grommit"));
5  push(@strings, "Wallace and grOmmit");

   foreach $item (@strings) {
       if($item =~ m/\"Grommit\"/ig) {
           print "$item matches\n";
10     }
       if($item =~ m/[G|g]rommit/ig) {
           print "$item matches\n";
       }
   }
15
   exit(0);
```

Metacharacters

Metacharacters are control sequences. They are not themselves matched but they alter the way that the system matches alphanumeric characters. If you want to match against a metacharacter you have to quote it with a backslash. I will explain how metacharacters work in Section 9.9.4. The list of metacharacters is:

```
\ | ( ) [ { ^ $ * + ?
```

To match for the pattern "Grommit$$$" try the following match:

```
1   #!/usr/bin/perl -w

    push(@strings, qw(Wallace and Grommit));
    push(@strings, qw(Wallace and Grommit$));
5   push(@strings, qw(Wallace and Grommit$$));
    push(@strings, qw(Wallace and Grommit$$$));

    foreach $item (@strings) {
        if($item =~ m/\"Grommit\${3}/ig) {
10          print "$item matches\n";
        }
    }

    exit(0);
```

Special Characters and Operators
Some ordinary characters can be used as operators. The set of characters is listed in Table 9.7, you met this table earlier when I was discussing regular expressions and JavaScript. I am reproducing it here to emphasize the similarities between the two languages in this respect.

Alternatives
If you need to match one, or more, from a set of patterns they are separated by |. The following example matches letters w through z or the string Wallace.

```
#!/usr/bin/perl -w

push(@strings, qw(Wallace and Grommit));
push(@strings, qw(wallace and Grommit));
push(@strings, qw(allace and Grommit));
push(@strings, qw(Walace and Grommit));

foreach $item (@strings) {
    if($item =~ m/[w-z]|Wallace/) {
        print "$item matches\n";
    }
}

exit(0);
```

Token	Description
^	Match at the start of the input string.
$	Match at the end of the input string.
*	Match 0 or more times.
+	Match 1 or more times.
?	Match 0 or 1 time.
a|b	Match a or b.
{n}	Match the string n times.
\d	Match a digit.
\D	Match anything except for digits.
\w	Match any alphanumeric character or the underscore.
\W	Match anything except alphanumeric characters or underscores.
\s	Match a whitespace character.
\S	Match anything except for whitespace characters.
[...]	Creates a set of characters, one of which must match if the operation is to be successful. If you need to specify a range of characters then separate the first and last with a hyphen: [0-9] or [D-G].
[^ ...]	Creates a set of characters which must not match. If any character in the set matches then the operation has failed. This fails if any lowercase letter from d to q is matched: [^ d-q].

Table 9.7 Special characters

	Meaning		Meaning
{n, m}	match between n and m times	{n, }	match at least n times
{n}	match exactly n times	*	match 0 or more times
+	match 1 or more times	?	match 0 or 1 time

Table 9.8 Pattern matching multipliers

Quantifiers

Sometimes you want to look for repeated patterns. The pattern matching operators attach only to the previous character, or set of characters if that set is placed inside parentheses. The quantifiers are shown in Table 9.8.

The next script shows how to specify the number of times a character must be matched. The first match looks for the string **allace** which must contain the repeated letter 1. The second match will only succeed if the string has a single 1:

```
1   #!/usr/bin/perl -w

    push(@strings, qw(Wallace and Grommit));
    push(@strings, qw(wallace and Grommit));
5   push(@strings, qw(Walace and Grommit));
    push(@strings, qw(allace and Grommit));

    foreach $item (@strings) {
        if($item =~ m/al{2}ace/) {
10          print "1. $item matches\n";
        }
    }
    foreach $item (@strings) {
        if($item =~ m/al?ace/) {
15          print "2. $item matches\n";
        }
    }

    exit(0);
```

Character Classes

It is possible to group together sets of characters when you want to perform the same operation using the whole set. Character classes are placed inside square brackets thus [class]. For instance, if you want a class containing all of the ASCII lower-case characters you would use [a-z]. Notice the minus sign which indicates that you want to use a range. The character class works exactly like the same set of individual characters separated by |. These are equivalent:

```
1   m/[a-e]/
    m/a|b|c|d|e/
```

Any of the special characters can be used in a class, and metacharacters are not interpreted as such inside square brackets. The exception to that is ^ which will be treated as a metacharacter if it is the first thing inside the brackets: it will invert the search so that it matches things not in the class. To match all of the metacharacters you could use:

```
1   m/[\|()[{^$*+?.]/
```

9.9.4 Rules for Matching

First it is probably important to realize that the matching algorithm is not intelligent – it simply applies patterns in the order that you specify along the string until it either runs out of string or matches successfully. The matching engine will keep trying things until the end of the string then back up to its last success, or the start of its last failure, and continue from there. Larry Wall codifies this behavior as *think locally, act globally*.[6]

rule one
> The engine matches as far left in the string as it can. Having found a match it will stop, unless you specify otherwise, it will not continue to search in the hope of finding a better match.

rule two
> The regular expression is a set of alternatives. If any one of the alternatives matches then the whole set is deemed to have matched. The alternatives are tried left to right in the order in which you specified them. Put the most likely alternative first and you will get more efficient code.

rule three
> An alternative will match if every item within the alternative matches in the left to right order.

rule four
> Each unit of the regex matches according to its type: brackets group items and store them for back-referencing. The dot . matches any character; a character class matches any character in the list.

---

 [6]These rules are abridged, simplified and further explained from the versions in *Programming Perl*.

9.9.5 A Few Other Things That You Should Know

backreferences

These are assigned according to sets of parentheses. A match from the first set will be assigned to $1, a match from the second set to $2 and so on. These backreferences are then available for further manipulation. Outside the pattern matching they are available as the scalars $1, $2 etc. The backreference holds the actual match, not the rules for that match taken from the regex.

Here is some code to swap the first two words in a string:

```
1  #! /usr/bin/perl -w

   $string = "here is a string string to test";
   $string =~ s/^([^ ]+) +([^ ]+)/$2 $1/x;
5  print "$string\n";
   exit(0);
```

How does that work? Here is the regex set out neatly with comments. Notice that the x flag lets me place comments inside the regex and set it out over a number of lines. I have included the flag in the one-line version simply to be consistent:

```
1  s/          # perform substitution
     ^          # at the start of the string
     ([^ ]+)    # find repeated non space characters
                # store that as \1
5    +          # move along the string
     ([^ ]+)    # find repeated non-space characters
                # store that as \2
     /$2 $1/    # substitute $2 for the value in
                # position 1 and $1 for the value
10              # in position two
     x;         # added to allow pretty printing
```

Backreferences – An Example

```
1  #! /usr/bin/perl -w

   my $string = "here is a string string to test";
   my $found = 0;
5  $found = ($string =~ m/\b(\w+)(\s+\1)+\b/ix);
   print "$found $1 $2\n";
   exit(0);
```

That is quite a complex regex. Before reading this explanation try to work it out for yourself.

```
1   m/          # it's a pattern match
      \b        # find a word boundary
      (\w+)       # followed by repeated word characters
                # save this as \1
5    (\s+\1)     # find repeated space followed by the
                # result of the first match
      +         # do this repeatedly
      \b        # finish at a word boundary
    /ix         # be case insensitive and allow pretty
10              # layouts
```

Does that make sense? Well the regular expression in there simply finds the first instance of a repeated word in the test string and displays it to the screen. Try reading the code again, now that you know what it does.

9.10 USING FILES

Perl makes using files very simple, certainly compared to the myriad subtle complexities of C or C++. The file is used through the mechanism of the filehandle. Filehandles are one of Perl's basic data types and are simply names which the programmer allocates to files, devices, sockets, or pipes. A large part of the complexity of using files is actually hidden behind the filehandle which presents a very clean interface.

open(FILEHANDLE, "[>|>>]filename")

open(FILEHANDLE)

To use a file you have to open it either for reading or writing. If you want to read from a file you supply a filehandle and the name of the file, which must be in quotes. To write to a file precede the filename by >, to append to the end of an existing file use >>. When you use the filehandle you can omit the $ sign, as you will see in the following examples. If the file does not exist then writing to the filehandle will create it. You will need to include error checking so that your script operates properly if you try to open a non-existent file:

```
1   $INPUT_FILE = "./datafile.dat";
    open($INPUT_FILE) or
        die("Unable to open $INPUT_FILE\n Program Aborting\n");

5   $OUTPUT_FILE = ">./storage.dat";
    open($OUTPUT_FILE) or
        die("Unable to open $OUTPUT_FILE\n Program Aborting\n");
```

You need an error message when trying to open a file for writing in case the operating system prevents you opening the file. Once you get this sort of major run-time error the only answer is to abort the program.

close(FILEHANDLE)

You can read from a file repeatedly until it is closed, although you would not want to read past the last line. If you try to open a file which is already open it will be closed then re-opened for you.

<FILEHANDLE>

To read from a file you use the line reading operator: <>. This reads and returns all characters up to and, including the newline. If you do not want the newline character, use chomp to remove it.

Create a simple data file containing:

```
1   cookies::chocolate::grahams
    cookies::fruit jelly::raspberry chewies
    cake::chocolate::black forest gateau
    cookies::plain::grahams
```

save it as cakes.dat and try the following script. This reads each line from the file, splits out the component substrings and prints them to STDOUT.

```
1   #!/usr/bin/perl -w

    $CAKES = "./cakes.dat";
    open(CAKES) or
5       die("Unable to open file $CAKES\n Program Aborting\n");

    print "Cake-a-base\n";
    while($line = <CAKES>) {
      chomp $line;
10     ($type, $filling, $style) = split(/::/, $line);
      printf("%s\t%s\t%s\n", uc($type), $style, $filling);
    }

    close CAKES;
15
    exit(0);
```

Hopefully that now makes sense. The line

```
while($line = <CAKES>) {
```

reads from the file until it reaches the end of the file. At this point the loop will terminate. When reading from file in this way the data comes out one line at a time. This is extremely useful because it means that processing file data does not require any extra effort on the programmer's part. Altering that program so that it writes its data into a file is very easy:

```
1  #!/usr/bin/perl -w

   $CAKES = "./cakes.dat";
   open(CAKES) or die("Unable to open source file $CAKES\n
5  Program Aborting\n");

   $NEWCAKES = ">./new.dat";
   open(NEWCAKES) or
       die("Unable to open target $NEWCAKES\n Program Aborting\n");
10
   print NEWCAKES "Cake-a-base\n";
   while($line = <CAKES>) {
     chomp $line;
     ($type, $filling, $style) = split(/::/, $line);
15   printf NEWCAKES ("%s\t%s\t%s\n", uc($type), $style, $filling);
   }

   close CAKES;

20 exit(0);
```

Writing to a file uses lines of text. In this script I use printf to write a formatted string to the file:

```
1  printf NEWCAKES ("%s\t%s\t%s\n", uc($type),
       $style, $filling);
```

When the end of the file is reached the line reader returns an undefined value, equivalent to false, and reading ceases. I use the close function in these programs to shut the files after I have finished with them. In Perl, unlike some other languages, you do not always have to *explicitly* close files but it is good practice to do so.

9.11 SUBROUTINES

Basic software engineering practice dictates that we do not write monolithic slabs of code. To make code readable, and hence maintainable, frequently used sections are placed in subroutines. If you are working through the book, you will already have used this idea successfully in JavaScript. In fact, if you have done much programming at all, you will have used subroutines, although they might have been called methods, operations, procedures, or functions in the language you were using. Subroutines are user-defined pieces of code which get used as if they were functions supplied with Perl, or downloaded as modules or libraries.

```
do subroutine([list])
use module_name
require expression
```

These are all ways in which code from another file can be included in the current script. In the chapters on CGI scripting, I will be demonstrating how to include other code in your scripts. Usually, though, you'll be using subroutines that you have defined and which live in the same file as the calling procedure.

```
sub function_name
```

Subroutines are declared like this. Simply put sub before the function name and enclose its code in brackets.

```
&subroutine([list])
```

Yet another funny symbol there. This is the way that you call subroutines. The ampersand is used to stop the namespace getting cluttered.[7] Strictly speaking the ampersand is not needed in Perl 5; however, I find that using it makes function calls nice and clear. You optionally pass a list of parameters into the subroutine. The list can, of course, contain just a single item:

```
1   #! /usr/bin/perl -w

    $a_number = 34.5;
    $square = &mysquare($a_number);
5   print "$square\n";

    exit(0);

    sub mysquare {
```

---

[7]You will find that this namespace stuff really stands out. Once you know what is going on it makes the code far more readable.

```
10      $in = @_[0];
        return $in * $in;
      }
```

Perl does not require function (or subroutine) prototypes so there is no way of knowing in advance (i.e., when interpreting the code) how many parameters a function will get. Each function receives its parameters as an arbitrary list, which is in fact passed as an array. This array of parameters is called @_ and can be manipulated just like any other array. Therefore parameters are accessible through @_[0] etc. (strictly that is $_[0] of course), and can be copied into scalars or into other arrays.

return expression

This is used to get values back from a subroutine. If you send just a single scalar as a parameter then you can only return a scalar; if you called the subroutine with a list of values then you will be able to get a list back.

local (expression)

Sometimes you want to temporarily manipulate a global variable before resetting it to its previous value. This is especially useful with arrays and hashes, and Perl provides a scoping mechanism to allow this. Within a subroutine, or any other block structure, you can declare a local version of the variable using the local keyword. This local variable can be manipulated in any way that you like but when you leave the block the global will still be there unaltered. Subroutines called from the block will see and be able to use the local version of the variable rather than the global one.

my(expression)

If you do not need the danger and power of local variables, or you want to declare a variable which can not be seen by subroutines you modify it using my. These private variables are not visible until after they have been declared so you have to take care to declare and initialize them before you use them.

9.11.1 Parameters into an Array

Subroutines are fairly straightforward to use once you understand the @_ array and how you can manipulate it. We have already looked at arrays in some detail, so this next example should be pretty straightforward. What you will notice is that the parameters are passed into an array inside the subroutine. Each parameter becomes a new array item. This is often more useful than passing the parameter values into a set of scalars as the array can be easier to manipulate. The mechanism also lets you pass a *lot* of parameters – try passing twenty parameters and then copying each one into a separate scalar!

The script takes a number of strings as arguments and returns the longest string and its length:

```perl
#! /usr/bin/perl -w

# find the longest of a set of strings
$fred = "Hello, I'm Fred";
$jack = "Hi!, Jack's the name";
$jill = "I'm Jill, but then you knew that anyway!";
$mary = "Wibble";

@answer = &Longest($fred, $jack, $jill, $mary);
$size = pop(@answer);
$long = pop(@answer);
printf("%s : %s\n", $long, $size);

exit(0);

sub Longest {
  my @param = @_;
  $long = shift(@param);
  $next = "";

  $size = length($long);
  foreach $next (@param) {
    if($size < length($next)) {
      $long = $next;
      $size = length($long);
    }
  }

  push(@it, $long, $size);
  return @it;
}
```

Notice that I call the subroutine with a list and am able to return an array. I use this to get two values back, rather as you might use a structure in C or a small class in C++ to get a set of values back from a function. The Perl implementation looks neat and is easy to use. As you use Perl more and more, you will find lots of these excellent design features. This probably results from its being an evolving language.

Once the parameters have arrived at the function, they need to be made available to it. Even if you are only passing a single value it will be passed as an array. Of course that array will only have one item, nonetheless you need to be aware that you are going to be handling arrays of parameters. The parameter array always has the strange name of @_. In the example I copy the values into a local array within the function using:

```perl
my @param = @_;
```

If I had only wanted to use a single parameter value inside the function I might have written something like:

```perl
my $param = $_[0];
```

Which would extract the first item from the parameter array. Remember if you want to use an array as if it were a single entity you need to refer to it with a $ rather than @.

9.11.2 Parameters into a Hash

The parameter set can be passed into a hash as well as a scalar and an array. If the data structure which is going to receive the parameters is a hash then Perl takes the parameters in pairs. The first parameter in each pair becomes the key, the second becomes the value. It is therefore important if you are going to use this technique that you supply pairs of parameters in the correct order.

```perl
1   #! /usr/bin/perl -w

    $fred = "Hello, I'm Fred";
    $jack = "Hi!, Jack's the name";
5   $jill = "I'm Jill, but then you knew that anyway!";
    $mary = "Wibble";

    @answer = &HashParam("fred" => $fred,
        "jack" => $jack,
10      "jill" => $jill,
        "mary" => $mary);


    exit(0);

15  sub HashParam {
        my %param = @_;
        foreach $key(keys %param){
            printf("%s : %s\n", $key, $param{$key});
        }
20  }
```

9.12 BITS AND PIECES
9.12.1 Operators

I have already used and described a few of the operators which Perl provides. Table 9.9 lists the others.

Op	Meaning	Op	Meaning
>	Numeric greater than	gt	String greater than
<	Numeric less than	lt	String less than
<=	Less than or equal	le	String less than or equal
==	Numeric equals	eq	String equals
!=	Numeric not equals	ne	String not equals
<=>	Numeric comparison	cmp	String comparison
&&	Logical AND	||	Logical OR
=	Assignment	+=	Add two values then assign the result to the operand on the left
-=	Subtract then assign the result to the operand on the left	*=	Multiply then assign the result to the operand on the left
/=	Divide then assign the result to the operand on the left	.=	Concatenate two strings then assign the result to the operand on the left
%=	Modulus division then assign the result to the operand on the left	++	Autoincrement
--	Autodecrement	!	Logical not
=~	Apply a pattern matching operation to a string		

Table 9.9 Logical operators (text and numerical)

When discussing scalar variables I used this simple script:

```
1  #!/usr/bin/perl -w
```

```
   $item = "3245.02e4";
   $item2 = $item;

5
   $item .= "12";
   $item2 = $item2 + "12";


   print $item."\n";
10 print $item2."\n";
   exit(0);
```

The numerical operation could have been written more concisely as

```
$item2 += "12";
```

Unless you have used languages such as C, C++ or Java, that is pretty cryptic stuff. It is not as awkward as it appears to be. In fact it is a more efficient way of incrementing and decrementing values. If you have not seen this sort of thing before, read this explanation carefully; this is an important piece of notation as the same idea is used with many string and regular expression operations.

First the easy case. It is common in programs to want to alter the value of a numeric variable by 1, for instance, when iterating through a loop or moving along an array. You could write that change as:

```
1  $variable = $variable + 1;
   $variable = $variable - 1;
```

but that can be time consuming, especially if you use meaningful variable names, which can get quite long. Therefore C and its descendants allow you to use what are called prefix and postfix incrementation and decrementation. To change a variable by 1 write this:

```
1  $variable++;
   $variable--;
```

You will see these conventions used in a lot of loops. In the for loop we write:

```
1  for($variable = 0; $variable < $enough; $variable++) {
   ...
   }
```

The value of variable is increased by 1 at the end of the loop, just before the closing bracket and is checked against the terminating condition just as the loop restarts. To move along an array we might use [8]:

---

[8]Yes, I could combine the increment and the print into one statement. I didn't do that because I wanted the code to be clear.

```
1   $count = 0;
    while($count <= $arraysize) {
        print $array[$count];
        $count++;
5   }
```

So that is the simpler example. What of $item += "12"? Well instead of increasing the value on the left by 1, here we are increasing it by more than 1. In this case $item becomes equal to its current value plus 12. Again, it is quick to type and, once you are used to it, this sort of notation is much easier to read when looking at a piece of code. So we use:

```
1   $variable += $amount;
    $variable -= $amount;
```

rather than:

```
1   $variable = $variable + $amount;
    $variable = $variable - $amount;
```

Other operations such as modulus division, multiplication and even string concatenation can work in similar ways. Strings are concatenated using the dot operator:

```
1   #!/usr/bin/perl -w

    $item = "Chris";
    $item .= " Bates";
5   print "$item\n";

    exit(0);
```

When using regular expressions, or performing more straightforward pattern matching, the operation has to be applied to a string. The following example shows how the notation is used:

```
1   #!/usr/bin/perl -w

    $string = "foobar was my Uncle";
    print "$string\n";
5
    $string =~ s/foobar/Fred/

    print "$string\n";
    exit(0);
```

The =~ operator applies the pattern matching operation on its right side to the string value on its left. In the example a string substitution is performed and the value held in the scalar is altered.

9.12.2 Comments

Any program that you write, apart from the sort of trivial examples I have used here, needs comments. Comments are useful when you are developing the code and even more so when you come back to maintain it. Start your scripts with some comments which describe what the program should do, who wrote it and when. Also if you are updating the script you need to include a version number so that users know they have the most recent. Each subroutine and any complex loops need comments explaining what you are trying to achieve. Perl can be fairly self-documenting but when you are using regular expressions it can also be pretty cryptic.

In Perl, comments start with the hash symbol # and run to the end of the line. They are easy, so use them!

9.12.3 Special Characters

Perl has many special variables which mean something to the interpreter. These are accessible to the programmer but you will probably never need most of them – they provide a shorthand for the gurus. These are the ones that you ought to recognize and be able to use.

$_

the default input, the default pattern-matching space. Perl often assumes that you want to use $_ unless you tell it otherwise. It will be used by:

- functions such as print,
- pattern matching operations such as s///, tr///, or m// if they are called without =~,
- the foreach loop as default iterator.

$0

The name of the script currently being executed.

$ARGV

The name of the current file when reading from <ARGV>.

%ENV

The hash containing the current environment. We'll be using this when we start writing CGI scripts.

9.12.4 Garbage Collection

Some of the commonest mistakes that all programmers make involve memory allocation and de-allocation. Languages such as Perl automatically manage memory for the programmer in a process called garbage collection. The mechanism used by Perl involves tracking references to variables: once they are no longer referenced they can safely be removed from memory.

You can create data structures which can never be deleted in this way: some tree structures, for instance, involve circular links. If you do not understand what I am writing then you probably could not create such a structure anyway. If you do know what I mean, take care with your complex data structures.

9.12.5 Command-line Parameters

Perl has various command-line switches. I have already shown you -w: here are some more that you might want to use:

-

   ends switch processing. Any switches which follow this will be ignored.

-c

   checks the syntax of the script and exits without executing it.

-d

   runs the debugger.

-e

   allows you to run scripts from the command line. If you use this switch then Perl will not bother looking for a filename on the command line.

-I

   followed by directories which are to be added to the search path for modules.

-S

   forces Perl to search your PATH environment variable. Can be useful if your operating system does not support #!.

-T

   switches on taint checking. This is useful when developing/running CGI scripts. See Chapter 10 for more on this.

-v

   prints the version of the Perl executable you are running.

-w

   prints useful warnings about the syntax of the script.

9.12.6 Things I Have Left Out

There is much to Perl that I have not covered. I have shown you enough of the language to start writing CGI scripts. These are relatively simple applications; if you want to know more, or all, about Perl buy one of the books listed in the reading list. I have not said anything about:

- references, hard and otherwise
- nested data structures, hashes of arrays or hashes of hashes or arrays of arrays or arrays of hashes
- objects, Perl is now an OO language too[9]
- cooperating with other languages such as C
- cooperating with shells
- the standard Perl libraries
- error messages.

EXERCISES

Perl

1. List five benefits that Perl can bring if used for solving text-based problems.
2. How does the flexibility of Perl affect the way that programmers attack problems?
3. Briefly outline the advantages and disadvantages of the open-source or free software model of development.
4. If you do not have access to Perl either install it on your own system or ask your site system administrator for help. Look through the documentation that accompanies your distribution. It is especially important that you find out how to use the perldoc utility to read POD documents.
5. Open a command shell and type `perl -v`. What happened?
6. Create a directory for your Perl scripts. Enter and execute a simple version of the classic "Hello World" program.
7. Try using a number of editors and find one that suits the way that you will work with Perl.

Basic Perl Exercises

1. Write a script which contains the various types of loop. Print out the loop counter each time that the script iterates.

---

[9]It's sort-of OO-ish, but not in the way that Smalltalk or Python (for instance) are.

2. Enter and execute the script from Section 9.7.1 which prompts for user input then displays the input back to the user. Try running the script using the -w flag.
3. Write a loop in which your code leaps out of the loop if a boolean condition is met.
4. Write an if ... elsif ... else structure which chooses between four alternatives.

Perl and Data

1. What are the basic data types in Perl?
2. Write a script which accepts different data types at the command line and performs some simple processing on them. Try some basic arithmetic functions and string concatenation to start with.
3. How can a Perl variable act as a string and a number?
4. What is an array?
5. Write a script which accepts inputs from the user, stores all of the strings in an array, and then displays them in reverse order.
6. Create a hash array of the days of the week. Print out the key:value pairs from the start of the array. Try printing individual values by accessing them through their key.
7. Make a list of six uses for each Perl data type.
8. Modify your script from Exercise 6, to read out the values from the hash and sort them into ascending alphabetical order.
9. Run the script from Section 9.6. Can you modify your days of the week script to split the syllable day from each value as it is read out?
10. Try this larger problem:
   Create two text files. Each needs to contain a number of lines of data. The first should be a list of unique identifiers (keys), names, and addresses. In the second file put the unique identifiers and information such as favorite food, hair color, shoe size. Separate the fields of each database table with pairs of colons : :.
   Write a pair of loops which read the data from the files into arrays and which display the contents of those arrays. You may choose to place whole lines into each array cell or to use arrays of arrays.
   Read all of the keys and one associated field from each file. You will have to use a pair of hashes for this. Now search the arrays and print out the keys and pairs of values. Do this only where a key occurs in both hashes. For instance:
   from file one the script reads:
   1 jack
   2 mary
   3 harry

```
34 mary2
56 fred
```

from file two the script reads:

```
1 beer
2 icecream
34 butterscotch
```

the script displays:

```
1 jack beer
2 mary icecream
34 mary2 butterscotch
```

Text Processing

1. List the text handling facilities which Perl provides.
2. Write a script which splits strings apart on predefined characters. This is the type of script that you might use to handle simple flat-file databases.
3. Modify your string-splitting script so that it will accept a sentence as input from the user and split it apart into individual words.
4. Now alter your script so that it builds a new string which is made by reversing the order of all of the words in the input string. Use only string-splitting and concatenating functions if possible.
5. Enter and run the date creation script from Section 9.8.3. Make sure that you understand how this works.
6. Modify your string-manipulating script so that alternate words appear as either all upper-case or all lower-case letters.
7. Using the script in Section 9.8.5 as a starting point write a script which manipulates the printing of numbers and strings through the `printf` function.
8. Try printing a large block of text by using the << operator.

Pattern Matching

1. The next few exercises all involve manipulating a string through pattern matching. Start off with this first example and once you understand it add in the code for succeeding examples. Do not move on until you understand what the code does *and* how it works.

```
1   #! /usr/bin/perl -w
    $replace = $ARGV[0];
    $line = "this is a test test string string";

5   if($line =~ /$replace/) {
        print("$replace was found\n");
    }
    exit(0);
```

```
2.  1   if($line =~ m/$replace/) {
            print("$line\n");
        }
```

```
3.  1   if($line =~ s/($replace#) \1/$1/g){
            print("$line\n");
        }
```

```
4.  1   if($line =~ /\b(\w+?)\s+ \1/mxgi) {
            print "Duplicate word: $1\n";
        }
```

```
5.  1   $line =~ s/^([^ ]*) *([^ ]*)/$2 $1/;
        print "$line\n";
        $line = "this is a test";
```

```
6.  1   $line =~ s/^([^ ]*) *([^ ] *)/$2 $1/;
        print "$line\n";
        $line = "this is a test";
```

```
7.  1   $line =~ s/^([^ ]*) *([^ ])*/$2 $1/;
        print "$line\n";
        $line = "this is a test";
```

```
8.  1   print uc($line)."\n";
        $line =~ tr/[a-z]/[A-Z]/;
        print "$line\n";
```

```
9.  1   $line = "this is a test";
        $line =~ s/(\w+)/\U$1/g;
        print "$line\n";
```

10. ```
    1  $line = "this is a test";
       $line =~ s/(\w+)/\u$1/g;
       print "$line\n";
    ```

11. Try to write a function which finds the first two pairs of matching words in a string.

File Handling

1. List the differences between a program file and a data file.
2. What is meant by the terms *reading* and *writing* when thinking about file handling?
3. What does *appending* mean?
4. To master file handling, code and run the "cake-a-base" example from this chapter.
5. What is a subroutine?
6. Can you list five reasons for using subroutines in your programs?
7. Can you think why code based around subroutines might be less efficient when the program is running?
8. Run the following simple example, then modify the code to perform some useful function!

```
1  #!/usr/bin/perl -w

   print "In the main program\n";
   &mySub();
5  &mySub();
   print "In the main program\n";

   exit(0);

10 sub mySub {
       print "\tNow in the subroutine\n";
   }
```

9. Next try running the following, more complex, example. Once it works modify the script so that the user can interactively choose which function is run. Can you also modify the script so that the selection of function takes place from the command line?

```
1  #!/usr/bin/perl -w

   $value = 32;
   print "Value starts as $value\n";
```
```

```
5   &mySquare($value);
    print "Value now $value\n";
    $value = &myCube($value);
    print "Value finishes as $value\n";
    exit(0);
10
    sub mySquare {
        $input = shift(@_);
        $square = $input * $input;
        print "Value of input to subroutine is $input\n";
15      print "Value of square is $square\n";
    }

    sub myCube {
        $input = shift(@_);
20      $cube = ($input * $input) * $input;
        return $cube;
    }
```

10. What does the shift function do?

CGI Scripting

10

T he Internet has become a network of interactive, distributed applications. Client software based anywhere in the world can access remote data stored on Web servers and can even modify that data. Clearly the majority of Web-based data is not modifiable, but when we design and build commercial Web sites we have to allow users to update our databases. That sounds rather worrying: it could be a security nightmare but I am not talking about allowing access to an organization's key data, rather I am simply suggesting that Web surfers must be able to give you information which you may choose to store and later use.

The basic mechanism for getting feedback from users is the HTML form which we looked at in Section 3.4. Having supplied a form through which the user can supply information, we must create applications which extract that data and process it. These might simply send an e-mail thanking the browser for their visit or might process credit card details, product orders, and address information, update stock databases, request delivery dates, and return an appropriate confirmation to the browser. Between these two extremes lie a plethora of approaches to making commercial Web sites interactive. In this chapter I will be examining some of the techniques that are used to process information and explaining some of the reasoning that lies behind them. In the accompanying exercises I will be demonstrating how to apply these ideas. By the end you will be capable of building a primitive site with some form of shopping cart application.

10.1 WHAT IS CGI?

CGI is an acronym for the Common Gateway Interface which is a standard protocol for running programs within a Web server. The CGI protocol allows external programs, those you develop, to interface with programs such as database management software and to access the networking facilities provide by the HTTP server software. HTML documents are generally static once created;[1] they do not change while displayed on the browser. CGI programs are dynamic; the state of their variables alters as they execute.

10.2 DEVELOPING CGI APPLICATIONS

A CGI script can be developed in any language. The only limitation is provided by the software that your Web server can run. You can write CGI applications in either interpreted or compiled languages so Perl, Basic, Python, Java, C, and C++ would all be good choices. There are security issues related to running compiled programs, and because CGI applications tend to be fairly trivial, large languages such as C++ and Java are often overkill. The general consensus is that interpreted languages provide the best solutions, with Perl and Visual Basic clearly leading the field.

The vast majority of Web servers run on UNIX boxes. Most CGI scripting involves manipulation of text data and many Web masters prefer to use software which is both free[2] and which has wide ranging technical support available on the Internet. Perl is the *de facto* standard CGI scripting language for all of these reasons, and as we saw previously it is also immensely powerful. Perl is continually being developed and enhanced, there are very many freely available modules created by other Perl users which support and ease the development of Web scripts. We shall be looking at a few of these modules later in this section.

Visual Basic is being heavily pushed by Microsoft along with the Active Server Pages (ASP) and .Net technologies. All of these are proprietary products, VB will not run on most servers, and the majority of HTTP server software does not support ASP at the moment. VB is an interface-driven development system, whereas CGI scripts are command-line based, leading to a fundamental conflict between what the product is designed to do and what CGI script developers require.

Having selected a development language, you need to choose a method for developing your scripts. The obvious choice is to hack some code, upload it to the Web server, and try to run it. Obvious, but not a good choice: imagine a script with a non-terminating loop. How would you spot that bug when running it remotely? How would you examine any error messages that you might be directing to STDERR? What sort of load would an unfinished script put upon the server? The sensible approach is to develop your scripts on your local PC or workstation, test that they run from the command-line, or a Web server installed on your PC, and only upload them to the server once the logic of the scripts has been debugged. The only areas left for bugs are then interaction with the server: parsing

---

[1] We have seen how to add dynamics on the client side through JavaScript applications.
[2] Free in the free-source sense rather than the monetary sense. Take a look at the Free Software Foundation Web site (http://www.fsf.org) for more details.

incoming data and returning data. If you have developed sensibly, even these will not be major problems.

10.3 PROCESSING CGI
10.3.1 Rationale

There are a number of libraries available from the Comprehensive Perl Archive Network, CPAN, sites which help with the problem of parsing input from the user. Whenever possible these should be used. They handle difficult MIME types very effectively. I will be discussing the most popular of these, `CGI.pm`.

Before looking at some code let us consider what CGI data is, where it comes from and how our scripts are expected to deal with it. When a user submits a Web form, the contents of that form are extracted by the browser and packaged as a message which is returned to a Web server. We saw in Section 3.4 that a form contains the URL of a server and the name of an application on that server. The browser transmits the data to the server. The server must then pass the data to the appropriate application for further processing. So what is a server? Well, in the example of a Web server, it is simply a piece of software executing on a machine which can process requests from Web browsers.

 NOTE *If you want to learn to develop CGI scripts, or ASPs or Java Servlets you will need access to the appropriate Web server. If you are learning this stuff at work or in education you may already have access to a Web server: ask the system administrator how to use it. If you are learning on your own machine you can download and install a Web server of your own. I am not going to tell you how to configure or administer your own set-up since the variations between systems are extremely complex. Most come with lots of documentation, and you can buy good quality texts about popular servers, such as Apache.*

Creating an application from the ground up, which can handle data sent from a Web form is a non-trivial piece of programming. It is not difficult once you have seen it done, on the other hand it does require quite a lot of code which is why, generally, it is handled by add-on modules. The code is split into two logical components:

- something to extract the data which is returned from a Web form,
- and something to create a new page which is sent back to the browser.

You cannot simply write a script which handles the first part but does not do the second. The CGI protocol expects that you are going to be sending some data back to the browser. If your script does not do this then the Web server will do it for you. The Apache server sends back an HTML page which says there has been an *Internal Server Error* due to a misconfiguration of the Web server. It also writes a message into the error log it maintains which on my systems says:

```
[Tues Sept 6 21:12:03 2005] [error] [client 127.0.0.1]
    Premature end of script headers:
    /home/httpd/cgi-bin/sample.cgi
```

That simply means that your script did not obey the protocol by returning a correctly formatted HTTP message in response to data from a Web form.

We are going to use CGI.pm to parse the data and to create the page which we will be returning to the browser. The module is very robust and complete and includes a lot of functionality which we will not be using. You should not worry if modules do things that you do not need. What is important is that the code in the module is robust and efficient and that it does what you want. Those parts of a module which you are not using will remain available for times when you do need them.

10.4 INTRODUCTION TO CGI.PM

CGI.pm is a library of routines that simplify the creation and processing of HTML Web forms. It has two aspects: the processing of data returned from client browsers and the dynamic creation of HTML pages containing Web forms. The ability to easily extract values from returned data and create dynamic forms gives the developer a relatively simple way of maintaining state across the Web. Later in this chapter I will give examples of how to do just that, one using cookies, others without.

Whenever you write a Web application you should use CGI.pm, at least for extracting data from forms. It does this safely and can handle POST, GET, and multi-part MIME data. Mostly you should use CGI.pm because it is safely and securely used by untold thousands of commercial sites around the Web and any problems with it have long since been ironed out.

Copious documentation is supplied with the CGI.pm module. If you want to do anything even remotely challenging with the module, you must read it. You can get at the documentation by giving the following command at a system prompt:

```
perldoc CGI
```

The CGI.pm can be used in a simple functional programming style or in an object-oriented way. The latter is more commonly used since most computing students are taught that way of programming as their main approach. Both give access to the same facilities within the module and the choice of which to use is left to the individual developer. Through this chapter I will use the object-oriented style. Here is a simple functional example which illustrates the difference.

```
1   #!/usr/bin/perl
    use CGI qw/:standard/;

    print header;
5   print start_html('hello world');
    print h1('hello world');
    print end_html;
```

A single CGI object is created automatically at the top of the script. This remains anonymous throughout the program. Access to its functions is implicit in each function call. The functions which the CGI module provides are accessed using their name. In this example an HTML page is being created and returned to the calling browser.

If you want to try it out put the code in a file called `hello.cgi` which is placed in a directory that your Web server can see and from which it can run CGI scripts. You will need to check the configuration files for the server if you are running your own to find out how to do this. By default, Apache has a directory called `cgi-bin` at the top of its installation hierarchy, for example under

        c:\Program Files\Apache Group\Apache2

Having the correct directory does not mean that Perl scripts will execute. You need to have a Perl interpreter and modules. Then you need to configure the server to find them and hand the processing of CHI scripts across correctly. This is sometimes configured for you when you install a Web server, more usually though you will need to read the documentation or find a local expert who will help.

If you are using a server which someone else administers you must ask them where to put the file and what to do to make sure that it is accessible.

Once installed and configured you can view the file using a Web browser with a URL such as

        http://localhost/cgi-bin/hello.cgi

In the object-oriented approach each script creates a CGI object. This has the same methods as the default one but you must make explicit calls to the object. Method calls in `CGI.pm` are written using the referencing notation – the arrow (->). Put the name of the CGI object, then the arrow, then the method with any parameters in parentheses:

        $cgiObject->method(parameters);

Most of the methods can accept a list of parameters, some or all of which may be optional. Here is an example, taken from the `CGI.pm` documentation, of how that might look in practice:

```
1   #!/usr/bin/perl
    use CGI qw/:standard/;
```

```
   $q = new CGI;
5  print $q->header,
          $q->start_html('hello world'),
          $q->h1('hello world'),
          $q->end_html;
```

10.5 CGI.PM METHODS

CGI.pm has a lot of methods. If you want to know how they all work you will have to read perldoc CGI. That is a long document and I do not feel that I need to cover the same ground here. Instead I will just cover the main points of extracting form data and creating simple pages. In the example that follows I will show how to use form data to maintain state between interactions without recourse to the dreaded cookie file. And at the end of the chapter I will show you how to use cookies too.

The main way that CGI.pm is used is to safely extract data and keywords returned from a Web form. These values may then be manipulated by any Perl script and can even form the basis of new HTML pages.

10.5.1 Creating CGI objects

The basic CGI object is created at the start of a script and contains all of the data and keywords that the form has returned. The following line of code parses the input and stores it in an object:

```
$query = new CGI;
```

Notice that you do not have to tell the program to extract the data. That is done automatically as part of the object creation routine. Sometimes you will want to create an empty CGI object. This is useful if you are dynamically creating an HTML page whose content is based upon the current state of your script. You might, for instance, want to do this so that you can send customized error pages back to users. To create an empty CGI object:

```
$page = new CGI("");
```

10.5.2 Extracting Parameter Names

If your object contains returned data, you need to be able to extract that data so that you can manipulate it. Again CGI.pm makes this *very* simple. The first thing that you must do is extract a list of the parameters from the GET or POST data. The following method call puts all of the parameter names into an array:

```
@parameter_array = $query->param;
```

The parameters are ordered as they were submitted by the user, which may not be the order that you expect. Therefore writing something like

```
$value = $parameter_array[0];
```

may not give you the outcome that you expected. The HTML form and CGI script will have been designed at the same time. This means that you know what parameters you expect to get from the client. There is no guarantee that they will have completed all of the fields on the form, which means that you cannot rely on the CGI object containing data for a particular field. Whilst you can use JavaScript to enforce completion at the client, server-side checking adds additional robustness to your system and is not a significant overhead.

10.5.3 Fetching Parameter Values
Once you have an array of parameter names you can start to extract the values that are associated with those parameters. Again this is easy with CGI.pm. Simply use the parameter name in a method invocation:

```
1   $name = $parameter_array[0];
    $value = $query->param($name);
    $value2 = $query->param('date');
```

To set the value of $value the parameters array is accessed and the returned parameter name used for the lookup. This is safer than the previous example simply because, having acquired the parameter name, it can be checked against expected names and processed properly. The second scalar $value2 is set using a call with an explicit parameter name. Often this is the way that you will extract values. Most of your CGI scripts will be responding to data from Web pages that you have also designed. Therefore you will know the names of the parameters that you are getting back and will not need to use the parameter array.

10.6 CREATING HTML PAGES DYNAMICALLY
Many of the methods that CGI.pm provides are designed to simplify the creation of forms based upon data values that have been returned by the client. You can look them up in the documentation. Instead I will concentrate on showing how to return a basic HTML page.

10.6.1 The HTTP Header
Remember that every page needs to send some MIME information to the browser so that it knows how to handle the data. Getting this bit wrong, or missing it altogether, causes the frustrating incomplete headers error messages that all CGI developers see so regularly.

To send the standard HTTP header using CGI.pm simply:

```
print $page->header;
```

That prints `Content-type: text/html`. If you want to send a different MIME type, for instance `image/gif` then you should supply it as a parameter:

```
print $query->header('image/gif');
```

10.6.2 Starting and Finishing a Page

Anything that you want to place in either the `<head>` section or the `<body>` tag must be passed as a parameter to the `start_html` method. Useful information that you can give here includes the page title, author name, meta information, address of the stylesheet (if any), and basic page formatting information.

The parameter-passing style used by `CGI.pm` is different to anything that you may have seen before. Within the parentheses the parameter name is preceded by a - sign. Parameter values are passed as quoted strings and are separated from the name of the parameter by the => notation, which is used when creating hashes.

The basic form of the method call is:

```
print $page->start_html(-parameter1=>'value',
                        -parameter2=>'value');
```

The following parameters are commonly used with the `start_html` method:

title

This sets the title of the document through the `<title>. </title>` attribute.

author

This sets the author through the `author` attribute of the document `<head>` section.

meta

This is used to create meta information. Multiple data items can be passed in the one parameter. Note the use of curly brackets to surround the list of values:

```
1  -meta=>{'keywords'=>'some important words',
           'expires'=>'expiry date'}
```

style

This identifies an external stylesheet that you want linked into the document.

```
-style=>{-src=>'somepath/somestyle.css'}
```

other parameters

If you pass in parameters which `CGI.pm` does not support it will include them in the `<body>` tag. Instances of this might include the use of `bgcolor` or `text` formatting attributes.

Here is some code showing how start_html can be used:

```
1   print $page->start_html{
      -title=>'A Web Page',
      -style=>{-src=>'./main.css'},
      -bgcolor=>'#e3e3e3',
5     -text=>'red'};
```

To finish off the page with the </body></html> tags use

```
print $page->end_html;
```

10.6.3 The Body of the Page

If you want to create non-form pages, then CGI.pm is not going to give much help with the body of your page. Although it has some *HTML shortcuts*, in my view these are actually more complex than writing your own print statements. Look at these two code fragments and decide which you prefer:

```
print a({-href=>'nextpage.html'}, "Next");
```

or

```
print "<a href="nextpage.html">Next</a>\n";
```

I will briefly describe how to use the shortcuts. For more detail, as ever, read the perldoc supplied with the module. To get access to these shortcuts you need to use a special declaration when including the module:

```
use CGI /qw:standard/;
```

Some HTML tags have attributes; most have values. These are provided as parameters to the shortcut. To give a value use:

```
    h1("A Title")
```

and to supply values for attributes:

```
1   a({-href=>'index.html',
      -target=>'_TOP'
    });
```

Notice that the attributes have their standard HTML names and are preceded by a dash. The values are passed in using the syntax that we saw when looking at hashes. Guess how the attribute-value pairs are stored?

Finally, you can pass an array of values to some shortcuts and magical things happen. Imagine that you wanted to create a list of items. Coding something like:

```
1  li(-type=>'square', "first");

   li(-type=>'square', "second");

5  li(-type=>'square', "third");
```

would be rather tedious. CGI.pm has the capability to distribute values for you:

```
li({-type=>'square', ["first","second","third"]});
```

would give the same set of list items. You will see some of this in action during the examples later in this chapter. The CGI.pm documentation includes the following example to show how this distribution of values can be used to dynamically create tables:

```
1  print table({-border=>undef},
        caption('Should You Eat Your Vegetables?'),
        Tr({-align=>"CENTER",-valign=>"TOP"},
          [
5          th(['Vegetable', 'Breakfast','Lunch','Dinner']),
           td(['Tomatoes' , 'no', 'yes', 'yes']),
           td($refval),
           td(['Onions'    , 'yes','yes', 'yes'])
          ]));
```

Well you can also create those arrays of parameters dynamically and pass references to them:

```
1  #!/usr/bin/perl -Tw

   use CGI qw/:standard/;
   use CGI::Carp(fatalsToBrowser);
5  use strict;

   my $page = new CGI;
   my $refval = ['Broccoli' , 'no', 'no',  'yes'];
   print(
10      $page->header(),
        $page->start_html("Menu"),
        $page->h1("Menu"));

   print table({-border=>undef},
15      caption('Should You Eat Your Vegetables?'),
```

```
          Tr({-align=>"CENTER",-valign=>"TOP"},
            [
             th(['Vegetable', 'Breakfast','Lunch','Dinner']),
             td(['Tomatoes' , 'no', 'yes', 'yes']),
20           td($refval),
             td(['Onions'    , 'yes','yes', 'yes'])
            ]));
    print $page->end_html;


25  exit(0);
```

10.7 USING CGI.pm – AN EXAMPLE

Some of the greatest benefits that CGI.pm brings include, of course, robustness and also a reduction in the amount of code which developers have to craft for themselves. The following simple script extracts the parameters from the HTTP request and displays their names and values in an unordered list. Notice that I am using a mixture of shortcuts from the CGI module and print statements to create the output page.

```
1  #!/usr/bin/perl -Tw

   use CGI qw/:standard/;
   use CGI::Carp(fatalsToBrowser);
5  use strict;

   my $page = new CGI;

   print(
10     $page->header(),
       $page->start_html("Parameters and values"),
       $page->h1("Parameters and values"));

   my @param_names = $page->param;
15 my $next;
   print "<ul>";

   foreach $next (@param_names) {
     print "<li>". $next ." => ". $page->param($next)."</li>";
20 }
```

```
print "</ul>";
print $page->end_html();
print "\n";

exit(0);
```

25

Running the script is easy. As an exercise you might want to create an HTML form and experiment with GET and POST. If you do not want to write any HTML just open a browser and enter the URL of the script. Parameters are separated from the URL using ? and from each other using &. Parameter names and values are joined using =. In this example I pass in a value which contains a space. This must be replaced with the appropriate escape sequence, %20 in this case.

```
http://localhost/~chris/cgi-bin/params.cgi?name=floyd&breed=scruffy%20mongrel
```

10.8 ADDING ROBUSTNESS

In Section 9.3 I said that you should develop your Perl scripts using the -w flag. That prints out some moderately useful warnings from the compiler which will help you to narrow down problems in your code. Using -w is only the first step that you can take in the process of creating good Perl scripts. In this book I am not going to describe how to use the Perl debugger – if you want information on that, try looking in the documentation that came with your Perl installation.[3] I am, however, going to give you some guidance through a few topics that will help. Most errors that you will make writing CGI scripts can be trapped, analyzed, and repaired fairly easily and you will probably only invoke the debugger on a few occasions.

Writing safe scripts has two aspects: first ensuring that your code is correct, and does what you expect; second ensuring that the data you are handling is not likely to corrupt or damage your system. I will deal with the data first.

10.8.1 Taint Checking

Any CGI script that processes information from users is a security risk. The biggest risk with such scripts is that unchecked variables supplied by the user can be passed directly to the operating system shell. Perl has a mechanism called taint checking which forbids such dangerous practices. Variables which are set using data from outside the script are tainted and cannot be used to set values outside your script.

---

[3]perldoc perldebug on UNIX, somewhere in the HTML documents if you are using the ActiveState port to Microsoft Windows.

If such care is not taken the taint can spread. Your tainted variable might be sent to the shell which opens a pipe to a shell command and passes your variable through. Now three different programs have been affected by an insecure value. When you use taint checking in Perl the script will fail, the Perl interpreter exiting, if you try to pass variables along like this. To use taint checking you change the shebang line on UNIX systems to:

```
#! /usr/bin/perl -Tw
```

The shebang will work on some Windows systems with some servers but is not guaranteed. If your Web server is running on Windows you should ensure that you run all of your CGI scripts with the -T flag as well as -w.

Having set taint checking you may find that your scripts die when they try to use external programs even if values are not being passed into them. If you get an error message like:

```
Insecure $ENV{$PATH} at line xx
```

you need to actually set a path at the top of the script. Using something like the following code at the top of your script avoids this problem:

```
$ENV{'PATH'} = '/bin:/usr/local/bin:/usr/bin';
```

but do not include the current directory . in this path. Once you have tainted a variable you cannot use it in system(), exec(), open(), or eval() or any function that affects external data through other programs. If you absolutely must use such a variable then you should first perform a pattern match on it to extract the substrings and rebuild the string. The importance of this is that, during the extraction process, you will be checking that you have received valid data.

10.8.2 Strict

Like most programming languages Perl supports the use of compiler directives. These are additional commands placed in the code which are used by the compiler rather than processed by it. The most useful of these for the CGI script developer is:

```
use strict;
```

This makes the compiler print an error every time that it encounters a potentially unsafe construct in your code. The benefit of this for the CGI author is that, to avoid these errors, you must properly scope all of your subroutines and variables. Typically this is done by making them all local to a package through the use of the my keyword. Some variables and references cannot be made safe so simply. Filehandles present a particular difficulty and must be *quoted* if you want your scripts to execute. The following code shows how to use strict in a simple script that reads data from a file and returns it inside an HTML page:

```perl
1   #!/usr/bin/perl -Tw

    # packages to be imported
    use CGI qw/:standard/;
5   use strict;
    use CGI::Carp;

    # first quote the filehandle
    # to reduce the warnings from strict
10  use vars qw($GBOOK);

    # next declare the local variables
    my ($name, $mail, $words, $line, $msg);
    my $msg = new CGI("");
15

    # finally the code starts here
    # ---------------------------

    $GBOOK = "./guestbook.dat";
20  open(GBOOK) or die("Unable to open guestbook.dat");

    print $msg->header;
    print $msg->start_of_html(-title=>''Guestbook'');

25  print <<EOT;
    <p>The guestbook for this site is shown below</p>
    <hr />
    <dl>
    EOT
30
    while($line = <GBOOK>){
       chomp $line;
       ($name, $mail, $words) = split(/::/, $line);
       print<<DONE;
35     <dt>$name [$mail]</dt>
       <dd>$words</dd>
```

```
        <br /><br /><br />
DONE
}
```

40

```
print "</dl>";
print $msg->end_html;
exit(0);
```

Using strict and -Tw might seem like a lot of effort. Actually it *is* a lot of effort in many ways, yet it is worth doing if it reduces the number of errors that your scripts write to the server logs and increases the safety of your applications and data. For an explanation of qw/:standard/ see Section 10.6.3.

10.9 CARP

CGI scripts tend to leave a trail of error messages in the error logs of the server when they die or fall sick. These messages need to be neatly formatted and timestamped if they are to be of any use. The Carp module provided with the standard distribution of Perl is used to provide error messages in the same way as warn() and die(). The important difference is that the error is not reported at the line where it occurred but in the calling routine. This behavior is provided so that library modules can act more like core functions in their error reporting behavior.

The CGI::Carp module is an extension of Carp() especially for use with CGI scripts. Neatly formatted, usable error messages can be provided. Usually HTTP servers write errors to STDERR which is actually the server error log; CGI::Carp allows you to redirect your error messages to other open filehandles and store them locally. What if you want to send a CGI error back to the browser? Well you can do that too. Whatever method you choose to handle your error messages, CGI::Carp will generate something like:

1

```
[Mon Sep 05 09:37:06 2005] show.cgi: Use of
uninitialized value at ./show.cgi line 30,
<GBOOK> chunk 9.
```

That message is highly informative – the developer now knows what error they had, what module caused it, which line of code had the problem, and when the error happened. Very little additional debugging information could ever be provided.

To get a meaningful error message back to the browser you must use some of the additional functionality provided by CGI::Carp. At the top of your script where you are listing the modules it uses, simply include the line:

```
use CGI::Carp(fatalsToBrowser);
```

Your fully robust CGI script will now start off something like

```
1    #!/usr/bin/perl -Tw

     # packages to be imported
     use CGI qw/:standard/;
5    use strict;
     use CGI::Carp(fatalsToBrowser);

     my $in = new CGI;
```

10.10 COOKIES

Tracking visitors is important, especially to commercial Web sites. You may want to gather information about your users for use in demographic analysis, for instance. Many sites ask first-time visitors to fill in a form about themselves before they get access to the site. Two models are then available to developers for tracking users. Some sites ask a visitor to go through a simple log-in procedure each time that they arrive. Others use cookies.

A cookie is simply a piece of textual information which rather than being stored on the server is actually stored on the client machine. The mechanism was developed by Netscape as a way of overcoming the stateless nature of the HTTP protocol and first appeared in version 2 of Navigator. Cookies are a rather controversial topic among both Web surfers and developers. The controversy is basically about control, as indeed are most Internet controversies. Many people resent the fact that remote servers are able to write data to their hard drive without even having to ask. Often that data is encrypted and it is a rare site which says it is using a cookie.

From the developer's point of view, cookies are excellent. They can be used to restrict access to whole areas, can be set to expire so that they provide a simple, and very insecure, form of access control, and they provide lots of information that businesses like. For example, without cookies you need to examine the server logs to see which parts of your site are popular. Do browsers simply ignore the catalogue for instance? How many people look at the page which contains all of your special offers? That information may not be available to you if your pages are hosted by an ISP. Use cookies though and you can find all of that and more. Let us say that your visitors all fill in an initial questionnaire. Using a cookie lets you find out which parts of the site are used by all of the high earners and which parts by poor, starving students. You can then tailor content to the needs of different audiences within the same site.

If you, as a Web user, object to cookies then you can configure your browser so that the entire mechanism is switched off. This may restrict the number of commercial sites that you can visit but at least you will keep your freedom intact. Although cookies are sent from the server they are stored by the browser. They are passed as part of the HTTP message header and hence can be safely ignored without corrupting the page content. For more information on the HTTP protocol turn to Chapter 16.

Developers do not have the luxury of choosing which mechanisms to implement. If a client wants to use cookies then you have to program them. It is easier than you might imagine.

10.10.1 Cookies in Detail

First let us see what all of the fuss is about. Netscape Navigator stores its cookies in a file called cookies.txt. Here is part of that file from one of my computers:

```
# Netscape HTTP Cookie File
# http://www.netscape.com/newsref/std/cookie_spec.html
# This is a generated file!  Do not edit

.amazon.com TRUE  /  FALSE 2082787201  ubid-main
    002-8015358-4455008
.yahoo.co.uk   TRUE  /  FALSE 1271361625  B
    97soiun7d3c42
www.homebuyers.co.uk FALSE /  FALSE 1293753600
    WEBTRENDS_ID 195.92.197.53-1125876848.29284862
```

Microsoft Internet Explorer stores each individual cookie as a separate file which makes manipulating them slightly harder for the user. At least with cookies.txt you can use a text editor to delete individual items if you do not want them in there. An Internet Explorer cookie file from the same machine looks like this:

```
ASGUID
1181408
activestate.com/
0
124316800
30056700
2387620512
29322478
*
```

Parts of these files are clear: they hold some domain names and some directory paths but a lot has meaning only to the server which created the cookie. Whilst we cannot *reverse-engineer* other sites cookies, we can learn to create our own.

10.10.2 The Parts of a Cookie

A cookie has six parts. Before I describe them I would like to make a suggestion about their content. If you *are* going to write information to visitor's hard drives, then you should be nice about it. A warning message somewhere on your site would be good, the option to turn cookies off would be very good but best of all make them expire within a reasonable time. Many sites create cookies which are designed to live for decades. This is ludicrous as most of them are only needed for a few minutes. It shows a lack of forethought on the part of the developers, and probably a lack of respect for their visitors. Finally do not pass encrypted data to your visitors. You are using *their* machines for *your* purposes. Get your cookies to write plain, legible text. I would even go so far as to suggest that this is an area where you could easily start to use XML within your sites.

But enough proselytizing, I hear you shout. Where is the code? Well, first let us see what the cookie is made from; then we will see how to bake it for ourselves.

Name

Each cookie needs to have a name. The name does not have to be unique as browsers can store up to 300 cookies. Some common names such as `my_cookie` or `the_cookie` will be used many times. Any alphanumeric characters except white spaces[4] are valid inside a cookie. This field is compulsory.

Value

The point of cookies is to store data. The data is held in name:value pairs. If you are thinking about implementing these things in Perl, as we are, then that ought to be making you think about hashes straight away. A cookie can have as many of these name:value pairs as you want.

Expiry Date

Each cookie has a finite life after which the browser can safely delete it. The cookie can be returned to your scripts at any point during its life. The expiry time is set using a time and date string in Greenwich Mean Time format. If no expiry time is set, the cookie will cease to be active when the browser is next shut down.

Domain

The cookie is only valid for one domain, or part of one domain. For instance, if you want your cookie to be used through your whole site you might set the domain attribute to `.shu.ac.uk`. Here the browser will happily return the cookie to servers such as `www.shu.ac.uk` or `mybox.cms.shu.ac.uk` but not to other machines in the `.ac.uk` domain. If the domain were

---

[4]Space, tab, newline, carriage return.

set to `www.shu.ac.uk` the cookie could not be accessed by `mybox.cms.shu.ac.uk` or any other machine in the `shu.ac.uk` hierarchy.

Path

The site further restricts the scripts which can access a cookie. By default it is set to `/` which means that all scripts in the domain may access the cookie. If you only wanted scripts in the directory `/cookie_handlers` to get at your cookie then the path would be set to `/cookie_handlers`. Scripts in directories like `/cgi-bin` would then not be able to use the cookie. This is a useful feature as it lets you create a variety of cookies for your site, each tailored to a slightly different set of needs.

Secure

If you only want your cookie used in secure communications, for instance, when SSL is being used, then set the secure flag to 1. Otherwise the cookie will be passed through normal TCP/IP communications inside HTTP messages.

10.10.3 Handling Cookies in Perl

The CPAN archive of Perl modules provides many different ways of handling cookies. I am going to demonstrate the approach taken by `CGI.pm`. If this does not meet your needs you should look at some of the alternatives such as `Cookie.pm`.

You will be familiar with the format of the `CGI.pm` methods if you have read Chapter 10. It works just like the commands for creating standard HTML elements but this time the data goes into the HTTP header rather than into the actual HTML document.

Creating a Cookie

Creating a cookie is easy. The simplest way is to make a cookie object and then to pass this into the routine which creates the HTML page header. Here is an example which I will explain in a moment:

```
1   #!/usr/bin/perl -Tw

    use strict;
    use CGI qw/:standard/;
5   use CGI::Carp(fatalsToBrowser);

    my %txtValues = ('Visit'=>'1');
    my $this_cookie = cookie(-name=>'ChrisCookie',
            -value=>\%txtValues,
10          -path=>'/',
```

```
        -expire=>'+2h');

    print header(-cookie=>$this_cookie);
    print start_html('Creating A Cookie');
15  print h1('Creating A Cookie');
    print end_html;

    exit(0);
```

The expiry time can be set to an explicit date and time or to a relative time. In the example shown above the cookie will expire two hours after it was first set. If you leave the expiry time unset then the cookie will be deleted by the browser when it is closed down.

Each cookie can hold a set of values: you do not have to use one cookie per value. If you *did* then building many e-commerce applications such as shopping carts would be almost impossible. Using CGI.pm the values are saved in a hash using a unique name for each as the key and the text string as the value. These are written to the cookie.txt file in a single long string with items separated by ampersands:

```
1  name&Chris&ordernum&123&itemnum&34
```

The hash is then added to the cookie using the reference notation. Simply place a backslash in front of the hash identifier and the module will handle the extraction and manipulation of the individual items.

Once a cookie has been created it can be amended by writing another cookie with the same name which contains different values. The new values overwrite the existing ones.

Reading a Cookie

If you are using cookies in e-commerce you will need to read the cookie back from the browser each time that the user makes some new selections. How do you get the cookie back? Again using CGI.pm this is very easy. Here is the code to read back a cookie and display all key:value pairs from the original values hash:

```
1  #!/usr/bin/perl -Tw

    use CGI qw/:standard/;
    use CGI::Carp(fatalsToBrowser);
5  use strict;

    my %data = cookie('ChrisCookie');

    print header;
```

```
10    print start_html('Reading Back A Cookie');
      print h1('Reading Back A Cookie');

      my @keys = keys %data;
      my @values = values %data;
15
      while(@keys){
          print("<p>");
          print(pop(@keys), " = ", pop(@values), "\n");
          print("</p>");
20    }


      print end_html;

      exit(0);
```

The cookie is read back by sending a request to the browser using just the name of the cookie. The returned data is then separated by the module into key:value pairs and stored in the hash:

```
my %data = cookie('ChrisCookie');
```

Do not expect intelligent processing from CGI.pm here. The first item is assumed to be a key, the second a value, and so on for the entire set of data. If you set the cookie using data in some other form then you will get rubbish back at this stage. This is especially important where cookies were set using some mechanism other than CGI.pm. If any tidying up is needed then you will have to do it once the data has been extracted into the hash.

In the example, I have written a trivial loop which extracts the keys and values into a pair of arrays. It then pops values off each array in turn until they are both empty and displays those values inside the HTML page:

```
1     my @keys = keys %data;
      my @values = values %data;

      while(@keys){
5         print("<p>");
          print(pop(@keys), " = ", pop(@values), "\n");
          print("</p>");
      }
```

which also shows you a different way of handling Perl hashes.

Deleting a Cookie

To delete a cookie you need to rewrite it with a date/time string that was sometime in the past. The easiest way of doing this is to send an expiry time of –1h:

```perl
1   #!/usr/bin/perl -Tw

    use strict;
    use CGI qw/:standard/;
5   use CGI::Carp(fatalsToBrowser);

    my %txtValues = ('Visit'=>'1');
    my $this_cookie = cookie(-name=>'ChrisCookie', -value=>\%txtValues,
        -path=>'/', -expire=>'-1h');

10  print header(-cookie=>$this_cookie);
    print start_html('Deleting A Cookie');
    print h1('Deleting A Cookie');
    print end_html;

15  exit(0);
```

EXERCISES

The CGI module

1. List six benefits of using a library such as CGI.pm rather than writing your own code.
2. Use CGI.pm to write a script which returns an empty HTML page.
3. Modify your guestbook applications so that they use CGI.pm.

CGI Scripting

1. Create a simple Web database application using CGI.pm. Use the database to hold details of your CD and MP3 collections.
2. Test your applications from the command line. Is this a useful way of testing and debugging scripts?

Cookies

1. Consider whether the use of a custom security application or the use of Web cookies gives better access control to a site.

2. Add cookie handling to a guest book application. Can you use it to extract information from a form and then display that information back to the user some time later?

3. Why do *you* think that people sometimes worry about the use of cookies? Are they right to do so?

Building Web Applications With Perl

11

nyone who has done a lot of programming will tell you that many of the things that you want to do in your programs have been attempted before. Most people who teach, or theorize about, programming regard code re-use as vitally important to the software industry. Simply put, there is no point re-inventing the wheel every time that you write a program. It is sensible to re-use code from previous projects wherever possible. Developers often build up large libraries of code that they will modify for new projects. Some people even write special code that can be used by anyone without modification. The Perl distributions come with varying amounts of such pre-written code.

In an interpreted language like Perl some mechanism is needed by which the namespaces of applications and library routines can be kept separate. If your application uses a variable name that has already been used in a library you are using, all sorts of unforeseen things (brown as side-effects) could happen. Perl provides the package mechanism to keep the namespace tidy. If you have to refer to a variable in a package then you use its fully qualified name:

```
$package::variable_name
```

A module is a special type of package. It is a package that is defined in a library file of the same name and in which the code is designed to be re-usable. The re-use of code may be done by exporting symbols or by functioning as a class. The two packages that I am concentrating on in this book (`CGI.pm` and Perl DBI) both operate as classes and allow the programmer to access their routines through method calls.

When a module supports the object style of interaction, you have to use a special notation to access its methods. You will be familiar with this if you have seen or written any code in C or C++. An *instance*[1] of a class is created using the new keyword. The methods of that instance are then accessed by using an arrow, ->. In practice it is fairly simple.

```
1   $instance = new PACKAGENAME;
    $instance2 = new PACKAGENAME;

    $instance->method_one;                # execute method_one
5   $temp = $instance->method_two;        # assign value
    $instance2->method_two($temp);        # method with parameter
```

Much useful documentation is available in perldoc perlmod, which you should read if you plan to write modules, and perldoc perltoot which gives an introduction to using OO ideas in Perl.

Getting Modules

If you run your own server, you will be able to install pretty much what you want to. For a Perl developer this is really an ideal situation. Not all of the modules I will discuss in this chapter are provided as part of a standard Perl distribution. Therefore you will need to download and install them. If you run your Web site on a server provided by an ISP or by your employer or college, then you will need to ask the System Administrator for help. You cannot install these modules in your user space and then access them from your CGI scripts. They need to be installed properly. A second problem is that some of them rely upon other libraries and applications being present on the server. The graphics modules also need a variety of pieces of software whose facilities they use. Your friendly administrator could well have a few hours work ahead if they are going to set everything up for you.

If you run your scripts on a UNIX machine, everything should work properly. If your server is running Windows 2000 or even MacOS you may have problems ahead. All of the software you need to complete this chapter was developed on UNIX boxes and ported to other systems. Installing and configuring some of these ports is, in my experience, fairly tricky even when they come as installable packages. It can be done, but plenty of patience and coffee are definitely required.

The Perl code for many hundreds of modules is available from CPAN and its myriad mirrors. You can view CPAN over the Web at http://www.cpan.org. Browse around the site to see what is available. The modules can be found listed by category and are generally provided in gzipped tar files. The following procedure is usually used to install modules on UNIX boxes, I will demonstrate with the fictitious mymod.pm module:

- you will need to be working as root or some other user who has administrative rights over the server and can install system software

---

[1] More OO terminology. This means the named example of a class (or module) that gets manipulated by the program.

- download `mymod.tar.gz` from CPAN
- create a temporary directory and uncompress the archive using:
  `gunzip mymod.tar.gz`
- now extract the files from the archive with:
  `tar -xf mymod.tar`
- that will create a directory below the current one called `mymod` which you should now change into
- the archive will contain a file called `Makefile.PL` which is used to create a makefile using the command:
  `perl Makefile.PL`
- now you can compile the module and documentation with:
  `make`
- many modules come with test scripts, try this:
  `make test`
- if the tests succeed you can install the module with:
  `make install`
- finally delete the archive, `mymod.tar` and the `mymod` directory.

If the tests failed you do not necessarily have to worry. On my Apple Mac they sometimes fail due to conflicts between the different versions of Perl that I have on there. The modules still work perfectly well. If the tests fail due to your set-up, ignore them. If they fail due to a problem with the module, such as a missing file or library, then you will need to do some digging to find a solution.

The module installation process should work under Windows but you will need to download `nmake.exe` from the Microsoft Web site and replace `make` with `nmake` in all of the instructions given above. You will probably also need to buy a utility such as WinZip to handle the archive for you.

11.1 UPLOADING FILES

I will start with a process which you might find on people's individual homepages or on corporate Intranets: the file upload. Most Web sites are *read only* for visitors. Authors take the view that the site is their work and they do not want it altered by random passing surfers. There are sites which take a different view and which are meant to be altered by readers. The most famous of these is probably the online encyclopedia Wikipedia. Many applications require a third type of site which, whilst it cannot be altered by readers, does allow them to add their own material.

Consider, for instance, an on-line photo album. You will see these all over the Web. People place scanned copies of their photos, or more commonly today digital photos onto their homesite so that friends and family can view them. This is really a very good idea but pretty time-consuming. It is also a one-way street: imagine that Auntie Mabel has some snaps of her holiday in the Caribbean to share and she wants to use your Web site to do it. How will she get the photos to you? Well she could send you a CD-ROM with the photos stored on it and a letter which lists all the captions she wants. She could email that same information to you, although the email would be prohibitively large, or she could place all the pictures on an FTP server so that you can download them. Whichever approach she takes is going to involve you in a lot of work. You will have to write the Web pages, copy all the files to their end location and deal with the inevitable changes which Auntie Mabel will require.

If the family photo album is a lot of hassle, what about the corporate Intranet? Here you have the same problem magnified many times over. Your users are creating reports and memos all day which others on the system *may* need to read. You want to archive all of this material so that it can be used in, for instance, later audit trails. If users simply email their memos to everyone, that quickly becomes irritating and after a while people stop reading the messages. Why not place all of the memos, reports, etc., on an Intranet site, so that co-workers can access them when they *need* to? Great idea, but potential implementation nightmare. How do the documents get onto the site? Your organization could employ someone to perform the uploads and maintain the site, you could buy a proprietary Intranet system such as Microsoft Exchange or Lotus Notes, or you could create upload pages on an internal Web site.

Building a full application based around a file upload page can be a very complicated process. For either of the applications I have just described, you will need to enforce access controls, restrict who is allowed to upload files, create a usable directory structure then index that, and finally use some sort of templating system to create the pages. You need:

- a form in which details of files are entered
- a script to perform the upload and save the file
- a database to hold the files and index them
- page templates created using the `HTML::Mason` module.

11.1.1 The HTML Page

OK, that is enough advertising, let us look at some code. I am going to show you how to write an HTML page which includes all of the fields you will need to upload files, and then a simple script which processes the data it gets from the browser. First the HTML page and the form:

```
1   <html>
    <head>
        <title>File Uploader</title>
    </head>
5   <body>
```

```
       <h1>File Uploader</h1>

       <form method="post"
             enctype="multipart/form-data"
10           action="../cgi-bin/upload.cgi">

       <table border="0" align="center">
         <tr>
           <th>Enter A File Name: </th>
15         <td>
             <input type="file"
                    name="original"
                    value="starting"
                    size="40"
20                  maxlength="120" />
           </td>
         <tr>
           <th>What Shall I Call The Saved Version?</th>
           <td>
25           <input type="text"
                    name="newname"
                    length="40"
                    maxlength="120" />
           </td>
30       </tr>
         <tr>
             <td><input type="submit" value="Submit File" /></td>
             <td><input type="reset" value="Reset Form" /></td>
         </tr>
35     </table>
       </form>
     </body>
     </html>
```

The HTML page has two new additions which you have not seen before. Firstly I am using a new attribute in the form tag:

```
1  <form method="post"
          enctype="multipart/form-data"
          action="../cgi-bin/upload.cgi">
```

We have no way of knowing how large the files are which users will try to upload. A maximum file size could be enforced with a client side scripting language such as JavaScript or Visual Basic, although those types of solution tend only to work on Windows based machines since they require access to operating system facilities. Instead we will let users send us as much data as they want to, the problem of sorting out how much to save is then left to the CGI script. Since files tend to be at least 1K bytes, the browser must use the post method to send data. The new attribute here is enctype which identifies the way in which the form will submit its data. In this case I am gong to send form data in multiple pieces.

Now we need a way for the user to tell us what file they are going to send. This is done using a file input field. This is a combined field which has a text box in which a file name can be typed, and a button which can be used to open file dialog to search for the file. This type of input is not standard HTML and may not be available in all browsers, although it works in all of those which I have used. Here is the code:

```
1   <input type="file"
            name="original"
            value="starting"
            size="40"
5           maxlength="120" />
```

When the file gets to the server it will need a new name. The name which accompanies it from the file box will be the complete operating system-dependent name. This will have no meaning on your server so you will need to save the data in a file with a different name. In the example, I get this information from another text box:

```
1   <input type="text"
            name="newname"
            length="40"
            maxlength="120" />
```

11.1.2 The CGI Script

When I came to write a script to process uploaded data files, I realized that there are many possible ways of handling this. You might want to save the data in a file, add it to a database or alter it before returning it to the browser. Data files may be plain text or one of hundreds of binary formats. They may be data or applications or images or... you get the picture. This is a complex area, much of the processing is application dependent. I have chosen to simplify the entire thing so that you can see the basic principles in action.

This CGI script reads in the data, saves it into a file on the server and copies the whole thing back to the browser inside an HTML page. If you read perldoc perlfunc and perldoc perlopentut, you will find more information about opening files than you can probably imagine ever needing. They will tell you how to safely handle binary data of all types.

As ever, read the script first, then I will explain it:

```perl
1   #!/usr/bin/perl -w

    use CGI qw/:standard/;
    use CGI::Carp(fatalsToBrowser);
5
    $in = new CGI();
    $INPUT = $in->param('original');
    $outtie = $in->param('newname');
    $OUTPUT = ">./$outtie";
10
    open (OUTPUT) || die "Unable to open file for writing";

    print $in->header();
    print $in->start_html("Thank You");
15  print "<h2>Thank You For Sending $INPUT</h2>";

    while($line = <$INPUT>) {
        print $line; # display contents back in browser
        print OUTPUT $line; # save in a file
20  }

    close OUTPUT;
    print $in->end_html();
    exit(0);
```

On the whole that is a pretty standard CGI script which uses the CGI.pm module. I start by creating a CGI object and extracting the parameter values from it. The value sent from the file input field is the *name* of the source file rather than the file itself. The output file is opened for writing:

```perl
1   $in = new CGI();
    $INPUT = $in->param('original');
    $outtie = $in->param('newname');
    $OUTPUT = ">./$outtie";
```

If it cannot open the file, the script dies:

```perl
open (OUTPUT) || die "Unable to open file for writing";
```

at which point an error will be logged and sent to the browser. If you are running this script on a UNIX server, you will need to set the permissions correctly so that it can write data to files.

Once the file is open I start to send an HTML page back, using some of the function provided by CGI.pm. The script loops through the incoming data, saving it into a new file and echoing it back:

```
1  while($line = <$INPUT>) {
       print $line; # display contents back in browser
       print OUTPUT $line; # save in a file
   }
```

That is all there is to performing file uploads. You can add plenty of refinement to the script to make it more robust, but the actual upload procedure never gets any more complex than this.

11.2 TRACKING USERS WITH HIDDEN DATA

HTTP is a *stateless* protocol. When you go to a Web site, you request a page, the server sends it right back, or sends an appropriate error code if it cannot. The server then forgets all about you. When you use a conventional desktop application, say a database input form, across a network, you log-on to a server. The server remembers you and is able to track and log all your actions until you log off. The database application contains some notion of a session simply because users will be interacting with it for a significant length of time. Interactions on the Web may only last for a single download. How can your CGI applications track users if the server does not provide any facilities? You might use cookies but some users do not like them. Instead, try placing information about users inside the pages you send to them and the requests which they send back to you. That is exactly what I am going to show you how to do in this section.

I have created a simple Web page containing an HTML form. It is basically a guestbook-type application which returns a number of data items to the server. The CGI script processes the data and creates a new Web page with another form. Embedded in *that* form is some of the information returned the first time around.

Let us consider some uses for this idea. First, if you *have* used a cookie file on your site, you probably read it when a visitor first arrives. You then want to track that visitor through the site. This is most easily achieved by using a hidden value, possibly as the only item in a non-displaying form. To make the idea work you need to create every page dynamically and place the hidden value in each page. That is not difficult: in fact many large commercial sites do just such processing. However, it may put an unacceptable overhead on your server.

A second, similar, use might be to track registered users after they log on to the site. Sometimes cookie files are used so that repeat visitors do not have to log on; many sites make each visitor go through the logging on procedure then track them with hidden values taken from the log-on form.

Thirdly, many users who are worried about privacy, turn cookies off in their browser. The only way that you can track these people through your site is by hiding data inside the pages which you send to them.

If you do this, be careful about which values you choose to hide in subsequent pages: anyone can access the source code of a page from disk cache and you do not really want to be giving users e-mail addresses or site passwords!

11.2.1 The Initial HTML Page

```
1   <html>
      <head>
        <title>The Initial Form</title>
      </head>
5     <body>
        <form action="./test3.cgi" method="post">
          <p>Enter Your Name Here
            <input type="text" name="visitor" value="name" size="48" max
              length="48" />
          </p>
10        <p>Enter Your Email Address Here (optional)
            <input type="text" name="email" size="48" maxlength="48"
              value="email" />
          </p>
          <p>Enter Your Comments Here
            <textarea name="msg" rows="20" cols="40"></textarea>
15          <input type="submit" value="Submit The Form" />
            <input type="reset" value="Clear The Form" />
          </p>
        </form>
      </body>
20  </html>
```

11.2.2 The CGI Script

The script does not have to do anything fancy here. I am just going to create an HTML page which includes a form. On that form I have a hidden field which has the value entered into the name field of the original form:

```perl
1   #!/usr/bin/perl -wT

    # packages to be imported
    use CGI qw/:standard/;
5   use strict;
    use CGI::Carp(fatalsToBrowser);

    # first quote the filehandle
    use vars qw($GBOOK);

10
    my $msg = new CGI;
    my $name = $msg->param('visitor');
    my $mail = $msg->param('email');
    my $words = $msg->param('msg');

15
    print $msg->header;
    print $msg->start_html(-title=>"Maintain State With CGI.pm");

    print<<EOT;
20  <h1>Maintaining State Through CGI.pm</h1>
    <p>You Entered the following values in the form...
    <table align="center" border="1">
       <tr>
          <td>Name</td><td>$name</td>
25     </tr>
       <tr>
          <td>Email Address</td><td>$mail</td>
       </tr>
       <tr>
30        <td>Comments</td><td>$words</td>
       </tr>
    </table>

    <h2>Next...</h2>
```

```
35   <p>Now select an item from the following list...
     EOT

     print $msg->start_form(-action=>'./proc.cgi');
     print $msg->hidden(-name=>'user', -default=>$name);
40   print $msg->popup_menu('next', ['apples', 'oranges',
                                      'pears', 'lemons']);
     print $msg->end_form;

     print $msg->end_html;
45   exit(0);
```

The hidden field does not display in the browser. If the user looks at the page source they will be able to see this hidden field. It is not encrypted or treated in any fancy way, it simply does not get displayed. When this second form is submitted, the value in the hidden field comes right back with it. The second script is able to relate the two sets of input right back to the same user.

11.3 USING RELATIONAL DATABASES

For the developers of large commercial Web sites, two issues override all others: security and data storage. The benefits of using the Web to conduct business disappear totally if you cannot efficiently store, retrieve, and manipulate the data from customers. Web sites which do not handle data are little more than glorified advertising opportunities – although they have a rather larger potential audience. All of the CGI code that I have shown so far has written data to simple flat files. For many applications that is fine. However, if you are handling complex data, complex processing or need to keep your data secure then using a relational database is probably the best solution.

Whilst I am not planning to show you how to program in SQL (the language used by most relational databases) I am going to give a couple of examples that will convince you that using a database is so straightforward you ought to consider doing so.

11.3.1 Introducing DBI

There are many types of relational database available – some of them are even freely available on the Internet. The multiplicity of such platforms could present the end-developer with a problem of potentially insurmountable proportions. Imagine developing an application which could talk to an Oracle database, only for your ISP or company to decide that they were moving from Oracle to SQL Server. If your application contained a lot of platform-specific code then you would have to rewrite the whole thing. That is not only time-consuming and expensive but potentially dangerous. All of the debugging and incremental improvements that had been made to the original Oracle application would have to be repeated for the SQL Server version. Fortunately, there is a database-neutral solution available for Perl.

11.3.2 RDBMS Neutral Database Applications

The Perl DBI module provides a neutral interface to many relational databases. It is an application programmer interface (API) which provides a library of functions, variables and conventions. According to the documentation with the modules these

> provide a consistent database interface independent of the actual database being used

The DBI routines do not actually perform much of the processing of the application-database connection. That functionality comes from a driver module which must be specifically developed for the database being used. Database drivers are available for most of the commonly used relational databases. The drivers do the actual work while the DBI API provides a framework within which those drivers can operate. The relationship between the application, API, driver, and database engine is shown in Figure 11.1.

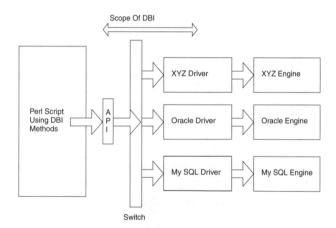

Figure 11.1 The Perl DBI

The great benefit for the application developer, of using the DBI module, is independence. If the database management system that you are using changes then you simply tell Perl DBI to use a different driver and leave the rest of your code totally unaltered. If the database driver has been developed properly, and those for the major databases have been around long enough now, then you should have no unexpected problems.

If you are working on UNIX systems then you have a wide range of RDBMS available. For the Web developer who uses Microsoft operating systems the choice was, until recently, rather more restricted. Today many of the popular Free Software databases are available as compiled Windows packages. Whichever system you use, once you have set up and configured your database under XP or Windows 2000 it will be as easy to use as it would be under UNIX. In fact, in one important aspect it is actually *easier* to use Windows. Microsoft has a technology called open database connectivity, ODBC, which provides a consistent interface to many relational database systems. A Perl DBI driver is available to talk to ODBC so that whatever back-end you use, once you have registered it with the ODBC manager you can access it through your Perl applications.

The implementation of DBI for each database system inherits and extends the methods of the generic Perl DBI package. You will see when I talk about connecting to databases that, rather than use the generic package, you should use the package developed for your database management system.

Most applications that use DBI adhere to the cursor model. Again for detail look at any good relational database text. Briefly, though, a cursor lets applications access sets of data returned by SQL queries. A cursor reads the next tuple (In effect, a row from a set) returned and all operations are performed against that tuple.

In the following descriptions of the Perl DBI, $dbh is used as a generic value for a database handle. The value $sth is used to indicate a handle to a statement. Suitable names for both of these, for your applications, should be submitted as appropriate.

11.3.3 Perl DBI Methods

Perl DBI is a module, so everything that was said in Section 10.4 when I described CGI.pm applies here too. I am not going to go into too much detail about how the module works. Once you have seen it in action it is pretty straightforward and you can, as always, get lots of useful information from the documentation. In this case perldoc DBI should do the trick. What follows is, therefore, a brief skim across the surface that should get you started.

Sessions

Perl DBI does not really have sessions in the database sense. There is not a continuous stream of operations from a specific, identifiable user to the database. Instead each connection into the database is identified by a handle (which is analogous to an object) whose methods are called by Perl scripts. Relational databases can support many types of data. To simplify data handling in the driver, all data is returned as string values. The application developer must manipulate those strings so that, for instance, numerical precision is not lost.

Often you will want to perform a number of operations on the same data set at the same time. Using Perl DBI you cannot perform more than one database operation at a time. If you want three consecutive operations then you must prepare and execute three statements. For more on using statements see "Preparing Statements", which follows.

As a final word of warning about Perl DBI, not all relational database systems support the same set of functions. For instance, the popular freeware database MySQL lacks both `commit` and `rollback`, so those operations are not supported by its driver. Therefore, you need to read the documentation for the DBI driver that you are using before you start coding. And if you do have to port your application to a new database you may have to rewrite any non-generic code that you have used.

```
$dbh = DBI->connect($data_source, $username, $password)
|| die $DBI::errstr
```

When a connection is opened to the database it returns a handle. The handle will be used for all database operations in a similar way to a filehandle. If the connection cannot be opened the driver will set a DBI error which the application can then use to fail gracefully. This set-up lets each application program establish multiple connections to multiple databases and to manage each of those connections independently.

`$data_source` is actually a colon-separated set of values which identify the driver, database, and host. The driver is called through `DBI:'driver name':` with the driver name being case-sensitive. The following example establishes a connection to a MySQL database called **webber** running on the local host.

```
1    $dbh = DBI->connect('DBI:mysql:webber:localhost', 'webber','pwd')
     || die 'Unable to connect to database $dbh->errstr\n';
```

The driver name may, on occasion, require the port number at which the database is listening. For instance

```
DBI:mysql:webber:localhost:7000
```

It may be that for your database, particularly during testing, no user name or password is needed. Obviously this is unacceptable practice on a production system but during testing you can use empty strings for these values.

The interpretation and use of the parameters to `$DBI->connect` is driver dependent and not considered here. If you want more details then look in the `perldoc` for DBI and DBD.

Once a connection has been established the DBI methods are accessed through the filehandle. In object-oriented parlance the handle is an *instance* of DBI.

$dbh->disconnect

When you have finished using a connection to a database, that connection should be dropped by calling the disconnect method of the handle. Most systems restrict the number of connections that can be made. Although the limit is high, an intensively used CGI application may soon reach it if connections are not released after use.

Some database systems will automatically commit any remaining changes when you disconnect. This is not defined anywhere so it is important that you specify, before disconnecting, whether any remaining changes are to be committed or rolled back. Of course if your DBMS does not support commit and rollback of transactions, disconnecting is likely to lead to unspecified behavior. You must write code in your application to validate your changes rather then relying upon the integrity of the system.

Attempting to disconnect from a database that has uncommitted changes will raise a warning. To avoid this, call the finish method before disconnecting.

$sth->finish

Is used to show that no more data will be returned from a statement handle. Calling this is a useful way of letting the database free resources.

Preparing Statements

You cannot simply write some SQL and run it against a database when using Perl DBI. Instead your SQL code must be prepared by the driver before execution.

$sth = $dbh->prepare($statement)
|| die $dbh->errstr

Prepares an SQL statement for execution and returns a handle to that statement to be held in $sth. The handle is then used in the execute statement. If the preparation fails, an error string will be returned by the driver. The prepare method should not generally be used to execute SQL statements. Some drivers *will* execute some statements from the prepare method. You should consult the perldoc for your particular driver for more information on this.

Not all database systems support the concept of prepared queries. If a system does not use prepared queries then the prepare method simply stores the SQL in the handle for processing by execute.

The DBI prepare method does not parse SQL statements. They will be passed onto the database engine and any errors returned from there. Note that your SQL statements should not generally be terminated by a semicolon when run from DBI.

Database Operations

$sth->execute || die $sth->errstr

All processing needed to complete the (prepared) statement is performed. If the statement is executed successfully true will be returned.

> **NOTE** *In many circumstances, when querying a database, a successful execution may not return any data. In database operations an empty set does not imply failure of a query. For more details on this consult any good database text.*

Select operations return the number of rows that the database will return to the application.

$sth->fetchrow_array

returns the next row from the set of rows returned by the database. The row is returned as an array of values which is available for processing as a normal array.

$dbh->selectrow_array($statement)

combines the prepare, execute, and fetchrow_array operations into a single statement. If the SQL statement in the $statement parameter has already been prepared, that step will not be repeated by selectrow_array.

$sth->rows

returns the number of rows that a query is returning. Often this will be an indeterminate value. A select operation simply returns rows until the set is empty; often even the DBMS will not know how large the return set *is*.

$dbh->commit || die $dbh->errstr

If the database supports transaction operations, this will force it to make the most recent set of changes permanent.

$dbh->rollback || die $dbh->errstr

If the database that is being used supports transactions, this command will undo any uncommitted changes that the application has made.

$dbh->errstr, $dbh->err

These are the database engine error string and error code, respectively. They correspond to the most recent driver function call.

$DBI::errstr, $DBI::err

These are generic versions of the errors just described. They always refer to the last handle used and so must be used with care if you have numerous handles open.

11.3.4 Using DBI and a Relational Database – An Example

This first example of using a database with Perl shows how to write a row of data to a MySQL database. In this case the table being written into has five fields. Four of them are text fields, the last one is a counter. The MySQL system supports an automatically incremented counter which always receives the value 0. The table being used in the examples here is a simple Web guestbook with fields for the visitor name, visitor IP address, e-mail address, and any comments that they may want to leave.

The second example reads data from the same table and prints it out to the screen. Notice how the returned values are accessed from $row just like any other array values.

It is easy to see how these database examples could replace some of the file handling code that I have shown throughout the CGI scripting chapters of this book.

Writing to a Database

```
1   #!/usr/bin/perl -w
    use DBI;

    $host = "DBI:mysql:webber:localhost";
5   $dbh = DBI->connect($host, 'webber','pwd')
       or die 'Unable to connect to database $dbh->errstr\n';


    $insert = <<DONE;
    insert into visitors values ('Bugs Bunny',
10                                'carrots\@home',
                                  '255.255.255.0',
                                  'An updated Row',
                                  0)
    DONE
15
    my $update = $dbh->prepare($insert);
    $update->execute
       or die 'Unable to execute SQL command. $dbh->errstr';

20  $dbh->disconnect;
    exit(0);
```

11.3.5 Reading from a Database

```perl
1  #!/usr/bin/perl -w

   use DBI;
   $host = "DBI:mysql:webber:localhost";
5
   $dbh = DBI->connect($host, 'webber','pwd') or die 'Unable to connect to
       database $dbh->errstr\n';

   $query = <<END;
   select name, comments
10   from visitors
     order by name
   END

   $cursor = $dbh->prepare($query);
15 $cursor->execute
       or die 'Unable to execute SQL command. $dbh->errstr';

   my $row;
   while($row = $cursor->fetchrow_arrayref) {
20   printf("[%s] [%s]\n", $row->[0], $row->[1]);
     }

   $cursor->finish;

25 $dbh->disconnect;
   exit(0);
```

The following code fragments are typical pieces of SQL:

```sql
1  insert into visitors values ('Bugs Bunny',
           'carrots\@home',
           '255.255.255.0',
           'An updated Row', 0)
```

and

```sql
1  select name, comments
     from visitors
     order by name
```

11.4 USING libwww

Sometimes you need to venture beyond the confines of your own Web site or databases. You need more data to provide more information on your site. Where are you going to get that data from? Why the Web, of course. Yes, strange as it may seem, there will be times when you want, or need, to create Web applications which can gather data from around the Web and incorporate that data into *your* pages. This seems like a strange concept, after all anything which surfs the Web is surely a Web client and I have been discussing and demonstrating the use of Perl in *server* applications. Did I not even imply that Perl was not a language you could use inside a browser? Well, yes I have been concentrating solely on Perl as a server language and I am *still* doing that. In this section I want to show how you can use Perl to build a script which can get information from other Web sites and then add that data to your pages.

You have probably seen this idea used around the Web. Many topical news sites are little more than dynamic lists of links to content on other sites. As the content changes, so the data those linked sites provide changes too. Even Web portals do this: Yahoo! provides endless links to news stories on sites run by organizations like CNN, the BBC and Reuters. Yahoo! goes even further by abstracting the first few sentences of the stories it is highlighting so that surfers can be selective about what they read. In the world of Open Source and Free Software, many Web sites list the latest updates to the Freshmeat archives (at http://www.freshmeat.net) and to stories being run on every computer nerd's favorite site: Slashdot (at http://www.slashdot.org). How are these things done? Well, in truth, I have no idea how large organizations like Yahoo! do this. For them it is really a trade secret, part of what makes them a distinctive brand. I do, though, know a way that you can get a foot in the door.

Perl has a set of modules which collectively are called libwww-perl. These are designed to be used when writing Web clients and replace low-level coding tasks involving things like sockets and ports with more high-level tasks involving URLs and whole Web pages. The best place to start with these modules is the documentation. Try `perldoc HTML::Simple`, to get an overview of what the modules can do, and to see some basic code.

I am going to show you an application which uses a combination of CGI scripting, libwww and XML parsing just to build a small HTML table. I am not going to explain the XML parsing here, you will just have to trust me that this works. If you want to know *how* it works, all of the gory details are on the way. For now I will concentrate on the networking aspects of building this client.

What does this client do? It incorporates a list of the current discussions at Slashdot into an HTML page. Sounds complicated doesn't it? Slashdot is a set of HTML pages, created using a whole load of Perl scripts. How can I find out what stories are running there and download the details of them into my own pages? A brute force solution to this problem might be to simply get hold of the HTML from the front page at Slashdot and strip out the bits I am interested in. But what I want are the titles of the stories and their URLs. If you take a look at the site you will see that it has a very complex structure and finding the information that I want would be next to impossible. Fortunately the people who run Slashdot provide an XML file which contains all of the information that I need and more. Here is a sample of that file (reformatted slightly to fit on the printed page):

```
<story>
    <title>CD-R Prices Could Triple This Summer</title>
    <url>
        http://slashdot.org/article.pl?sid=01/05/09/0236235
    </url>
    <time>2001-05-09 03:03:03</time>
    <author>timothy</author>
    <department>stock-several-spindles</department>
    <topic>money</topic>
    <comments>168</comments>
    <section>articles</section>
    <image>topicmoney.gif</image>
</story>
```

All I have to do, therefore, is connect my script to the Slashdot Web server, download this file, which is called slashdot.xml, and process it in whatever way I need to. One final thing, before I get into the coding, the Slashdot site has an extremely high load. If you are going to practise writing a Web client using my code *please* download the slashdot.xml file just once, save it on your own Web server and work on that version. Once you have a working script you can use the real file. Right, here is the code:

```
1  #!/usr/bin/perl -w

   use CGI qw/:standard/;
   use CGI::Carp('fatalsToBrowser');
5  use XML::Parser;
   require LWP::UserAgent;

   $ua = new LWP::UserAgent;
   $rq = new HTTP::Request('GET', 'http://www.slashdot.org/slashdot.xml');
10
   $title = 0;
   $url = 0;
```

```perl
    @linktext = "";
15  @urls = "";
    $j = $k = 0;

    $response = $ua->request($rq);

20  if($response->is_success) {
        $parser = new XML::Parser;
        $parser->setHandlers(
                        Start => \&elStart,
                        End => \&elEnd,
25                      Char => \&elChar);
        &makePage($response->content);
    } else {
        print $response->error_as_HTML;
    }
30
    exit(0);

    sub makePage {
        $parser->parse($_[0]);
35      $page = new CGI;
        print $page->header;
        print $page->start_html("Slashdot.xml");
        print "<h1>Slashdot Stories</h1>\n";
        print qq(<table border="0">);
40
        for($i = 0; $i < $k-1; $i++) {
            print "<tr><td>";
            print "<a href=\"$urls[$i]\">$linktext[$i]</a>\n";
            print "</td></tr>";
45      }

        print "</table>\n";
        print $page->end_html;
    }
50
```

```
    sub elStart {
        ($expat, $item, %atts) = @_;
        if($item eq "title"){
55          $title = 1;
        } elsif($item eq "url"){
            $url = 1;
        }
    }
60

    sub elEnd {
        ($expat, $item, %atts) = @_;
        if($item eq "title"){
65          $title = 0;
        } elsif($item eq "url"){
            $url = 0;
        }
    }
70

    sub elChar {
        ($expat, $item, %atts) = @_;
        if($title == 1){
75          $linktext[$j] = $item;
            $j++;
        } elsif($url == 1){
            $urls[$k] = $item;
            $k++;
80      }
    }
```

The part of that script which creates the Web client, connects to the remote server and handles the response, is shown below:

```
1   #!/usr/bin/perl -w

    require LWP::UserAgent;

5   $ua = new LWP::UserAgent;
    $rq = new HTTP::Request('GET',
```

```
         'http://www.slashdot.org/slashdot.xml');
     # variables cut here

10   $response = $ua->request($rq);

     if($response->is_success) {
         # XML handling code removed from here
         &makePage($response->content);
15   } else {
         print $response->error_as_HTML;
     }


     exit(0);
```

Let us take that piece by piece and see what it is doing. The developers of libwww have taken an object-oriented approach to its development. The code has been broken down into a set of classes which each perform distinct functions. Each class can be used separately but most applications will use more than one of them. That is the case here, where I need to create an HTTP request, transmit it and handle the response from the Web server. Therefore I am using a class called LWP::UserAgent which encapsulates (an object-orientation term which means includes) the HTTP::Request, HTTP::Response and LWP::Protocol classes. The script starts by creating an instance of the LWP::UserAgent which will perform most of the work for us.

$agent = new LWP::UserAgent
constructs an instance of the UserAgent class and returns a reference to it.

The next step is to create a request. As you might guess, an HTTP request consists of a request line, some headers and potentially some content.

$rq = new HTTP::Request(method, URI[, header[, content]])
$rq = HTTP::Request->new(method, URI[, header[, content]])
$rq = HTTP::Request->new(method => URI[, header[, content]])

These constructors all work in the same way. Really the choice of which to use is down to personal preference. The request can handle either GET or POST forms as the method parameter. The URI parameter is the URI of the document which you want to retrieve. If you need to pass in any headers with your message these go as the third parameter. They should be wrapped inside an HTTP::Headers object. Next the request has to be processed.

```
request($request[, $arg[, size]])
simple_request($request[, $arg[, size]])
```

LWP::UserAgent has two ways of submitting a request to a server. Actually, they work in the same way. The Request method can send more than one request and can handle operations such as redirections. The simple_request is much less complex and is used to submit just a single request. The first parameter should be a reference to an instance of the HTTP::Request class. The, optional, second argument, $arg, controls the way that the response from the server is to be handled. This must be either the name of a file in which you want the response stored, or a reference to a subroutine which will handle chunks of data as they arrive. If this parameter is missing, as in my example, the data is stored in the HTTP::Request object.

An HTTP request returns an error code alongside any data. These return codes can be used to control how your script operates. For instance, if you get an error message back from the server then you will not want to show it on your page will you? These return codes become part of the HTTP::Response object and are accessed through its methods.

```
$response = HTTP::Response->new(code[, message[, content[, header]]])
```

constructs an HTTP::Response object with the specified code and, optionally a message, some content and a header. In the example script this object is created automatically when the request returns and then made available to us. The HTTP::response object has a number of attributes which we can access from our scripts.

```
$response->code()
```
returns the code which was sent from the server.

```
$response->message()
```
returns the message sent from the server.

```
$response->base
```
gives the base URI for the response. This actually returns a reference to a URI object.

```
$response->is_success
$response->is_error
```

return boolean values indicating the status of the request which was sent to the server.

```
$response->error_as_HTML()
```
returns a string which contains a complete HTML page giving details of which error occurred and why. Generally this method will only return anything useful if is_error

has returned true. In the example this must have happened if the check of is_success failed.

11.5 TEMPLATE-BASED SITES WITH HTML::MASON

Dynamic Web sites usually have three elements. These are the HTML which the browser displays, the scripts which create the dynamic parts of the site and some form of data storage. By now you are familiar with all of those pieces. So far, in the scripting sections of the book, I have shown you how to place HTML inside Perl code. This seems sensible to experienced programmers, we tend to think in terms of algorithms and data structures.

But what if you are not a programmer, or if you are a Web designer? You will probably think firstly about HTML files, page layout and site structure. You will want to use scripting to support HTML, rather than using HTML to present the results of your scripts. A number of technologies are available which work like this. Most of these involve learning a new language. If you have worked your way through to here then you have already invested a significant amount of time in learning Perl, so finding that you now need to learn PHP could be more than a little irritating. Fortunately there is at least one solution which lets you use all of the facilities of Perl and, at the same time, get blistering levels of performance out of your Web server.

Mason is an open source Web engine which supports the development and delivery of large, complex sites. It is being developed by Jonathan Swartz and can be downloaded from http://www.masonhq.com where you will also find HTML versions of the documentation, mailing lists to join and the beginnings of a useful FAQ. Mason is a Perl module with attitude. It is designed specifically to work with the Apache Web server and the mod_perl extension to it. The combination of Apache and mod_perl is vital since it provides extremely high throughput levels and extremely low response times. If you use those two pieces of software, the Perl interpreter lives in memory as do compiled versions of your scripts. There is little or no initiation time required when a script is called and performance levels approach those of native code.

Installing and configuring Mason is quite straightforward once you have Apache and mod_perl running. I will leave the details to the supplied documentation. Take a look at:

```
1   perldoc HTML::Mason
    perldoc HTML::Mason::Admin
    perldoc HTML::Mason::Devel
```

the last of those being the documentation for developers.

I am going to show you how to get a simple Mason page up and running, look at how you use the module to intertwine HTML and Perl, and finish by presenting a complex example. First, though, some more background. Mason is a sort of pre-processor which takes small pieces of code, called *components*, and joins them together to make a complete HTML page. Each component is stored in a separate file and may contain HTML, Perl or a combination of the two. When the pre-processor encounters Perl code inside a component it processes that code as if it were a script and uses the result in the page it is building. When it encounters HTML it places the code directly into the new page. The beauty of components is that they are easily re-used. If you create a menu based upon a dynamic search of your system, it can be included in every page on your site with a simple Mason statement. You get all of the flexibility of a frameset with none of the annoyance to your users. Life as a developer is also simplified. If you need to update part of your site, for instance to change a logo, you make the change once and it spreads through all your pages without you doing any work at all.

11.5.1 A Basic Application

I am not going to show you the simplest of Mason pages, a *Hello World!* type application, since you can find examples of that in the perldoc supplied with the module. Instead I will show you a more fully featured, yet still quite trivial, application.

You may remember from earlier that operating systems store details about the current system environment. This data can be accessed from Perl scripts using a builtin hash called %ENV. The following script displays those details in an HTML page. It also accepts a parameter from the browser, sent using either GET or POST, which controls the number of lines of data that are displayed. If you have got Mason installed try saving the script in your Mason directory as environ.html and running it using:

```
http://localhost/mason/environ.html?num_lines=12
```

although the exact path will change depending upon how you have configured your installation. Here is the code:

```
1   <& header, title=>' is now', bgcol=>'red' &>
    <table border="1">
    % foreach my $key (sort keys %ENV) {
    <tr>
5      <td>
          <b><% $key %></b>
       </td>
       <td>
          <% $ENV{$key} %>
10     </td>
    </tr>
    %last if(--$num_lines <= 0);
    % }
```

```
    </table>
15
    <& footer &>

    <%args>
    $num_lines=>10
20  </%args>
```

As well as the HTML file, you will need to create and save two Mason components in the same directory. These are called `header` and `footer` and are shown below:

header

```
1   <html>
    <head>
    <title>Current environment <% $title %></title>
    </head>
5   <body bgcolor="<% $bgcol %>">
    <h2>Current Environment <% $title %></h2>

    <%args>
    $title
10  $bgcol=>'yellow'
    </%args>
```

footer

```
1   <hr />
    <p>This site &copy; 2005, Chris Bates.</p>
    </body>
    </html>
```

So how does that work? And, what is all the funny syntax about? Mason adds some more syntactic salt to the soup of symbols and meanings which is Perl. Fortunately there are only a couple more things to learn and they are pretty straightforward. Since Mason makes HTML pages from components, it needs to be able to identify which component to include and where to place its content. This is done by placing the component name in this format:

```
<& footer &>
```

Sometimes you will need to pass parameters to a component, the construct used is familiar from `CGI.pm` and numerous other Perl modules:

```
<& header, title=>' is now', bgcol=>'red' &>
```

where the parameters form a comma-separated list of keys and values. The component receives its parameters by declaring them in a <%args> block:

```
1    <%args>
     $title
     $bgcol=>'yellow'
     </%args>
```

The same approach is used by a *top-level* component to receive parameters from the browser. In the example, the browser can send a parameter called num_lines back to the script. This is accepted using this declaration:

```
1    <%args>
     $num_lines=>10
     </%args>
```

with the variable given a value in its declaration. This value will act as a default if the parameter is not passed in. The arguments now need to be used in the component. This is done by placing them in <% %> tags:

```
<title>Current environment <% $title %></title>
```

with the current value held by the variable, $title in this case replacing the tag. When you want to execute lines of Perl, you place a % sign in the first column of the line. Do not leave any white space before the symbol though, as then the code will not be executed.

```
1    % foreach my $key (sort keys %ENV) {
     %     last if(--$num_lines <= 0);
     % }
```

11.5.2 Mason In Action

I decided I would create a more complex application to show you some more of the features of Mason. I also wanted to demonstrate that a Mason page can be made from lots of components. Figure 11.2 shows the results of my efforts. I am not going to take you through the whole set of code. It is included below so that you can find out how the page was created. I will pick out one or two highlights along the way. Probably the best way of finding out how that page is made would be to recreate it for yourself then start changing bits. See what happens as it breaks and you will soon learn how it all works.

main.html

The main page is a table and seven Mason components. Notice how components can be placed inside the table yet still work perfectly. This type of structure leads to really clean

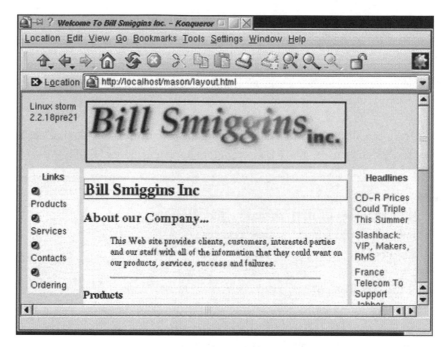

Figure 11.2 Using Mason

and readable code; once you have seen a couple of examples the structure of a page becomes obvious. Compared to this, CGI scripts are almost unreadable.

```
1   <& thetop &>
    <table border="0" width="95%" cellpadding="2" align="center">
      <colgroup>
        <col width="100">
5       <col>
        <col width="100">
      </colgroup>
      <tr valign="top">
        <!-- main header -->
10      <td><& motd &></td>
        <td><& logo &></td>
      </tr>
      <tr valign="top">
        <!-- content -->
15      <td><& links &></td>
        <td><& thebody &></td>
```

```
        <td><& headlines &></td>
     </tr>
   </table>
20  <& footer &>
```

thetop

I could have placed all the HTML which starts the page into the main file. I've deliberately split it out so that you can see that Mason components can be pure HTML.

```
1  <html>
     <head>
       <title>Welcome To Bill Smiggins Inc.</title>
       <link rel="stylesheet" type="text/css"
5            href="../html/test.css" media="screen" />
     </head>
   <body bgcolor="#f0e68c">
```

motd

UNIX systems include a file called motd which contains a piece of text called *the message of the day*. This is sometimes used by system administrators to display a message to all users as they log-on to the system. In this component I read the contents of that file and show them on my page.

```
1  <table border="0" cellpadding="0" cellspacing="0" align="left">
           <tr><td><% $motd %></td></tr>
   </table>

5  <%init>
   my($MOTD, $motd, @tmp);

   open MOTD, 'etc/motd' or die "Message of the day is unavailable";
   while (<MOTD>) {
10   @tmp = split /#/, $_;
     $motd = $tmp[0];
   }
   </%init>
```

The Perl code is placed inside <%init> tags. These create a special type of Mason element which is called as soon as the component is loaded. If you want to perform a lot of Perl processing inside a component, using <%init> is a very good idea. It lets you cleanly separate the HTML and Perl and makes the source much cleaner.

logo

More HTML, this time including a link to an image:

```
1  <table border="0" align="left">
     <tr>
       <td bgcolor="#000000">
         <img src="../html/logo.gif" height="80" width="352" />
5      </td>
     </tr>
   </table>
```

links

This table of links is also used in Chapter 15:

```
1  <table border="0" align="left" cellpadding="0" bgcolor="#fff8dc">
     <tr><th>Links</th></tr>
     <tr><td><img src="../html/bullet.gif" />  Products</td></tr>
     <tr><td><img src="../html/bullet.gif" />  Services</td></tr>
5    <tr><td><img src="../html/bullet.gif" />  Contacts</td></tr>
     <tr><td><img src="../html/bullet.gif" />  Ordering</td></tr>
   </table>
```

thebody

```
1  <div style="background: #fff8dc">
     <h1>Bill Smiggins Inc</h1>
     <h2>About our Company...</h2>

5    <p>This Web site provides clients, customers, interested parties and our
     staff with all of the information that they could want on our products,
     services, success and failures.</p>

     <hr />
10   <h3>Products</h3>

     <p align="center">We are probably the largest supplier of custom
     widgets, thingummybobs and bits and pieces in North America.</p>

15   <hr width="50%" />
   </div>
```

headlines

The most complicated component on the page is used to include headlines from Slashdot. I am reusing a lot of the code from Section 11.4. I have, though, had to change the code which processes the XML file. In the Mason version I am using regular expressions to pick out the rows of data which I am interested in. I can do this because slashdot.xml is a well-defined and neat XML document. If I wanted to do this in anger I would have to use proper XML processing code.

You are probably wondering why I went to the trouble of rewriting perfectly acceptable code which works well. Unfortunately I was faced with a limitation of Mason. You cannot place Perl functions inside Mason components and make calls to them. Mason converts each component into a Perl object and places code in such functions as *it* requires. If you create a function of your own, it may get wrapped inside Mason's function definition so that it no longer works. There are two solutions to this problem. First, as I have done here, write your code so that it does not require function calls. Mason lets you call built-in Perl functions and those in Perl objects and modules. This leads to alternative two, which is to define a class which encapsulates the functions you require. You then use that class inside your components. For large problems or industrial strength code, the latter alternative is by far the better approach. Since I have not shown you how to implement object orientation in Perl I am using the first alternative here.

```
1  <table border="0" align="left" bgcolor="#fff8dc">
   <tr><th>Headlines</th></tr>
   % for($i = 0; $i <= $k; $i++){
   <tr>
5    <td>
       <a href="<% $urls[$i] %>"><% $linktext[$i] %></a>
     </td>
   </tr>
   %}
10 </table>

   <%once>
   my($ua, $rq, @linktext, @urls, $j, $k, $i);
   my($response, $item, @lines);
15 </%once>

   <%init>
   require LWP::UserAgent;
```

```
20   $ua = new LWP::UserAgent;
     $rq = new HTTP::Request('GET', 'http://www.slashdot.org/slashdot.xml');

     @linktext = "";
     @urls = "";
25   $j = $k = 0;
     $response = $ua->request($rq);

     if($response->is_success) {
       @lines = split /\n/, $response->content;
30     foreach $item (@lines) {
         if($item =~ m/<title>(.+)<\/title>/) {
           push @linktext, $1;
           $k++;
         }
35       if($item =~ m/<url>(.+)<\/url>/) {
           push @urls, $1;
         }
       }
     }
40
     </%init>
```

I have used a new Mason construct in there. The <%once> ... </%once>, block is used to define code which is executed exactly once[2] when the component is loaded. Here I use it to scope the variables to the file and so avoid lots of error messages from the strict module.

footer

The final component on this page is the footer. It includes all of the HTML elements which are needed to complete a document and it displays the current time and date. I am reusing the code from Section 9.8.3 to create these. However, because you cannot easily place calls to functions within Mason components I need to slightly rearrange this code. The code needs to be copied from the GetTime function and placed inside an <%init> block:

```
1    <hr>
     <p>The time is <% $time %> on <% $today %> </p>
     <p>This site &copy; 2005, Chris Bates.</p>
     <hr>
```

[2]No surprise there, then.

```
5   </body>
    </html>

    <%init>
     my ($sec, $min, $hour, $mday, $month, $year,
10       $wday, $yday, $isdst, $day, $today, $time);

    # put the time and date generation routine here

    </%init>
```

11.6 CREATING AND MANIPULATING IMAGES

The Web is awash with graphics. The vast majority of pages include at least one static image, some include so many that waiting for their download to complete can be a nightmare. Images can be animated, used in navigation systems or included to provide vital information. Let's face it, the Web is a graphical medium. It was not always, in the early days the Web was purely text-based and a minority of users and developers would like to see a return to that era. In one respect, at least, many sites remain text-based. Most CGI scripts return a page of text to the browser, few programmers even bother to add decorative images. This is not because the technologies do not exist, after all you can place hyperlinks which point to image files inside your CGI `print` statements. It is more likely that CGI programmers simply do not think about using images on their pages.

Since we are using Perl to develop our CGI scripts, we ought to investigate the facilities which it provides for graphics programming. If the language has any useful modules then we could try using them inside our Web pages. I hope you are already ahead of me here and have guessed that amongst the myriad things you can do with Perl, you can write programs which create and manipulate graphics. It is surprising at first glance that Perl, a text processing language, has graphical libraries. In fact if you look in the CPAN archive, you will find that there are Perl modules for just about everything. The language has evolved. In so doing it has become a real general purpose language which can be used for many different classes of task.

What sort of image processing might you want, or need, to perform on your Web site? You might want to create images from scratch or you might want to alter existing images. Before writing any code you should be aware that this type of work can be extremely processor intensive. If you do a lot of graphical processing on your server you will place a high load on it and slow down other work. One good solution is to farm image processing out to another, dedicated, server. That is a great idea if you run your own servers, but generally it is not possible. You will need to optimize your image processing code wherever you can and investigate profiling and performance-enhancing tools before you do any serious work.

In my view, scripted image manipulation on Web sites can be used successfully in two areas. First, you can take existing images and alter them in some way. Creating image files can be difficult and time consuming. If you have gone to the effort of placing your digital photos onto your Web server, you probably do not want to have to edit each of those images in Adobe Photoshop to add a copyright message. You probably do not want to sort through and crop them all individually or add a sepia tint to each. You will probably want to preserve the image in its original state so that it can be used in different ways in different situations. It is important to remember that image files are just data files. When you alter the image you alter the data. Therefore if you change the color depth or file type you will be losing data from that file. Once that data has gone, it cannot be restored. Thus making those changes programmatically whilst preserving all of the image data is very appealing.

The second thing you can try is actually creating an image from scratch. The best use of this is probably the creation of graphs based upon data stored elsewhere. There are many situations in which you might need to present graphs of your data. You may want to demonstrate loading on your Web server, total sales over the last twelve months or absence rates amongst your coders on sunny days. Those data sets may be stored in plain text files on the Web server or inside proprietary software, such as Excel spreadsheets or Oracle databases. If you can rely upon your users having the appropriate application, for instance the spreadsheet, on their machine then you might just as well use it. What if you need to present that data to sales staff who are on the road and have only a mobile phone and PDA with them? And what about download times? A spreadsheet is a large chunk of data to download, especially if you only need to scan a single graph. A small image, on the other hand, remains a small image however it is downloaded or viewed. The image can present exactly the same information as the spreadsheet graph, so why not use it?

Hundreds of different image formats are available. It sometimes seems that there is a rule somewhere stating that every single graphics package has to have a proprietary data format. Saving data in the native format of your graphics package ensures that you are saving the maximum amount of information possible about the image. Unfortunately it also means that the image is unlikely to be very portable. In fact, if you want to display an image in a Web browser you are really restricted to three data types: GIF, JPEG and PNG.

The GIF format was invented by Compuserve but uses a compression algorithm which Unisys had previously patented. This means that the developers of any software which can manipulate GIF files *must* pay royalties to Unisys. For a number of years the Unisys patent was widely ignored and many software applications were developed to manipulate GIFs. These included a number of Perl modules based around Thomas Boutell's GD library, which is written in C, and the ImageMagick library. Unisys has recently been much more assertive over its rights and these libraries no longer read or write GIF files.

NOTE *The controversy over the Unisys patent does not mean that you cannot use GIF files on your Web pages. It simply means that the authors of any software you use to create or manipulate those files must pay Unisys.*

The loss of GIF as a format for the Web developer is important. GIFs have many advantages over other data types: they are nice and small and have just enough clarity to display well inside Web pages. GIF is a particularly nice format for logos, cartoons and graphs. JPEG, on the other hand, is designed for images of near photographic quality. A JPEG file will tend to be much larger than the same image stored as a GIF. The PNG format was developed as an open, patent-free replacement for GIF and is supported by version 3 and later of both Internet Explorer and Navigator. It is the format which I am going to be using in the examples in this chapter.

I am going to show you three different things you might want to try, and in doing so I hope to give you a brief introduction to the facilities in some of the Perl modules. I am *not* attempting to provide you with a user guide to those modules. Instead I will give you enough information to get you started and to help you over some of the initial hurdles. Much more information can be found in the POD provided with the modules. If you want to go further, I would also recommend checking out Shaun Wallace's book *Programming Web Graphics* (published in spring 1999). That was written when the modules still supported GIF files, but much of the detail remains appropriate and useful today.

First, I will show you how to write some text onto an image using the GD.pm module. Then I will show you how to create a simple graph with GD::Graph. Finally I will demonstrate how you can filter and crop an existing image using ImageMagick.

11.6.1 Using GD

The GD module is a port to Perl of the GD library which was written by Thomas Boutell. The original version of the module was simply a wrapper around a set of calls to Boutell's C code. Later versions of the module include a complete port of the library to Perl. This means that the library includes everything you need to draw and manipulate images. If you want to compile your own version then you will need access to the header files and libraries from GD, if you are using a version someone else compiled, you will not. The module is available as a package for most Linux distributions and, from ActiveState, for Windows. By default, the GD.pm module produces PNG format images. Until recently the module could produce GIF files, older versions are available from its homepage. The port of GD was carried out by Lincoln Stein who also wrote CGI.pm.

Simple Applications

I will start by looking at a simple piece of code which writes a text string into a file as a PNG image. The process of creating an image has five stages:

- import the GD module into your script
- create an image
- create a color table which holds information about the colors that you will use in the image
- draw the image
- output the image either to a file or to STDOUT for further processing elsewhere.

The following application shows those stages:

```perl
1  #!/usr/bin/perl -w

   use GD;
   use strict;
5
   my ($newim, $red, $white, $OUT);


   $newim = GD::Image->new(115, 20);
   $white = $newim->colorAllocate(255, 255, 255);
10 $red = $newim->colorAllocate(190, 0, 0);
   $newim->string(gdLargeFont, 0, 0, "This is a test", $red);


   open(OUT, ">gdtest.png") || die ("Unable to open $OUT");
   binmode OUT;
15 print OUT $newim->png;
   close OUT;


   exit(0);
```

Unlike many of the earlier examples, much of that will not make any sense at all without some explanation. I will go through the code piece by piece and introduce the features of GD.pm along the way. The script starts with:

```perl
1  use GD;
   use strict;
   my ($newim, $red, $white, $OUT);
```

This tells the interpreter to use the GD module and to rigorously apply the rules of the language with the strict module. GD.pm includes three classes, each of which encapsulates a different set of functionality. These can be imported individually by writing, for instance:

```
use GD::Polygon;
```

or all of them can be included by using the statement shown in my script.

GD::Image

> is used to read, store and write image data. This class provides access to many primitive graphics routines.

GD::Font

> holds information about fonts and is used when rendering text.

GD::Polygon

> The polygon class is used to hold details of polygonal shapes. It stores a list of the vertices of the polygon which is rendered elsewhere.

```
$newim = new GD::Image(115, 20);
```

In graphics programming an image is a representation of a picture in memory. Before your scripts can perform any manipulations you need to create an image. This can be empty, as in the example, or based upon the contents of an existing file.

$image = GD::Image->new([width, height])

> This creates a new image which contains no data. The width and height parameters are optional but if given they indicate the size of the image in pixels. If the parameters are omitted the image will be 64x64 pixels.

$image = GD::Image(*FILEHANDLE)

> This creates an image based upon the contents of a filehandle. The filehandle must already be open.

$image = GD::Image($filename)

> This creates an image based upon the contents of a file.

Once the image has been created the next stage is to allocate the colors:

```
1   $white = $newim->colorAllocate(255, 255, 255);
    $red = $newim->colorAllocate(190, 0, 0);
```

This is done using the colorAllocate() method in the newly created image object. In the example I create two colors, the first one will be used for the background, the other for the foreground.

NOTE *The first color that you create is* always *used as the background color for the image.*

`$image->colorAllocate(red, green, blue)`

This function creates a color and returns its index in the color table. The parameters each take an integer value from 0 through to 255.

`$image->colorDeallocate($index)`

This marks the color at the given index as unused so that it can be re-allocated.

`$image->colorClosest(red, green, blue)`

This will return the index of the allocated color which is closest to the one specified by the parameters. If no colors have been allocated the function will return -1.

`$image->transparent($index)`

All pixels which use the color at the supplied index are made transparent.

Now that the colors are allocated, it is time to create the image:

`$newim->string(gdLargeFont, 0, 0, "This is a test", $red);`

In this case I am simply drawing a text string. I could have been using any of the dozens of drawing functions which the module provides.

`arc(cx, cy, width, height, start, end, $index)`

This draws an ellipse centered on position (cx, cy) with the specified height and width. The visible portion of the ellipse is given by the start and end positions. The arc is drawn in the color found at $index in the color table.

`fill(x, y, $index)`

This will fill a region starting at pixel (x, y) with the color found in the color table at the given index. The fill stops when it reaches any pixel which has a different color to the one at position (x, y).

`line(x1, y1, x2, y2, $index)`

This draws a line from the pixel at position (x1, y1) to the pixel at (x2, y2) in the color found at the given index.

`polygon($polygon, $index)`

This draws the polygon, which is described by the polygon object in the first parameter, in the color found at $index.

rectangle(x1, y1, x2, y2, $index)

This draws a rectangle whose top left corner is at (x1, y1) and whose bottom right corner is at (x2, y2). The rectangle is drawn in color $index.

string($font, x1, y1, string, $index)

This will draw a string starting at position (x1, y1) in the color at $index. The font can be any of:

- gdGiantFont
- gdLargeFont
- gdMediumBoldFont
- gdSmallFont
- gdTinyFont

stringUp($font, x1, y1, string, $index)

This works just like string but rotates the text through 90 degrees clockwise.

Finally the image is saved to a file:

```
1  open(OUT, ">gdtest.png") || die ("Unable to open $OUT");
   binmode OUT;
   print OUT $newim->png;
   close OUT;
```

Writing to the file starts by opening it in a conventional way. Because some operating systems, at least all variations of Microsoft Windows, distinguish between binary and text files, we need to set the filehandle to binary mode. This is done with:

```
binmode OUT;
```

Finally the data is written to the file using the print function and the filehandle closed.

Working On The Web

The previous example is not very Web-aware. In fact the created image is saved to a file rather than being sent back to the browser. There is almost no point in performing a manipulation like that on your Web site but not letting the user see the results instantly. In fact, getting the data back to the browser is very easy. You should remember that Web servers redirect STDOUT so that anything printed to it goes to the browser. The following code incorporates a couple of changes to get the output right:

```
1  #!/usr/bin/perl -w

   use GD;
```

```
use strict;

my ($newim, $red, $white, $OUT);

$newim = GD::Image->new(115, 20);
$white = $newim->colorAllocate(255, 255, 255);
$red = $newim->colorAllocate(190, 0, 0);
$newim->string(gdLargeFont, 0, 0, "This is a test", $red);

print ("Content-type: image/png\r\n\r\n");
binmode STDOUT;
print $newim->png;

exit(0);
```

Notice that before running the `binmode` command I print a MIME type declaration:

```
print ("Content-type: image/png\r\n\r\n");
```

If I did not do this, the browser would have no way of knowing that it was receiving an image file. Instead, it would attempt to show the characters inside the file as ASCII text. To avoid this, we need to warn the browser that it has to process the data as an image and display it properly.

If you comment out the printing of the MIME type, you can redirect the output of this script to a file or to another program so that you can check it is working. On a UNIX system[3] I can run the script and show its output in the ImageMagick `display` utility:

```
gdtest.cgi | display
```

or save the image in a file with:

```
gdtest.cgi > gdtest.png
```

Manipulating Existing Images

The next situation which needs examining is the opening and alteration of an image which is stored in a file. The result may be written back to the file or sent to STDOUT from where it can be redirected. In the following example, I read in an existing file then draw a small blue triangle on top of it. Read the script then I will explain it:

[3]So far as I know, you cannot do this on a Windows box. You will need to save the image in a file instead.

```perl
1   #!/usr/bin/perl -w

    use strict;
    use GD;
5
    my ($IMGFILE, $im, $OUT, $triangle, $blue);

    open(IMGFILE, "./logo.png") || die "Unable to open source file";
    $im = newFromPng GD::Image(\*IMGFILE) || die "Unable to read image file";
10  close IMGFILE;

    $triangle = new GD::Polygon;
    $triangle->addPt(10, 5);
    $triangle->addPt(50, 18);
15  $triangle->addPt(25, 4);

    $blue = $im->colorAllocate(0, 0, 190);
    $im->filledPolygon($triangle, $blue);

20  print ("Content-type: image/png\r\n\r\n");
    binmode STDOUT;
    print $im->png;
    exit(0);
```

This script uses a different approach to creating an image. Rather than using the methods I outlined earlier, this time I use a specialized function:

```perl
$im = newFromPng GD::Image(\*IMGFILE)
```

newFromPng GD::Image(FILEHANDLE)

> This function creates a new image based upon the contents of a PNG file. A *reference* to a filehandle is passed in as the parameter. The function calls binmode when that is appropriate but does not automatically close the filehandle.

newFromJpeg GD::Image(FILEHANDLE)

> This will create a new image based upon the contents of a JPEG file. JPEG is a 24-bit format but GD uses 8-bit images so this method will lose data.

newFromGd GD::Image(FILEHANDLE)

> This creates an image based upon the contents of file in native GD format.

newFromXpm GD::Image(FILEHANDLE)
> Will create an image based on the contents of an XPM file. This method will not work in all versions of the GD module.

The next stage in the script is to create a triangle which I will then draw on top of the image. The polygon object is an instance of the GD::Polygon class. Once created it is populated with a set of points. Each point represents one of the vertices of the polygon:

```
$triangle = new GD::Polygon;
$triangle->addPt(10, 5);
$triangle->addPt(50, 18);
$triangle->addPt(25, 4);
```

addPt(x, y)
> adds a point to the polygon,

setPt(x, y)
> changes the value of an existing vertex,

deletePt(x, y)
> deletes an existing vertex and returns the deleted value,

length
> returns the number of vertices in the polygon,

vertices
> returns a list in the polygon. Each item in the list is an array containing x and y co-ordinates.

The script concludes by writing the new image to STDOUT. Notice that this script leaves the original image in its original state.

11.6.2 Creating Graphs With GD::Graph

The GD module is clearly stocked with useful routines. These have been used by Martien Verbruggen in his creation of the GD::Graph module. This is a direct replacement for the earlier GIFgraph module. If you find that on your system, try to get an upgrade to the latest version of GD::Graph. Output formats mirror those of GD and, of course, data can be streamed back to a user so that the graph appears in their Web browser.

GD::Graph supports several types of graph and chart: line, point, area and bar graphs and pie charts. Individual data sets are displayed in different colors and you can supply titles, legends and titles for each axis. If you want a slightly different outcome there is also GD::Graph3D available which, you will not be surprised to learn, draws three-dimensional graphs.

A Simple Application

Again, I am going to explain the module through a simple example. The following code draws a bar graph which contains two data sets. IT demonstrates the use of the key features of the module and should be enough to get you started:

```perl
1   #!/usr/bin/perl -w

    use strict;
    use GD::Graph::bars;
5
    my (@data, @legend, $graph, $OUT, $drawn);

    @data = ([qw(MON TUES WED THURS FRI SAT SUN)],
             [12, 356, 67, 346, 8, 0, 189],
10           [45, 45, 45, 678, 45, 45, 5]
             );

    @legend = ('Orders', 'Returns');
    $graph = GD::Graph::bars->new();
15  $graph->set(x_label => 'Week Day',
                y_label => 'Volume',
                title => 'Returns and Orders (by day)');
    $graph->set_legend(@legend);

20  my $format = $graph->export_format;

    print STDOUT("Content-type: image/$format\r\n\r\n");
    binmode STDOUT;
    print STDOUT $graph->plot(\@data)->$format();
25
    exit(0);
```

Let us look at some of the highlights.

I start of by deciding what type of graph I want to draw. The GD::Graph module supports several types, each implemented as a class. You must specify the type of graph you're going to create in your use statement:

```perl
use GD::Graph::bars;
```

GD::Graph::area

is a graph which shows data as the area under a line,

GD::Graph::bars

    where data items are shown as bars,

GD::Graph::lines

    where data is represented by lines joining the data values,

GD::Graph::linespoints

    combines the features of a line and a point graph,

GD::Graph::pie

    in which data is represented as segments of a pie,

GD::Graph::points

    where data is represented by points.

The first stage in creating a graph must be the definition of the data set. Data is specified in an array which has to have a very particular format.

NOTE *If you get the array structure wrong,* GD::Graph *will not be able to draw anything.*

```
1  @data = ([qw(MON TUES WED THURS FRI SAT SUN)],
          [12, 356, 67, 346, 8, 0, 189],
          [45, 45, 45, 678, 45, 45, 5]
          );
```

The array consists of a series of arrays, each enclosed in square brackets. Each array *must* have the same number of items, if you do not have a value for one location use undef, do not leave a space. The next thing to do is to create a legend which is done using an array of strings, one for each data set that will appear on the chart:

```
@legend = ('Orders', 'Returns');
```

Now we are ready to create the graph.

GD::Graph::type->new([width, height])

    This creates a new graph object. Replace type in the definition with the class of graph which you want to create. The width and height parameters are optional, if you omit them the graph will be 400x300 pixels. The class of the graph will be one of lines, points, area, bars, linespoints or pie.

set(attribute => value ...)

Once a graph object exists we can start to modify its default attributes. This is done using the set method which takes attribute/value pairs as parameters:

```
1    $graph->set(x_label => 'Week Day',
                 y_label => 'Volume',
                 title => 'Returns and Orders (by day)');
```

set_legend(@legend)

This sets the legend for your graph to the values in the array @legend,

$graph->export_format

The GD library defines a data type which it will use to export, that is to *output*, the finished graph. This function queries the library to find out what that format is and returns it, usually as a scalar,

plot(data)

This plots the graph and returns a GD::Image object,

Printing the graph is best done by combining the plot() and a call to the format object:

```
print STDOUT $graph->plot(\@data)->$format();
```

Of course, GD::Graph has many more options than I have shown you here. You can find out all about them in a command shell with:

```
perldoc GD::Graph
```

11.6.3 Using ImageMagick

Our final graphical application is included to show you the sort of thing which you can achieve if you use the correct module. ImageMagick is a set of tools which mostly run from the command line. These are truly industrial-strength tools, they can manipulate just about every graphics format that you can think of. They can perform conversions, filtering, help create animations and much more besides. Unlike GD, there is no direct Perl replacement for ImageMagick. Instead, there is a Perl wrapper which is used to call the native C code routines inside the ImageMagick tools. The Perl module you will need is called PerlMagick At the time of writing, version 6.2 is available from CPAN.

The sample application I have created here takes an image in PNG format, inverts and crops it and filters it so that it looks like an oil painting. The two images are displayed inside a Web page. The result of all that processing is shown in Figure 11.3.

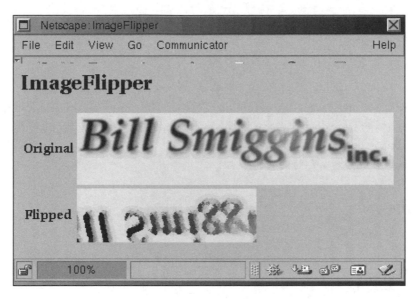

Figure 11.3 Using Image::Magick

A Simple Application

This little application has two pieces of code for us. An HTML page, and a CGI script.

The HTML Page

```
1   <html>
      <head>
        <title>ImageFlipper</title>
      </head>
5     <body>
        <h1>ImageFlipper</h1>
        <table border="0">
          <tr>
            <th>Original</th>
10          <td><img src="./logo.gif"
                height="80"
                width="352"
                alt="Logo" /></td>
          </tr>
15        <tr>
            <th>Flipped</th>
            <td><img src="../cgi-bin/flipper.cgi" /></td>
```

```
        </tr>
      </table>
20    </body>
</html>
```

There is nothing particularly new in that HTML. The important thing to notice is that the source of an image does not have to be a graphic file. In this example one of the sources is a CGI script:

```
<img src="../cgi-bin/flipper.cgi" />
```

The Script

```
1  #!/usr/bin/perl -w

   use strict;
   use Image::Magick;
5
   my($image, $OUT, $blue);

   $image = Image::Magick->new;
   $image->Read('./logo.png');
10
   $image->OilPaint(radius=>3);
   $image->Crop('200x60+50+10');
   $image->Flip();

15 print("Content-type: image/png\r\n\r\n");
   $image->Write('png:-');
   exit(0);
```

I have got absolutely no intention of going into any detail about that script. ImageMagick is extraordinarily complete and you really need to read its documentation before you attempt to use it. There is a Web site which has plenty of information, you can find it at:

```
http://www.imagemagick.org/
```

Only limited documentation is supplied with the PerlMagick distribution since it is effectively the same as ImageMagick. What you will notice from the script I have given you is that reading, writing and manipulating images this way is pretty straight-forward. Although ImageMagick itself is complicated, the API it offers is nice and clean.

EXERCISES

Perl and Modules

1. What are the main features of the Perl module approach to library development?
2. Identify and describe the benefits which programmers get from the use of namespaces in programming languages.

File Uploads

1. Create an on-line photo album to hold images of yourself, your family and friends.
2. Develop an HTML form through which pictures can be uploaded to the site. Information about the image such as its size, a suitable title and the name of the photographer should accompany the image.
3. Generate dynamic Web pages which automatically include new images as they are added to the album.

Relational Databases

1. List six benefits that arise from using relational databases in Web applications.
2. What is the Perl DBI module? How does it support database-independent applications development?
3. What is meant by the term session in conventional database usage? How does a DBI session differ from this?
4. Under what conditions would an application run more efficiently when using flat files rather than a database?
5. What is a prepared statement? Why must statements be prepared by DBI?
6. Alter your guestbook application so that it uses a relational database instead of flat files.
7. Write a database application using Perl DBI. How easy is it to build such an application so that it can be queried and updated from a Web page?

libwww

1. If it is not already available on your system, install libwww and configure your system to use it.
2. Write a script to access the contents file at Slashdot. Display the contents of the file in your own Web page.
3. Write a script which will download an arbitrary Web page, extract its body section and display it inside a new Web page.

4. Modify your previous example so that the page contents are saved into a file.

5. Are there any legal or ethical objections to copying other sites in this way?

6. Write a script which measures the response times of various Web servers by seeing how long each takes to return the file `index.html`.

HTML::Mason

1. Install and configure the `HTML::Mason` module. You may need to get hold of a copy of the Apache Web server before this works easily.

2. Create a simple page which uses two components: one for the header and one for the body. Check that a browser can access this page correctly via the Web server.

3. Create a guestbook which uses components to display comments from visitors.

4. Create an on-line photo album which is structured using Mason components.

Manipulating Images

1. Download, install and configure the GD and PerlMagick modules. You may also need to install a version of ImageMagick.

2. Write a script which sepia tints the pictures in your on-line photo album.

3. Add a copyright message to each image as it is being downloaded from your site.

PART V

PHP

An Introduction to PHP

P rocessing Web data using CGI and related technologies has a relatively long history. A number of alternatives have been developed by big commercial software houses including Microsoft, IBM, Sun, and Allaire. Personally, I am interested in what the Free Software movement has to offer since excellent tools such as Perl and Apache come from that community.

Almost all non-CGI approaches to Web programming involve some form of *templating system*. Templates are outline HTML pages which have calls to scripts or programs embedded within them. When the page is requested, the scripts are executed and the result of that execution replaces the original code. This is really the reverse of CGI. In CGI processing the script is called and it creates the HTML page. Why does it matter if the script or the markup come first? From a pure performance point of view the two approaches are really pretty similar. At runtime the server has to do quite a lot of work, but if you are using an Apache extension such as mod_perl you will get great performance. The big difference really comes during development.

Large Web sites tend to be created by teams of people, each of whom brings their own specialized skills to the project. A really large site may need HTML authors, programmers to create scripts for both the server and the client, graphical designers and artists and, finally, content creators. If you are working for an organization like CNN or the BBC, you may only meet your collaborators at weekly team meetings, yet the work that each of you do is closely coupled to the work of everyone else. Consider the programmer and the HTML author. If a script is creating the HTML, who is leading the work? Is it the HTML author who decides what scripts are needed or the programmer who requests a particular HTML structure? And who does the design? Most programmers can create good code but their pages are likely to be poorly set out. HTML coders, on the other hand, may create great pages but lousy scripts.

This is where templating systems enter the picture. All of these systems place HTML and some scripting inside the same file but separate them so that they can be developed independently. The HTML author is able to write calls to scripted functions which a programmer can develop later. When the page is returned to a browser the script call is replaced by its result. That is enough introduction, this chapter is about PHP, so what is it?

12.1 PHP

The acronym PHP is one of the recursive kind favored by free software projects[1] and stands for *PHP Hypertext Processor*. The PHP project has a home on the Web at `http://www.php.net` where you can get source code, compiled binaries for systems like Microsoft Windows and a large, quite well written manual.

PHP is a development from a project called Personal Home Page Tools which was started by Rasmus Lerdorf in 1994. The original version consisted of a set of unique macros, a parser and some tools. The parser was rewritten in 1997 when a wider project was based around Lerdorf's original work. This parser was the basis of PHP3 which gained phenomenal popularity. Version 4 had another new parser and continued the growth in usage. The latest release, version 5, adds better support for object-orientation.

If you have never heard of PHP, you may be wondering just how popular it is. That is not a question which can be answered easily. It is possible to measure how many servers have PHP enabled and then calculate how many Web sites are hosted on those servers. In August 2005, the Netcraft Survey[2] said that PHP is available on over 1.3 million servers and used in over 22 million domains. The Apache module which integrates PHP into the World's most popular Web server is used four times more often than the `mod_perl` module.

The reasons for the popularity of PHP are manifold:

- PHP is Web specific which makes it more attractive to many than, for instance, a more powerful generic tool like Perl
- PHP is free software and has been ported to a vast range of operating systems,
- PHP works extremely well with many different Web servers, unlike the `HTML::Mason` Perl module which works best with Apache
- PHP scripts can use many standard network protocols since libraries are supplied for IMAP, NNTP, SMTP and POP3 as well as HTTP
- almost everything that Perl can do on the Web can be done by PHP including setting and reading cookies and image manipulation
- PHP is able to work with a vast range of database systems from UNIX DBM through relational systems such as MySQL to full size commercial solutions like Oracle
- PHP has the ability to process XML data and RSS feeds out of the box.

[1] After the example of GNU which stands for GNU is Not Unix.
[2] Which can be found at `http://www.netcraft.com`.

The PHP language is described in its documentation as a mixture of Perl, C and Java. That sounds like a recipe for disaster but it is not, simply because you only have to use those facilities which you actually need. If you want to create classes and objects, you can. If you want to connect to a relational database on a remote server, you can. If you just want to parse data from a form and return an acknowledgement, you can do that too.

PHP is a large language but you can achieve a lot using just a small subset of it. I am not planning to give you much more than an introductory overview in this book. I hope that I will show you enough to enable you to get to grips with some quite complex scripting – you will certainly see enough to help you to understand the documentation that is supplied with the PHP distribution. One important omission is the use of object-oriented development techniques. PHP can be used as a procedural language or it can be used to create complex object systems. I will take a very brief look at how classes and objects work in PHP but you will find that a simple approach pays dividends when you are learning a new language. If you do need to learn about PHP and objects, you will find the discussion of object-orientation and JavaScript in Chapter 6 gives you a very useful primer.

12.2 INTRODUCING PHP

Before looking at the details of PHP, I am going to show you how to use it. As ever you need some examples so that the explanation makes sense . . . but the examples will not make sense until you have read the explanation.

I do not want to spend time describing how to download, install and run PHP. You can get instructions from the project's homepage but you will find that configuring it to run with your particular Web server may be quite complex. Each Web server needs a different configuration – there is no such thing as a standard set-up on the Web. If you are using Apache, make sure that you also install the mod php extension which will give greatly improved performance. In my experience, most systems seem to want developers to place their PHP files in the same directory tree as their HTML. Many of these same systems want CGI scripts in a special directory, usually called cgi-bin. This fits nicely with the PHP philosophy which places so much importance on HTML.

 Unlike Perl's CGI.pm *module, you cannot normally run PHP as a stand-alone processor. If you want to use PHP you will need a running Web server.*

Once you have got PHP installed on your Web server, you need to test it. Create a file called info.php and put this code in it:

```
1   <html>
        <head><title>Details of PHP</title></head>
```

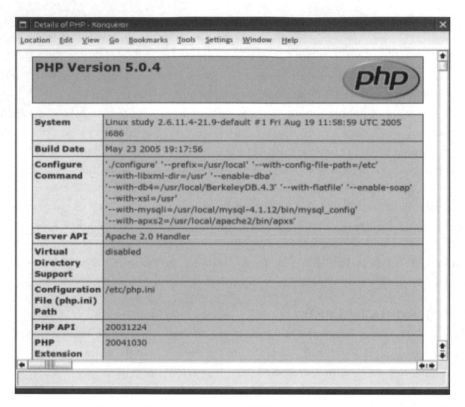

Figure 12.1 Testing a PHP installation

```
    <body>
        <?php phpinfo() ?>
5   </body>
</html>
```

Make sure that your Web server is up and running, then try to access the file through your Web browser. For instance, on my desktop machine the address is:

```
http://localhost/~chris/info.php
```

Figure 12.1 shows part of the result on my system. If you do not get a similar result, you will need to do some work on your configuration. If you have worked through some of the earlier programming examples in this book, then you have probably guessed that `phpinfo()` is some sort of function. It is one of many which are provided as part of the language. In this particular case it prints out vast amounts of information about your PHP installation, operating system and Web server. As an exercise try typing `phpinfo` into your favorite Web search engine. You will find links to numerous copies of the PHP documentation, you will also see lots of people revealing fascinating things about their servers.

12.3 INCLUDING PHP IN A PAGE

Once you have got PHP up and running, it is time to try creating a Web page. The following code is about the most simple you will find anywhere. Save it in a file called `simple.php` and access it from the Web:

```
1   <html>
        <head>
            <title>Hello</title>
        </head>
5       <body>
            <?php
                echo "<h1>Hello</h1>";
            ?>
        </body>
10  </html>
```

The PHP instructions are placed inside special HTML tags. All PHP instructions have to be placed inside such tags, although you can place large blocks of code inside the same set. You do not have to use a new tag for each line of code. The inclusion of PHP within HTML files is called *escaping* in the PHP documentation. The PHP interpreter looks for any of the escape sequences shown below, processes the code within them and replaces them with the result of that processing.

Four different methods are provided for escaping from HTML:

- `<? echo("<h1>Hello</h1>"); ?>`
- `<?php echo("<h1>Hello</h1>"); ?>`
- `<script language="php">`
  `echo("<h1>Hello</h1>");`
  `</script>`
- `<% echo("<h1>Hello</h1>"); %>`

The first method is only available if your PHP installation has been configured to allow *short tags*. The second method is the most legible and is the one that I shall use in this book. The third method is useful if you find an environment which supports mixed scripting languages inside the same HTML file, most do not. The final method uses the ASP syntax and is also reliant upon server configuration.

When you want to display text in the browser the command you need is `echo()`. PHP shows its derivation from C and similar languages because lines of code are terminated using semi-colons and blocks of code are enclosed within braces (curly brackets). Unlike JavaScript or Perl, PHP supports comments which span more than a single line of code:

```
1  <html>
       <head>
           <title>Comments</title>
       </head>
5      <body>
           <?php echo("<h1>PHP Comments</h1>");
           // this comment only lasts for a single line
           /*
           * this comment spans more
10         * than one line
           */
           ?>
       </body>
   </html>
```

Comments are ignored by the interpreter when it parses your code. This means that you can use them in the *normal* way to describe your program, but you can also use them to *comment out* pieces of code which you do not want to execute.

12.3.1 Variables

Creating variables is easy. Variable names follow the usual rules: alphanumeric characters are used plus the underscore and hyphen. Spaces are not allowed in variable names. There is one piece of syntax to note, variable names *always* start with the dollar sign:

```
1  $a_variable;
   $name = "Chris";
   $age = 36;
   $height = 1.778;
```

If you are used to a programming language such as Java or C++ then you may wonder where the data types are. In those languages variables are given explicit data types and may only hold data of their assigned type. In PHP, variables can hold any type of data, and the data type can change during the execution of the script. This is a common feature of interpreted languages.

PHP variables can reference other variables so that both names point to the same piece of memory. Changing the value of one variable changes the value of both. The name of the variable which is being referenced is preceded with an ampersand, &.

```
1   $name = "Chris";
    $alias = &$name;
    echo "$name is also $alias";
```

12.3.2 Accessing HTTP Data

Creating Web pages which you can send back to the browser is pretty easy in PHP, what about getting hold of data that has been sent back from your Web forms? Again this is exceptionally straightforward. PHP automatically creates a number of global arrays. The most important of these hold data which is sent using either the HTTP get or post methods. In the former case the data is appended to the URL of the PHP page, in the latter it is sent within the HTTP message. The browser selects the method which it is going to use because the HTML form elements has amethod attribute. The arrays of returned data are called $_POST and $_GET. PHP arrays are covered in lots of detail in Section 12.6. For now you just need to know that you access array elements using their names.

In the case of $_GET, for example, it holds data sent within a URL. Those data items come from HTML forms where they are identified using the name or id attribute. We can simulate the same thing by creating the complete URL ourselves. Here is an HTML page containing a form, and a PHP script to process the return data. After you have looked at the code I will show how to do the same thing but by modifying the URL.

```
1   <html>
        <head>
          <title>Web Forms in PHP</title>
        </head>
5       <body>
          <h1>Web Forms in PHP</h1>

          <form action="http://localhost/~chris/guest.php" method="GET">

10          <table border="0">
              <tr>
                <td>Your Name:</td>
                <td><input type="text" maxlength="32" size="20"
                    name="user"></td>
              </tr>
15            <tr>
                <td>Your Email Address:</td>
                <td><input type="text" maxlength="32" size="20"
                    name="mail"></td>
```

```
          </tr>
          <tr>
20            <td><input type="submit" value="Submit Details"></td>
              <td><input type="reset" value="Reset The Form"></td>
          </tr>
        </table>

25      </form>
      </body>
   </html>
```

Notice that the return data is going to be sent to a PHP script. Here that is:

```
1   <html>
        <head>
          <title>Your Data</title>
        </head>
5       <body>
          <h1>Your Data Processed By PHP</h1>
          <table border="0">
          <tr>
            <th>Your Name:</th>
10          <td><?php echo $_GET["user"]; ?></td>
          </tr>
          <tr>
            <th>Your Email Address:</th>
            <td><?php echo $_GET["mail"]; ?></td>
15        </tr>
          </table>
        </body>
   </html>
```

If you want to test the PHP script but do not want to create a form you can modify the URL:

```
http://localhost/~chris/guest.php?user=Chris&email=chris@email.home
```

The parameters follow the server address, from which they are separated by a question mark. Elements and values are separated using an equals sign. Finally, element:value pairs are kept apart using ampersands.

12.4 DATA TYPES

The use of variables is at the heart of all programming. Unlike Perl, where almost everything is either a scalar or an array, PHP variables have distinct types which means that they can be numbers, characters or strings. When PHP is interpreting your script it differentiates between these data types so that, for instance, you cannot generally add a string to a floating point number. Note, though, that you do not have to explicitly assign data types in your scripts. The PHP interpreter can work these things out for you. This means that a particular variable can hold numbers or strings or point to an array as the need arises.

Broadly speaking, variables must have unique names which can contain a mixture of letters and numbers. Variable names are case-sensitive and cannot start with a digit. Case-sensitivity means that $fred is a different variable to $fRed.

PHP variables are different from those found in languages like Java or C. They are much closer to the types of variable which we have encountered in JavaScript and Perl. Like those two, PHP is an interpreted language so nothing inside a script is really fixed until it runs.

12.4.1 Numbers

PHP supports two different numerical types. Most often you will use *integers*. If you have not programmed before, the terminology may confuse you, but an integer is simply a whole number. They can be positive or negative values. The range (maximum and minimum values) of integers in PHP is defined by the operating system and generally runs from approximately − 2000 000 000 up to 2000 000 000. In computing terms that is $\pm 2^{31}$. PHP integers can be declared in base 10, base 8 (octal) or base 16 (hexadecimal):

```
$positiveInt = 14;
$negativeInt = -78;
$octalInt = 0421;
$hexadecimalInt = 0x1c;
```

The second numerical data type in PHP is the floating-point number. Floating point is a computer representation of positive and negative decimal numbers. They can be expressed as simple decimals or as exponential values. In PHP, floating point values are system dependent in the same way that integers are; however, the range is far larger. Floating points are 64 bit numbers with a range of approximately $\pm 1.8e38$. That is more than big enough for most Web scripts you will ever write. Declaring floating point values is straightforward. The second example here uses the letter e to indicate that it is holding an exponential value:

```
$floater = 23.567;
$bigger = 4.6e7;
```

12.4.2 Boolean

These hold the values TRUE and FALSE. Booleans are most often used in controlling the flow of a program. Boolean values exist in a number of situations where no Boolean has been explicitly created by a program. In these cases the implicit Boolean can be used in a logical expression such as an `if`. Typically this is done when evaluating the return value from a function call. The following values always evaluate as FALSE, everything else is TRUE:

- Boolean variables holding FALSE
- integer 0
- float 0.0
- an empty string
- a string containing just "0"
- an array of length zero
- NULL.

12.4.3 Strings

Most of the data that gets manipulated on the Web is text. In PHP, text is stored in strings. These must be surrounded with quotes so that the interpreter does not mistake them for commands. PHP lets you use either single or double quotes around a string. If you use double quotes, any PHP variables inside the string are replaced by their value. Here are a few strings:

```
1  $str = "A Simple String";
   $str2 = 'Another String';
   $str3 = "This is $str2";
   $str4 = $str;            // copy by value
5  $str5 = &$str;           // copy by reference
```

Like most programming languages, certain character sequences carry special meaning in PHP. For instance, you need some way of telling the system to insert a newline inside the current piece of text. Such control characters must be replaced with *escape* sequences in your scripts. When the interpreter finds an escape sequence, those characters are replaced with the appropriate control code. Table 12.1 lists the possible escape codes in PHP.

Joining strings together is done by the process of *concatenation*. PHP uses the dot operator to concatenate strings, as does Perl:

```
1  $str1 = "Have A Nice";
   $str2 = "Day\n";
   $str3 = $str1 . " ";
   $str3 .= $str2;
```

Line three appends a string consisting of a single space onto the end of `$str1` and stores the result in `$str3`. The operation uses `$str1` but does not alter its value. In line four the value in `$str2` is appended onto the value in `$str3` and the result stored in `$str3`. PHP has a lot of operations which store their result in one of the original values, although most of these actually work with numbers, not string.

Escape Sequence	Meaning
\n	Insert a newline character
\r	Carriage return
\t	Horizontal tab
\\	Backslash
\$	Dollar
\"	Double quote

Table 12.1 Escape sequences in PHP

Here Documents

Often you will want to manipulate, especially display, a string which naturally spans more than one line of code. You can do this by placing a call to the echo() function before each line, but that is really pretty inefficient. Sending data to a browser like that may result in many calls to the interpreter and will certainly degrade performance. If the string is to be displayed pretty much *as is*, without any alteration, you are much better off using a *here* document. Unlike Perl, PHP will expand variables inside here documents. You are generally better off not doing this but instead keeping them in separate echo() statements to simplify code maintenance. In PHP a here document is delimited by <<< and a string token. The token is repeated at the end of the string to terminate printing. Again, unlike Perl, the terminating semi-colon appears after the terminating delimiter in PHP. The terminator must start in the first column of your code. Here is an example:

```
1   <html>
        <head>
            <title>Using Here Docs</title>
        </head>
5       <body>
    echo <<<_DONE
        <h1>Using Here Docs</h1>
        <p> The string which is being displayed in the browser can span several
            lines.</p>
    _DONE;
10      </body>
    </html>
```

12.4.4 Changing Data Type

Strings can be evaluated as if they were numbers, in the right circumstances. If a string contains only digits it can be used in mathematical expressions as if it were the equivalent number. For instance '12.561' automatically gets treated as 12.561. Optionally, such strings can start with '+' or '-' signs. If a string contains either 'e' or 'E' followed by one or more digits, it will be treated as an exponential value. Conversion of the string to a number stops when any characters are encountered which cannot normally be found in a number. Numbers, of course may be represented in base 10, 8 or 16. The following code shows some string conversions. The result is shown in Figure 12.2:

```
1   <html>
        <head>
            <title>Strings Into Numbers</title>
        </head>
5       <body>
            <h1>Strings Into Numbers</h1>
            <ul>
            <?php
                $n = "0x237a";
10              echo "<li>".$n."</li>";
                echo "<li>".($n * 3)."</li>";
```

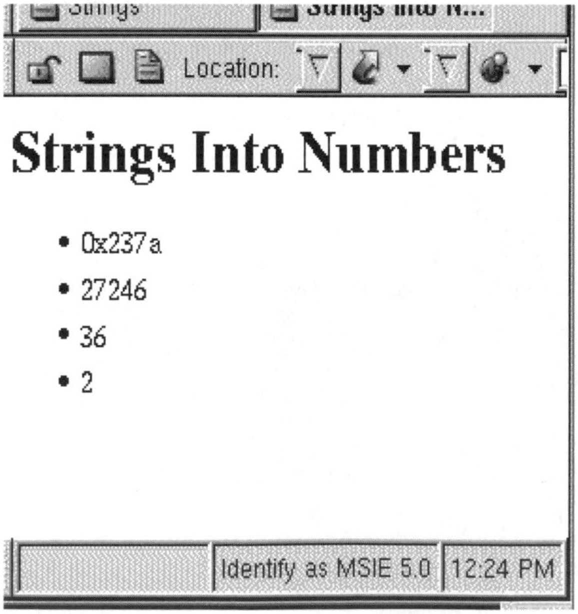

Figure 12.2 Converting strings to numbers

```
            $n2 = "34re5";
            echo "<li>".($n2 + 2)."</li>";
            $n3 = "boo";
15          echo "<li>".($n3 + 2)."</li>";
        ?>
        </ul>
    </body>
</html>
```

PHP also supports *type casting*. This process involves dynamically changing the type of a data item. You might need to do this if your variable holds an integer but you want to use it in floating point arithmetic. These type casts can be automatic. For instance, if you add a double to an integer, the result will be a double even if you are storing it in the original integer variable:

```
1   <?php
        $int = 32;
        $float = 12.67;
        $int = $int + $float;
5       echo $int;
    ?>
```

But you can be explicit about type casts too. This is done by putting the type you want the variable to become in parentheses before the variable name:

```
1   <?php
        $int = 32;
        $float = 12.67;
        $res = $float + (float)$int;
5       echo $res;
    ?>
```

12.4.5 Other Useful Functions

A variable can hold different types of data during the execution of a script. This may mean that there are times when you need to know the data type before performing your processing. PHP includes a set of functions which can do just that.

is_array(var)

    returns TRUE if the variable is an array,

is_double(var)

    returns TRUE if the variable is a double,

is_float(var)

   returns TRUE if the variable is a floating point number,

is_int(var)

   returns TRUE if the variable is an integer,

is_string(var)

   returns TRUE if the variable is a string,

is_object(var)

   returns TRUE if the variable is an object.

12.5 PROGRAM CONTROL

PHP scripts require structure in the same way as those written in JavaScript and Perl do. Like those two languages, PHP is structured in blocks of code with each block delimited by curly brackets. Programs are much more than blocks and variables. Within a program you need to make choices about what will happen and decide how often things happen. You might want your program displaying an error message if a visitor fails to enter their email address in the appropriate field of your form. You may want to print out a list of items which a shopper has placed in their cart.

   Program control is provided by a set of structures which let you make choices and decisions. Broadly, these program elements can be split into two sets: operators and control structures. Operators generally take two arguments and return a result. Most programming languages provide an addition operator which takes two numbers, adds them together and gives you back the answer. In PHP we also get operators which work on string data. I have already introduced you to the dot operator which is used to join strings together, for example. Table 12.2 lists the operators which PHP provides.

   Program control is provided through a set of branching and looping constructs. PHP provides the same set as many other languages.

if ... [elseif ...] else

   Many things inside programs are optional. As programs run they are continually having to make decisions about what to do. Generally these decisions are based upon the state of variables or the value of expressions. The program is being asked to evaluate expressions such as "if the value entered was greater than ten, do A, otherwise do B". In programming, such a statement is simplified to:

```
1    if(value > 10) {
        A
     } else {
        B
5    }
```

Op	Meaning	Op	Meaning
>	Greater than	>=	Greater than or equal to
<	Less than	<=	Less than or equal
==	Equal to	!=	Not equal to
=	Assignment	+	Addition
/	Division	*	Multiplication
-	Subtraction	%	Modulus division
&&	Logical AND	||	Logical OR
!	Logical NOT	+=	Add two values then assign the result to the operand on the left
-=	Subtract then assign the result to the operand on the left	*=	Multiply then assign the result to the operand on the left
/=	Divide then assign the result to the operand on the left	.=	Concatenate two strings then assign the result to the operand on the left
%=	Modulus division then assign the result to the operand on the left	++	Increment a value by one
--	Decrement a value by one		

Table 12.2 Logical operators (text and numerical)

The if ... else structure makes choices based upon the value of the expression which follows if. Such expressions are called Boolean because they evaluate to either TRUE or FALSE. When the expression is TRUE, the code which follows if is executed. When the expression is FALSE, the code following the else clause executes.

If you have more than two choices, you will need a slightly different construct. PHP provides an elseif clause which expands the number of choices you can make:

```
1   <html>
        <head>
```

```
            <title>Welcome</title>
        </head>
    5   <body>
            <h1>Welcome</h1>
            <p>
            <?php
                if($name == "Chris"){
   10               echo "Hi Chris!";
                } elseif($name != ""){
                    echo "Hi $name";
                } else {
                    echo "Please enter your name";
   15           }
            ?>
            </p>
        </body>
    </html>
```

Save that code in a file called names.php in the directory where you normally keep your PHP/HTML files. Run it by typing the URL of the file and supplying a name as parameter. On my system I use:

http://localhost/html/names.php?name=Chris

You can have as many elseif clauses as you need in there. If you are making a lot of decisions in the same place, you will probably find using switch instead makes your code much more readable.

 NOTE *In PHP we use* elseif, *in Perl we use* elsif *for the same thing. If you mix those up, you'll get syntax errors thrown up by the parser.*

while

The while loop is used when you want to perform a set of operations repeatedly whilst a condition is TRUE. The following example uses two array functions: list and each. These are described in detail in Section 12.6. For now you need to know that list assigns the values held in an array to a set of variables and that each iterates across an array, returning FALSE when it reaches the end of the data.

```php
1  <?php
       $test = "cookies::multipack::chocolate::brownies";
       $parts = split("::", $test);

5      echo "<ul>";
       while(list($key, $val) = each($parts)) {
           echo "<li>$val</li>";
       }
       echo "</ul>";
10 ?>
```

for

The for loop also repeats. It is used in a more controlled fashion because we are explicit about the number of times that we want the loop to iterate:

```php
1  <?php
       for($i = 0; $i < 10; $i++) {
           echo "Hi $name";
       }
5  ?>
```

foreach

Looping over arrays can be done in a number of ways. I have already shown you how to use each, but that can lead to quite clumsy code. Using foreach leads to cleaner code. The basic syntax is:

foreach($array as $value)

which puts the next element of the array into $value on each loop. The statement has an implicit loop counter which is used to track the element that is currently being used. Each time that a foreach statement is reached the loop counter is reset to zero. This means that the statement always starts by accessing the first element of the array. If you have an associative array, you will need to extract both the key and the value. The foreach statement has a rather strange syntax when working with an associative array. In this situation foreach is used to extract both the key and the value which it points to.

foreach($array as $key => $value)

Here is the cookie example again:

```
1   <?php
        $test = "cookies::multipack::chocolate::brownies";
        $parts = split("::", $test);

5       echo "<ul>";
        foreach($parts as $val){
            echo "<li>$val</li>";
        }
        echo "</ul>";
10  ?>
```

break

Not all loops need to run until their scheduled end. If you want to leap out of a loop, do so using break. The following code will print out the name which the user enters ten times unless that name is "Chris", that only gets printed once:

```
1   <?php
        $count = 10;
        while($name) {
            echo "Hi $name";
5           if(--$count == 0) {
                break;
            }
            if($name == "Chris") {
                break;
10          }
        }
    ?>
```

switch

When you need to select between lots of options, an if ... elseif ... else structure can become unwieldy. The switch statement is much more usable.

```
1   switch(expression) {
        case label:
            statement;
            [statement;]
5           break;
```

```
     [case label:
         statement;
         [statement;]
         break;]
10   [default:
         statement;]
   }
```

A switch selects between a number of choices depending upon the value of the expression. The choices are identified by case statements, each has a label which equals one of the potential values of the expression. If none of the cases matches the expression, the optional default may be used instead.

The Sieve of Eratosthenes

Here is a more comprehensive script which uses several different program control structures. The Sieve of Eratosthenes is an algorithm for calculating prime integers. Prime integers are whole numbers which are divisible only by themself and 1. This method uses an array to perform the calculation and is adapted from an exercise set by Deitel and Deitel in their *How To Program* books. The algorithm is:

- an array is created, the length set by a parameter passed to the script
- all elements of the array are initialized to 1
- starting at the third element of the array, the first two being 0 and 1
  - the index is stored
  - the array is looped through
  - all elements whose index is a multiple of the stored value are set to 0
- the index of each element whose value is 1 are displayed.

```
1  <html>
       <head>
           <title>Prime Numbers</title>
       </head>
5  <body>
           <h1>Sieve of Erastothenes</h1>
           <ul>
           <?php
               if($_GET['len'] > 1000) {
10                 echo "<h2>Use only values up to 1000</h2>";
               } else {
```

```
                    $counter = 1;
                    $array[0] = 1;
                    while($counter < $_GET['len']){
15                      $array[] = 1;
                        $counter ++;
                    }
                    for($i = 2; $i < $_GET['len']; $i++) {
                        if($array[$i] == 1) {
20                          $inc = $i;
                            for($j = $i + $inc; $j < $_GET['len']; $j += $inc){
                                $array[$j] = 0;
                            }
                        }
25                  } // for $i=2
                    for($i = 0; $i < $_GET['len']; $i++) {
                        if($array[$i] == 1) {
                            echo "<li>$i</li>";
                        }
30                  } // for $i=0
                } // else
            ?>
            </ul>
        </body>
35  </html>
```

12.5.1 Using Multiple Source Files

You may have code which you need to use in more than one PHP script. Placing the code in every script which needs it is generally considered a bad idea for all but the most trivial situations. If the code needs changing or optimizing you will have to look across all of your files to find it. Making lots of identical changes leads to errors, it also means that you must retest all of the code which you have deployed and which relies upon the changed scripts. On a personal Web site that is a tedious process, on a commercial one it becomes too expensive to contemplate. The solution is to put pieces of code in files which act as libraries that can be included in any script that needs them.

include(file)

Loads the code from the file and evaluates it. The function returns a warning if the code fails. The file is specified using either an absolute path or a URL. The use of URLs depends upon the configuration of your PHP installation rather than your script.

The `included` file will be processed in HTML mode. Any PHP code inside it must be contained inside valid PHP start and end tags.

require(file)

Works in the same way as include but gives a fatal error if the code inside the `required` file fails.

12.6 ARRAYS

When you need to store more than one data item in a list you will need to use an array. An array is a structured list of data items which are accessed via an index value. PHP supplies two different array types: the basic array uses a numerical index to order its contents, the associative array uses a text string. The PHP associative array works exactly like the hash array in Perl, in fact it is the same thing[3]. You can actually mix and match the two array types in the same array in PHP so that some items are accessed by their index and others by a key value. I'm going to discuss them separately for clarity.

12.6.1 The Basic Array

Array operations are exactly the same as those found in JavaScript or Perl. Assignment to the array is done through index values. If you use empty brackets in an assignment operation, the new value is added onto the end of the array. PHP arrays can grow dynamically but if you want to remove items from the middle of an array you will need to write your own function for doing so. Indexes in a PHP are placed in square brackets after the array name in exactly the same fashion as in Perl or JavaScript.

```
1   <html>
        <head>
            <title>Array Operations</title>
        </head>
5       <body>
            <h1>Array Operations</h1>
            <ul>
            <?php
                $array[0] = "Fido";
10              $array[1] = "Rover";
                echo "<li>".$array[1]."</li>";
                $mydog = $array[0];
                echo "<li>".$mydog."</li>";
                $array[] = $array[0].$array[1];
```

---

[3]Strictly speaking, in Perl a hash is called an associative array.

```
15          echo "<li>".$array[2]."</li>";
        ?>
        </ul>
    </body>
</html>
```

12.6.2 Associative Arrays

In an associative array, each item is indexed with a key value. The key must be a unique string. Here is a simple example which can be dropped into the previous code:

```
1   <?php
        $array["pet"] = "Fido";
        $array["friend"] = "Rover";
        echo "<li>".$array["friend"]."</li>";
5       $mydog = $array[0];
        echo "<li>".$mydog."</li>";
        $array[0] = $array["pet"].$array["friend"];
        echo "<li>".$array[0]."</li>";
    ?>
```

If you try running that code you will find that the line

```
$mydog = $array[0];
```

does not lead to any output. Although the two PHP array types can be mixed together, once you have created a key value for an array item you will need to use that key to get at the data value. You cannot assume that the data items are placed in the array in the order in which you supply them.

An associative array can be created using a syntax which will be familiar if you have worked through the Perl material:

```
1   <?php
        $array = array(
            "pet" => "Fido",
            "friend" => "Rover");

5
        echo "<li>".$array["friend"]."</li>";
        $mydog = $array["pet"];
        echo "<li>".$mydog."</li>";
        $array[0] = $array["pet"].$array["friend"];
10      echo "<li>".$array[0]."</li>";
    ?>
```

I will look at the array() function in a while. What I want you to notice from that example is that key:value pairs can be passed to the array constructor using => to link them. The key:value pairs are passed in as a comma-separated list to the constructor.

12.6.3 Multidimensional Arrays

Sometimes data is nice and simple. For instance if you wanted to list all of the items sold by a grocer, you could use a simple array:

```php
<?php
    $veg[0] = "peas";
    $veg[] = "carrots";
    $veg[] = "purple sprouting broccoli";
```

but real data is often more complex than that. Consider the example of Fido and Rover. A dog's home might want to record more information about them such as their color, weight, or temperament. Possibly the easiest way of storing this data is to create a multidimensional array. This is really an array of arrays in which each item, for instance the dog's name, leads to more items, such as her details. In PHP both indexed arrays and associative arrays can be multidimensional. Here are examples of both in action down at the pound. First the associative array:

```
1   <html>
        <head>
            <title>Pooches</title>
        </head>
5       <body>
            <h1>At The Dog's Home Today</h1>
            <ul>
            <?php
            $array = array(
10              "pen1" => array(
                    "name" => "Fido",
                    "color" => "brown",
                    "temperament" => "quiet"),
                "pen2" => array(
15                  "name" => "Rover",
                    "color" => "white",
                    "temperament" => "noisy"),
                "pen3" => array(
                    "name" => "Patch",
20                  "color" => "brown and white",
                    "temperament" => "friendly"));
```

```
            echo "<li>".$array["pen2"]["name"];
            echo "<ul><li>".$array["pen2"]["color"]."</li>";
25          echo "<li>".$array["pen2"]["temperament"]."</li>";
            echo "</ul>";
            echo "</li>";
        ?>
        </ul>
30    </body>
</html>
```

Next, the PHP code from the indexed array:

```
1   <?php
        $array[0][0] = "Fido";
        $array[0][] = "brown";
        $array[0][] = "quiet";
5       $array[1][0] = "Rover";
        $array[1][] = "white";
        $array[1][] = "noisy";
        $array[2][0] = "Path";
        $array[2][] = "brown and white";
10      $array[2][] = "friendly";

        echo "<li>".$array[1][0];
        echo "<ul><li>".$array[1][1]."</li>";
        echo "<li>".$array[1][2]."</li>";
15      echo "</ul>";
        echo "</li>";
    ?>
```

The associative array is much *cleaner* than the indexed version. That is partly a function of the data I am using here. It is also because remembering that you want to access the color of the dog in pen2 is far easier than remembering that you want data item 1 of array item 1. Notice that when I was creating the associative array, I was able to nest calls to the array function. Each call was separated from the following one with a comma just as the data items were in the single-dimensional associative array.

12.6.4 Array Functions

PHP supplies a rich set of built-in functions which can be used to operate on arrays. You will find that using these built-in operations takes a lot of the pain out of the array data structure.

In other languages, C for instance, handling arrays is fraught with difficulty. PHP is more like JavaScript in this respect: the language developers have done a lot of the hard work for you.

array(var1[, var2[, varn]])

>   creates a new array which contains all of the values that are passed in as parameters.

array_intersect(array1, array2[, arrayn])

>   returns a new array which contains all of the elements from array1 which are also present in *all* of the other arrays. This function works best with associative arrays since it preserves the values of keys and the new array can be accessed via the key of array1. Here is an example:

```php
1   <?php
        $pen1 = array("Fido" => "brown", "quiet");
        $pen2 = array("Rover" => "brown", "noisy");
        $new_array = array_intersect($pen1, $pen2);
5       echo "<li>".$new_array["Fido"]."</li>";
    ?>
```

>   That code sets $new_array to the key:value pair "Fido" => "brown".

array_keys(array)

>   returns an array containing all of the keys from the associative array which is given as the parameter.

array_merge(arr1, arr2[, arrn])

>   merges all of the arrays which are given as parameters. If the arrays have common keys, the values from later arrays will override those from earlier ones.

array_pop(array)

>   removes the last element from the array and returns it. This operation reduces the length of the array by 1.

array_push(array, var1[, varn])

>   adds one or more elements onto the end of the array.

array_reverse(array)

>   returns a new array which contains all the elements from the original array but now in reverse order.

array_shift(array)

returns the first element in the array, removes it from the array and so shortens the array by one item.

array_slice(array, offset[, length])

returns a subarray starting at the position indicated by the *offset* parameter. If no length is given, all elements to the end of the array are returned. If length is negative, the copy will stop that many elements from the end. Here is a small example which copies the last two elements from an array:

```php
<?php
    $fido = array("brown", "quiet", "small", "one-eyed");
    $tmp = array_slice($fido, 2);
    echo "<li>".count($tmp)."</li>";
    echo "<li>".$tmp[0]."</li>";
    echo "<li>".$tmp[1]."</li>";
?>
```

array_unshift(array, var1[, varn])

pushes one or more elements onto the *start* of the array.

asort(array)

sorts an associative array and in doing so preserves the association between each key and its value.

count(var)

returns the number of items in the variable. Usually the variable will be an array, if it is not then count() will return 1. If the variable has not been set, count() will return 0.

each(array)

returns the next key:value pair from an array. Usually you will want to assign these returned values into a set of variables.

in_array($var, array)

returns TRUE if the variable, $var is present in the array.

is_array(var)

returns TRUE of the variable is an array, FALSE if it is not.

key(array)

returns the key value for the item at the current index.

list(var1, var2[, varn])

assigns a set of values to variables as if they were an array. This means that you can pass a set of variables into list, assign it to an array and each variable will hold one array element. Here is an example.

```php
<?php
$original = array('cookies', 'multipack', 'chocolate', 'brownies');
echo "<p>$original<p>";
list($a, $b, $c, $d) = $original;
echo "<p>$a, $b, $c, $d</p>";
?>
```

sizeof(var)

returns the number of elements in the array.

sort(array)

sorts the items in an array into ascending order and returns the sorted list.

The following code shows a number of the array functions in action. The output is shown in Figure 12.3:

```html
<html>
    <head>
        <title>Pooches</title>
    </head>
    <body>
        <h1>At The Dog's Home Today</h1>
        <h2>Indexed Array</h2>

        <?php
            $fido = array("brown", "quiet", "small", "one-eyed");

            echo "<p>";
            for($i = 0; $i < count($fido); $i++) {
                echo $fido[$i]." ";
            }

            echo "</p><p>";
            while(list($key, $val) = each($fido)){
                echo $val." ";
```

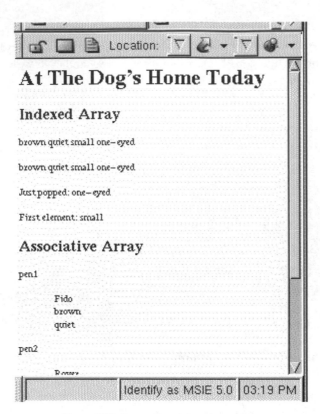

Figure 12.3 Converting strings to numbers

```
20          }
         echo "</p>";

         $tmp = array_pop($fido);
         echo "<p>Just popped: ".$tmp."</p>";
25       $tmp = array_reverse($fido);
         echo "<p>First element: $tmp[0]</p>";
     ?>

     <h2>Associative Array</h2>
30
     <?php
         $array = array(
             "pen1" => array(
                 "name" => "Fido",
```

```
35              "color" => "brown",
                "temperament" => "quiet"),
            "pen2" => array(
                "name" => "Rover",
                "color" => "white",
40              "temperament" => "noisy"),
            "pen3" => array(
                "name" => "Patch",
                "color" => "brown and white",
                "temperament" => "friendly"));
45

        echo "<dl>";
        while(list($key, $val) = each($array)){
            echo "<dt>$key</dt><dl>";
            while(list($k, $v) = each($val)){
50                  echo "<dd>$v</dd>";
            }
            echo "</dl>";
        }
        echo "</dl>";
55      ?>
    </body>
</html>
```

The code demonstrates the use of both array types. I start by displaying the indexed array in two different ways. First, I use a simple for() loop exactly as you have seen me do in JavaScript and Perl. The second variant uses some PHP functions:

```
1   while(list($key, $val) = each($fido)){
      echo $val." ";
    }
```

This is a normal while() loop which uses some interesting functions to control iteration. The each() function is used to control movement across the array. When the end of the array is reached, this function will return FALSE and the loop will terminate. The function returns a key:value pair, in an indexed array it returns the array index and its associated value. I use the list() function to copy these into two variables. I am not interested in the keys since I know that they are simply numerical values, so I ignore them in the print statement.

Printing out the contents of the associative array is slightly more complex. In part this is due to the nature of the data structure I have created.

```
1   while(list($key, $val) = each($array)) {
        echo "<dt>$key</dt><dl>";
        while(list($k, $v) = each($val)) {
            echo "<dd>$v</dd>";
5       }
    }
```

This code has two loops. The outer one iterates across the main data structure, $array, copying the keys and values into two variables. Because the data structure I am using is a multidimensional associative array, the values here are, themselves, arrays. I want to print out the values in these subarrays so I iterate across each of them. I extract the data values and finally display them.

12.7 USER-DEFINED FUNCTIONS

Large scripts tend to repeat the same operations as they run. When writing a script like that you *could* repeat the same code in numerous places throughout the script. The difficulties with doing that have been well documented since the 1960s, broadly there are two which need concern us here. Firstly, the repeated code will make your scripts larger, they will take longer loading and being interpreted which must be offset against the cost of function calls, put an increased load on your server and reduce performance of your Web site. Secondly, whenever you repeat code you increase the possibility of transcription and typing errors and of introducing errors of logic. These lead to buggy code which takes longer to develop.

The solution is to extract the repeated code, place it into special blocks called *functions* and place *calls* to those functions into the main body of your script. Functions can have arguments, values which are passed to them, and can return the result of their processing. Here is an example:

```
1   <html>
        <head>
            <title>Functions</title>
        </head>
5       <body>
            <h1>Using Functions in PHP</h1>
            <?php
            $array = array(
                "pen1" => array(
10                  "name" => "Fido",
                    "color" => "brown",
                    "temperament" => "quiet"),
                "pen2" => array(
```

```
                   "name" => "Rover",
15                 "color" => "white",
                   "temperament" => "noisy"),
               "pen3" => array(
                   "name" => "Patch",
                   "color" => "brown and white",
20                 "temperament" => "friendly"));

        foreach($array as $key => $val) {
            $name = showDog($val);
        }

25
        function showDog($dog) {
            foreach($dog as $key => $val) {
                if($key == "name") {
                    $ret = $val;
30              }
                echo "$key -- $val<br/>";
            } // foreach

            echo "<br/>";
35          return $ret;
        } // end of function

        ?>
        </body>
40   </html>
```

The function showDog() is passed an array and returns a string. I do not actually do anything with the string ... it is there to show how return values work. Notice that in PHP you do not have to define a function before you call it.

12.7.1 Variable Scope

Variables are not automatically available throughout your program. If a variable is declared at the top of a piece of PHP it is said to be *global*. This means that any code in the current HTML file can use it, including code which comes from external files through the include or require keywords. However, within user-defined functions variables are locally scoped. This means that they are only available within the function in which they are declared. If you access a variable in one of your functions and it has the same name as a global function the *local* version is used.

global $var1 [,$varn]

> The `global` keyword takes a comma-separated list of variables as its parameter. The global version of any variable named in the list is used instead of a local version.

static $var

> When execution of a function ends, all of its local variables are lost. If you need to remember the value of a variable between function calls you must declare that variable as `static` within the function.

12.8 BUILT-IN FUNCTIONS

PHP includes thousands of useful pieces of code in functions and libraries. I do not have the time or the space to describe them all in this book. Fortunately the PHP distribution includes a manual which outlines them all. I have attempted to show you some of the most useful PHP functions, but I have really tried to concentrate on those which have near-equivalents in Perl so that you can fairly compare the two languages.

In fact, one of the great things about developing using open source scripting languages is the sheer volume of useful code that you have at your disposal. When you install PHP you are getting the basic language, an interpreter and copious libraries. Look around the Web for a short time and you will find even more code – there is a large repository of libraries at the PHP Web site to get you started. In fact almost any programming task that you need to achieve on a Web site can be done with PHP.

One of the great benefits of PHP is said to be the ease with which your scripts can access relational databases. When you have used a few languages for the same task you find that PHP is nearly as good in this respect as more established languages like Perl and Python. Its facilities far exceed those of Java, C++ or Visual Basic. In fact you can get at virtually any database from inside a PHP script, all you need to do is use the right library. This is where one of the limitations of the language appears. In Perl there is a standard database interface for all relational systems which use SQL. Once you have learnt how to connect to Access on a PC, you can use exactly the same knowledge to connect to Oracle across a network. PHP is slightly less *developer friendly*, there is not the same common interface. None of the libraries are too complex though and much of your knowledge transfers pretty easily.

In this section I am going to examine some of the facilities which the PHP libraries provide. I have tried to concentrate on those libraries which you can start using straight away. I am *not*, though, looking at database access. I will examine how to use PHP with mySQL in the next chapter.

12.8.1 Output

echo [(] string1 [)][, stringN]

> outputs its parameters embedded within the HTML page. Strictly, `echo` is part of the PHP language rather than a function. It can accept any number of strings or variables

as parameters. The parameters must be in a comma-separated list. Parentheses are optional, but can only be used if just one parameter is being passed in.

Variables and expressions can be evaluated within echo but since echo is not a function it cannot be used within an expression. The following examples are all valid:

```
1   echo ("hello");
    echo "hello", "world";
    $h = "hello";
    $w = "world";
5   echo $h, $w;
    echo 'The message is $h $w';
```

Single quotes around a variable name prevent its evaluation. The variable name is displayed instead of its content:

```
1   $h = "hello";
    echo 'The message is $h';
```

print [(] string1 [)][, stringN]

Like echo this is part of the language, not a function. The two can normally be treated as synonyms except that print returns a value to the calling code. This has two effects. First, it makes echo marginally faster; second, it means that print can be treated as a function so that its result is evaluated in expressions.

printf(format string [, arg1 [, argn]])
sprintf(format string [, arg1 [, argn]])

If you have programmed in C, C++ or Java 5 you will have encountered the idea of formatted print strings. If you have not used those languages you should be prepared for a surprise. Print statements can do an awful lot more than simply displaying strings.

The printf function, and sprintf which works in the same way, takes a format string as its first argument and a comma-separated list of values and variables as its other arguments. The format string consists of plain text mixed with control sequences. Arguments from the list are converted into values and replace the control sequences. The replacement happens in order, so that the first control sequence is replaced by the first argument from the list, and so on. The number of additional arguments must *exactly* match the number of control sequences in the format string. Let us look at an example[4] before we examine the control sequences.

---

[4]You might have seen this in Section 9.8.5

```
1    <html>
         <head><title>Printf</title></head>
         <body>
         <?php
5
     $string = "Using printf:";
     $number = 76523;
     $decimal = 34.5612;
     $float = 23.08e35;
10   $hex = 0x23a7;

     print("<p> Using print: $number, $decimal, $float, $hex </p>");

     printf("<p> %s %d <br/> %f <br/> %e <br/> %x </p>", $string,
15         $number, $decimal, $float, $hex);

     printf("<p> %s %d <br/> %3.3f <br/> %1.3e <br/> 0x%X </p>",
           $string, $number, $decimal, $float, ($hex + 0xa));

20       ?>
         </body>
     </html>
```

Which on my system produces the output shown in Figure 12.4.

The control sequences have a number of components but all start with a compulsory percentage sign. Table 12.3 contains the other elements.

12.8.2 String Function

Strings are complex objects. Non-programmers might disagree, to them a string is just an ordered collection of characters. To programmers, though, strings are more often things which they need to manipulate in a variety of ways. PHP comes with code which you can use to perform all of the most common string manipulations.

strlen(string)

returns the number of characters in the string.

trim(string [,character set])

removes whitespace and related characters from the start and end of the string. You can supply a list of characters to remove as the second parameter.

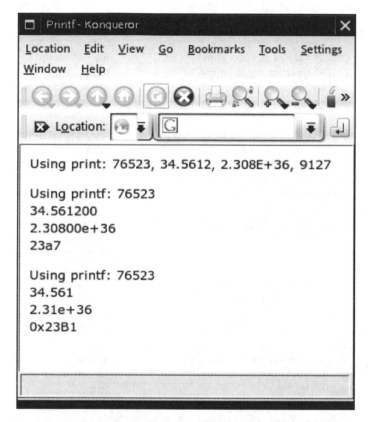

Figure 12.4 Using printf in PHP

By default the set of characters which are removed is

- space
- tab
- new line
- carriage return
- vertical tab
- null.

substr(string, start [,length])

returns a part of the original string beginning at the character whose location is given by the second parameter. A negative number can be given as the second parameter. This sets the offset from the end of the original string rather than from its beginning. If the third parameter is given it indicates the number of characters to extract.

Code	Meaning	Code	Meaning
%	Outputs a percentage sign. This is needed because the formatting codes start with percentage.	+ or –	Forces a sign for a numeric value. Negative numbers are only ever given.
Padding	Results can be padded to a given size. By default a space is used. Any character can be substituted but must be preceded by '	Alignment	By default padded output is aligned to the right. A minus sign can be used to align it to the left.
Width	Gives the minimum width of padded output	Precision	Controls the number of decimal places used for a floating point number.
b	The argument is an integer which is to be treated as binary.	c	The argument is an integer which is treated as an ASCII code with the appropriate character displayed.
d	The argument is an integer which is displayed as a signed decimal.	e	The argument is a number which is in scientific notation.
u	The argument is an integer which is displayed without sign.	f	Floating point number.
o	The argument is an integer which is displayed in octal format.	s	The argument is a string.
x	The argument is an integer which is displayed in hexadecimal.		

Table 12.3 PHP `printf` formatting codes

`ucfirst(string)`

> returns a copy of the string with the first character converted to upper case.

`ucwords(string)`

> returns a copy of the string with the first character of each word converted to upper case. Words are delimited by whitespace.

strtolower(string)

returns a copy of the string with all characters converted to lower case.

strtoupper

returns a copy of the string with all characters converted to upper case.

strstr(string, search_term)

hunts for the search term in the string. If the search term is found the substring from its beginning to the end of the string is returned. If the search is unsuccessful FALSE is returned.

strcasecmp(string1, string2)

lexigraphical comparison of two strings. Returns zero if the strings are the same. A value less than zero is returned if the first string is less than the second. A value greater than zero if the second string is greater than the first.

strtok(string, token)

splits a string into substrings. The splits occur when any character in the second parameter, token, is encountered. The strtok function will be repeatedly called in a loop which moves across the string. The string parameter is only used on the first call. Thereafter the function both remembers the string which it is tokenizing and its current position in that string.

```php
<?php
    $testString = "It's not what you say, it's how you say it    ";

    $word = strtok($testString, " "); // string AND token
    while ($word) {
        echo "$word<br/>";
        $word = strtok(" "); // token only
    }
?>
```

str_replace(search, replacement, source)

This function replaces all instances of a search term with a replacement term in a string. If the search and replacement parameters are arrays, values from each are used in turn.

split(pattern, string)

splits the string using a regular expression which is given in the first parameter. If the power of regular expressions is not needed explode is a faster alternative since it does not use the regular expression engine. If complex regular expressions are required the preg_split is both faster and uses expressions which are compatible with Perl.

explode(token, string)

splits the string at each occurrence of the token which is given as the first parameter. The function returns an array which holds the elements split out of the string.

implode(join character, array)

returns a string which contains all of the elements in the array joined together using the character supplied in the first parameter.

join

An alias for implode.

The following code demonstrates some of the string manipulation functions which PHP provides. Figure 12.5 shows the output of this code.

```
1   <html>
    <head><title>String Functions in PHP</title></head>
    <body>
    <ul>
5   <?php
        $testString = "It's not what you say, it's how you say it    ";

        echo "<li>The string is <b>". $testString ."</b></li>";

10      echo "<li>The string has ". strlen($testString) ." characters</li>";

        $trimmedString = trim($testString);
        echo "<li>After trimming it has ". strlen($trimmedString) ."
            characters</li>";

15      $iTrimmedString = trim($testString, "iI");
        echo "<li>After trimming &quot;i&quot; or &quot;I&quot; it has    ".
            strlen($iTrimmedString) ." characters</li>";

        echo "<li>Substring from character 2 to 5 is <b>".substr($testString,
            2, 5) ."</b></li>";

20      echo "<li>Substring from character -8 <b>".substr(trim($testString),
            -8) ."</b></li>";
```

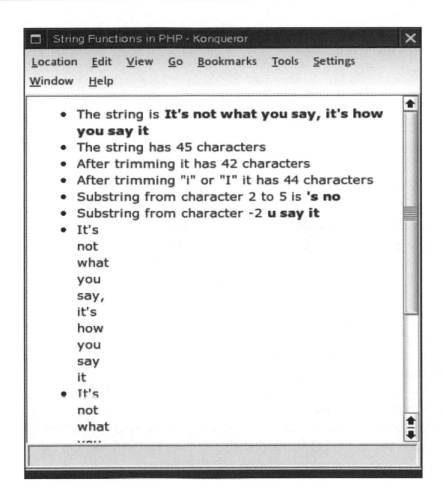

Figure 12.5 String manipulation in PHP

```php
echo "<li>";
$word = strtok($testString, " ");
while ($word) {
    echo "$word<br/>";
    $word = strtok(" ");
}
echo "</li>";

echo "<li>";
$words = explode(" ", $testString);
```

```
            foreach ($words as $item)
                echo "$item<br/>";
            echo "</li>";
35    ?>
     </ul>
    </body>
    </html>
```

HTML Character Functions

strip_tags(string, allowed)

removes all HTML elements and PHP tags from the string. Any tags which you want to leave in the output are listed in parameter two. The function does no validation so you may get unexpected results from badly formatted HTML strings.

htmlentities(string)

A string is returned which contains the contents of the parameter string. Every character in that string which can be converted into an HTML entity will have been changed.

htmlspecialchars(string)

In HTML some characters have special meanings. For example, the ampersand, &, is used at the start of HTML entities. The htmlspecialchars function converts all of those characters into the appropriate HTML entity.

urlencode(string)

This is not a String function but one which operates on Strings. Any non-alphanumeric characters in the input string are converted to hexadecimal values preceded by a percentage sign. You will have seen this encoding used in URLs which contain parameters.

urldecode(string)

Converts hexadecimal escape sequences back into non-alphanumeric characters.

12.8.3 Math Functions

abs(number)

returns the absolute value of a number. If the argument is a floating point number, the return value will also be a float. Otherwise it will be an integer.

acos(float)

> returns the arc cosine in radians.

asin(float)

> returns the arc sine in radians.

atan(float)

> returns the arc tangent in radians.

ceil(float)

> returns the integer which is directly higher than the argument. ceil(34.56) would return 35.

cos(float)

> returns the cosine in radians.

exp(number)

> returns e raised to the power of the argument.

floor(float)

> returns the integer directly lower than the argument.

log(float)

> returns the natural logarithm of the argument.

log10(float)

> returns the base 10 logarithm of the argument.

max(arg1, arg2[, argn])

> returns the largest of its arguments.

min(arg1, arg2[, argn])

> returns the smallest of its arguments.

pi()

> return the value of π.

pow(arg1, arg2)

> returns arg1 raised to the power of arg2.

rand([min[, max]])

> returns a pseudo-random number. If max or min are set, they place limits upon the range in which the number will be generated. Before calling rand() you *must* call srand() to seed the random number generator.

round(float[, precision])

> rounds the floating point number. If no precision is specified, the number is rounded to the nearest whole number. For instance, round(3.6) will return 4.0 and round(3.2) will return 3.0. If the precision is provided, it sets the number of decimal places in the result.

sin(float)

> returns the sine in radians.

sqrt(number)

> returns the square root of its argument.

srand(integer)

> Seed the random number generator using the supplied value. Random number generators are not really random. If left to their own devices and called repeatedly, they actually produce a sequence of values. At some point the sequence will repeat, the trick in writing a random number generator is to make the sequence before repetition very long. The sequence, and its length, are determined by the *seed* value which is supplied. Therefore to get the appearance of a random sequence you must re-seed the generator each time that you use it.

tan(float)

> Returns the tangent in radians.

12.8.4 Dates and Times

PHP has a decent set of functions for manipulating times and dates. Most often you will want to get the current time and date to use as a timestamp either on a page or in a database. These functions are provided:

date(format[, timestamp])

> Formats a timestamp as a date. If no timestamp is supplied, the current time is used. The format is defined by a string which uses the set of characters shown in Table 12.4. The following example displays a neatly formatted date:

```php
<?php echo(date("l dS F, Y")); ?>
```

> The result of that code is shown in Figure 12.6. If you want formatting that is suitable for your locale, you should investigate the strftime() function.

getdate([timestamp])

> returns an associative array containing the elements of the date. If no timestamp is given, the current time is used. The keys for the array are:

Character	Meaning	Character	Meaning
a	Display am or pm	A	Display AM or PM
B	Swatch Internet time (invented by the Swiss watchmakers Swatch)	d	Day of the month as a pair of digits
D	Day of the week as three letters	F	Month as text
g	Hour in 12 hour format with no leading 0	G	Hour in 24 hour format with no leading 0
h	Hour in 12 hour format *with* leading 0	H	Hour in 24 hour format with leading 0
i	Minutes	j	Day of the month as integer
l	Day of the week in long text format	m	Month as integer
M	Month as three letters	n	Month as integer without leading 0
r	Date formatted according to RFC 822	s	Seconds
S	Ordinal suffix (such as "th" or "nd")	t	Number of days in the month
T	Timezone of the machine	U	Seconds since midnight on January 1st, 1970
w	Day of the week as integer	Y	Year in four digit format
y	Year in two digit format	z	Day of the year as integer

Table 12.4 Time and date formatting characters

- seconds
- minutes
- hours
- mday (day of the month)
- wday (day of the week)

Time and Date

Tuesday 29th May, 2001

Figure 12.6 Formatted date string

- mon (numeric month)
- year (numeric year)
- yday (day of the year as an integer)
- weekday (as text, using the full name of the day)
- month (as text using the full name).

localtime([timestamp[, associative]])

Returns an array containing the elements of the timestamp. If no timestamp is given, the current time is used instead. If the Boolean value `associative` is TRUE the array will be returned as an associative array. The keys will be:

- tm_sec
- tm_min
- tm_hour
- tm_mday
- tm_mon
- tm_year
- tm_wday
- tm_yday

mktime(hour, min, sec, month, day, year)

returns a UNIX timestamp in seconds for the given date and time. All parameters are supplied as integers. The last day of a month can be expressed as day 0 of the *next* month.

time()

returns the a UNIX timestamp which represents the current time in seconds since midnight on January 1st 1970.

12.9 REGULAR EXPRESSION

A regular expression, which may also be called a regex or regexp, is a string which denotes a search pattern. The search pattern is applied to text strings inside your script. Regular expressions have been used for many, many years in computing but are still, in some ways, considered a bit of a black art. PHP regular expressions use identical syntax to those found in

Perl, in fact they are based upon the Perl version. Since Perl regular expressions also heavily influenced the development of the JavaScript regex *engine*, the PHP and JavaScript versions work in the same way too. This happy coincidence means that I do not have to spend a lot of time here describing the syntax of the things since I have already done so elsewhere. Therefore, before reading this section I would like to refer you back to Section 7.2 and Section 9.9.

Whilst the mechanism for creating the patterns which make up a regex are the same in all three languages, the way in which they are used differs. Having created the pattern, you will need to use some PHP-specific functions if you want to apply it.

preg_match(pattern, string[, matches])

hunts for strings which match the supplied pattern in the string subject. This match will stop once it has found a target. Optionally an array can be supplied as the third parameter. This will be used to store matches. The first item in the array, item 0, contains the text which matches. Any text-matching patterns which are placed in parentheses[5] will be placed into subsequent array items. Here is an example:

```php
1   <?php
        $test = "This is a test";
        if(preg_match("/(\ws)\s(\ws)/", $test, $matches)){
            echo "</h3>Matched<h3>";
5           echo "$matches[0],<br/>";
            echo "$matches[1],<br/>";
            echo "$matches[2].<br/>";
        } else {
            echo "<h3>Did not match</h3>";
10      }
    ?>
```

The program outputs Matched is is, is, is., formatted suitably, of course. The text his is contains the matched strings. It is stored in the first element of $matches. The two strings in parentheses in the regular expression describe the substrings that I want to store. The two matches are any single letter followed by the letter s, and must, themselves, be separated only by a single space. If the sample string $test were changed so that more than one space separated each word, it would not match the regular expression.

---

[5]Compare this with backreferences in Perl.

preg_match_all(pattern, string)

> works like `preg_match()` but matches *all* occurrences of the pattern in the string.

preg_replace(pattern, replacement, string)

> If the regex pattern is found in the string, it is replaced by the string supplied as the second parameter.

preg_split(pattern, string)

> splits the string at all points which match the pattern. Returns an array of strings containing all of the substrings it creates.

Let us start by looking at a simple pattern match.

```
1   <html>
      <head><title>Regexes</title></head>
      <body>
        <h1>Using Regexes in PHP</h1>
5       <?php
          $pattern = "/target/";
          $string = "Can you find the target?";
          if(preg_match($pattern, $string)) {
            echo "Found it";
10        } else {
            echo "Didn't find it";
          }
        ?>
      </body>
15  </html>
```

The pattern match could also have been written:

```
if(preg_match("/target/", "Can you find the target?"))
```

which is rather closer to the sort of thing you will see in Perl. One thing about PHP which is slightly different to other languages, is that the pattern has to be inside quotes *and* it has to have delimiters. I have used slashes since, by convention, they are used in most other pattern matching languages. Here is a match which stores its results:

```
1   <?php
      $pattern = "/([a-z]+\?)/";
      $string = "Can you find the target?";
      if(preg_match($pattern, $string, $matches)) {
```

```
5         echo "Found $matches[0]";
      } else {
          echo "Didn't find it";
      }
   ?>
```

The pattern matches repeated lower-case characters followed by a question mark. Clearly this will only match target? in the string. The pattern is placed inside parentheses and gets stored in the first element of the array $matches. This example shows a simple replacement:

```
1  <?php
      $pattern = "/[a-z]+\?/";
      $string = "Can you find the target?";

5     if($new = preg_replace($pattern, "replacement", $string)) {
          echo "$new";
      } else {
          echo "Didn't find it";
      }
10  ?>
```

Again, I am looking for the string target?. If the string is matched, it will be changed for replacement. This operation returns a new string and leaves the original, $string unaltered. Splitting strings work as you might expect. Here is one of the earlier Perl examples rewritten in PHP. Figure 12.7 shows the result:

```
1  <html>
      <head><title>Regexes</title></head>
      <body>
          <h1>Using Regexes in PHP</h1>

5
          <?php
          $test = "cookies::multipack::chocolate::brownies";
          $parts = preg_split("/::/", $test);

10        echo "<ul>";
          while(list($key, $val) = each($parts)) {
              echo "<li>$val</li>";
          }
          echo "</ul>";
```

```
15            ?>

        </body>
    </html>
```

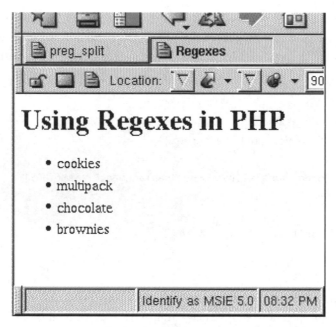

Figure 12.7 Splitting strings

12.10 USING FILES

Most of your scripts will need to store data at some point. You may only need to write data into a temporary file which gets deleted once the script has completed, or you may want to store many megabytes of data gathered from all the visitors to your site. Much of the literature and many of the tutorials which discuss PHP talk about storing all of this data in a relational database. If you surf the Web looking for PHP tutorials you will see the same combination of PHP, Linux and MySQL described over and over again. For many applications a database is an irrelevance: they are designed to store and manipulate large volumes of data and many simultaneous connections. If you have a low volume site with few connections and relatively little data you will not get any benefits from a database. Instead if you are creating a guestbook or an online diary, you are far better off saving your data in simple files.

PHP has many functions which handle files and directories. I am going to show you just a few which you can use to open files, save data to them and read that data back. One really nice thing about the file routines in PHP is that they handle remote files as efficiently as they do local ones. From the point of view of a traditional programmer, these might seem like weird ideas, but in the world of the Web they make perfect sense as you will see.

A file is a collection of data stored on a disk and accessed via a unique name. The full name of the file includes the path to it. Generally when we talk about files we mean stored data on the local machine or on a machine which appears to be the local machine. On a Windows PC you may store all of your data on the C: drive and have a CD-ROM called drive D:. When you log on to a network at college or work, your PC may have access to a whole collection of servers around the organization. These servers will appear to be more drives and directories on the local system. For instance at work I get access to drives named F: through Z:. Providing they have the correct access permissions, your applications can open and read files from those drives as if they were stored on the C: drive of the machine.

What about files on other systems? If I have some files stored on a server which is run by my ISP rather than my employer, how can I get to those files? Generally, the answer is that I need to use FTP to download a copy of each file and to upload the new version when I have finished with it. That is a well used and successful idea, but what happens if my Web application needs to alter the data in that file? Languages such as Perl can be used to automate an FTP connection but writing the code requires a certain amount of prior knowledge and experience. What if the file is residing on a Web server somewhere? Again, Perl has modules that can be used to automate that process. But what about PHP?

PHP is designed for the Web, it is supposed to work in a connected, Web world. Can it be used to manipulate files on remote servers? The answer to that is an emphatic *yes*, and what is more, the process is almost transparent. The fopen() function which is used to open files is described and demonstrated below. At this stage I would just like to outline its Internet facilities.

Opening a file is done with fopen(filename) which accepts a filename as the first of its parameters. If the filename is a standard directory/file combination such as these:

```
$data = c:\\MyFiles\\data\\guests.dat);
$data = fopen(/home/chris/data/guests.dat);
```

the file is assumed to be on the same machine that the script is on. Actually, and to be more rigorous, it is assumed to be *mounted* by the operating system and available as if it is on that machine.

 NOTE *On Windows machines, backslashes in the path to a file must be escaped or replaced with forward slashes.*

If the filename starts with http://, the file is assumed to be on a remote Web server. A standard HTTP connection is opened to the server and the file is retrieved. When you access data like this you are not really working with the original file. The *open* file is really the data sent back by the HTTP response. You are actually going to be working on a copy of the data. This has important implications since the file might change whilst you are working on it. You can never assume that remote data is bang up to date; generally, though, this does not matter. Web data will give you a snapshot of the state of a system which is accurate enough 99 per cent of the time.

Filenames which start with ftp:// are assumed to be on FTP servers. They can be accessed for reading and writing, although not at the same time. If the remote machine is not running an FTP server you will get an error if you try to use the FTP protocol to read or write a file on it. When you are using FTP you will need to make *two* connections if you want to update a file: the first connection is made to download a *copy* of the file, the second to upload the amended version. During the period that your script is creating the amended file, the original is available to other users. As with HTTP access, you cannot assume that you have got the latest version. "Ah," you may say, "but I'm the only person who can access those files directly." That is fine, but how many copies of your script are executing concurrently? You really have no way of knowing. If concurrent access, especially to update the file, is likely to be important then you ought to consider using a database which enforces transactions and data integrity.

The files on FTP servers are protected by usernames and passwords. You may have downloaded files from FTP servers in the past via your Web browser without entering either a username or a password. Your Web browser will have done this for you automatically. Many file repositories around the Internet support *anonymous FTP* which lets anyone log on to the system as user *anonymous* provided they give their email address as a password. Files can then be downloaded from the server. If you are using remote files as part of a Web application, they will not be accessible via anonymous FTP, you will need an account on the FTP server. The filename becomes a combination of username, password and file:

```
$data = fopen("ftp://chris:password@ftp.shu.ac.uk/guests.dat");
```

with the username and password separated by a colon.

The full set of PHP file functions is described in the supplied documentation. I am only going to describe some of the more important functions and show you a simple example.

copy($source, $dest)

copies the contents of $source into $dest. The two parameters are the names of the files. If the copy fails, the function returns FALSE, otherwise it returns TRUE.

fclose($fp)

closes the file which is pointed to by $fp. The parameter $fp is a file handle, created using fopen() *not* the name of the file.

feof($fp)

> checks if the end of file has been reached. Returns TRUE if it has, otherwise it returns FALSE;

fflush($fp)

> writes all buffered output to the file which $fp points to. You should always call fflush() before you close a file because the operating system may buffer data without your knowledge. By calling this function you ensure that all data gets written out.

fgets($fp, length)

> reads up to length-1 bytes of data from $fp. The call to fgets() ends when a newline character or the end of file marker is reached. Newline characters are returned as part of the string.

fgetss($fp, length)

> works like fgets() but strips any HTML tags out of the data as it is read.

file(filename)

> reads the complete contents from the file and stores them in an array. Each line of data makes up a separate element in the array.

file_exists(filename)

> returns TRUE if the file exists and FALSE if it does not. This function will not work on remote files such as those you might try to access with FTP or HTTP.

flock($fp, operation)

> locks a file so that access to it can be controlled. This function works under most UNIX systems and Microsoft Windows. Many similar functions in other languages are unavailable on Windows. Operation takes one of the following values:
>
> • LOCK_SH denotes a shared lock – used for reading a file
> • LOCK_EX denotes an exclusive lock – for writing to a file
> • LOCK_UN releases a file lock.

fopen(filename, mode)

> opens the file. Works on local and remote files as described above. The modes are listed in Table 12.5.

fputs($fp, string[, length])

> writes the string to the file pointed to by $fp. If the optional length is given, that many bytes are written. Otherwise the entire string is written.

File Mode	Meaning
r	Opens the file for reading. Reading starts at the beginning of the file.
r+	Opens the file for reading and writing. The file pointer starts at the beginning of the file.
w	Opens the file for writing. Places the pointer at the start of the file and sets the file length to zero. This means that all data previously in the file will be deleted unless you have previously copied it elsewhere. If the file does not exist, it will be created.
w+	Opens the file for reading and writing. Places the pointer at the start of the file and sets the file length to zero. This means that all data previously in the file will be deleted unless you have previously copied it elsewhere. If the file does not exist, it will be created.
a	Opens the file for writing. The file pointer is placed at the end of the file. If the file does not exist, it is created.
a+	Opens the file for reading and writing. The file pointer is placed at the end of the file. If the file does not exist, it is created.

Table 12.5 File modes

fread($fp, length)

> reads up to length bytes from $fp. This operation is suitable for reading either text or ASCII data on systems such as Windows which distinguish between the two.

tmpfile()

> creates a temporary file which is ready to be written to. The function returns a filehandle to the new file. The file is deleted when fclose() is called on it.

unlink(filename)

> deletes the file whose name is given as parameter. Return FALSE if there is an error.

The following code operates on the simple cookie database that I created in Section 9.10 for use with small Perl applications. This code reads through the database and echoes the contents out to the browser:

```
1    <html>
        <head><title>Biscuit Database</title></head>
        <body>
```

```
          <h1>The Biscuit Database</h1>
5         <?php
              makeContent();
          ?>
      </body>
   </html>
10
   <?php
      function makeContent() {
          $fp = fopen("cookies.dat", "r");
          if($fp) {
15            while(!feof($fp)){
                  $row = fgets($fp, 1024);
                  $bicks = preg_split("/::/", $row);
                  echo "<h3>Next Row</h3><ul>";
                  for($i = 0; $i < count($bicks); $i++) {
20                    echo "<li>";
                      echo $bicks[$i];
                      echo "</li>";
                  ]
                  echo "</ul>";
25            } fclose($fp);
          }
      } // makeContent
   ?>
```

EXERCISES

1. Install PHP 5 and configure your Web server to use it. Test the installation by using `<? phpinfo() ?>`.
2. Write a guestbook in PHP. Your page should accept input from users through a form and return a message to them. Hold the data in a file.
3. Modify your guestbook so that all messages are saved in a file.
4. Write a script which reads the guestbook data back out of the storage file and displays it, neatly formatted, in a new page.

5. Add a search facility to your guestbook so that visitors can search for messages left by other people whose names they know.

6. Add a stylesheet to format your guestbook.

7. Use PHP to display the current time of day at the server within a Web page.

8. Write PHP routines which validate all data entered into your guestbook.

9. Implement the Sieve of Eratosthenes method for discovering prime numbers in PHP.

10. Create an HTML page which has form fields for name, age and full address including zip code. Send the contents of the form to a PHP script using HTTP post. Validate the returned data in your PHP script, ensuring that it is suitable for your locale. For example, ages should be positive integers in the range 0 to 12 months and 0 to 130 years. Return a neatly formatted page which contains the transmitted data and which highlights any errors that the user might have made.

11. What differences would a user note if you switched from using HTTP get to using HTTP post? What changes would you have to make to your PHP scripts?

12. Create an HTML form which you can use to enter a list of your friends names, include both forenames and surnames. Pass the data to a PHP script. Display the names in the order in which they were entered and in descending alphabetical order. Store the unordered names in a cookie. Let the user enter another name, display it correctly in the sorted list, taking the other names from the cookie.

Building Web Applications With PHP

13

In Chapter 11, I showed some of the things which can be done using readily available Perl libraries. The PHP community has created an equally vast collection of resources. In this chapter I will look at some common Web programming tasks and show how they can be achieved using PHP. Most of the code you will see in this chapter uses extensions which can be compiled directly into the PHP interpreter. Others use standard extensions which are almost always available.

Very little here requires the installation of additional components after you have installed the main system. In this sense PHP is far easier to manage than Perl. The basic Perl system is a powerful text and system manipulation language. Code which can handle image data, XML or Web protocols is available from CPAN, the Comprehensive Perl Archive Network, sites around the World. The existence of CPAN means that Perl can be kept up-to-date and extended very quickly as new technologies come along.

Any serious Web server programming needs to be as extensible and flexible as Perl. For example, if PHP could only speak to a single relational database it would not, could not, be widely used. Large organizations use many different database technologies and applications developers need to be able to talk to all of them. The same applies across many aspects of applications development including networking, graphics and multimedia. With this in mind the PHP community has created an extension system and library of code called PEAR. PEAR, PHP Extension and Application Repository, gives PHP developers access to:

- a library of open-source code
- a way of packaging code, maintaining packages and distributing them
- PECL, the PHP Extensions Community Library, for extensions to the basic PHP system written in C

- support for developers through forums and Websites
- coding standards.

13.1 TRACKING USERS

Users have to be tracked through many Web sites. Shopping baskets, security or simple curiosity about the parts of a site that users like, require this. The easiest and commonest way of tracking users is with a cookie. If you have been reading through this book sequentially you will have already encountered cookies in both JavaScript and Perl. If you though that they were easy in those languages, you will find that they are even more straightforward in PHP.

In this section, I will demonstrate how to use cookies in your PHP scripts and how to uses PHP sessions, essentially an in-built implementation of cookies, to restrict access.

13.1.1 Cookies

A cookie is a text string which is stored in your visitor's PC by *your* script. Cookies are both useful and controversial. If you are running a large site or doing e-commerce, then cookies are an excellent way of tracking users and can be a help in managing transactions. Many shopping cart applications are based around cookies, using them to track the items that a shopper has ordered. Users, especially those concerned with civil liberties in cyberspace, are worried about the widespread use of cookies. They are often used by advertisers, especially those selling banner advertising, to track users through sites. Whilst the advertiser will not know who is viewing their banners, they will be able to build a picture of the type of viewer they are attracting. I suppose that whether this offends you or not, depends upon your philosophical outlook. The important consideration for a developer is that if you use cookies too widely, you may drive potential customers away – or worse yet, make it impossible for them to do business with you.

Creating cookies in PHP is easy. Simply place a call to the setcookie() function before the HTML tag at the top of your page. It needs to go there because cookies are sent as part of the HTTP header message which is sent *before* the HTML page.

setcookie(name[, value[, expiry]])

> Each cookie has to have a name. Generally all cookies from each area of your site will have the same name so that you can retrieve them and track your visitors. If you do not pass a name to the function, you will get an error. If the only parameter that you give to the function is the name, the cookie will be deleted.

> Cookies are designed to expire after a preset length of time. That expiry time is set using the third parameter which is an integer value. The time value should be created using either mktime() or the time() function so that it has a valid value. If you use an empty string the cookie will be deleted. If no time is supplied the cookie will expire when the browser session is closed.

Cookies are automatically returned to the site which created them. They are accessed from an array called $_COOKIE using their name.

This code reads in and displays a cookie, and sets it with a new value which was passed to the script as a parameter. The cookie will expire after 20 minutes:

```
1   <?php
        setcookie("CookieTest", $_GET['value'], time()+1200);
    ?>
    <html>
5       <head><title>Functions</title></head>
        <body>
            <h1>Using Cookies</h1>
            <?php
                echo "<h2>The cookie is: ". $_COOKIE['CookieTest'] ."</h2>"
10          ?>
        </body>
    </html>
```

Try saving that as a file called cookie.php. Run it using:
http://localhost/html/cookie.php?value=something

Cookies really do not get much more complicated than that. Access to them can be restricted to certain parts of a server or domain although by default they operate only on the directory which contains the script that creates them. If you need to use a cookie to control access to other parts of your server then look in the PHP documentation for full details.

The following listing creates a cookie which lasts for two minutes. The cookie can be viewed, reset or deleted using an HTML form. Read through the code then read the detailed explanation which follows. As you read the code, notice that I use only one PHP script to do all of the work. I could have written the code so that separate pages were need to write, view or delete the cookie. Users sometimes want to avoid even the least intrusive security schemes. If your pages hide behind a single URL like this in which the server-sided code is performing redirection, you are keeping a lot of structural information away from users. This gives you a little more security against the casual or accidental hacker.

```
1   <?php
        $name = $_POST['user'];
        $pwd = $_POST['pwd'];

5       if ($_POST['on']) {
            if ($name && $pwd) {
                $content = $name ."&". $pwd;
                setCookie("UserDetails", $content, time()+120);
```

```
            }
10
      } elseif ($_POST['off'])
          setCookie("UserDetails", '');
   ?>


15

   <html>
      <head><title>Access Control with Cookies</title></head>
      <body>
          <h1>Access Control with Cookies</h1>
20

          <?php

   if ($_POST['__check__']) {
      checkForm();
25 } else {
      printForm();
   }



30 function checkForm() {
      global $name,$pwd;

      if ($_POST['show']) {
          echo "<h3>Cookie contains ". $_COOKIE["UserDetails"] ."</h3>";
35    } else {
         if (!$name || !$pwd)
            echo "<h3>Please enter username and password</h3>";
         else
            echo "<h3>You submitted $name and $pwd</h3>";
40    }

      printForm();

   } // checkForm
45
```

```
   function printForm() {
     $thisURL = $_SERVER[PHP_SELF];

50   echo <<<_DONE
     <form action="$thisURL" method="post">
       <table>
         <tr>
           <td>Enter Your Name</td>
55           <td><input type="text" length="20" name="user"></td>
         </tr>
         <tr>
           <td>Password</td>
           <td><input type="password" length="10" name="pwd"></td>
60         </tr>
         <tr>
           <td><input type="submit" name="on" value="Log On"/></td>
           <td><input type="submit" name="off" value="Log Off"/></td>
         </tr>
65         <tr>
           <td colspan="2" align="center">
             <input type="submit" name="show" value="Show the Cookie" />
           </td>
         </tr>
70         <input type="hidden" name="__check__" value="1" />
       </table>
     </form>
   _DONE;


75 } // printForm


         ?>
     </body>
   </html>
```

The first piece of code that I am going to examine is the printForm function which creates an HTML input form by echoing a *here* document. Any HTML form has two important parameters: the method by which data will be returned and the URL of the script which will handle that data. In this example we are returning data using HTTP post. We are going to return data to the script which created the form so that it handles both parts of the process. The URL of the script could be hard-coded in the action attribute of the form element, but if the script is moved from one server to another the code will immediately break. PHP provides a nice way of discovering this information programmatically. It has an autoglobal array called $_SERVER which contains information provided by the server about itself and the script. One of the values in there is called PHP_SELF which is the relative name of the current script. That name is relative to the root of the document tree and will remain valid if the Website is moved to another server.

 NOTE

Before version 4.2 of PHP many global variables including data sent back in HTTP requests was automatically available. Since then PHP installations default to using autoglobal arrays for control information. This behavior can be changed through the register_globals directive in the configuration file for your PHP installation.

The URL is assigned to the action attribute using these two lines of code:

```
$thisURL = $_SERVER[PHP_SELF];
<form action="$thisURL" method="post">
```

One other thing that you should notice is a hidden value in the form:

```
<input type="hidden" name="__check__" value="1" />
```

When the page loads for the first time, no values are sent from the browser back to the server in the HTTP GET request. Later requests for the page using the buttons on the form will contain data which we want to use. Needless processing of non-existent values with the first request is avoided using this hidden value. After processing the HTTP header and starting to write HTML the hidden value is checked. The appropriate PHP function is chosen depending upon the existence of the hidden value in the returned data.

```
23  if ($_POST['__check__']) {
        checkForm();
25  } else {
        printForm();
    }
```

When the page is initially loaded any cookie data is processed. If the user completed the HTML form data will have been sent back to the server and will be available from the $_POST autoglobal array.

```
1  <?php
       $name = $_POST['user'];
       $pwd = $_POST['pwd'];
```

```
5     if ($_POST['on']) {
          if ($name && $pwd) {
              $content = $name ."&". $pwd;
              setCookie("UserDetails", $content, time()+120);
          }

10
      } elseif ($_POST['off'])
          setCookie("UserDetails", '');
    ?>
```

The script first extract the contents if the user and pwd fields. check that the fields
were completed before processing the data. In a production system I would use JavaScript
on the client to ensure that these fields were completed then add a further check here. The
field values are copied into variables at this stage. Because the $name and $pwd variables are
outside any PHP functions they are *global* and will be available to later PHP sections in this
page.

The HTML form contains buttons named on, off and show. These select different
pieces of processing. The first two are checked at this stage. If on was pressed the cookie is
created and given a life of two minutes. If off was selected the expiry time is set to an empty
string which causes the deletion of the cookie. Processing proceeds on to the first HTML
section of the script.

The checkForm function on line 30 is selected if the hidden field __check__ was returned
by the client.

```
30    function checkForm() {
          global $name,$pwd;

          if ($_POST['show']) {
              echo "<h3>Cookie contains ". $_COOKIE["UserDetails"] ."</h3>";
35        } else {
              if (!$name || !$pwd)
                  echo "<h3>Please enter username and password</h3>";
              else
                  echo "<h3>You submitted $name and $pwd</h3>";
40        }

          printForm();

      } // checkForm
```

On line 36 the code will need the values which were entered into the form by the user. These were copied into global variables. Programmer-defined global variables are different to PHP autoglobals. The latter are always available to a script. The former have scope and are not automatically available inside functions. To access them we place the keyword `global` before a list of the variable names that we need to use at the top of the function:

`global` $name,$pwd;

The function then displays the contents of the cookie or a message about the submitted data. Finally the function which prints the HTML form is called and the user can repeat her actions if she so chooses.

13.1.2 Sessions

A session is a way of preserving information between page and across page accesses. The same things can be done using hidden data on a form or through cookies but PHP sessions provide some advantages:

- The most important of these is that the really hard work has been done for you. Using sessions gives access to robust, efficient code.
- The session library provides two ways to do the same thing: using cookies or rewritten URLs. This lets you choose which is the more appropriate approach to take for your situation.
- Using a standard API is much safer then developing your own. It reduces the maintenance effort required to keep your code running because you can trust the underlying implementation.
- Other developers who work on your code will know the same API which will make *them* more efficient.

The PHP session gives each visitor a unique ID. This is either added to the URL of each page that they request within your site or is stored in a cookie on their browser. You can use the session ID to restrict access, for example, by making it *timeout* after thirty minutes, after which time they must login once more. Because the ID is passed as plain text, sessions are not secure. You cannot guarantee that other people will never see a user's cookie, which is just a text file, or the rewritten URL. Therefore you should not trust sessions where you need absolute security. However, if you need an easy way to link a shopping cart to a user, or to allow or disallow postings to a blog or forum, the session is perfect.

A session is created using a call to the built-in `session_start()` function. Because sessions are either cookie or URL based they are working with HTTP header information. This means that you must create the session before performing any processing which transmits data back to the user. The easiest way of ensuring this is to create the session at the very start of the PHP file. Everything then works as for cookies but using a different autoglobal array. If you look at the following example you will see that most of it is identical to the cookie code from Section 13.1.1.

```php
<?php
    session_start();

    $name = $_POST['user'];
    $pwd = $_POST['pwd'];

    if ($_POST['on']) {
        if ($name && $pwd) {
            $_SESSION['user'] = $name;
            $_SESSION['pwd'] = $pwd;
            $_SESSION['counter'] += 1;
        }
    } elseif ($_POST['off']) {
        unset($_SESSION['user']);
        unset($_SESSION['pwd']);
        unset($_SESSION['counter']);
    }
?>

<html>
    <head><title>Access Control with Sessions</title></head>
    <body>
        <h1>Access Control with Sessions</h1>

        <?php

if ($_POST['__check__']) {
    checkForm();
} else {
    printForm();
}


function checkForm() {
    global $name,$pwd;
```

```php
        if ($_POST['show']) {
            echo "<h3>Session contains ". $_SESSION['user'] ." and ".
                $_SESSION['pwd'] ."</h3>";
            echo "<h3>You have logged on ". $_SESSION['counter'] ." times</h3>";
40      } else {
            if (!$name || !$pwd)
                echo "<h3>Please enter username and password</h3>";
            else
                echo "<h3>You submitted $name and $pwd</h3>";
45      }

    printForm();

} // checkForm
50


function printForm() {
    $thisURL = $_SERVER[PHP_SELF];

55  echo <<<_DONE
    <form action="$thisURL" method="post">
        <table>
            <tr>
                <td>Enter Your Name</td>
60              <td><input type="text" length="20" name="user"></td>
            </tr>
            <tr>
                <td>Password</td>
                <td><input type="password" length="10" name="pwd"></td>
65          </tr>
            <tr>
                <td><input type="submit" name="on" value="Log On"/></td>
                <td><input type="submit" name="off" value="Log Off"/></td>
            </tr>
70          <tr>
                <td colspan="2" align="center">
                    <input type="submit" name="show" value="Show the Session" />
                </td>
```

```
            </tr>
75          <input type="hidden" name="__check__" value="1" />
        </table>
    </form>
_DONE;


80  } // printForm


    ?>
    </body>
</html>
```

The important differences lie in the way that the data is saved to the session and the way that the session is ended. When working with cookies we used a call to the `setCookie` function. In session code values are assigned directly to the `$_SESSION` array. Each value must have a unique name and may hold any valid value but may not hold a reference.

```
    $_SESSION['user'] = $name;
10  $_SESSION['pwd'] = $pwd;
    $_SESSION['counter'] += 1;
```

Removing data from the session is done through a call to the `unset` function:

```
    unset($_SESSION['user']);
15  unset($_SESSION['pwd']);
    unset($_SESSION['counter']);
```

You should be able to see many possible uses for sessions. Try them on some of your pages.

13.2 USING DATABASES

Relational databases are central to most commercial Web development. Databases are used to store, manage and efficiently query large volumes of data. They are complex pieces of software built on a relatively simple programming model. A full explanation of how to design and implement relational data structures, use different database packages and access stored, data is beyond the scope of this book. I will provide an introduction to some of the database facilities which you can use in PHP but for more detail you will need to go elsewhere.

13.2.1 LAMP

Large-scale Web systems are most often based on J2EE, a version of Java which has the features you need to run enterprise systems. J2EE is massively complex since it tries to be all things to all enterprises. Smaller organizations often use Microsoft products throughout and tend to build their systems using the .Net framework which is rich and powerful but not as fully-featured as J2EE.

Both J2EE and .Net are proprietary technologies aimed at business developers. Both have problems of complexity and bloat. There are a number of open source alternatives to them both. One popular approach is to run a server which has the GNU/Linux operating system, an Apache Web server, a MySQL database and one of the programming languages PHP/Perl/Python. This particular combination has taken on the acronym LAMP.

The LAMP suite of technologies are all popular both together and individually. One great aspect is that they can all be downloaded and installed free of charge. This gives you the opportunity to learn about them at home without the pressure of work deadlines and standards.

13.2.2 Introducing MySQL

The MySQL database engine has been around for about 10 years now. It is one of the great successes of the open-source software movement. According to its homepage, http://www.mysql.com the software has been downloaded over 100 million times, hundreds of books have been written about it and it is used daily by major organizations such as CERN, Wikipedia and the Human Genome Project.

Depending upon the system that you are using and the software that you have installed, using MySQL can be a more or less daunting experience. On my Linux system I access it through a command shell, typing commands directly into the database. There a number of tools which provide graphical interfaces. These often aspire to provide the same levels of abstraction and ease of use that Microsoft Access has. If you are new to database software then using a friendly graphical tool will make the whole experience far less painful. Because MySQL can be used in many different ways I am not going to show you how to use it. Your local installation will have lots of documentation to help you through the process.

One thing which you do have to be aware of is the concept of the database. In working with software such as MySQL we *overload* the word database to give it two different meanings. We talk about a database when we mean the software which stores and manipulates our data. Developers will ask each other what database they are using when really they mean to ask about a *database engine* or *database software*. More correctly database is used to mean a particular collection of tables, queries and views which are related to each other. We may have a customer relations database or an accounts database, a suppliers database or a parts database. Each of these is an independent collection of tables but all of them can exist on the same server and be used by the same database software.

Using MySQL

Relational databases are manipulated using a language called SQL[1]. This is an acronym for Structured Query Language but no-one ever calls it that. SQL only really makes sense in the context of a relational database and it is best learnt when you are learning about database technology. There is not enough space here to describe the language in much detail. I will just talk through a few of its key parts.

The SQL commands can be used both from the MySQL interface and from within PHP scripts.

Unlike most programming languages, keywords in SQL ares not case sensitive. By convention, SQL commands are entered as uppercase. Both MySQL commands and SQL instructions are terminated with a semicolon from the command line but *not* when inside PHP code.

SHOW DATABASES;

> is a MySQL command which lists all of the databases which are available on the system.

USE name

> selects one of the available databases. Subsequent commands will apply only to this database.

CREATE DATABASE name

> creates an empty database with the name which is supplied as the parameter.

DROP DATABASE name

> deletes the named database.

CREATE TABLE tableName (column1 type[,column2 type[, ...]])

> creates a new table called `tableName`. The table has columns whose names are supplied in the comma-separated list. Each column name is followed by the data type to be used for that column. Data types which you may commonly use include:

- **BOOLEAN** non-zero values are `true`, zero is `false`.
- **INTEGER [UNSIGNED]** holds integer values in the range of $\pm 2^{31}$. Unsigned integers can range from 0 to 2^{32}.
- **MEDIUMINT** holds integer values in the range of $\pm 2^{23}$. Unsigned integers can range from 0 to 2^{24}.

---

[1]You may hear this pronounced by spelling out the letters or as the word *sequel*

- **DOUBLE[(m,b)] [UNSIGNED]** is a double precision floating point number accurate to 15 decimal places. If m is specified in parentheses it indicates the display width of the number. A b in the parentheses gives the preferred precision. if both m and b are given they should be separated using a comma.
- **DECIMAL[(m,d)] [UNSIGNED]** indicates a decimal number, m gives the total number of digits, d the number of decimals.
- **DATE** a date in YYYY-MM-DD format.
- **CHAR** an ASCII character.
- **VARCHAR(m)** is a variable length string. m gives the length of the string in the range 1 to 255.
- **TEXT** a piece of text of maximum length 65 535 characters.
- **ENUM('value1'[, 'value2'[, ... ,]])** an enumeration. A comma-separated list of values is given in parentheses. The column must take one of these values.

When columns are defined within tables they can be modified, as the next example shows. Some of these columns are given the modifier NOT NULL which means a value *must* be entered into that column. The id column is defined as being AUTO_INCREMENT. You do not need to enter a value into this column, it will be automatically assigned one each time a new row is inserted into the table.

Each table has a primary key. This is a value which the database software uses when building indexes and which is often used as the main criterion in a search. The primary key for each row of the table must be unique. In this example the id column is the primary key.

```
1   CREATE TABLE user (
        id MEDIUMINT NOT NULL AUTO_INCREMENT,
        email VARCHAR(255) NOT NULL,
        forename VARCHAR(32),
5       surname VARCHAR(32),
        type ENUM ('user','administrator','owner','guest') NOT NULL,
        PRIMARY KEY (id)
    );
```

DESCRIBE table

lists the columns and data types which make up the table. The table outline created using the code shown above has the following description (which has been slightly reformatted to fit the printed page).

```
mysql> describe user;
+---------+-----------------+----+----+--------+---------------+
|Field    |Type             |Null|Key |Default |Extra          |
+---------+-----------------+----+----+--------+---------------+
|id       |mediumint(9)     |    |PRI |NULL    |auto_increment |
|email    |varchar(255)     |    |    |        |               |
|forename |varchar(32)      |YES |    |NULL    |               |
|surname  |varchar(32)      |YES |    |NULL    |               |
|type     |enum('user',     |    |    |        |               |
|         |'administrator', |    |    |        |               |
|         |'owner','guest') |    |    |user    |               |
+---------+-----------------+----+----+--------+---------------+
5 rows in set (0.00 sec)
```

INSERT INTO tableName (column1[, column2[, ...]]) VALUES (value1[, value2[, ...]])

inserts values into the table. Each value in the second set of parentheses is assigned to the corresponding column from the first set.

```
1   INSERT INTO
        user (email, forename, surname, type)
    VALUES
        ('chris@home', 'Chris', 'Bates', 'owner'),
5       ('floyd@dogs.com', 'Floyd', '', 'user'),
        ('null@nowhere', 'Guest1', 'Guest', 'guest');
```

SELECT column1[, column2[, ...]] FROM tableName [WHERE condition]

returns the chosen columns from the table. If a WHERE condition is given, only rows which match the condition are returned. If no WHERE condition is supplied, all rows of the table are returned. To return all columns simply use a wildcard asterix instead of column names. Here are some examples.

```
1   SELECT email FROM user WHERE forename='Floyd';
    SELECT email,type FROM user;
    SELECT * FROM user;
    SELECT * FROM user WHERE surname='Bates';
```

```
UPDATE tableName SET column1=value1[, column2=value2[, ...]] [WHERE
condition]
```

changes the value of rows and columns which are already present in the table.

```
 1   UPDATE user SET type='administrator' WHERE forename='Floyd';
```

```
DELETE FROM tableName
```
deletes all data from the table called `tableName`. This command cannot be reversed.

```
DELETE FROM tableName WHERE condition
```
deletes all rows from the named table which match `condition`.

13.2.3 Accessing MySQL from PHP

Using databases is a very complicated activity. Giving comprehensive examples and instructions would require a book of its own. Since I do not have the space here to do justice to the subject I am going to provide a quick overview. This example shows how to connect a PHP script to a MySQL database. It is a simple application which stores name, email address and a role taken from a drop-down list. Data is entered using an HTML form. This lets users query the database, delete or amend existing records and add new data. The complete listing is nearly 160 lines of code. I have placed it in Appendix A because of its length and will cover just the most important aspects here.

I have included two versions of this application. The first uses the standard PHP interface to MySQL. The second, in Section 13.2.4 uses the Pear DB extension.

The application starts by connecting to the database server. The connection is made using the `mysqli_connect` function. This takes a number of parameters. In this example I pass in the most common ones: URL or address of the database server, user name, password and the name of the database. The function returns an object which represents the connection.

```
 1   <?php
         $db = mysqli_connect('127.0.0.1', 'username', 'pwd', 'database');
         if (!$db) {
             die("Unable to connect to database: ". mysqli_connect_error());
 5       }
     ?>
```

If the attempt to connect to the database is unsuccessful `false` is returned instead of a connection object. You always need to test for this return value so that you can display a meaningful error message to the user. Here I call `die` and pass in a string with the error which the MySQL driver returns concatenated onto it.

If you look at the complete listing in Appendix A you will see that the bulk of the code prepares and manages the HTML form. The real work of the application is done by the handleForm method. This code extracts the values which the user returned from $_POST and copies them into local variables. Notice the use of global to gain access to the database connection object.

```
1  function handleForm() {
       global $db;

       $forename = $_POST['forename'];
5      $surname = $_POST['surname'];
       $email = $_POST['email'];
       $role = $_POST['role'];
```

The printForm method which redisplays the entry form takes four parameters. If the database search has been successful these will contain the extracted values. By passing the returned data into printForm I am able to display them in the form. Thus the user can easily edit the data.

```
1  if ($_POST['save']) {
       // save one record

   } elseif ($_POST['amend']) {
5      // alter one record

   } elseif ($_POST['delete']) {
       // delete one record

10 } elseif ($_POST['view']) {
       // show one record

   } else {
       // must be showall
15 }
```

If you look at the submit buttons on the form you will see that five operations are permitted. The code chooses between these using if... elseif... else. If the return values were integers this code could be replaced with a switch statement. The problem with integers as return values is that their meaning is unclear, which complicates code maintenance.

The first operation is the insertion of new data into the database. The SQL statement is assigned to a string.

NOTE *When you place an SQL statement within PHP code you must **not** terminate it with a semicolon.*

The variables which contain the values for insertion are placed directly into the SQL statement. The PHP interpreter will perform *interpolation*. That simply means that each variable name will be replaced by the value of the variable at runtime. In this example all of the values are strings. In SQL statements strings must be surrounded by quotes therefore the variable names are placed inside quotes.

The two commonest mistakes which I see amongst my students are missing or mismatched quotes and semicolons in the SQL string. You must be careful with these – the error message which you get back from the database will generally be cryptic. Finding a mismatched quotation mark can be frustrating and time-consuming.

mysqli_query(database, statement)

The query is executed using the standard mysqli extension. This function returns true or an object containing the results of the SQL statement if it executes successfully. The result object is returned from SELECT, DESCRIBE or SHOW statements.

PHP has two extensions which can handle connections to MySQL databases. The older one is called mysql. Its operations take the form mysql_query. In these examples I am using the improved MySQL interface mysqli. This version should be used when you need to access version 4.1.3, or later, of MySQL.

This code sample executes the INSERT then checks the return value and displays an appropriate message. You must always give useful feedback to the user when they have submitted data. Be aware of two things, though. First, most users will not know that your backend uses a database and will not want to know this. Do not show them a message which mentions the database (this does but it is just an example). Second, never return a complete database or PHP error to a user. Few things are more pointless than getting an SQL error which you do not understand and which you cannot act on.

```
1   if ($_POST['save']) {
        // save one record
        $statement = "INSERT INTO user (forename,surname,email,type) VALUES
            ('$forename','$surname','$email','$role')";
        if ($result = mysqli_query($db, $statement)) {
5           echo "<h3 style='color: green'>One row added to the database</h3>";
        } else {
```

```
        echo "<h3 style='color: red'>There was a problem saving your
            data</h3>";
    }
```

Changing the data already stored uses an UPDATE statement. Again the parameters are placed in quotes and the interpreter performs the interpolation. Deletion works in the same way as insertion and updating. In this case I have changed the error message to make it slightly more meaningful. Here are the key parts of each operation.

```
1  // alter one record
   $statement = "UPDATE user SET forename='$forename', surname='$surname',
       type='$role' WHERE email='$email'";
   if ($result = mysqli_query($db, $statement)) {

5  // delete one record
   $statement = "DELETE FROM user WHERE email='$email'";
   if ($result = mysqli_query($db, $statement)) {
```

Viewing data is slightly different. When the SELECT query executes, the rows which it returns are held in the result object.

```
1  } elseif ($_POST['view']) {
       // show one record
       $statement = "SELECT * FROM user WHERE email='$email'";
       if ($result = mysqli_query($db, $statement)) {
5          echo "<h3>Your query returned</h3>";
           $data = mysqli_fetch_object($result);
           $f = $data->forename;
           $s = $data->surname;
           $e = $data->email;
10         $r = $data->type;
       } else {
           echo "<h3 style='color: red'>There was a problem finding the row.
               Please check that you entered the correct email address</h3>";
       }
```

mysqli_fetch_object(result)

> returns the result set as an object. The object has attributes which have the same names as the columns in the result set which they represent. If you attempt to read past the last row of the data set null will be returned.

mysqli_fetch_row(result)

> returns an array which contains the current row.

mysqli_fetch_array(result, type)

> an extended version of `mysqli_fetch_row`. The method can store data in an array and use either numeric or associative indices to access it. In an associative array the names of the fields are used as the keys.
>
> The type field can take one of the constants MYSQLI_NUM, MYSQLI_ASSOC or MYSQLI_BOTH.

If the result set may have returned more than one row, for example, following SELECT * FROM table; the program must iterate across the returned rows and display them all. The easiest way of doing this is to use a while loop as the following fragment shows.

```
while ($data = mysqli_fetch_object($result)) {
```

The `mysqli` extension is large and complex. I have not even begun to scratch at its surface. The documentation in the PHP manual is comprehensive and contains good examples. If you plan to explore further into the inner recesses then that should be your starting point.

13.2.4 Using Pear DB

Database-specific interfaces which can talk to MySQL, Oracle or SQL Server are great. With them you can get really close to the specifics of your database server which lets you optimize your code for speed, memory usage or maintainability.

If you are creating a system which uses more than one type of database server or your code is likely to be moved between servers, these extensions can cause problems. If you are moving code between database systems you need to find and rewrite all of the database-specific sections of your PHP. There are many things that you can do to ease the pain involved but there will definitely be some pain.

If you are working with a number of database backends from different manufacturers you must learn the intricacies of several extension packages. This is obviously time-consuming and can be confusing.

In truth, commercial systems almost never move between database servers from different manufacturers. At the requirements gathering or analysis phases of a project, decisions are made about the technologies that will be used. Just as a decision to use PHP instead of Java is made early, so the choice between SQL Server and MySQL is made. You are more likely to meet situations in which your PHP applications are talking to different databases. Typically organizations have *legacy* systems. These are systems which they have been using for a number of years, which the manufacturer may regard as long past their end of life. They are often mission-critical to their users and so live on.

Pear DB provides a consistent interface to a wide range of database backends. You write code in the same style whether you are talking to MySQL, mSQL, PostgreSQL, Oracle or many others. Pear DB uses the appropriate PHP driver for each database system.

connect(dsn)

opens a connection to the database. It returns an object which encapsulates the connection if successful. On failure it returns a DB_Error object.

data source name

This is not a Pear DB object. It is a string which names and identifies the database to which you are connecting. The DSN has the following components:

- Database type.
- SQL syntax. For ODBC connections this identifies which style of SQL syntax is in use.
- Protocol to use which may be TCP, Unix or other variants.
- The host name and, optionally, a port.
- The name of the database.
- The user name.
- Password.

Examples of the use of these can be found in the documentation.

setFetchMode(mode)

tells the extension how you want to receive data from your queries. This method sets a property of the database connection. The available modes are:

- DB_FETCHMODE_OBJECT returns an object. The properties of the object are named after the columns returned.
- DB_FETCHMODE_ORDERED data is put into an ordered array. The order of items matches the order of the select statement.
- DB_FETCHMODE_ASSOC data is placed in an associative array with column names as keys.

The code in Appendix B reworks the example from Section 13.2.3 to use Pear DB. The code fragments and descriptions which follow show how much more straightforward this database agnostic approach is.

```php
1   <?php
        require 'DB.php';
        $db = DB::connect("mysqli://user:password@address/database");
        if (DB::isError($db)) {
5           die("Unable to connect to database: ". $db->getMessage());
        }
        // returned values are available as object
        $db->setFetchMode(DB_FETCHMODE_OBJECT);
    ?>
```

We start by loading the DB module. If it is not available the user will get a standard PHP error message. The connection is opened. In this example I am passing in a straightforward DSN string. The connection is going to piggyback on the improved MySQL extension mysqli which was used on the previous example. The connection returns an object which is checked to make sure that is not an error. If a connection was not established the reasons for the failure are returned to the user.

The connection is set to use an object-based interface rather than one of the array forms. Using objects makes the rest of the code cleaner and reduces future maintenance overheads.

The process of inserting data into the table shows most of the functionality that you will need in simple programs.

```
if ($_POST['save']) {
    // save one record
    $statement = $db->query("INSERT INTO user
        (forename,surname,email,type) VALUES
        ('$forename','$surname','$email','$role')");
    if (! DB::isError($db)) {
        echo "<h3 style='color: green'>One row added to the
            database</h3>";
    } else {
        echo "<h3 style='color: red'>There was a problem saving your
            data</h3>";
    }
```

The SQL statement is passed into the query method of the database connection object. The query method is a utility function which prepares and executes SQL statements in a single step. If you need to execute the same statement repeatedly throughout your code this method is rather inefficient. Instead you should call prepare at the top of your script and then use repeated calls to execute to run the prepared statement. The mixed prepare—execute cycle is the more flexible approach since it lets you pass different values into the SQL statement each time that it is run.

Once query has run your SQL it returns one of three things. If it is unable to execute your code form some reason it gets a DB_ERROR object. If the code succeeds a DB_OK object is returned if the code has simply manipulated the database. If the SQL returns a set of data, that will be placed in DB_result object.

Statements such as INSERT, UPDATE or DELETE manipulate data but do not return a result set. Instructions such as SELECT return a result set. It is worth noting that a SELECT can execute successfully but not return any data. You may be trying to select data which does not exist in the database!

You always need to check for errors. If your SQL is incomplete or the number of values does not match the number of parameters, for example, you will get an error from the database. Programs should check the return type to see if it is an error. Remember the error message which you return to the user should be meaningful to them. You may want to include a code number so that you can track what is happening when the user reports their problem to you. Never return the raw error message to them.

The code to update and delete records is shown below. If you look at the full listing you will see that these fragments are also followed by error checks.

```
1    // alter one record
     $statement = $db->query("UPDATE user SET forename='$forename',
        surname='$surname', type='$role' WHERE email='$email'");


     // delete one record
5    $statement = $db->query("DELETE FROM user WHERE email='$email'");
```

Finally we have the selection of data. At the top of the program we selected an object-based style of data. The data object returned from the query can contain many rows. It has an accessor function called fetchRow to get the next row of data. Place this in a while loop and access the properties of each rows as we did in Section 13.2.3.

```
1    } elseif ($_POST['view']) {
         // show one record
         $statement = $db->query("SELECT * FROM user WHERE email='$email'");
         if (! DB::isError($db)) {
5            echo "<h3>Your query returned</h3>";
             while ($data = $statement->fetchRow()) {
                 $f = $data->forename;
                 $s = $data->surname;
                 $e = $data->email;
10               $r = $data->type;
             }
         } else {
             echo "<h3 style='color: red'>There was a problem finding the
                row. Please check that you entered the correct email
                address</h3>";
         }
```

The code described above and shown in Appendix B contains a lot of error-checking code. You can get the Pear system to handle all of this for you. Place the following code at the top of your script just after you check that the connection to the database has been made successfully.

```
1   // handle errors automatically with pear DB
    $db->setErrorHandling(PEAR_ERROR_DIE);
```

If you are using the Pear error handling routines you do not need to add your own error-checking logic. Of course you will sacrifice customization, flexibility and control but you will gain code which is easier to develop and maintain.

The Pear DB extension is large and complex. The only way that you can get maximum benefit from using it is to spend some time reading the documentation. You can get the documentation for all of the Pear extensions from the Web site at `http://pear.php.net`.

13.3 HANDLING XML

The ability to move data between platform and to share it across applications within different parts of an organization is one of the most important drivers in the development of distributed computing systems. The most important distributed systems in use today is the Internet and its most important applications are based on HTTP. Everywhere that you look in large organizations you will see the Web being used in some way. The Web is no longer used solely by surfers using Web browsers such as Internet Explorer. Today software applications are talking directly to each other using the Web infrastructure to facilitate their communications. To do this the different pieces of software need to use the same data structures.

Applications have always communicated across networks and have always been able to share data. Sharing data used to mean that unique data structures were developed for every new set of communications. The applications at each end had to be able to parse the data structures, extract and handle the data that they contained and to build messages which were correctly formatted. Obviously that lead to a proliferation of unique message formats which, in turn, meant that applications could not share data in *ad hoc* groupings. Standard structures were defined for common applications such as email or Web traffic.

Data structures are designed to be used by software. They are not, generally, readable by humans. That is not normally a problem but if something goes wrong in a communication it can become one.

The solution to these problems is to find an efficient way of structuring which is usable by software but also usable by humans. The data structure should be designed so that pieces of software can parse new applications of it so that *ad hoc* communications can evolve. All of these goals, and many more, are met by XML. XML is described in detail in Chapter 14.

13.3.1 PHP's XML Facilities

PHP has excellent facilities for manipulating XML. By default the language includes the **expat** processor library written by James Clark. This can be disabled during the compilation of PHP but generally it will be available. Using **expat** based processing is quite hard work. The underlying library provides raw access to the XML document, you have to write functions which look for elements in the XML document, extract and manipulate their attributes and which handle the content of those elements. Finding sample code to do those things is not difficult but making sure that the code is robust and ensuring production quality is a different matter.

The Document Object Model provides a uniform interface to XML documents. A DOM implementation is available in PHP 5. PHP 4 had many of the same facilities in an extension called DOM XML.

The DOM extension gives access to an API which implements DOM Level 2 through an object-oriented interface. Once again the API is rather low-level. You will need to understand the XML document in detail. If you have used functions such as `getElementByID` in JavaScript the DOM implementation will be familiar and comfortable. DOM can be useful when you are creating XML documents in your programs since it includes methods to create elements, add attributes and validate documents. A complete discussion of the usage of PHP to manipulate the DOM is beyond the scope of this book. If you need to know how it works there is copious documentation in the PHP manual.

Most programmers working on Web development do not need all of the facilities of a DOM implementation and do not want to work at the level of raw XML. They need a nice, clean interface which lets them extract information from XML documents with the minimum of effort. PHP 5 includes an extension called `SimpleXML`. This extension loads an XML document from a string, file or DOM object and provides object-oriented facilities to access it.

SimpleXML

`simplexml_load_string(string)`

If the parameter is a string which represents an XML document this method returns an object of type `SimpleXMLElement`. The properties of the returned object have the names of the elements from the XML and contain their data, attributes or children.

If the parameter string cannot be formatted as an object of type `SimpleXMLElement` the Boolean value `false` is returned.

The contents of the `SimpleXMLElement` object can be displayed using the standard PHP `var_dump()` method. The following example shows how this works:

```
1   <html>
    <head><title>Using SimpleXML</title></head>
    <body>
        <?php
5           $strDoc = <<<_DONE
    <?xml version="1.0" ?>
```

```
      <message>
          <sender>Chris Bates</sender>
          <recipient>Readers of Web Programing 3</recipient>
10        <content>Hello, why not try using PHP 5!!</content>
      </message>
      _DONE;

          $xml = simplexml_load_string($strDoc);
15        echo var_dump($xml);
      ?>


      </body>
      </html>
```

Which produces output like this:

```
1   <html>
    <head>
        <title>Using SimpleXML</title>
    </head>
5   <body>
        object(SimpleXMLElement)#1 (3) {
            ["sender"]=>string(11) "Chris Bates"
            ["recipient"]=>string(27) "Readers of Web Programming 3"
            ["content"]=>string(32) "Hello, why not try using PHP 5!!"
10      }
    </body>
    </html>
```

simplexml_import_dom(object)

If your script contains an XML document as a DOM object, this method will load the properties of that object into a SimpleXMLElement object.

simplexml_load_file(URI)

Although you will often have XML data in your script as a string or DOM object, for example after a database query, this is not always so. Sometimes you will want to load a file which contains the XML at runtime. The file may be available on the local filesystem or remotely via a URL. This method encapsulates all of the functionality which is needed to find and import the file and to create the SimpleXMLElement object. If loading or importing the data fails the method returns false.

The underlying implementation uses the Libxml 2 library. This converts the URL so that escape sequences are converted back into characters. To pass in characters such as & as part of the URL you must encode them first using `urlencode`.

`SimpleXMLElement->asXML()`

takes the properties of the `SimpleXMLElement` object and returns an XML document which contains them. In the earlier example this will return an XML document which is identical to `$strDoc`.

`SimpleXMLElement->attributes()`

returns the attributes, if any, of the object. These can be iterated across using a `foreach` loop.

`SimpleXMLElement->children()`

returns the children, if any, of the object so that they can be iterated across.

`SimpleXMLElement->xpath(expression)`

This method accepts an XPath expression as its parameter. The element is evaluated against the expression. The result is returned as an array of `SimpleXMLElement` objects.

13.3.2 Processing RSS Feeds

Many Websites have very dynamic content. Some areas of the BBC news Website, `http://news.bbc.co.uk`, are updated almost every minute of every day. Users of such highly dynamic sites typically want to know when content is updated and what the new content is so that they can decide if they are going to go and view it. RSS is an XML file format which is used to describe and syndicate the content of Websites, blogs and Podcasts.

The RSS format has undergone a number of revisions, many of which are incompatible with each other. The acronym stands for different things depending upon which version is in use:

- Rich Site Summary covers RSS 0.91
- RDF Site Summary is used for RSS 0.9 and 1.0
- Really Simple Syndication is RSS 2.0.

RSS is widely used. Sites provide RSS feeds listing their updates and content. People who are interested in the site use a piece of software called an aggregator to gather the headlines. Most people will set their aggregator to access the RSS feeds from a number of sites each day. Aggregators are built to understand all of the different formats which they encounter and to hide those differences from the user.

If we want to write our own RSS aggregator we have either to handle all of the available formats or decide on a subset with which we will work. This example handles only RSS 2.0 compliant feeds, but could be extended to cope with others.

Before we can begin to write code to process the RSS data we need to know how it is
structured. We could do this by getting a copy of the specification document or a suitable
schema or DTD. In this case I have downloaded a sample document and will be working
from that.

```
1   <?xml version="1.0" encoding="ISO-8859-1" ?>

    <rss version="2.0">
    <channel>
5       <title>BBC News | Entertainment | Film | UK Edition</title>
        <link>http://news.bbc.co.uk/go/rss/-/1/hi/entertainment
            /film/default.stm</link>
        <description>Updated every minute of every day</description>
        <language>en-gb</language>
        <lastBuildDate>Fri, 16 Sep 2005 09:58:43 GMT</lastBuildDate>
10      <copyright>Copyright: (C) British Broadcasting Corporation, see
            http://news.bbc.co.uk/1/hi/help/rss/4498287.stm for terms and
            conditions of reuse</copyright>
        <docs>http://www.bbc.co.uk/syndication/</docs>
        <ttl>15</ttl>

        <image>
15          <title>BBC News</title>
            <url>http://news.bbc.co.uk/nol/shared/img/bbc_news_120x60.gif</url>
            <link>http://news.bbc.co.uk</link>
        </image>

20      <item>
            <title>Actress ends marriage</title>
            <description>Actress RZ and singer KC seek an annulment after four
                months of marriage.</description>
            <link>http://news.bbc.co.uk/go/rss/-/1/hi/entertainment
                /film/4251388.stm</link>
        <guid isPermaLink="false">http://news.bbc.co.uk/1/hi/entertainment
            /film/4251388.stm</guid>
25      <pubDate>Fri, 16 Sep 2005 07:41:15 GMT</pubDate>
        </item>
    </channel>
    </rss>
```

The content of the document is inside an rss element. The object which is created when the document is parsed will represent this top-level element. The content of the XML document becomes the properties of the SimpleXMLElement object. This means that the object will have properties called title, language, ttl, etc. These properties will take the values BBC News | Entertainment | Film | UK Edition, en-gb and 15 respectively. Elements which have children, such as item, themselves become SimpleXMLElement objects which are accessed by references from the main object. This sounds confusing but should become clearer when we look at the PHP code.

The PHP code is shown below. This script takes the URL of an RSS file as the value of its parameter, url. For example:

http://localhost/rss.php?url=http://rss.cnn.com/rss/cnn_world.rss

Read through the code then I will explain the key parts.

```php
1  <?php
       $url = urldecode($_GET['url']);
   ?>


5  <html>
       <head>
           <title>rss.xml</title>
       </head>
       <body>
10         <h1>Using RSS Feeds</h1>
           <p>The news at
           <?php
               echo date("h:ia") ." on ". date("l jS F, Y") ."</p>";
               makeIndex();
15         ?>
       </body>
   </html>


   <?php
20     function makeIndex() {
           global $url;

           if ($url)
               parseData();
25         else
               returnError("<span style='color:red'>No resource URL
                   supplied</span>");
```

```php
      } // makeIndex

30
      function parseData(){
          global $url;
          $xml = simplexml_load_file($url);

35        if ($xml) {
              echo "<h2>Channel: <a href='"
                  . $xml->channel[0]->link
                  . "'>"
                  . $xml->channel[0]->title
40                . "</a></h2>\n";

              echo "<ul>";

              foreach ($xml->channel[0]->item as $item) {
45                echo "<li><i><a href='"
                      . $item->link
                      . "'>"
                      . $item->title
                      . "</a></i> "
50                    . $item->description
                      . "</li>\n";
              }
              echo "</ul>";
          } else
55            returnError("<span style='color:red'>Unable to load $url</span>");

      } // parseData


60    function returnError($msg) {
          echo "<h2>Due to fatal error ". $msg ." we are unable to process your
              request</h2>";
      }
  ?>
```

The script starts by extracting the URL from the HTTP GET parameter. When the script is accessed through a Web browser the URL will have been escaped. The escape sequences must be replaced with characters before processing can begin. This is done by the URL decode function. The resulting string is a global variable so functions which need access to it must use the keyword global.

The parseData function does the majority of the work in this script. Data is loaded from the remote site, or from a local file, using

$xml = simplexml_load_file($url);

If the resource cannot be loaded and parsed $xml will be set to false. This value is checked before processing begins. It is always a bad idea to try processing data which does not exist. You will inevitably return error messages to your users which have no meaning to them and which they cannot act on. Checking for the presence, or absence, of critical values lets you return meaningful messages to your users.

The most complex part of the script is two echo statements. The first displays the name of the RSS resource and makes it into a clickable hyperlink.

```
1    echo "<h2>Channel: <a href='"
        . $xml->channel[0]->link
        . "'>"
        . $xml->channel[0]->title
5       . "</a></h2>\n";
```

The variable $xml has properties which represent the whole of the RSS document. If you look back at the RSS sample you will see a single channel element. This will become an *object* called channel which is, in turn, a property of $xml. Since an RSS feed may contain more than one channel, there will be an array of channel objects. Access to the channel property of the $xml object is gained using the arrow operator,->. Since channel is an array we must specify the particular element on which we are operating. In this case we use element zero.

Having found the channel we could copy it into a variable:

$channelObject = $xml->channel;

However, object creation has a significant runtime overhead even if you are merely creating a reference to the object. In this example I avoid that by directly accessing the object. The code shown above extracts the link and title parameters and embeds them in some HTML. Although typing $xml->channel[0]-> is long and time-consuming, it is clear and maintainable. There is no room for doubt over which objects and elements are being manipulated. Therefore, I would not bother to simplify short pieces of code such as this.

Each channel contains a number of items, I am going to extract and display details from each. The details of each new item are formulated as hyperlinks placed within an unordered list.

The items are properties of the channel which are contained in an array. They are extracted using a foreach loop which creates a reference to the next element of the array.

```
1   foreach ($xml->channel[0]->item as $item) {
        echo "<li><i><a href='"
            . $item->link
            . "'>"
5           . $item->title
            . "</a></i> "
            . $item->description
            . "</li>\n";
    }
```

The observant amongst you will see that when I was extracting the channel information I did not use a reference because I wanted speed. Here I am using a reference, so what is different? In this case I am using the foreach construct which is optimized and efficient. Language constructs are implemented in native code and will run very quickly. If you create a reference in your PHP it has a significant performance overhead because it runs within the PHP interpreter. A built-in feature will always outperform code written in PHP.

The SimpleXML extension provides most of the basic facilities that you will need to work with XML. If you want fine-grained control or access to control information such as processing instructions you will have to look at other options that the language provides. The DOM extension is very good if you need all of its power and if you understand it. If you want to work with documents at the lowest level then you have the basic XML extension. However you need or want to get at your XML, PHP provides the extensions to get you started.

 # EXERCISES

Cookies and Sessions
1. Give two reasons why PHP sessions are better than cookies for tracking users.
2. How does a PHP session store its data?
3. Cookies are client-side text strings, are they secure?
4. Write an application which uses cookies and sessions to mimic a shopping cart.

Databases
1. List three reasons why you would use Pear DB.

2. Identify three situations in which you would not use Pear DB.
3. Create a simple Web database application using Pear DB. Use the database to hold details of your CD and MP3 collections. Ensure that you can add, delete and update your records.
4. This exercises uses a relational database system. You may use any software which you have access to. Build a database of musicians, CDs and tracks. You will need at least the following set of tables:

Table Name	Fields
Musician	musicianID, name, instrument
CD	CdID, title, release date, highest chart position, genre
Track	trackID, title, length, rating
Musician to CD	musicianID, cdID
Track to CD	trackID, cdID

Write SQL statements to insert data into the database, to delete items and to query the database. You should write query statements which will select
- all musicians,
- all musicians who play a particular instrument,
- all CDs,
- all CDs on which a chosen musician plays,
- all tracks on a chosen CD.

Create PHP pages which can be used to execute your SQL statements and to display the results with appropriate formatting.

XML

1. What are the advantages which RSS has compared to taking headlines from HTML files?
2. Create a Web application which uses XML to store details of television programs.
3. Write a small application which is able to parse both RDF and RSS 2 files. Use your code to display content from four different Web sites.

PART VI

Miscellany

XML: Defining Data for Web Applications

14

O ver the years many technologies have excited the computer industry. Artificial intelligence, structured programming, databases, interfaces, networks have all had an impact beyond their designer's expectations. The current big thing on the Web is not some fancy multimedia application or new access technology, it is a way of describing data. Why does the Web need *another* way of describing data? Is that not what HTML is for? Read on and I hope that I can clarify the situation and excite you to the possibilities that the Extensible Markup Language (XML) presents.

Data can easily be saved and presented as plain text and for many applications nothing else is needed. For instance, configuration files such as Windows `.bat` files are rarely viewed by systems users, they provide control information for applications, and plain text is the perfect way of handling them. A word-processed document on the other hand is meant to be displayed, edited, and printed *and* to look good in each of those situations. Data often only has structure which must be recognized and remembered such as those Windows `.bat` files. In some situations applications need to present just the raw data while in others they are showing formatted data. The difficulty for developers is to combine all of these requirements into a single file type. Fortunately there is a standardized way of doing exactly that.

Back in the 1970s, organizations were already suffering from large volumes of data which could not be shared between applications. Each program used its own proprietary format and those formats had a worrying tendency to change with new versions of the software. IBM developed a *markup*language which could be used to add structural and formatting information to data and which was designed to be simple enough to be included in any application. That markup language was adapted to be suitable for general use and in 1986 the Standard Generalized Markup Language was adopted as standard 8879 by the International Organization for Standardization (ISO).

So what is a markup language? Well, a markup is a set of instructions, often called *tags*, which can be added to text files. When the file is processed by a suitable application the tags are used to control the structure or presentation of the data contained in the file. Most commonly tags are used by applications when presenting data. There are many, many different types of presentational markup such as Microsoft Rich Text Format (RTF), Adobe Portable Document Format (PDF), and HTML. Each of these is a useful powerful solution to the problem of displaying information but all have the same limitation: they describe how the data *looks* but give no information about *what* it is.

This is the point at which XML enters the picture. XML is a subset of SGML, which simply means that it is composed of parts of the SGML specification. The designers of XML chose to include only those parts of SGML which are used most often and which can help to structure data and documents. This means that any valid[1] XML document is also a valid SGML document, which is useful as lots of tools have been written over the years to create and manipulate SGML. SGML tools are often far more sophisticated than HTML editors. They include facilities for validating data, for creating tags, and for describing documents. Such tools can use data written by any other SGML editor and some can even be embedded into other applications.

Whilst markup systems such as HTML set out a standard set of rules which are applied to all documents, XML and SGML are a little different. XML is a sort of *meta-markup*: a grammar for creating other markup languages. By applying the rules of XML to a particular need, developers can create their own markup languages which conform to an international standard and can be manipulated by many applications but which are exactly tailored to a specific set of needs.

RULE OF THUMB

XML is used to describe the structure of a document not *the way that it is presented.*

XML is a *recommendation*[2] of the World Wide Web Consortium (W3C). The current version of the standard is 1.0 but this is a fast-moving area, so expect new versions in the near future. A large number of other technologies and ideas are closely related to work on XML. Therefore anything written about the topic will soon be superseded. For the most accurate and up-to-date information on all of the technologies that I discuss in this chapter see http://www.w3c.org.

[1] Here valid means that the document conforms to its specification. I will look at this in more detail later.
[2] Their version of a standard.

Although XML is a very young technology it has caught the imagination of many developers. Two areas in which XML appears to have potential are structuring data for storage where a relational database is inappropriate, and structuring data for presentation on Web pages. If a system is handling small quantities of data or if the data lacks a *relational* structure[3] programmers have usually resorted to creating their own data formats. For example, configuration files on many systems take a form like the following, which comes from the Ghostview PostScript viewer on a PC running Windows NT:

```
[Devices]
bit=72,96
bitcmyk=72,96
bitrgb=72,96
bj10e=360x360,360x180,180x360,180x180
bj200=360x360,360x180,180x360,180x180
bjc600=360x360,360x180,180x360,180x180
bjc800=360x360,360x180,180x360,180x180

[cdj500]
dBitsPerPixel=24
dBlackCorrect=4
dShingling=2
dDepletion=1
```

Here is a simple database which uses pairs of colons to separate the parts of each data item and newlines to separate items themselves:

```
cookies::chocolate::grahams
cookies::fruit::raspberry chewies
cake::chocolate::black forest gateau
cookies::plain::grahams
```

Many programmers use characters such as the vertical bar, |, instead of colons. The important point is that none of these characters used as separators appear in the actual data. Manipulating any of these data files needs the facilities which are provided by languages like Perl: regular expression parsing, string matching and replacement, and iteration through repetitive structures. XML is used to create structured data and hence it is also very suitable for manipulation with Perl.

Through the rest of this chapter I am going to talk about the individual pieces which make up the XML jigsaw, describing each and showing how they fit together. I will be

---

[3]See any introductory database text for a description of relational structures.

demonstrating XML with a simple application: a recipe book. I will show how to build the necessary data structures, how to create a grammar in XML to describe those structures, and how to use styles to Web enable the recipe book. In Section 14.6 I will take the recipe book further and show how you can start to build a dynamic application to handle searching and displaying of recipe data using XML and Perl.

14.1 BASIC XML

You have already seen a lot of markup in this book so you probably have a good idea what XML is going to look like. If your idea is that XML closely resembles HTML then you are correct. Here is the start of a structure for our recipe book:

```
1   <?xml version="1.0"?>

    <recipes>
      <category type="loaf">
5       <name>Basic Farmhouse</name>
        <ingredient></ingredient>
        <cooking>
          <time></time>
          <setting></setting>
10      </cooking>
        <serves></serves>
        <instructions>
          <item></item>
        </instructions>
15    </category>
    </recipes>
```

That is not too complicated – but does it work? Is it *really* XML? Well Microsoft ships an XML parser as part of Internet Explorers, so we can find out. All that you have to do to display your XML files is to open them with one of those browsers. Figure 14.1 shows what my recipe book looks like. The formatting there is not too special and some funny things have happened to the XML but it all seems to be there. Notice the small hyphens before some of the items? Those items are containers which hold other XML elements. IE5 lets you hide or display the contents of container elements by clicking those hyphens with your mouse.

Look back at the code and, in particular, the first line. This is a *Processing Instruction* which tells applications how to handle the XML. In this case it also serves as a version declaration

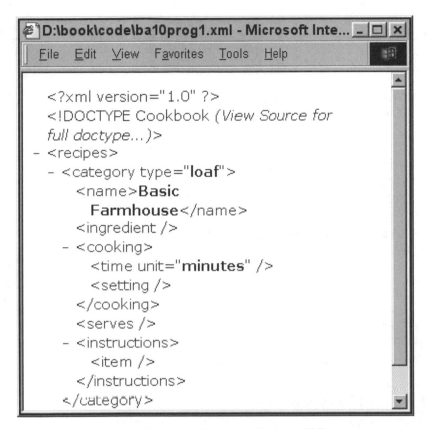

Figure 14.1 Internet Explorer 5 displaying XML

and says that the file is XML which should adhere to the rules for XML version 1.0. All of your XML applications *must* include a similar declaration, formatted in the same way:

```
<?xml version="1.0"?>
```

What happens if you break the rules? How do parsers cope? The rules state that the parser must halt when it finds an error and that it may return a message back to the calling application. Let us make a change in the recipe book so that it is no longer well formed. Change the line

```
<serves></serves>
```

into

```
<serves></servs>
```

and run the file through the browser once more. This time Internet Explorer displays the message shown in Figure 14.2.

Figure 14.2 Internet Explorer 5 displaying an XML error

14.1.1 Valid or Well Formed?

XML documents may be either valid or well formed. These terms imply different levels of conformance between the document, the DTD, and the XML standard. A well formed document is one which follows all of the rules of XML. Tags are matched and do not overlap, empty elements are ended properly, and the document contains an XML declaration. There are many such rules which are available in the XML recommendation document. A valid XML document has its own DTD. The document is well formed but also conforms to the rules set out in the DTD.

Many XML parsers and libraries have been written in the last few years. A few of these are *validating*. They check that the document and its DTD are in agreement. Others such as Microsoft Internet Explorer 5 simply check that the document is well formed. The parser or library that you choose to use depends upon your needs. Although in this book I use non-validating parsers, simply because they are what I have available, all of the XML *is* actually valid.

14.1.2 XML Elements

XML documents are composed of just three things: elements, control information, and entities. Let us look at each of those in turn. Most of the markup in an XML document is element markup. Elements are surrounded by tags much as they are in HTML. The content of the document has a structure imposed by the rules of XML although this structure is quite loose. Each document has a single *root* element which contains all of the other markup. You have already met this idea in HTML where all documents are enclosed inside `<html></html>` tags. The document is then composed of a number of *sections*, each of which is enclosed between tags. The sections themselves are also elements, of course.

Nesting Tags

Even the simplest XML document has nested tags (tags inside tags). Unlike HTML these *must* be nested properly and closed in the reverse of the order in which they were opened. The following code is invalid XML because the order of the tags has become confused, with tags overlapping:

```
1  <category type="loaf">
       <name>Basic Farmhouse</name>
       <ingredient></ingredient>
       <cooking></cooking>
5      <serves>
       <instructions></serves>
       </instructions>
   </loaf>
```

Each XML tag has to have a closing tag, again unlike HTML (see Section 3.6 for a description of the way that HTML parsing is moving.). There is no way that a parser can extract control information from the structure of the document. In HTML a parser will, for instance, assume that a `<td>` tag has been closed if it reads a `<tr>` tag. That is only possible because the parser is working within the context of HTML. It is not a general principle to be applied elsewhere.

Case Sensitive

HTML lets you use mixed upper- and lower-case letters inside markup. XML is case sensitive and you must use lower case for your markup. You will use some upper-case letters inside control information but not inside your tags.

Empty Tags

Elements usually have content. A recipe without ingredients would make no sense after all and there would be no point in including empty `<ingredient></ingredient>` pairs in a recipe book. Elements may be empty though, if you are formatting data retrieved from a database or entered by a user. Where the content of the element is missing the tag becomes:

```
<ingredient />
```

Look back at Figure 14.1 and you will see that is how Internet Explorer displayed the empty tags in my skeleton document.

Attributes

Sometimes it is important that elements have information associated with them without that information becoming a separate element. Again this is an idea you have met before:

```
<img src="../images/uncle_fred.png" height="120" width="34" alt="Uncle Fred">
```

The markup would be very messy if all of those *attributes* and *values* were pulled out into individual tags:

```
<img>
    <src>../images/uncle_fred.png</src>
    <height>120</height>
    <width>34</width>
    <alt>Uncle Fred</alt>
</img>
```

Isn't that awful? Making the img element into a *container* adds nothing to our understanding of the data and may actually make handling it more complex.

The next piece of code adds some attributes to the ingredient tag of the recipe book:

```
<ingredient amount="200" unit="ml">milk</ingredient>
```

Notice that the values associated with each attribute are in quotes. Again that is an XML rule that does not apply in HTML. Attributes are actually not as easy to use as you might think. You need to spend some time thinking about whether an item really *is* an attribute or if it should be an element itself. Consider how you are going to be processing the item, how it might be stored and if it can stand alone. For instance, if I wanted my recipe book to find all occasions on which 200 ml of a liquid was used, then I would make amount an element rather than an attribute. Searching on an element rather than an attribute of element is logical and simple to me. Elements have more context and meaning than attributes. Attributes simply describe properties of elements. Unfortunately these design decisions cannot be resolved through a set of simple rules so you are on your own when it comes to designing your structures.

14.1.3 Control Information

Although you will not know this yet, you have already seen all of the XML control information. There are three control structures: comments, processing instructions, and document-type declarations.

Comments

XML comments are exactly the same as their HTML cousins. They may span several lines or be contained on just a single line of the page. All take the form:

```
<!-- comment text here -->
```

The same type of comment is used in both XML source files and in Document Type Definition (DTD) files, which we will look at in Section 14.2. It is important that you thoroughly comment XML and DTD to aid in development and maintenance. Whilst your carefully crafted `ingredient` attribute might be obvious when you first create a document it may not be so clear when you come to edit that data in 10 years' time!

Processing Instructions

Processing Instructions (PI) are used to control applications. In this book I am only scratching the surface of XML and I am only going to use one PI. We met this earlier:

```
<?xml version="1.0"?>
```

Remember? That instruction tells the application that the data in the file follows the rules of XML version 1.0. Whether the file is being parsed or validated it must obey the XML 1.0 rules. This instruction must be the first instruction in your XML file because if it is not, the parser will not have any rules to work with and will simply return an error to you. Some parsers, such as the Microsoft one, make assumptions if you omit the version information and assume that you are using version 1.0. It is far safer to force this behavior than to leave it to chance.

Document Type Declarations

Each XML document has an associated Document Type Definition. The DTD is usually held in a separate file so that it can be used with many documents. You *can*, though, place a DTD inside the XML file. I will show you how to do that in a while but for now I will concentrate upon the more useful external DTDs.

The DTD file holds the rules of the grammar for a particular XML data structure. Those rules are used by validating parsers to check that, not only is the file valid XML, but that it also obeys its own internal rules. HTML has a set of DTDs which it can be validated against. Here is how you use them in XML:

```
<!DOCTYPE Recipes SYSTEM "recipe.dtd">
```

This declaration tells the parser that the XML file is of type `Recipes` and that it uses a DTD which is stored in a file called `recipe.dtd`. Furthermore the location is actually a URL[4] so the application knows that it should retrieve the DTD from the current directory.

---

[4]Strictly the W3C uses the term Uniform Resource Indicator (URI) when discussing XML. A URL is a *type* of URI. In this chapter I shall use the more familiar URL so as to avoid confusing readers too much.

The keyword SYSTEM is quite important in there. Some DTDs are available as International *standards*, such as those recommendations of W3C which relate to HTML. Other DTDs are developed by individuals and organizations for their own use. Each of these has a different effect on the application processing the document. Internationally agreed DTDs are denoted by the use of the keyword PUBLIC; any DTD which you develop yourself or have developed for you is denoted by the keyword SYSTEM.

14.1.4 Entities

The final part of an XML document *may* be one or more entities. An entity is a *thing* which is to be used as part of the document but which is not a simple element. An example of an entity is something like an image or an encrypted signature which you wish to use frequently. Rather than having to create some XML each time that the signature is used, the entity itself can be included in the XML. The processing application is then able to handle the inclusion of the entity in an appropriate way.

14.1.5 Putting it All Together

Here is a rather more complete recipe book. If you try this code for yourself, you will find that you get an error unless you also create and save the DTD described in Section 14.2.

```
1   <?xml version="1.0"?>
    <!DOCTYPE Cookbook SYSTEM "recipe.dtd">

    <cookbook>
5   <category type="loaf">
      <recipe>
        <name>The Basic Loaf</name>
        <ingredient>
          <qty amount="825" unit="ml"/>
10        <item>Warm water</item>
        </ingredient>
        <ingredient>
          <qty amount="20" unit="g"/>
          <item>Granulated Dried Yeast</item>
15      </ingredient>
        <ingredient>
          <qty amount="20"/>
          <item>Sugar</item>
        </ingredient>
20      <ingredient>
          <qty amount="450"/>
```

```
            <item>Stoneground wholemeal flour</item>
         </ingredient>
         <ingredient>
25           <qty amount="900"/>
             <item>Strong white bread flour</item>
         </ingredient>
         <ingredient><qty amount="20"/>
             <item>Salt</item>
30       </ingredient>
         <ingredient>
             <qty amount="55"/>
             <item>Fresh Lard</item>
         </ingredient>
35       <cooking>
             <time>15</time>
             <gas>8</gas>
             <electric>230c</electric>
         </cooking>
40       <cooking>
             <time unit="minutes">30</time>
             <gas>6</gas>
             <electric>200c</electric>
         </cooking>
45       <serves />
         <instruction>
             <ins>Add the yeast and sugar to the warm water and
             leave to activate</ins>
         </instruction>
50       <instruction>
             <ins>Sieve the flour and salt into a large bowl</ins>
         </instruction>
         <instruction>
             <ins>Crumble the lard into the flour until it has a
55           "breadcrumb" texture</ins>
         </instruction>
         <instruction>
             <ins>Mix the liquid into the flour</ins>
         </instruction>
```

```
60      <instruction>
            <ins>Turn onto floured surface and knead for 300
            strokes</ins>
        </instruction>
        <instruction>
65          <ins>Form into a ball, place in a warm place until
            doubled in size</ins>
        </instruction>
        <instruction>
            <ins>Knead for another 100 strokes</ins>
70      </instruction>
        <instruction>
            <ins>Form into a ball, place in a warm place until
            doubled in size</ins>
        </instruction>
75      <instruction>
            <ins>Form into five loaves and leave to rise for 30
            minutes</ins>
        </instruction>
        <instruction>
80          <ins>Bake!</ins>
        </instruction>

    </recipe>
    <recipe>
85      <name>Wheatgerm Bread</name>
        <!--
            NOTE that this recipe is incomplete. I included it
            so that you will see how the processing works with
            multiple data items
90      -->
    </recipe>
    </category>
    </cookbook>
```

I must admit that I am not totally satisfied with that XML structure. Where I have used:

```
<cooking>
    <time unit="minutes">30</time>
    <gas>6</gas>
```

```
        <electric>200c</electric>
</cooking>
<instruction>
<ins>Form into a ball, place in a warm place until doubled in
size</ins>
</instruction>
```

I would have preferred something like:

```
1   <cooking>
        <time unit="minutes">30</time>
        <setting type="gas" value="6"/>
        <setting type="electric" value="200c"/>
5   </cooking>
    <instruction>
    Form into a ball, place in a warm place until doubled in size
    </instruction>
```

which also happens to be valid XML. The reason that I have used the former version is[5] XSL. When I came to write a stylesheet for the original version I discovered either the limitations of XSL or of my XSL programming abilities. Whatever the reason, I took a pragmatic decision to write working code rather than elegant code. You will make many similar decisions as *you* work with these infant technologies.

14.2 DOCUMENT TYPE DEFINITION

Writing the XML is only half the story. The XML has neither meaning nor context without a grammar against which it can be validated. The grammar is called a Document Type Definition (DTD). The DTD has quite a complex structure which makes sense given the difficult and important nature of its role. Writing a good DTD is probably the most difficult aspect of using XML in your applications. Before I look at the details here is a DTD for my recipe book:

```
1   <!ELEMENT cookbook (category+)>
      <!ELEMENT category (recipe+)>
      <!ATTLIST category
        type CDATA #REQUIRED>

5
      <!ELEMENT recipe (name, ingredient+, cooking+, serves?,
      instruction*)>
        <!ELEMENT name (#PCDATA)>
```

---

[5]Extensible Stylesheet Language. See Section 14.5 for more details.

```
10      <!ELEMENT ingredient (qty, item)>
          <!ELEMENT qty (#PCDATA)>
            <!ATTLIST qty
              amount CDATA #REQUIRED
              unit CDATA "g">
15        <!ELEMENT item (#PCDATA)>

        <!ELEMENT cooking (time*, gas*, electric*)>
          <!ELEMENT time (#PCDATA)>
            <!ATTLIST time
20          unit CDATA "minutes">
          <!ELEMENT gas (#PCDATA)>
          <!ELEMENT electric (#PCDATA)>

        <!ELEMENT serves (#PCDATA)>
25
        <!ELEMENT instruction (ins*)>
          <!ELEMENT ins (#PCDATA)>
```

Looking at that DTD there is quite a lot to explain – and I have not used all of the possibilities which XML provides. Before I start the explanation, if you have access to a copy of Internet Explorer, try saving the recipe book source (as recipes.xml) and DTD file (as recipe.dtd). View the XML by opening recipe.xml in the browser. It should all work nicely. You can even omit all attributes which say (exactly) unit="g" or unit="minutes" and the file will still display as intended. Figure 14.3 shows what you might get.

Just like the XML source, the DTD actually only has a few components, it is the way that those components are assembled which leads to complex structures like the recipe book.

DTDs can be included in the XML file. The XML source file will then look like the next example:

```
<?xml version="1.0"?>

<!DOCTYPE recipe[
  <!ELEMENT cookbook (category+)>
  <!-- Rest of DTD here -->
]>

<cookbook>
  <!-- Rest of XML here -->
</cookbook>
```

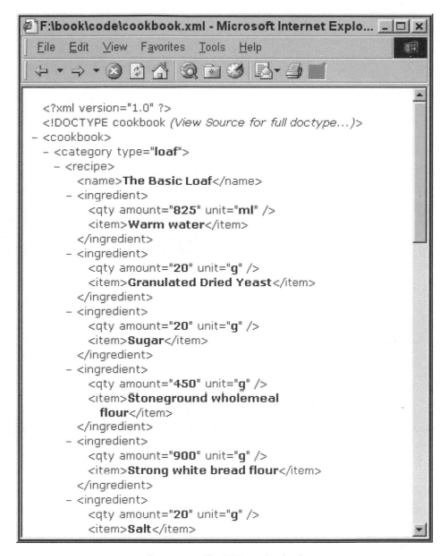

Figure 14.3 The XML recipe book

The DTD is all placed inside a single DOCTYPE tag and is surrounded by square brackets [...].

14.2.1 Elements

The XML document is composed of a number of elements. Each of those elements may itself be made from other elements and some of the elements in the document may contain attributes. This structure is reflected in the DTD. The first *node* of the XML document is called the *root node*. It contains all other nodes of the document and each XML document

Symbol	Example	Meaning
Asterix	`item*`	The item appears zero or more times.
Comma	`(item1, item2, item3)`	Separates items in a sequence in the order in which they appear.
None	`item`	Item appears exactly once.
Parentheses	`(item1, item2)`	Encloses a group of items.
Pipe	`(item1 | item2)`	Separates a set of alternatives. Only one may appear.
Plus	`item+`	Item appears at least once.
Question mark	`item?`	The item appears once or not at all.

Table 14.1 DTD elements which control repetition

must have exactly one root node. In the recipe book, the root node is called *cookbook* and all of the nodes which it holds are called *category*. Defining that in XML is straightforward:

```
<!ELEMENT cookbook (category+)>
```

All elements are declared using the same format. The element tag starts with an exclamation mark and the word ELEMENT in upper-case letters. This is followed by the name of the element. The element ends with some information in parentheses. Each element can either be a container which holds further elements or it can define data. In the case of container nodes, the parentheses hold a comma-separated list of sub-elements. Each sub-element can also be associated with a control character indicating how often it appears. These control characters are listed in Table 14.1.

The root node contains at least one other element definition with that element appearing at least once in the XML document. In the recipe book I have defined just one node, `category`, appearing below the root but that node is itself quite complex. Concentrating on the ELEMENT tags for now, the `category` element is defined as:

```
<!ELEMENT recipe (name, ingredient+, cooking+,
    serves?, instruction*)>
```

which is a list of elements. The name appears just once, at least one ingredient and one cooking element are required, only a single serves element is allowed but as many instructions as the recipe requires can be used.

Elements which contain data items are declared using the format:

```
<!ELEMENT name (#PCDATA)>
```

In this case the parentheses contain the data type of the element. The data type must be preceded by a # symbol. Although XML documents can contain many data types, the more complex such as gif are included as entities. Elements basically hold one of two data types: PCDATA and CDATA. CDATA is plain text character data which is not passed through the engine of the XML parser. PCDATA is parsed character data which may contain XML markup and hence has to be handled by the parser. The default data type for elements is PCDATA but CDATA can be very useful. If the content of the element contains any of the characters which are used for markup such as < or > you will not want the parser to handle these. If they are parsed then you may get errors about the structure of your document.[6] The use of CDATA lets you avoid parsing.

Attributes

So far we have seen that an XML element can contain other elements or data items. Some elements are more complex than this and have attributes which may be optional. This idea is well established in HTML where tags such as

```
<a href="http://www.shu.ac.uk">A hyperlink</a>
```

have important information inside the tag. In the case of the HTML address tag the content of the element is the text or image which the user selects with the mouse. The address which the tag points to is an attribute of the element.

Attributes are important and useful when you are handling complexity. Some XML elements need to hold more than one piece of information. Some of that information will be displayed or handled by applications but other pieces are used to control the behavior of the application. The latter types are best included as attributes. In the recipe for bread the ingredients all have attributes:

```
<qty amount="825" unit="ml">Warm water</qty>
```

The most important information about an ingredient is *what* it is. If we wanted to search the recipe book to find all recipes which need, for instance, onions, then we need onion to be the content of the ingredient. It is unlikely that we would want to search for all recipes which contained a pinch of something or which use grams as a unit of weight. The amount of onions in a recipe is an attribute; as information it is less important than the fact of using onions.

---

[6]As in HTML these characters can be replaced with entities such as <.

Once you have decided that some of your XML elements have attributes, then you need to include this information in the DTD. Associated with the element declaration is an ATTLIST which may contain:

- the name of the element
- the name of each attribute
- the data type of the attribute
- any value which will be used as a default if the attribute is omitted from the XML source
- control information about the use of the element.

```
<!ATTLIST qty
  amount CDATA #REQUIRED
  unit CDATA "g">
```

This attribute declaration shows an element with two attributes. The first one is called amount. This element is of type CDATA which means that it holds plain text which will not be passed through XML parsers. The attribute is REQUIRED which means that it *must* be included when the element is used. Failure to do so will result in the parser raising an error. The second attribute, unit is also of type CDATA. This element is optional but a default value, "g", is shown. If the attribute is omitted from the XML the default will be used instead.

As well as the REQUIRED and default controls, attributes may be FIXED, in which case, as with default, a specific value will be used if the attribute is not included. Finally, attributes can be IMPLIED. These are optional and can be safely ignored if no value is given.

14.2.2 Entities

You have already seen, in HTML, that some markup elements can contain complex data. These elements are called entities. Think of an entity as a container which will be filled with some form of content. The content may be included in the XML file, an *internal* entity, or stored in another file, an *external* entity. As with attributes and elements, entities may be either parsed or non-parsed. All complex data items which do not need to pass through the XML parser should be defined as non-parsed.

Internal Entities

Internal entities are used to create small pieces of data which you want to use repeatedly throughout your schema. For instance, in the recipe book it may reduce the size of the source files if we declare an entity like this:

```
<!ENTITY POS "Pinch of salt">
```

which could then be used in an instruction like this:

```
<item>Finally add the &POS;</item>
```

When an entity is included, the name is preceded by an ampersand and followed by a semicolon. That is also the way that HTML control characters such as < (<) or © (©) are included in documents. In fact, this is the same idea but with user-defined entities.

External Entities

Almost anything which is data can be included in your XML as an external entity. Here is a quick example which shows how to create a container for a Portable Network Graphic (png) image in an XML schema.

```
<!ENTITY myimage SYSTEM "unclefred.png" NDATA PNG>
```

You may remember from the discussion of XML that the SYSTEM keyword shows that we have created the data for our local application. This picture of Uncle Fred is not part of some internationally agreed standard. The address of the image is given in URL format so that the processor knows where to find the data object. The end of the entity declaration is NDATA PNG. NDATA tells the processor that we have created a notation for this type of data. Notations are important because the XML parser and most XML applications will only handle a limited range of data types. Where an application uses a data type which the XML parser does not understand a *helper application* must be specified. The data will then be passed to this helper for processing. The same model is, of course, used by Web browsers with multimedia data. Declaring the helper looks like this:

```
<!NOTATION PNG SYSTEM "xv">
```

That passes the image to a paint program for viewing (the standard UNIX xv application in this case).

14.2.3 Namespaces

If everything in your XML document is an element, then how does the parser identify items? It uses the element name to create an internal representation as described in Section 14.4. No problem so far, but what happens if two different elements which represent different types of object have the same name? Look at this example:

```
<staff>
  <name>Chris Bates</name>
  <dept>
    <name>Faculty of Arts, Computing, Engineering and Sciences</name>
  </dept>
  <room>2323</room>
</staff>
```

Here I have two elements called name but they each represent different things and have different meanings. Applications could confuse these two items, thus rendering the whole

XML document useless. In a small document that is not a problem as you can simply invent a new name for one of the elements. What happens in a large organization where, potentially, there are hundreds of different XML schemas? The answer is to use *namespaces*.

A namespace is a way of keeping the names used by applications separate from each other. Within a particular namespace no duplication of names can exist. Applications may use many different namespaces at the same time. The implementation of namespaces is system dependent. Scripting languages such as Perl create internal data structures to manage these. Compiled languages rely upon the compiler to alias names statically as the program is compiled. XML developers can specify their own namespaces which can be used in many applications. A namespace is included in the XML in the same way as a DTD:

```
1   <?xml version="1.0"?>
    <!DOCTYPE Recipes SYSTEM "recipes.dtd">
    <!xml:namespace ns="http://URL/namespaces/breads" prefix="bread">
    <!xml:namespace ns="http://URL/namespaces/meats" prefix="lamb">
5   <recipes>
       <category>
         <bread:name>Basic Loaf</bread:name>
       </category>
       <category>
10        <lamb:name>Roast Lamb</lamb:name>
       </category>
    </recipes>
```

Each category of recipe has a name element. However, because the namespaces have been declared there is no chance of an application confusing the two names.

You will not need to use namespaces until your XML documents become quite large or your applications are processing many different schemas at the same time. More information is available from the W3C Web site (http://www.w3c.org).

14.3 XML SCHEMA

Document Type Definitions have been successfully used in SGML applications for many years. From the XML view, though, they appear to have a number of limitations. The most important objection to DTDs is that they are too document-centric. As the name implies a DTD is created to describe the structure of a text document, which is what SGML files are. XML, on the other hand is not intended as a way of describing text documents. Instead XML is used to define any form of structured information, which may range from a love letter through to the interface of an application. Secondly, and related to the first point, DTDs assume that the content of an element will be either text or a child element. That is not the case in some XML applications where elements may hold binary data, for instance. Finally, writing DTDs is not easy. They use a grammar and syntax all of their own. If you are planning to use XML plus DTD you will have to learn more and deal with more complexity.

So what are the benefits, if any, of DTDs? Primarily they are successful because they are well understood. You will find a wealth of information on the Web and in textbooks and magazines describing how to use and create a DTD. You will also find plenty of tools which support their creation and use, all serious SGML and XML editors support DTD editing as well. Many tools require a DTD if they are going to validate your documents. Given these benefits, anything which comes along to replace DTDs has a hard job. It is going to have to provide all of the facilities of a DTD, yet be easier to author. At the same time the replacement must be easy to build into existing tools. If it does not get support from the tools manufacturers, technical excellence will count for nothing since it just will not be used.

A number of candidates have been proposed over recent years with a clear winner emerging recently. The W3C developed a technology called XML Schema which they accepted as a recommendation in Spring 2001. XML Schema is itself an XML application which means when you use it you only need a single grammar and can use your normal XML editor to create it. At the time of writing few tools are available which can use XML Schema to validate XML documents. Automated support is sure to start to appear soon. XML Schema is a complicated language and since it cannot easily be used at the moment I am not going to describe it in too much detail. Instead, I shall reformulate the recipe book DTD and point out one or two useful features.

14.3.1 Schema for the Recipe Book

The complete XML Schema definition of the recipe book is a very long piece of text. I am only going to include a partial schema in this book to save space. Writing the remainder is, as they say, left as an exercise for the reader.

```
1  <?xml version="1.0" encoding="utf-8" ?>
   <xsd:schema xmlns:xsd="http://www.w3.org/2001/XMLSchema">
     <xsd:element name="cookbook">
       <xsd:complexType>
5        <xsd:sequence>
           <xsd:element name="recipe">
             <xsd:complexType>
               <xsd:sequence>
                 <xsd:element name="name" type="xsd:string"/>
10
                 <xsd:element name="ingredient">
                   <xsd:complexType>
```

```
                    <xsd:sequence>

15                       <xsd:element name="qty">
                           <xsd:complexType>
                             <xsd:attribute name="amount"
                             type="xsd:decimal" />
                               <xsd:attribute name="unit"
20                             type="xsd:string" />
                           </xsd:complexType>
                         </xsd:element>

                         <xsd:element name="item"
25                             type="xsd:string"/>
                       </xsd:sequence>
                     </xsd:complexType>
                   </xsd:element>

30               </xsd:sequence>
               </xsd:complexType>
             </xsd:element>

           </xsd:sequence>
35         </xsd:complexType>
         </xsd:element>
       </xsd:schema>
```

This schema defines a namespace for its elements. Elements and some attributes, those which define data types, all exist in that namespace. XML elements are defined within XML Schema as being either simple types or complex types. A complex type contains other elements or has attributes. Notice that, when you define the attributes of a complex element, these definitions must follow those of any child elements which it may have.

A simple type defines an element which is a container for data. Within a complex type the individual components form a sequence which must be defined in the schema document. Elements and attributes may have a data type which is defined as an attribute of the element definition, although if the element is designed to be empty, this will be omitted. The XML Schema recommendation lists a range of data types from traditional integers and strings through to day, month and XML types such as NMTOKEN. Although my example does not show this, you can restrict the number of times which an element must appear in a valid document. Such restriction is done by setting two attributes, minOccurs and maxOccurs in the schema.

XML Schema looks to be an important tool for XML developers. It will not replace the DTD since they continue to be used by SGML authors, but you will see more of them used as tool support appears. You can find lots of useful documentation, including a comprehensive primer, on the W3C Web site at `http://www.w3c.org`.

14.4 DOCUMENT OBJECT MODEL

XML parsers can handle documents in any way that their developers choose – up to a point. The W3C recommendations for XML specify the *external* behavior that parsers must have. That simply means that a parser has to structure its output in a specific way, has to pass certain messages to applications, and has to handle specified types of input. However the *internal* behavior of the parser, such as the data structures which it uses or the types of algorithm used to handle XML parsing, are not specified. This is important because it means that developers can use whatever language they want, or need to, when implementing a parser, but that parser will have standard behavior.

Two models are commonly used for parsers: SAX and DOM. SAX parsers are used when dealing with *streams* of data. The data, XML documents, are passing from one place to another with the parser acting as an intermediate way-point. Typically this model is used when passing XML data across a network between applications and is widely used by Java programmers. SAX-based parsers do not have to build large static models of the document in memory and are intended to run quickly.

The SAX model is, though, unsuited for use on Web sites where repeated querying and updating of the XML document is required. Here it is sensible to build some sort of representation which can be held in memory for the duration of the use of the application. In such cases a DOM-based parser is the better route, which is the way that the Microsoft parser (`msxml.dll`) in Internet Explorer works. So what is DOM? The acronym stands for the Document Object Model which is a concept which you should be pretty familiar with by now.

The DOM is an Application Program Interface (API) for XML documents. If you are not a programmer you may well be wondering what an API is supposed to be. Basically an API is a set of data items and operations which can be used by developers of application programs. The Microsoft Windows environment has a very rich API which is used by developers when creating Windows programs. Rather than create their own functionality for buttons, for instance, they use the functionality which Microsoft has already created. However, access to that functionality is restricted by the API: if the API does not let something happen then it cannot be done, even if technically it is a good idea.

How does the idea of an API work with XML? Well the DOM API specifies the *logical* structure of XML documents and the ways in which they can be accessed and manipulated. If you write an application which uses a DOM-compliant XML parser, i.e., one which sticks to the standard API, then your application will function in a certain way. Changing the parser you use for another DOM-compliant parser, possibly written in a different language, will leave the operation of your application totally unaffected. That sounds fanciful and optimistic but really does work in practice. It is possible to swap a parser made by Sun, for example, with one made by IBM and to rebuild and run the application without changing any code.

The DOM API is just a specification. There is not a single reference piece of software associated with it which everyone must use. This is unlike Microsoft Windows where all developers use a standard set of libraries which contain the Windows code. Anyone can write an XML parser in any language. All of those parsers can be implemented in different ways. What is important is that they all present the same interface to other applications.

DOM-compliant applications include all of the functionality needed to handle XML documents. They can build static documents, navigate and search through them, add new elements, delete elements, and modify the content of existing elements. The DOM views XML documents as *trees* like that shown in Figure 14.4, but this is very much a *logical* view of the document. There is no requirement that parsers include a tree as a data structure. What is important is that each node of the tree, each XML element, is modeled as an object. This means that the node encompasses both data and behavior and that the whole document can be seen as a single complex object.

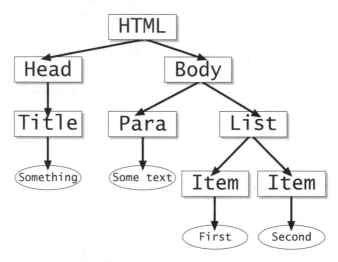

Figure 14.4 Sample document object model

Object-oriented theory lets each object have a unique identity which means that some very useful options are open to the DOM processor. If each node has a unique identity, then the tree can be searched for individual nodes. To an application the document then becomes simply a structured set of data items which it may manipulate. That may not be very beneficial when handling a Web page but it certainly *is* when your XML contains a database.

The DOM *exposes* the whole of the document to applications. It is also *scriptable* so applications can manipulate the individual nodes. If you worked through the JavaScript and Dynamic HTML chapters, you have used this idea before. HTML documents can also be viewed as XML documents and accessed through a DOM structure. Languages such as JavaScript can easily be used within Web clients to manipulate the components of a Web page. XML takes the same sort of idea much further but the DOM is *not* DHTML. The current version of the DOM specification makes no inclusion of events. It is the ability to respond to events which gives DHTML its power; hopefully this ability will be included in later versions of the DOM.

14.5 PRESENTING XML

All of the Web presentation technologies are moving towards an implementation-independent paradigm. There is an increasing tendency to keep the data and formatting information separate from each other. We have seen this in the Web development sphere where formatting information is kept in styles, often stored in stylesheet files which may optionally be applied to the HTML text by the browser. The importance of using styles cannot be overstated: the same data can be formatted differently for any number of devices and, importantly, that formatting can be appropriate for the device and its user.

Stylesheets are an attractive and seductive idea which the specifiers of XML have been keen to adopt. The *Extensible Stylesheet* is a language used to express stylesheets which are then used to present XML documents.

XSL stylesheets are *not* the same as HTML Cascading Stylesheets. Rather than create a style for a specific XML element or class of elements, with XSL a template is created. This template is used to format XML elements which match a specified pattern. Usually the template is a page design *or* the design of part of a page. The application simply substitutes the template for a marker in the formatted page. It is a seductive idea which is actually rather complicated in practice.

I want you to be able to actually *use* some of the ideas from this chapter. To that end I am going to be working with Internet Explorer. The XML parser in IE5 was developed to output HTML from a combination of XML and XSL. I will show you how to take the XML recipe book and make it look more like a conventional Web page.

 NOTE *Although these examples produce HTML output, XSL could be used to produce any type of markup from LATEX through to Rich Text Format.*

I will start by showing you some code and then discuss it bit by bit. XSL is pretty complex and I do not have the space here to show you everything that it can do. What I am going to concentrate on is a *transformation* from XML to HTML. Basically what XSL does is transform one data structure into another. You start out with some XML code and then, by applying the rules from the XSL, you output something else. If you read the documentation from the W3C Web site you will see that these transformations involve tree-based data structures. Remember from the discussion of XML that these are *logical* trees and that applications can implement them in any way that they need to. So let us look at the code, which takes a perfectly acceptable XML cookbook and converts it for display within a Web page.

We need to start by altering the XML so that the parser knows that it needs to use a stylesheet. I will be using the XML code from Section 14.1.5 and the DTD from Section 14.2. The DTD does not need to change. Here is the change that the XML requires:

```
1   <?xml version="1.0"?>
    <!DOCTYPE Recipes SYSTEM "recipe.dtd">
    <?xml:stylesheet type="text/xsl" href="recipe.xsl"?>


5   <cookbook>
    <category type="loaf">
```

I have added a single line of code which is a reference to a stylesheet called recipe.xsl. Notice that the reference is actually a URL even though the stylesheet is, in this case, on the same drive as the XML file. Now for the stylesheet itself:

```
1   <?xml version="1.0"?>

    <xsl:stylesheet xmlns:xsl="uri:xsl">
    <xsl:template match="/">
5   <html>
      <body>
        <h1>The Cookbook</h1>
        <xsl:for-each select="cookbook/category">

10      <table border="1">
          <xsl:for-each select="recipe">
          <tr>
            <th colspan="3" style="font-size:25;color: purple">
            <xsl:value-of select="name"/></th>
15        </tr>
          <tr><th colspan="3">Ingredients</th></tr>
          <tr style="color:red; font-style:italic;
          text-align:center">
            <td colspan="2">Item</td><td>Amount</td>
```

```
20      </tr>

        <xsl:for-each select="ingredient" order-by="ingredient/item">
        <tr>
           <td colspan="2"><xsl:value-of select="item"/></td>
25         <td>
           <xsl:value-of select="qty/@amount"/>
           <xsl:value-of select="qty/@unit"/>
           </td>
        </tr>
30      </xsl:for-each>

        <tr><th colspan="3">Instructions</th></tr>

        <xsl:for-each select="instruction">
35      <tr>
           <td colspan="3"><xsl:value-of select="ins"/></td>
        </tr>
        </xsl:for-each>

40      <tr> <th colspan="3">Cooking Instructions</th></tr>
        <tr style="color:red; font-style:italic; text-align:center">
           <td colspan="2">Setting</td><td>Time</td>
        </tr>
        <tr style="color:blue">
45         <td>Gas</td>
           <td>Electric</td>
           <td></td>
        </tr>

50      <xsl:for-each select="cooking">
        <tr>
           <td><xsl:value-of select="gas"/></td>
           <td><xsl:value-of select="electric"/></td>
           <td>
55           <xsl:value-of select="time"/>
             <xsl:value-of select="time/@unit"/>
           </td>
```

```
        </tr>

60      </xsl:for-each>
        </xsl:for-each>
      </table>
      </xsl:for-each>
    </body></html>
65  </xsl:template>
    </xsl:stylesheet>
```

Even if you have followed everything so far, I imagine that it is pretty cryptic. Certainly my first experience of reading an XML stylesheet left me wondering just what I was seeing. When the XML file `recipe.xml` is loaded into Internet Explorer 5 the browser produces some very reasonable output. If you have access to IE5 try saving the DTD, XSL, and XML then loading the XML file into the browser. If you do not have IE5 take a look at Figure 14.5 to see what you are missing.

Remember when you look at the sample output that I am using IE5 because it handles XML *now*. I do not have to write any code of my own and I do not have to wait for other developers to create XML handling applications. Microsoft is there already.

Before I dive into some of the intricacy of the recipe stylesheet I will just make a couple of points about using XML and XSL. First, where I have declared default values for attributes within the DTD, I have to use those attributes in the XML. When the application processes the XML it automatically includes the default if no alternative value is given. That is standard XML, but it is nice to see it working as specified even when using XSL. Second, I have found XSL to be an awkward technology. XSL *seems* to include normal programming techniques such as repetition and selection, but if the XML is not structured in a way that XSL likes, incompatibilities start to appear. It is *much* easier to rewrite the XML than get XSL to do what you want. In addition you cannot easily debug XSL. If the stylesheet includes an error then the browser will probably display a blank screen. Finding the error can sometimes become a nightmare.

14.5.1 The Recipe Book XSL Explained

The stylesheet begins with a declaration which tells the application exactly what it is handling. Right at the top the application needs to know that this file is a stylesheet. It cannot rely upon the link from the XML file to *know* that these instructions form a stylesheet. In the XML file we have a line like

```
<?xml:stylesheet type="text/xsl" href="recipe.xsl"?>
```

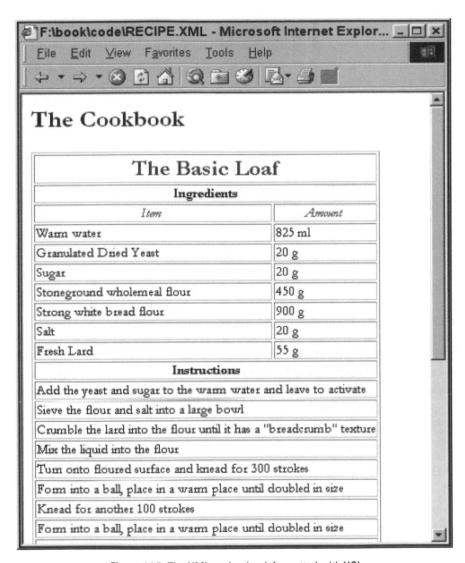

Figure 14.5 The XML recipe book formatted with XSL

which is an instruction telling the application to fetch a specific file and to use that file as a stylesheet. If the link is wrong then the application has no way of knowing. Instead it may start parsing the file and give parser errors. Much better, surely, if the application looks for a stylesheet declaration inside the linked file and returns a sensible error if it cannot find one.

```
<xsl:stylesheet xmlns:xsl="uri:xsl">
```

The declaration not only says that the file is a stylesheet, it also creates a namespace. Stylesheets are valid XML documents and may contain markup which is also present in the XML document. To avoid this problem all XSL elements are contained within one namespace. In the case of our example the namespace is called xsl.

```
<xsl:template match="/">
```

The next element declares an XML template. To briefly recap, a template acts as a set of instructions to transform an XML document into a particular output document. A stylesheet may contain many templates for use in different situations. Where multiple templates are found inside one stylesheet, XSL can be used to select between them.

In the recipe book I only declare a single template which I apply to the whole XML file. This is done through the attribute match="/". This is a pattern-matching command. Whenever you need to select XML elements within your template a pattern is created. Any elements which match the pattern will be subject to the transformations which it includes. Think of the XML document as a hierarchy of these patterns, each separated by a slash. For instance:

```
/cookbook/category/ingredient/item
```

Once the whole document has been selected for transformation, the actual work can begin. I am transforming the recipe book into an HTML document. To do this I create the framework of an HTML page with empty spaces in which I will place my XSL elements. Here is part of that framework:

```
1  <html>
     <body>
       <h1>The Cookbook</h1>
       <!-- for each category -->
5
       <table border="1">
         <!-- for every recipe -->

         <tr>
10          <th colspan="3" style="font-size:25; color: purple">
             <!-- display the name of the recipe -->
           </th>
         </tr>

15          <!-- end every recipe -->
       </table>
```

```
      <!-- end each category -->

20    </body>
      </html>
```

The plan is that I will display the whole recipe book within an HTML table. I will start by moving through all of the recipes in one category, then move onto the next category. I am making no assumptions about the structure of the data: the structure is closely controlled by the DTD so I *know* that I have categories which contain recipes. I do not attempt to check that a recipe is in the correct category: that type of processing requires more powerful code than XSL can provide.

Once inside a category I will move in turn through the recipes. Notice that, as well as indicating where the XSL processing happens, I include an HTML comment showing where a piece of processing ends. Finally I will display the name of the recipe inside the table as an HTML <th> element.

Moving through all elements of one type is easy. The XSL namespace that I am using here has an xsl:for-each element which does exactly that. Processing occurs inside this element and looping terminates once the pattern no longer matches. The first pattern match I need is to find categories inside the cookbook:

```
<xsl:for-each select="cookbook/category">
```

Once this pattern matches, processing moves inside the HTML table. Here I look for all recipe elements and loop through those which I find:

```
<xsl:for-each select="recipe">
```

Finally I need to look for recipe names and display them. The display happens automatically whenever I find a name. The search is also straightforward. Again it happens through a pattern match:

```
<xsl:value-of select="name"/>
```

This time the text string which the XML element holds will be returned *if* the name of the element matches the pattern name. That is confusing at first. Let us break it into pieces.

1. Find the next unprocessed recipe.
2. Read each element in turn.
3. If the element name does not match the pattern name ignore the element.
4. When an element such as <name>Wheatgerm Bread</name> matches the pattern, extract and return the content of the element. In this example the content is the text string Wheatgerm Bread.

The xsl:value-of element is an empty element. It is not a container for markup or data. Instead the value which it returns is substituted for it in the output document. In the example shown above, the text string Wheatgerm Bread is placed into the th element of the HTML document. Searches can hunt attributes as easily as elements. The xsl:value-of element includes the name of the element which contains the attribute we are interested in. The names are split by a slash and an ampersand:

```
<xsl:value-of select="qty/@amount"/>
```

XSL transformations use this simple algorithm:

- The parser searches for a pattern.
- If it finds the pattern it either processes further instructions or returns the text held in an XML element.
- Where text is returned, that is placed into the output document at the same point that the XSL element occupies in the template.

14.5.2 XSL Elements

I have used a few XSL elements in this chapter. These are commands which the XSL processor understands. More commands will undoubtedly be added as the technology matures. Here are definitions of those which are currently supported. Most of these elements select data from the XML document, although a few are used to control the processor. Where data must be selected the XSL element takes the form:

```
xsl:element select=value
```

The value is usually a pattern which matches a node or set of nodes within the XML structure.

xsl:apply-templates

A stylesheet can contain a number of templates. Each of these can be directed toward a different output format. This command directs the processor towards the most appropriate template for the situation.

xsl:attribute

This creates an attribute node. The attribute is then applied to the output element. Usually the attribute is based upon an attribute value from an XML element.

xsl:cdata

A CDATA section is added to the output document.

xsl:choose

The condition of an element can be tested. The result of this test can then be used by commands such as xsl:when.

xsl:comment

This copies the target node from the input source to the output.

xsl:copy

A comment is added to the output document. The application will usually not display these.

xsl:define-template-set

A set of templates is defined. These can be given *scope*.

xsl:element

This creates an element in the output.

xsl:entity-ref

This creates an entity reference in the output.

xsl:eval

This evaluates a piece of text. This element means that scripts can be embedded into the template adding plenty of flexibility to the processing.

xsl:for-each

A single template is applied to a set of XML elements.

xsl:if

Boolean conditions can be tested. For instance, you may choose to produce output only when an attribute takes a specific value.

xsl:node-name

The name of the current node (XML element) is inserted into the output.

xsl:otherwise

This is used for conditional testing of element or attribute values.

xsl:pi

A processing instruction is inserted into the output.

xsl:script

Global variables and functions can be declared within a template.

xsl:stylesheet

This defines a set of templates.

xsl:template

This defines a single template for output based on a specific pattern.

xsl:value-of

This evaluates an XSL element. The element is specified in the `select=` attribute of the command.

xsl:when

This is used in conditional testing.

14.5.3 Styling XML With Cascading Stylesheets

Formatting XML using XSL means that you need a complex processor to get any meaningful output. Generally, at the moment, authors are converting their XML into either HTML or PDF for display. Some Web browsers are able to parse XML, although those parsing capabilities may quite limited in practice. If you want to display your XML in a Web browser there is an alternative which has a very low overhead. XML files can be combined with cascading stylesheets, such as those described in Chapter 4. When displayed in a browser the XML file will display just as if it were HTML.

In the following example I am going to style the index file from Slashdot which I used in Section 11.4. The resultant output is shown being displayed by Opera in Figure 14.6. All of the processing was performed by the Web browser which received both the XML and stylesheet files from the server.

Before I show you the stylesheet, you need to know how to include it in your XML file. The following line of code will be familiar from the XSL examples that you saw earlier:

```
<?xml-stylesheet type="text/css" href="slash.css"?>
```

but notice that the MIME type has been changed to reflect the correct data type. The stylesheet is pretty straightforward:

```
1  story{
       font-family: "arial", "helvetica", "sans-serif";
       font-size: 4pt;
   }
5
   title{
       font-family: "times", "times new roman", "serif";
       font-size: 24pt;
       padding-top: 15pt;
10     color: #002312;
       background: #fffff0;
```

Figure 14.6 Opera displaying CSS formatted XML

```
        display: block;
    }

15  url {
        font-family: "Courier";
        font-size: 14pt;
        color: #ab0000;
        background: #fffff0;
20  }

    author {
        font-size: 18pt;
        font-variant: small-caps;
25      text-decoration: underline;
        display: block;
    }

    time {
30      font-size: 10pt;
```

```
    font-style: italic;
}

department {
    font-size: 16pt;
    color: #0000ce;
    display: block;
}
```

Instead of creating styles for individual HTML elements such as td or h1, I create styles for the individual elements inside the XML file. All of the attributes which could be used when creating styles in HTML can be used here. The best way of finding out what works is to try the example for yourself and then modify parts of it. The only thing that you may not have seen before is the use of the `display` attribute.

display: block|inline

XML elements are not automatically mapped into paragraphs when the browser displays the file. In fact all of the elements inside the file are strung together into a single very long line. Clearly, though, by displaying the file inside a browser you are envisaging some sort of hierarchy of information. This necessarily involves the placing of some elements on new lines, whilst others may be displayed next to each other.

If you want an element to appear on a line by itself you must make that element a `block`. In HTML elements such as headings and paragraphs are regarded as blocks. When the end tag of the element is encountered, a blank line is drawn. The same thing happens with XML blocks.

By default, XML elements are treated as `inline` elements. These are displayed within the flow of the text without new lines. An `inline` element is really analogous to an HTML span element.

Cascading stylesheets provide limited formatting of XML. You cannot use them to create lists or tables. If you need those more complicated elements then you should seriously consider using XSL. If you only need a simple way to view an XML file on the Web, CSS looks like a good alternative.

14.6 HANDLING XML WITH PERL

Perl and XML go so naturally together that a large number of modules have already been made available which perform many of the most fundamental XML tasks. The list of modules stored on CPAN is large and growing. Here is a selection of the latest versions in early 2000.

Because these modules are created by volunteers, their rates of development will vary but it is clear that a lot of work is being done.

```
Index of /modules/by-module/XMLIndex
Name                      Last modified        Size

Parent Directory          25-Jan-2000 10:07       -
XML-Catalog-0.01.tar.gz   10-Jun-1999 22:37      3k
XML-DOM-1.25.tar.gz       24-Aug-1999 09:46    120k
XML-DT-0.11.tar.gz        30-Jul-1999 06:04     18k
XML-Dumper-0.4.tar.gz     19-Jun-1999 23:50      5k
XML-Edifact-0.40.tar.gz   26-Feb-2000 00:34    297k
XML-Encoding-1.01.ta..>   27-Dec-1998 01:22    185k
XML-Filter-Hekeln-0...>   01-Mar-2000 19:18      8k
XML-Generator-0.5.ta..>   08-Sep-1999 20:14      4k
XML-Grove-0.46alpha...>   09-Sep-1999 16:06     27k
XML-Handler-YAWriter..>   01-Mar-2000 19:18     23k
XML-Node-0.09.tar.gz      15-Nov-1999 12:23      7k
XML-Parser-2.27.tar.gz    25-Sep-1999 15:43    380k
XML-QL-0.07.tar.gz        26-May-1999 13:43      8k
XML-RSS-0.8.tar.gz        27-Dec-1999 01:09     19k
XML-Registry-0.02.ta..>   25-Oct-1998 23:09     47k
XML-Simple-1.03.tar.gz    05-Mar-2000 12:58     25k
XML-Stream-0.1b.tar.gz    16-Feb-2000 12:42      8k
XML-Template-1.0.3.t..>   24-Feb-2000 21:00     10k
XML-Twig-1.9.tar.gz       17-Feb-2000 16:39     21k
XML-Writer-0.3.tar.gz     09-Dec-1999 10:09     11k
XML-XPath-0.16.tar.gz     28-Feb-2000 02:42     21k
XML-XQL-0.61.tar.gz       02-Aug-1999 16:08    106k
XML-XSLT-0.19.tar.gz      09-Feb-2000 08:26     92k
XML-miniXQL-0.04.tar.gz   16-Jun-1999 03:46     11k
libxml-perl-0.07.tar.gz   22-Feb-2000 14:31     52k
xslt-parser-0.14.tar.gz   16-Dec-1999 07:14     79k
```

I am going to show you just two ways that you can marry XML and Perl. First, I will use a simple parser to move through the XML recipe book; second, I will use a DOM parser to achieve the same results. It will, hopefully, be clear how the XML structures created by these parsers can be transformed into HTML documents.

Transforming XML into HTML is only one thing that can be done with Perl. Whilst the same can be achieved with XSL, using Perl means that you can add querying and updating capabilities. Perl also has significant performance benefits over XSL. Most importantly, if you use Perl for these tasks, then most of the work is done by the server.

- Where the *client* is doing the work, as with XSL, more data may be sent. This adds to the load on the network and reduces security because you must reveal all of your data before the client-side parser can start to work on it.
- If the transformation from XML to HTML is complex then it may take quite a while on lower powered PCs. On a powerful server the same transformation could be very fast. Users do not like waiting for data but they *really* dislike waiting while their PC processes data.
- If many of the visitors to your site will use the same data then you will want a persistent data structure on the server. Combining Perl, `mod_perl`, Apache and XML lets you build a structure based upon passing the data through the parser just once. Accessing this persistent data structure will be fast but will also lend itself to further optimization.

14.6.1 Parsing XML with Perl

Earlier I made the claim that Perl and XML are well suited to each other. Perl is a text-manipulating language, XML is data expressed in a textual form. Using one to program the other seems fairly natural, and indeed it is. This does not mean that manipulating XML is in any way *easy*. In fact the Perl scripts I use in this section are the most complex in this book. Each introduces new ways of working and new features of the language that I have not previously shown you. When you are learning a new programming language, adding new features gradually is important. It is also sensible to learn those new features only when you actually *need* to. There is no point in confusing yourself right from the start. If you have struggled with Perl so far, take your time over these programs. I have tried to explain their key features but you will still need to use the online documentation.[7]

Parsing

The process of taking a file and breaking it into its components is called *parsing*. The components are defined by a grammar, the rules of the language, although this may be implied by the file structure rather than formally specified. Parsing is one of the commonest activities carried out by software. Whether an application is reading in configuration information from a text file, manipulating simple databases or reading in a complex formatted document, it must perform parsing.

---

[7] `perldoc` man pages, HTML files from ActiveState.

Earlier I demonstrated the use of text databases. A simple file structure in which data items were separated by pairs of colons was parsed like this:

```
1   SEARCH:while($line = <DB>) {
        chomp $line;
        ($type, $filling, $style) =
                        split(/::/, $line);
5       if( ($type = $search) || ($filling = $search)
                                || ($style = $search)){
            $found = 1;
            last SEARCH;
        }
10  } # while
```

Parsing XML

Instinctively, a brute-force approach seems like it will be successful when parsing XML documents. After all they are just structured data files with items separated by <tag> ... </tag> pairs. Why not use regular expressions to find start and end tags and take the parsing from there? The reality is that you are definitely better off *not* handling the parsing yourself. XML is not a simple data structure and cannot be handled with regular expressions for these reasons:

- White space and newlines have no meaning in XML. They are used to make handling the markup easier for humans but are ignored by parsers.
- XML elements will often span a number of lines of text.
- Perl regular expressions cannot handle arbitrary nesting.
- XML documents can contain external entities which the parser must include in its operation.
- Matching pairs of tags is not straightforward in complex documents.
- XML elements may contain optional parameters and your parser must be equally adept at handling their presence and absence.

The most important reason for avoiding XML parsing is that Perl already has a very functional XML parser module available for free. Why spend time writing a parser when you can use the work of other people? Your time will be better spent working on your own application which uses the parser. This does not mean that you should not try to write an XML parser, just that if you have a job to do you should use the existing tools rather than try to reinvent them.

XML Parsers

There are four parameters which can be used to categorize parsers. They may be validating, non-validating, stream-based, or tree-based. A validating parser uses both an XML file and a DTD to check that the XML adheres to the rules of the application. If the XML breaks the rules by straying from the DTD then the parser will create an error and stop processing the files. Non-validating parsers are much more tolerant. They only use the XML document and are quite content if it is *well formed*. A well formed document is one which sticks to the general rules for XML, such as having only one top-level element and no overlapping tags. At the moment all available Perl-based parsers are non-validating.

The parser can operate using either a stream or a tree of data. Stream-based parsers must read the entire document each time that an operation is requested and send a message to the controlling application when specific events occur. I will show you how to do this in Section 14.7. A tree-based parser builds a static representation of the document which corresponds to the structure of the original XML. This tree may be updated by adding, removing, or modifying the *nodes*, which are the internal representations of XML elements, at run-time. You may read elsewhere about SAX and DOM parsers. SAX is an informal specification for stream-based parsers which was primarily written for use with Java programs. DOM is a recommendation of W3C for use with tree-based parsers. In Section 14.8 I will use a DOM-compliant parser to manipulate the XML recipe book.

14.7 USING XML::PARSER

The basic components of each XML document *may* include

- elements
- a list of attributes and their values for each element
- processing instructions
- comments.

I am going to show you simple applications which concentrate on extracting elements, attributes, and values and reformatting them as plain text.

The first example uses the XML::Parser module. This comes as standard with the ActiveState distributions and the latest versions are always available for download from CPAN. XML::Parser can of course be added to any up-to-date Perl installation which lacks it. Although I only have enough space to provide a quick overview of the module and its facilities you can get comprehensive documentation by using perldoc XML::Parser. ActiveState provides the same information in both POD [8] and HTML formats.

---

[8] Plain Old Documentation: the platform-neutral system for documenting Perl modules and libraries.

XML::Parser was originally written by Larry Wall, who was the man responsible for creating Perl in the first place, and is now maintained by Clark Cooper. It is based upon a module called XML::Parser::Expat which provides a low-level interface to the Expatlibrary, which in turn was written by James Clark. Expat was written in C and is widely used as the foundation of XML parsers. Fortunately the underlying complexity is hidden from applications developers. You may choose to find out how XML::Parser works its magic if you want to. On the other hand you may just want to use its facilities without knowing how it does what it does.

XML::Parser implements a number of methods and *event handlers*. I discussed methods and events when introducing JavaScript, although JavaScript calls methods *functions*. Look back at Chapter 6 for more information. The important thing to remember when using XML::Parser is that it is event-driven. The parser will read through your XML file and when it reaches certain pieces of markup it will signal your application. The parser is generating a message in response to an event; you may have built your application to respond to that type of message, in which case the code that you write inside an *event handler* will now be executed. If you have not written an event handler for a given event, the parser will continue working through the XML document.

14.7.1 XML::Parser Methods

new(OPTION=>VALUE)

The constructor method which creates a new, named parser. With all of these methods, lists of optional parameters are allowed. Each parameter is passed as a keyword=>value pair and items are separated by commas. The following options are the most useful of those allowed:

style=>debug|subs|tree|object|stream

The parser can operate in a number of ways. Each has a different effect.

debug

This displays the document in outline form.

subs

At the start of elements a subroutine from an external package is called. At the end tags of elements another subroutine is called. This routine has an underscore appended to its name. The external package is included through the Pkg option.

tree

A parse tree is returned to the application.

object

This works like the **tree** style but creates a hash object for each element.

stream

> This uses routines from Pkg. It looks for routines called StartDocument, StartTag, EndTag, Text, PI, and EndDocument.

Handlers

> This option takes an anonymous hash as its value. The hash contains the names of events as keys and the names of subroutines as values. The subroutine will be called if the named event occurs. Each handler gets passed a reference to the underlying Expat parser as its first parameter.
>
> For instance in:
>
> $p = new XML::Parser(Handlers =>(Start=>\&getStart))
>
> the parser will call the getStart subroutine each time that the Start event occurs.

Pkg

> This includes a package of subroutines. These are used instead of event handlers if the subs style has been set.

ErrorContext

> If this is set then errors will be reported in context. This option accepts an integer value which sets the number of lines of code to display on either side of the line which contains the error.

ProtocolEncoding

> This selects one of the following protocol encodings: UTF-8, UTF-16, ISO-8859-1, or US_ASCII

Namespaces

> If this is set to true, the parser will process namespaces.

setHandlers(TYPE, HANDLER)

> Event handlers can be registered using this method rather than as parameters to the new method. Handlers which are set by setHandlers over-ride handlers set earlier in the program.

parse(SOURCE [option=>value])

> This runs the source through the parser. The source is either a string containing the XML document or an open IO::Handle to a file containing it. Any of the constructor options which pass to Expat may be specified here. They will only apply for the duration of this method.

parsefile(FILE [option=>value])

> This opens FILE for reading, parses, and then closes it. Again Expat options may be specified for the duration of this method call.

14.7.2 XML::Parser Event Handlers

The module has many event handlers. Each handler accepts a reference to the Expat parser being used as the first parameter. Usually your code will ignore this parameter. Most of the handlers are listed below:

Start(Expat, element[attr, val])

> This is created when a start tag has been found. element is the name of the XML element; attribute:value pairs are created for each attribute of the element.

End(Expat, Element)

> This is generated when an XML end tag is found. Calls to empty elements will generate both start and end events.

Char(Expat, string)

> Non-markup has been recognized. The text is passed in as the string parameter. This handler may be called on more than one occasion by the same piece of non-markup.

Proc(Expat, target, data)

> A processing instruction(PI) has been found.

Comment(Expat, data)

> An XML comment is found in the source.

CdataStart(Expat)

> This is called at the start of a CDATA section.

CdataEnd(Expat)

> This is called at the end of the CDATA.

Default(Expat, string)

> This is called for all characters which do not have a specified handler either because they are not part of the markup or because no handler has been registered for them.

ExternEnt(Expat, base, sysid, pubid)

> An external entity is referenced by the source, the base URI is used when resolving relative addresses, sysid is the system ID, and pubid the public ID.

Entity(Expat, name, val, sysid, pubid, ndata)

> This is called when an entity is declared. For internal entities val contains the value of the entity with the last three parameters undeclared. If ndata has a value it contains the notation used by the entity.

Element(Expat, name, model)

> This is called when an element declaration occurs.

```
Doctype(Expat, name, sysid, pubid, internal)
```
This is called if a DOCTYPE declaration is found. If an internal subset was declared it will be in the `internal` parameter. Otherwise this parameter will be undefined.

14.7.3 XML::Parser and the Recipe Book

To demonstrate the use of XML::Parser I have created a simple application which reads through the recipe book and displays its contents. The primitive output from the application is in the form:

```
Element=>ingredient
Element=>qty
        Attributes: (unit=>ml) (amount=>825)
End=>qty
```

You will find the later discussion of the code much more straightforward if you first enter it into an editor and then run it. Save the code in a file called `parser.pl` and execute it from a command line using:

```
parser.pl recipe.xml
```

Try running other XML files through this application. You should find that it works for all well formed XML files. Here is the complete code:

```
1   #! /usr/bin/perl -w

    # include the modules etc. that we need
    use strict;
5   use XML::Parser;

    # create a globally scoped parser
    my $parser = new XML::Parser;

10  # and define what it's going to do
    $parser->setHandlers(
            Doctype => \&getDoctype,
            Start => \&getStart,
            End => \&getEnd,
15          Char => \&getChar);

    # now get the file name from the command line. This is
    # the data to actually parse
```

```perl
    $file = $ARGV[0];

    # parse the XML file
    $parser->parsefile($file);

    # and look for a specific string - change the parameter
    # if you use a different XML file
    $parser->parse('<name>Wheatgerm Bread</name>');

    # for details of the parameters passed into these handler
    # functions see perldoc XML::Parser
    sub getDoctype {
        printf("DTD => %s : file => %s\n", $_[1], $_[2]);
    }


    sub getStart {
        my $key = "";
        my $value = "";
    # put the attributes & values into a hash. They will pair
    # up nicely and correctly if they are correct in the
    # original XML file
        my ($expat, $item, %atts) = @_;

        print "Element=>$item\n";

    # now extract the attribute=>value pairs and display them
        if (%atts) {
            print "\tAttributes: ";
            foreach $key (keys %atts) {
                $value = $atts{$key};
                print "($key=>$value) ";
            }
            print "\n";
        }

    } # getStart

    sub getChar {
```

```
        my $str = $_[1];
     # need to handle repeated calls to the handler with empty
     # strings so: find repeated word characters at the start
60   # of the string
        if ($str =~ /^\w+/) {
            print "\tValue $str\n";
        }
     }

65
     sub getEnd
        { print "End=>$_[1]\n"; }


     exit(0);
```

Read carefully through the code and much of it will make sense to you. I will just discuss the pieces which you may be finding difficult. If you want to be sure that your ideas are correct put some debugging information into the code. Adding print statements liberally throughout the source is a useful way of finding out exactly what is happening under the hood.

Having created a new parser I give it some work by adding handlers:

```
1  $parser->setHandlers(
            Doctype => \&getDoctype,
            Start => \&getStart,
            End => \&getEnd,
5           Char => \&getChar);
```

When the parser encounters doctype elements, start and end tags, or character data, processing passes to a subroutine. The subroutines are declared in the parser.pl file but the setHandler method is using a new notation to access them. Unfortunately the explanation of this notation will get rather complicated. If you have never been exposed to object-oriented techniques before you may have to read through this a few times before it makes sense.

The parser object $parser was created by using the new method of the XML::Parser class. Once the object has been created (The OO term for this is *instantiation*) Perl code can access it by name. Think of the object as a distinct and unique thing within the system. I have written some subroutines which are going to handle processing of the XML in response to events from the parser. The easiest way to implement this is to let the parser know the identity of those routines so that it can use them itself. The alternative might be to write a handler routine which receives notification of all events from the parser and selects the appropriate routine. Such an approach would be extremely messy and would run counter to object-based programming techniques.

I have written the routines, the parser has been created, and now I need to tell the parser that the routines exist. This is done by creating a *reference* to each routine and passing the reference to the parser object. A reference is, as the name suggests, a data item which refers to another thing. It is rather like a unique name for an item but has a slightly different effect. In most programming languages if the name of anything is passed around then the whole of the *thing* goes with it. The processor performs lots of memory management to manipulate such data movements. A reference is a small data item which is easily manipulated.

To create a reference to an item a backslash is placed in front of the name of the item. References can be created to any scalar, array, or hash, and to subroutines. For lots of information on using references and accessing the data which they point to see:

```
perldoc perlref
```

The code Doctype => \&getDoctype creates a reference to a subroutine called getDoctype. This reference is associated with a key called Doctype within the parser. Now when the parser finds a doctype element in the XML it knows the name and (memory) address of a routine which can further process the element.

The parser can operate on any XML file as it does nothing that might be considered application specific. The name of the file is passed as a command-line parameter when the parser is invoked. Command-line parameters get stored in an array called ARGV and are extracted using:

```
$file = $ARGV[0];
```

Once the parser has been created and the name of the XML document extracted it is time to do some parsing. I get the parser to run through the whole of the document using:

```
$parser->parsefile($file);
```

which displays the whole of the document. But XML::Parser can be used for other purposes too. To search for a specific element within the document I use:

```
$parser->parse('<name>Wheatgerm Bread</name>');
```

The getStart subroutine starts by extracting all parameter values:

```
my ($expat, $item, %atts) = @_;
```

The $expat scalar is not used in the example program. $item holds the name of the element and the hash %atts holds the attributes – if there are any. Extraction of the attributes uses a technique which should be familiar from earlier Perl chapters:

```
1  foreach $key (keys %atts) {
       $value = $atts{$key};
       print "($key=>$value) ";
   }
```

The final piece of cryptic coding occurs in the `getChar` routine. This routine displays character data and ought to be pretty straightforward. It gets two parameters: a reference to the instance of `Expat` and a string. It ignores the first and displays the second. Easy. Except there is a problem. `XML::Parser` calls this subroutine a lot. A single piece of character data in the XML document may lead to many `Char` events and hence to many calls to their handler, which in this case is `getChar`. Again surely there is no problem? But there is: many of those calls consist of empty strings. If they are all printed out then the program ends up printing lots of blank lines.

There is no way of knowing in advance how many empty strings will be passed for each piece of character data so we cannot write code which, for example, prints the third string while ignoring all others. Instead we need to check if the string passed in is empty. If it is then ignore it, otherwise use it. Remember that XML parsers ignore white space at the start and end of lines – it's only use in source files is to make them legible. Therefore we know that the string passed into `getChar` must start with a character so let us use a regular expression to find it. If the string is empty the code passes on by:

```
1   if ($str =~ /^\w+/) {
        print "\tValue $str\n";
    }
```

Even this simple application is capable of a lot of work. For instance, it is easy to see how the print statements might be altered to output HTML code which could be streamed to a browser. More querying capabilities might easily be added; the data could be reformatted on its way to (or from) a database. The only problem is that the whole source file has to be read through each time you need to perform an operation. That is a big performance hit on a Web server handling large XML files. Fortunately DOM parsers let you build static data structures which are often more useful.

14.8 HANDLING THE DOM WITH PERL

The `XML::DOM` module is a DOM level 1 compliant parser which extends the `XML::Parser` module. The DOM parser creates a tree-style data structure composed of *nodes*. Each node may, depending upon its type, contain other nodes and subtrees. Nodes which represent documents and elements can contain other nodes; nodes representing attributes, text, comments, CDATA, etc. cannot. `XML::DOM` extends the facilities specified for DOM level 1 but I do not intend to discuss any of those extensions here.

The module is composed of a great many methods which are subdivided into categories. Methods are available to handle any situation that may arise while manipulating XML, but because the module is so complex I will not be listing all of the methods available in each subclass here. In fact I am only going to look at a very small subset. This subset will be enough to help me explain a simple example and should serve to whet your appetite for discovering more.

The XML::DOM module is not provided as standard in Perl distributions. It can be downloaded from CPAN or installed in an ActiveState Perl distribution using the Perl Package manager (ppm). Complete documentation is supplied with the code and can be viewed by using perldoc XML::DOM. ActiveState supply the same documentation in HTML format; if you install the module using PPM it will automatically be added to the documentation index.

14.8.1 XML::DOM

Constant integer values are used to identify the type of each node. Table 14.2 shows the constants, hopefully their meanings are self-explanatory!

Typically these values are used in Boolean operations to control processing.

```
if ($elem->getNodeType == ELEMENT_NODE) {
    $nodename = $elem->getTagName;
}
```

The XML::DOM class has the following subclasses and interfaces:

- XML::DOM::NodeList (interface)
- XML::DOM::NamedNodeMap (interface)
- XML::DOM::DOMImplementation (subclass)
- XML::DOM::XMLDecl (subclass)
- XML::DOM::ElementDecl (subclass)
- XML::DOM::AttlistDecl (subclass)
- XML::DOM::AttDef (subclass)
- XML::DOM::Node (subclass). This class is further extended by
  - XML::DOM::Attr (subclass)
  - XML::DOM::Element (subclass)
  - XML::DOM::ProcessingInstruction (subclass)
  - XML::DOM::Notation (subclass)
  - XML::DOM::Entity (subclass)
  - XML::DOM::DocumentType (subclass)
  - XML::DOM::DocumentFragment (subclass)
  - XML::DOM::Document (subclass)
  - XML::DOM::CharacterData (interface). This class is extended by
    * XML::DOM::Text (subclass)
    * XML::DOM::Comment (subclass)
    * XML::DOM::CDATASection (subclass)

Name	Value
UNKNOWN_NODE	0
ELEMENT_NODE	1
ATTRIBUTE_NODE	2
TEXT_NODE	3
CDATA_SECTION_NODE	4
ENTITY_REFERENCE_NODE	5
ENTITY_NODE	6
PROCESSING_INSTRUCTION_NODE	7
COMMENT_NODE	8
DOCUMENT_NODE	9
DOCUMENT_TYPE_NODE	10
DOCUMENT_FRAGMENT_NODE	11
NOTATION_NODE	12
ELEMENT_DECL_NODE	13
ATT_DEF_NODE	14
XML_DECL_NODE	15
ATTLIST_DECL_NODE	16

Table 14.2 Constants used in XML::DOM

14.8.2 XML::DOM::Node

The node class provides a range of methods which can be used to process any type of node. In the standard object-oriented fashion, when methods apply only to a specific type of node they are provided by subclasses. For instance, only XML elements have unique names. These names are accessed through the getTagName method of XML::DOM::Element.

Methods of the Node class are mostly concerned with manipulating the document tree. Working with the document tree involves moving from node to node. If the current node is a document or an element then it may have further nodes below it forming a subtree. This subtree is manipulated through the methods of the XML::DOM::Node class. When a method has no data to return it will return the Perl value undef, which for the purposes of XML::DOM acts as a null value.

The methods available through XML::DOM::Node include:

getNodeType

> This returns an integer indicating the type of the current node. The list of available types is shown in Table 14.2.

getNodeName

> This returns the name of the node. It may be a property of the node or hard-coded in. The name is found by calling a method belonging to one of the subclasses of XML::DOM::Node.

getParentNode, setParentNode(parentnode)

> These manipulate the node immediately above the current one in the tree. If the node is new and has not yet been added to the tree then setParentNode() method adds it as a child of the named node. Until a node is actually added to the tree its parent will be undef.

getChildNodes

> returns a list of all of the children of the current node. This is returned as a NodeList object which has its own methods.

getFirstChild

> returns the first child of the current node.

getLastChild

> returns the last child of the current node.

getPreviousSibling

> returns the node immediately before the current node.

getNextSibling

> returns the node immediately after the current node.

getAttributes

> returns a NamedNodeMap containing the attributes of the current node.

insertBefore(newnode, refnode)

> inserts the new node immediately before the current node which is passed as the refnode parameter.

replaceNode(newnode, oldnode)

> replaces the node in its second parameter with that in its first.

removeChild(child)

> removes the child node from the tree.

appendNode(child)

> appends the child to the end of the list of children of the current node.

hasChildNodes

> returns true if the current node has children.

getElementsByTagName("tag")

> returns all elements which have the name supplied as a parameter. To return all of the elements in a tree, use the parameter "*". The parameter is a string which must be quoted.

14.8.3 XML::DOM::NodeList

A NodeList is a collection of nodes. The class does not specify how the nodes are collected together but they are stored in the order in which they appear in the XML document.

item(int)

> The contents of the list are accessed by the index of their position in the list. These indexes start from 0. If you try to access an item which is greater than the size of the list, undef is returned.

getLength

> returns the number of items in the list. Because the indexes start from zero, this will be one greater than the index of the final item.

14.8.4 XML::DOM::NamedNodeMap

The NamedNodeMap is a collection of nodes which can be accessed directly via their name. Nodes in the collection are unordered.

getNamedItem(name)

> returns the item named in arg or undef if it is not found.

setNamedItem(name)

> adds a node to the collection. The nodeName is passed as the parameter and used the as key within the collection.

14.8.5　XML::DOM::Element

The majority of items within a DOM tree will be elements. XML::DOM::Element class inherits from XML::DOM::Node and so can use its methods. For instance, getAttributes can be used to return all of the attributes associated with a particular element.

getTagName
> returns the name of the element. This is the value used inside the XML tag: the element <cookbook> has the name cookbook.

getAttribute(name)
> returns the value of a named attribute.

setAttribute(name, value)
> creates a new attribute with the specified name and value. If the element already has an attribute of that name its stored value is changed to the value of the parameter.

removeAttribute(name)
> deletes the named attribute.

getAttributeNode
> returns an Attribute node associated with this element.

setTagName(name)
> changes the name of the element.

14.8.6　XML::DOM::Text

If the majority of items in the tree are elements, then the second most numerous are text items. Objects of type XML::DOM::Text represent character data. Any markup found inside the text will be used to create a subtree below the current node.

14.8.7　XML::DOM and the Recipe Book

The DOM approach to handling XML is far more flexible than the stream approach and this is reflected in the XML::DOM module, which provides a comprehensive feature set. Developers are helped through these features by the excellent structure of the module. At any time it is obvious where you need to look for help. If you are handling a node, then the methods available to you come from the node class or one of its superclasses. If you use the strict directive and the -w flag when running your programs you will get useful messages. For instance, if you try to use a method which a class does not provide, the interpreter will tell you exactly what you are doing wrong, although it may find a cryptic way of doing so.

I have written a small DOM program which, like the previous example, reads through an XML document and displays its contents. Before reading the discussion of the code, I recommend that you try it out. Save the script in a file called domparse.pl and run it using:

```
domparse.pl recipe.xml instruction
```

Now change instruction to fred. What happens this time?

```
1   #!/usr/bin/perl -w

    # include the modules etc. that we need
    use strict;
5   use XML::DOM;

    # create a parser
    my $parser = new XML::DOM::Parser;

10  # parse the file and create the DOM tree
    my $doc = $parser->parsefile($ARGV[0])
        or die ("Unable to parse $ARGV[0]\n");

    my $nodes = $doc->getElementsByTagName("*");
15
    # start by parsing the whole file
    &parseCookbook;

    # find a specific element supplied at the command line
20  my $found = 0;
    &searchCookbook($ARGV[1]);
    if ($found == 1)
        { print "$ARGV[1] found in file $ARGV[0]\n"; }
    else
25      { print "$ARGV[1] NOT found in file $ARGV[0]\n"; }

    exit(0);

    # ------------ ## ------------ #
30  # ------------ ## ------------ #

    sub parseCookbook {
```

```perl
       # declare some vars
       my ($i, $j, $l);
35     my ($elem, $kids, $child, $val, $nodename, $attrs);
       my ($nodevals, $attval);

       # first find the elements
       for $j (0 .. ($nodes->getLength - 1)){
40         $nodevals = "";
           $attval = "";
           $elem = $nodes->item($j);
           if ($elem->getNodeType == ELEMENT_NODE) {
               $nodename = $elem->getTagName;
45         }

           # then find their children
           if ($elem->hasChildNodes){
               $kids = $elem->getChildNodes($i);
50             for $i (0 .. ($kids->getLength - 1)){
                   $child = $kids->item($i);
                   if ($child->getNodeType == TEXT_NODE){
                       $val = $child->getNodeValue;
                       # only print this if not an empty string
55                     if (($val) && ($val =~ /^\w/m)) {
                           $nodevals .= "$val ";
                       }
                   }
                   $attrs = $child->getAttributes;
60                 if ($attrs){
                       for $l (0 .. ($attrs->getLength - 1)) {
                           $val = $attrs->item($l)->getNodeValue;
                           # only print if not an empty string
                           if (($val) && ($val =~ /^\w/m)) {
65                             $attval .= "$val ";
                           }
                       }
                   }
               }
           }
70     }
```

```
            if (($nodevals ne "") || ($attval ne "")){
                print "$attval $nodevals\n";
            }
        }
75  } # parseCookbook


    sub searchCookbook {
        my ($i, $elem, $nodename);
        my $hunt = $_[0];
80
        for $i (0 .. ($nodes->getLength - 1)){
            $elem = $nodes->item($i);
            if ($elem->getNodeType == ELEMENT_NODE) {
                $nodename = $elem->getTagName;
85              if ($nodename eq $hunt){
                    $found = 1;
                }
            }
        }
90  } # searchCookbook
```

The DOM application takes two parameters: the name of an XML document and an XML element which the program will attempt to find in the document. The program begins by creating a new parser. This parser then runs through the XML document and creates a tree. This is done through the parsefile method of the underlying XML::Parser class.

```
my $doc = $parser->parsefile($ARGV[0])
```

The result which parsefile returns is a representation of the XML document in a format which the XML::DOM methods can manipulate. The first operation is to extract nodes from the tree. Remember you can extract just a subset of the tree if that is all that you need. In this case I am going to extract all of the nodes as I want to work with the whole document:

```
my $nodes = $doc->getElementsByTagName("*");
```

I now have a list of nodes stored in the imaginatively named $nodes which I can start to work on. I am going to work through the entire document printing out the names of the XML elements, the contents of those elements, and their attributes. The first step is to find out how many nodes the document contains using getLength. The program then iterates through that list using the index value as a controller. Iteration stops after position (getLength - 1) as this is the last item in the list:

```
for $j (0 .. ($nodes->getLength - 1))
```

If the node is an element node then its name is saved for later use. The node type is compared to one of the global constants from XML::DOM:

```
if ($elem->getNodeType == ELEMENT_NODE) {
    $nodename = $elem->getTagName;
}
```

Next I check to see if the node has children. If it *does* then I will work down the tree:

```
if ($elem->hasChildNodes){
    $kids = $elem->getChildNodes($i);
```

If a child node exists and it is a text node then the content is extracted. If the content is anything other than an empty string, it is saved:

```
1   if ($child->getNodeType == TEXT_NODE){
        $val = $child->getNodeValue;
        # only print this if it's not an empty string
        if (($val) && ($val =~ /^\w/m)) {
5           $nodevals .= "$val ";
        }
    }
```

Next, I extract any attributes that the node has and save them. I use the extraction on all nodes. If the node does not have children the extraction operation will return undef, which I check for:

```
1   $attrs = $child->getAttributes;
    if ($attrs){
        for $l (0 .. ($attrs->getLength - 1)) {
            $val = $attrs->item($l)->getNodeValue;
5           # only print this if it's not an empty string
            if (($val) && ($val =~ /^\w/m)) {
                $attval .= "$val ";
            }
        }
10  }
```

EXERCISES

XML and XSL

1. What are the practical differences between general markup schemes such as XML and proprietary systems such as Rich Text Format?
2. Create an XML document which holds a diary of appointments. You should include day, date and time of events, and details of each event and of other people who may be involved. Load the XML file into a parser, such as Microsoft Internet Explorer 5 to check if it is well formed.
3. Create a Document Type Definition for your diary.
4. Why do applications use a DTD when the XML document follows the same structure?
5. Can you list three benefits of the Extensible Stylesheet (XSL) mechanism?
6. Complete the XSL framework from Section 14.5.1.
7. Write an XSL stylesheet to transform your diary into an HTML page.

Parsing XML

1. Why does XML use both streaming and tree-based parsing?
2. List three benefits of using Perl to manipulate XML.
3. If you have not yet installed the XML::DOM module, do so now either by downloading it from CPAN or by using ppm if you have the ActiveState installation.
4. Modify the parser shown in Section 14.7.3 to output HTML rather than plain text.
5. Modify the DOM application from Section 14.8.7 so that it outputs formatted HTML.

Good Design

15

The technical aspects of HTML are relatively straightforward. It is not difficult to program, and in fact many tools let you create Web pages as easily as you might word process a letter. What separates the good Web sites from the bad is the way that they have been designed.

Web design is complex and subjective. Few good resources exist to help the neophyte designer and I am not about to write one. I do, though, think that having written a bit of HTML I am in a position to give some general guidelines. I am also willing to look for advice from higher authorities. In this case the guru of Web design and usability is Jakob Nielsen, I will be referring to some of his ideas in this discussion. Nielsen fights hard against the trend towards multimedia content all over the Web. He does this not because he disapproves of the use of sound, animated images or Java applets, but because the widespread use of these technologies restricts the use that can be made of the Web. I will discuss more of these ideas in Sections 15.3 and 15.4. For now I will just mention a couple of things.

Firstly, there is the discipline of *usability*. This is the study of how using technology can be made easier, what is sometimes called *user-friendliness*. Large media companies such as the BBC, http://www.bbc.co.uk, and software houses such as Microsoft spend millions of dollars annually on their Web sites. If the site is difficult to navigate or does not work as a visitor expects, that money has been wasted. To get best value from their Web sites, many companies perform the same sort of testing and evaluation as is done for pieces of software like word processors. This testing comes under the general heading of usability. I am not suggesting that you should do a lot of testing on your personal Web sites, but if you are developing sites for clients or expecting lots of visitors, such testing is definitely something which you should investigate. A good place to start your investigation is Jakob Nielsen's site which can be found at http://www.useit.com. You might also consult his books, especially

Designing Web Usability which, as well as presenting many good ideas, shows some examples of both good and bad practice.

The second important consideration is the technology which your potential users have available to them. The entry bar is being raised all the time on the Web. The modern generation of browser is a large and complex piece of software. Running these beasts requires a relatively fast processor and plenty of memory. If, on top of that, you expect your users to have a PDF viewer, a Java virtual machine and Shockwave installed, you should not be too surprised if few people actually enter your site. You might argue that *everyone* has a powerful PC these days, and anyway the modern PC is an incredibly cheap commodity device. That is true in Western Europe and North America, but what about the rest of the World? Web designers need to start preparing now for the massive potential audience they have in Asia and South America. It is possible that as these markets grow, people there will be acquiring fast machines because that is what is being made. They may even get higher bandwidth connections than we have in Europe or North America. Equally, though, these areas may grow through use of technologies which are three or four years behind the leading edge. Do you want to lose visitors simply because the expectations you have of them are too high?

You may have a target audience in mind when you write your pages. This is particularly true if you are writing for a corporate Intranet or writing for a few people. For instance, if you are writing for an audience of scientists who use the same software then you can target your design towards them and their platforms. For example, if your audience is going to be using UNIX workstations it is unlikely that they will have access to a QuickTime viewer so there would be no point in using QuickTime movies. Similarly, many Web users continue to use platforms which do not support Java. If you want to attract business from the casual passer-by then avoid using too much Java for the moment.

Download times matter. If your pages take a long time to download over a 33.6 Kbps modem line, people will go elsewhere. Several famous examples leap to mind. Boo.com, for instance, was created to sell designer clothing on-line. Their site was heavily dependent upon the use of Macromedia Flash animations which took an eternity to download. The site was rendered unusable on a home PC, even if customers existed for the Boo.com concept, the site was so slow they went elsewhere.

Images are important. They offer information and decoration, which is why designers like them. Images also take a long time to download. If someone is paying for their access to the Web they will not enjoy downloading your *small* 200K JPEG.

Sound can brighten a Web page. It can also annoy the reader and their colleagues. Do not rely upon sound to get information across as anyone browsing from an office or Internet café may not be able to hear it. Music is similarly difficult to get right. You might find a piece of music relaxing, it may remind a potential customer of the death of a loved one. Sound files are included in pages using the `object` tag.

Use colors, use background images but be careful. Make sure that your text remains clear and legible when viewed with 256 colors. Remember that many PC users set their screen resolution to 800 by 600 pixels and use 16 000 or fewer colors.

15.1 STRUCTURE

It is important that your site is structured sensibly. Remember the purpose of any Web site is to impart information or to get a reaction, which will hopefully be sales if it is a commercial site. If the structure of the site is not clear users will not be able to navigate to the information in which they are interested. Unlike a book or paper catalogue you cannot flick though a Web site to find something. There are a number of commonly used techniques for aiding navigation. Most commonly an index is given at the top of the page, or a set of buttons is provided at the top and bottom. Remembering that this is hypertext, you should provide copious links from the body of your documents, although too many can make them crowded. When you provide a hyperlink make sure that you design a way in which the reader can get back.

One popular navigational aid is called a breadcrumb trail. The idea is that each page has a line of hyperlinks along the top which refer back to previous pages in the hierarchy. The user is able to quickly move back to previous sections without going near the back button of the browser. A breadcrumb trail works best on sites which have large amounts of well-structured pages. They are particularly popular with on-line magazine sites such as http://www.zdnet.com. Figure 15.1 gives a small example.

Figure 15.1 A breadcrumb trail

The easiest way to navigate is probably the use of frames or tables. Using a table is an interesting approach to page layout that is commonly found on classy Web sites. Using frames makes moving through the site even easier. With a frame you can make sure that links to pages are always available on the screen. Using well-designed navigation tools means that the visitor never has to get lost within your pages.

Whichever navigational scheme you use, you should be aware of the difficulties which visually-impaired users might have with your site. Of all the groups which can struggle on the Web, the visually-impaired probably suffer more difficulties than just about anyone else. The browsers which these people use can have problems with framed sites and those which use lots of tables. The sites which seem to be least usable are those which have lots of images acting as hyperlinks. Whenever you use an image, especially if it provides meaningful content, you should use the `alt` parameter:

```
<a href="./history.html">
<img src="../images/history.png" alt="Link to history.html">
</a>
```

so that even if the browser cannot handle the image, it can get useful information from the tag.

15.2 TABLES VERSUS FRAMES VERSUS . . .

Frames are simple, provide excellent navigation, and ought to be highly popular. In fact many Web surfers hate using frame-based sites. The reasons for this are not difficult to discover. Sites over-use frames, each frame takes up space on the visitor's screen for borders and scrollbars: more frames equals less space for information. More importantly, though, if you are not careful you can easily create a situation in which other Web sites appear inside one of your frames. If a visitor selects a link to an external site from one of your frames, that site will appear inside your frame. Often the only way that a user can rectify this is to restart the browser. I will show one solution to this problem in Section 15.2.2.

The problem with using a table to provide the structure of the page is that it makes the design of the page much more complex. If you decide to use a table then you have to be sure to get it right – if you make a mistake the page will look really terrible.

Well, that is the controversy. How do you go about writing a Web page based inside a table? To demonstrate the techniques I will build the same page in a table and in a set of frames and you can make your own mind up about which is preferable.

15.2.1 The Code
Using a Table

```
1  <html>
     <head>
       <title>Bill Smiggins Inc</title>
     </head>
```

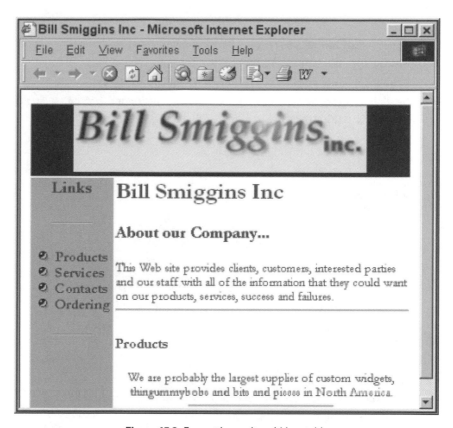

Figure 15.2 Formatting a site within a table

```
5    <body bgcolor="#ffffff" text="#362e00">
     <! -- start of the table -->

     <table>
        <! -- first of all the logo -->
10      <tr>
           <td colspan=2 align="center" bgcolor="#000000">
              <img src="./logo.gif" />
           </td>
        </tr>
15      <tr>
           <td bgcolor="#7cb98b" width="20%" valign="top">
           <! -- and then the links -->
           <h2 align="center">Links</h2>
           <hr width="50%" />
```

```
20          <h3>
              <img src="./bullet.gif" />   Products
            <br>  <img src="./bullet.gif" />  Services
            <br>  <img src="./bullet.gif" />  Contacts
            <br>  <img src="./bullet.gif" />  Ordering
25          <br><hr width="50%"/>
            </h3>
            </td>

            <td width="70%">
30          <! -- and finally the information -->
            <h1>Bill Smiggins Inc</h1>
            <h2>About our Company...</h2>
            <p>
            This Web site provides clients, customers, interested
35          parties and our staff with all of the information
            that they could want on our products, services, success
            and failures.</p>
            <hr />
            <h3>Products</h3>
40          <p align="center">We are probably the largest supplier
            of custom widgets, thingummybobs and bits and
            pieces in North America.</p>
            <hr width="50%" />
            </td>
45       </tr>
      </table>
      </body>
    </html>
```

Using Frames
File One containing frame definitions

```
1   <html>
      <head>
         <title>Bill Smiggins Ltd</title>
      </head>

5
      <frameset rows="25%,75%">
         <frame name="TOP" src="./banner.html" scrolling="no" />
```

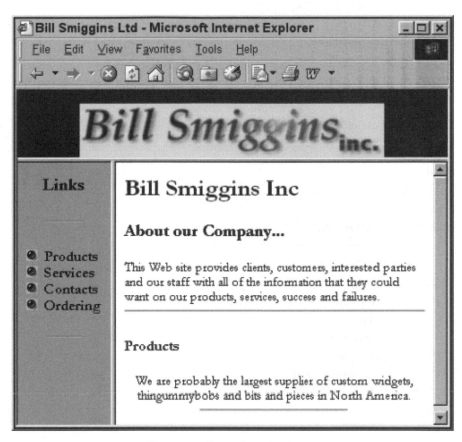

Figure 15.3 Formatting using frames

```
        <frameset cols="15%,75%">
10          <frame name="A" src="./links.html" scrolling="no" />
            <frame name="B" src="./headers.html" />
        </frameset>

    </frameset>
15
</html>
```

File Two containing contents for frame TOP

```
1   <html>
      <head>
        <title>Banner</title>
```

```
      </head>
 5    <body bgcolor="#000000">
         <p align="center"><img src="./logo.gif" /></p>
      </body>
   </html>
```

File Three containing contents for frame A

```
 1 <html>
      <head>
         <title>Links</title>
      </head>
 5    <body bgcolor="#7cb98b">
         <h2 align="center">Links</h2>
         <hr width="50%" />
         <h3>
            <img src="./bullet.gif" />  Products
10          <br /><img src="./bullet.gif" />  Services
            <br /><img src="./bullet.gif" />  Contacts
            <br /><img src="./bullet.gif" />  Ordering
            <br /><hr width="50%"  />
         </h3>
15    </body>
   </html>
```

File Four containing contents for frame B

```
 1 <html>
      <head>
         <title>Bill Smiggins Inc</title>
      </head>
 5    <body>

         <h1>Bill Smiggins Inc</h1>
         <h2>About our Company...</h2>

10       <p>This Web site provides clients, customers,
         interested parties and our staff with all of the
         information that they could want on our products,
         services, success and failures.</p>
```

```
15        <hr />
          <h3>Products</h3>

          <p align="center">We are probably the largest
          supplier of custom widgets, thingummybobs and bits
20        and pieces in North America.</p>

          <hr width="50%" />
      </body>
  </html>
```

15.2.2 Escaping from Framesets

If you have ever been trapped inside a frameset you will know how irritating it can be. When users leave your site you should try to be nice to them. If you are not careful they will be viewing the new site inside just one of your frames. It is easy to avoid this problem. On every link to an external page simply put_TOP as the `target`. When the link is clicked it will open up in a new window. Easy!

```
<a href="some URL" target="_TOP">Click here</a>
```

15.2.3 Discussion

First of all I should issue a caveat about those images: to get everything usefully legible I have shrunk the browser down and then put *life-size* screen captures in. Therefore, not everything in the images is arranged as nicely as it would be in a full-screen browser window. I mention this so that I can discuss the relative merits of the techniques without having to get sidetracked into discussing the placement of the bullet point GIFs and the text. What are the issues that matter here? Table 15.1 neatly summarizes the differences between the approaches.

Ultimately, frame-based Web sites are a straightforward extension of *conventional* sites. Table-based sites require a lot of input into the design process and are more likely to be static. The Web should be dynamic – content should be updated regularly. Frames make this simple and therefore ought to be the better solution. The fact that Web designers can debate the merits of the approaches suggests that nothing is as simple as it could be. This debate will continue.

15.3 ACCESSIBILITY

As I mentioned earlier, blind or partially sighted Web surfers can find the Web an extremely unfriendly and unusable place. Too much information is contained in images when it could easily have been expressed as text. Too often, images are used as the source of hyperlinks yet no alternative text is provided. One might, rightly, ask how disabled users are supposed

Frames	Tables
Need multiple source files.	A single source file.
Code is easy to read and it is clear where any piece should go.	The code can be confusing, especially when you are putting data tables inside your formatting table.
Writing the code is time consuming, but not too difficult.	Coding for tables like this can be very difficult, the code is not easily maintained.
It's easy to add new pages or new sections to your site.	Changing the structure of the site can involve a major re-write of the code for the table.
Each frame can be scrolled independently. Borders, if used, can look messy.	You have to scroll the whole page to move around. No borders are used, but you have to be careful with padding cells which can waste screen space.
Users can get stuck inside your frameset if you are not careful.	Tables behave like any non-formatted page.
The screen can look cluttered.	A very clean look.

Table 15.1 Contrasting frames and tables

to use these sites. Conversely, developers may argue that it is not *their* job to provide access to everyone and that better software might provided solutions to many of these difficulties.

If you are developing a private Web site for your own interests, that last point is perfectly valid. If you are creating a commercial Web site then it is not. Legislators throughout Europe and North America have passed a series of laws which give disabled people the right to equal access to computer systems. Whilst these laws are most likely to be applied to corporate Intranet systems, customers visiting any commercial Web site can surely expect equality of treatment. If you are using the Web to generate sales, for customer support, or to provide information about your products you really *ought* to take on board the equal access message.

Jakob Nielsen lists five components which must be considered when creating a usable Web site:

- Learnability which means users can achieve their tasks when they first use the site.
- Efficiency describes how easily a user who knows the site can perform tasks.
- Memorable means that the site should be structured so that a returning user can quickly become as adept at using the site as on their previous visit.
- Errors made by users have differing degrees of severity and importance.
- Satisfaction that users get from using the site.

All of these are subjective criteria but all can be tested using volunteers. If every tester has an unsatisfactory experience, then finding what they dislike, what does not work for them and why, is useful information. Testing is not difficult. As few as half a dozen users who represent a cross-section of the expected user community can give enough feedback to make real improvements in design and usability.

Developers, especially those with a design background, sometimes worry that creating an accessible site means creating an ugly one. That is not the case at all, there are many things which you can do to make your site work for all users whilst keeping all of those nice design flourishes. The basic rules for accessible Web design are:

- Use markup to express meaning, not to control appearance.
- When HTML elements have attributes such as `alt` which can add meaning, use those attributes.

Detailed guidance on all of these issues is available from the Web Accessibility Initiative. Their Web site can be found at:

```
http://www.w3c.org/WAI
```

Making a list of the things that can go wrong with Websites is surprisingly easy. Even sites which appear to be really complex, such as Amazon.com, are basically a mix of text and images. Making a list of things which annoy you, or which you regard as bad design is a very useful exercise. Try doing that for some of your favorite sites. Here are a few well-established pointers to help you get started.

- Reading large blocks of undifferentiated text is not a problem in a book. On screen, though, most people find this difficult. The effort required to read content makes it harder to remember what the content is about. Break text into manageable chunks based around small sections, lists and tables.
- Be consistent in your design. If all of your pages are consistent in the way that they interact with users then they will be easier to use. If they are easier to use then visitors will come back. Remember that there are millions of Web pages. If you want users to return then yours need to have better content and be easier than those of the others.

- Searching Websites can be a pain. If you have a search box, and any commercial site must have one, then make it flexible. In your index, allow for obvious misspellings, missing hyphens and plural words. If it is important that users enter exact terms then make suggestions when they make mistakes. Give priorities to search results. Return the mot important documents at the top of the list. Those which match most accurately are not necessarily the most important.
- Do not open new browser windows. Ever. Users hate this, most modern browsers let them disable it. Why open a new Window? What not find another way to display its content?

The simplest rules for Web design are based upon the requirements and abilities of the assistive software which visually impaired users, in particular, have available to them. Browsers have been available for a few years now which *read* Web pages out loud. Screen readers have been used for a number of years, but they are general purpose and can read many different applications. The Web is, obviously, very different to a word processor. The requirements which it places on software are much greater, using a dedicated application is the best choice. If you want to implement accessible design, try this guidance:

- Set a high contrast between the background color and the colors which you use for your text.
- If you *must* use a background image, make it pale and simple.
- Make sensible use of headings to add structure and meaning. Use <h1> for the main title of the page and <h2> and <h3> for sections and subsections.
- If you have a long page, provide an index at the top and hyperlinks to allow movement within the page. Do not make users scroll needlessly.
- Place all formatting information in stylesheets, users may then choose not to load these.
- Use relative font sizes rather than absolute ones. Users can then make text as large as *they* need.
- Test your pages with very large font sizes, 24 point, for instance.
- Test your pages with *Bobby* from the Center for Applied Special Technology. This excellent application can be found at `http://www.cast.org/bobby`.
- Test your pages with a range of users, including someone who is red-green colorblind.

I have not considered access for those with physical disabilities in this section. That is quite deliberate. Most physical disabilities lead to difficulties using input devices such as mice or keyboards. A range of alternative control devices are available and Web browsers, such as Internet Explorer, are relatively easy to configure and control. In general, at the moment the physically disabled are well catered for and can use most Web sites, even those which rely on Java applets or ActiveX.

15.4 INTERNATIONALIZATION

The Web is an international phenomenon. Whereever you go in the World you can access the Web. I would not be surprised to find that astronauts on the International Space Station spend those long evenings between space walks surfing for cheap holidays and on-line dates. Sure, at the moment most Web users are American and most of the rest speak English as either their first or second language. At the moment. As the growth in the number of Web users peaks in North America, it starts to take off elsewhere. The next surge in numbers is likely to come from Eastern Europe, South America or China. Those users will have Spanish, Chinese and German as their common languages. Pretty soon the Web will cease to be the sole preserve of English speakers, actually they will be in the minority before too long.

How you react to the changing nature of the Web depends upon what you want to use it for. If your Web site is based around your hobby and you are only ever going to be visited by fellow enthusiasts, you can use any language that you like. If your business is in Idaho and all of your potential customers live within 200 miles then English is probably the ideal language for your Web catalog. If, on the other hand, you aspire to rival Amazon.com then your Web site had better be available in a variety of languages.

You need to use the widest possible set of characters on your pages. Web browsers support the Unicode character set which uses 16 bits per character for an alphabet with thousands of letters. You also need to think about things like formatting dates, times and numbers. State locations alongside times, for instance: 3:00 p.m. New York time. Be aware that 1,500 and 1.500 can mean the same or radically different things depending on who is reading the number.

Having an international Web site involves more than simply translating the page content. If you want visitors, and their business, from Birmingham to Bahrain and Bali you need to be sensitive to their cultures. This obviously applies to the main textual content of your pages. It also means that any icons or other images you use should avoid giving offense. Do not expect your customers to make the effort of *not* being offended. If you want their business, *you* need to be the one making the effort.

EXERCISES

Web Design
1. Make a list of factors that affect the design of a Web page.
2. Convert the list you have just made into a series of guidelines that encompass *best practice* in Web site design.

3. Is HTML development a process which encourages good design, or does the relatively simple nature of the process mean that developers are more likely to simply throw a site together?

4. Think about Web sites that you have visited. Do you prefer a table-based or frame-based layout? Try to give three reasons for your choice.

5. Take a page that you have already developed and recreate it based firstly around a table and then around a frameset. From a developer's perspective which is preferable?

6. Run your Web pages through a validator such as Bobby (`http://www.bobby.org`).

Protocols

16

Web development is all about making use of networks. Networking lies at the heart of everything that I have written about in this book but most people, even most software developers, know little about the subject. In this chapter I will try to fill in some of those gaps. This is not meant to be a comprehensive guide to networking, just a discussion of a few relevant technologies.

Most computer users are familiar with the idea of a network. It is simply a set of computers which are connected together in some way, often so that some resource can be shared between them. What is a resource? Well, it can be many things, usually though it will be something like a printer or a scanner, or a server which holds a whole load of applications. In the latter case the applications will be available for use by anyone who is authorized to log on to the network. If you have worked in a modern computerized business or studied almost anywhere in the last five years you will have used these types of *network resource*. Commonly they are found on small networks within a single department or building. Such networks are called Local Area Networks, LANs for short. A large organization, such as a university, may have a great many LANs but they all work in the same way, and they can even be interconnected so that resources can be accessed from anywhere in the organization.

Access to LANs has to be controlled. Network security, and the security of the data on those networks, is big business today. Users are typically given a *log-on code* which allows them to access some, or all, of the facilities provided by the network. Organizational networks have their own operating systems which provide many of the facilities needed to administer the network, involving control and management of hardware, software, and users. Popular examples in wide usage today include UNIX, NetWare from Novell, and Microsoft NT. Each of these systems was developed independently and they all work in different ways, leading to employment opportunities for many highly trained specialist engineers.

You are more likely to be familiar with using networks to share data. The World Wide Web is an application which allows data sharing across interconnected Wide Area Networks, WANs. Most home users, and many business users too, store all of their applications on the hard disk of their desktop PC. Most data will also be stored on PCs, but there are times when we all need to share data with colleagues who are physically distant from us. In such cases data must pass from our local machine across other networks to our remote collaborator. We may access the Web from home via a modem and the local telephone network. Both of these are examples of using the Internet, which is just a nice name for the global interconnection of smaller networks. This raises two problems:

- How can machines which use different operating systems, applications, and hardware communicate?
- How can applications find individual machines when many millions are connected together?

In Section 16.2 I will look at the problem of finding a specific machine but first, communication protocols.

16.1 PROTOCOLS

If you read anything about networks you will find yourself reading about *protocols* at some point. They seem important, vital even, as they are mentioned so often, but what is a protocol? Put simply, a protocol is a set of rules which govern how computers can communicate. The protocol dictates the way that addresses are assigned to machines, the formats in which they will pass data and the amount of data which can be sent in one go (data is sent as *packets* which have set minimum and maximum sizes). Think of a protocol as a common language. Without it each application must be able to translate into, and out of, the formats of any machine which it talks to. With the protocol everyone is talking the same language.

Here is an analogy which might be useful. At inter-governmental bodies like the United Nations each government brings along some of its translators. As each speech is made, the appropriate translator renders the words legible. But there is a problem. The world has many hundreds of languages and there are not enough well-trained translators for all of them. In fact, for some languages finding anyone who could do the translation might prove impossible. Think how much easier life at the UN would be if everyone spoke French or Japanese or Esperanto. Of course, using a common language would bring problems too. Not everyone would be fluent in the chosen standard language, and if they were, there might still be difficulties over exact meanings,[1] and someone would be certain to stick to their own mother tongue. The ideas that could be expressed in this way would be simpler yet less clear than those under the current system.

---

[1] English speakers cannot even agree on how we should spell many common words, such as colour/color!

That simplicity is *just* like computer communications. Everyone uses certain common standards. These may not be the best technical solutions but each manufacturer is able to implement them efficiently . Where a network uses only a single product such as Microsoft NT, the supplier is free to implement the best technical solution that they can. Where networks interconnect, manufacturers use the agreed format. This sounds like a recipe for disaster but in fact it works *extremely* well. The whole of the Internet is underpinned by just two protocols: the Internet Protocol (IP) and the Transmission Control Protocol (TCP). The World Wide Web adds a couple more into the mix: Hypertext Transfer Protocol (HTTP) and the Common Gateway Interface (CGI). And that is pretty much that. Let us look at those protocols and see why they are so important.

16.2 IP AND TCP

The two protocols upon which the whole Internet runs are Internet Protocol and Transmission Control Protocol. Between them these provide all of the requirements to transmit and receive data across complex WANS. Networks are made of layers with each layer providing a different type of functionality. Each layer *abstracts* the layer below it, adding functionality while hiding complexity. Figure 16.1 shows how some of the most important of these layers fit together.

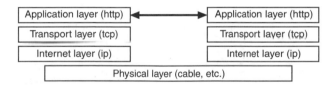

Figure 16.1 Layers of a network protocol

The physical layer is made from the actual hardware (cables, network interface cards, etc.) and the drivers which are required to run that hardware. For our purposes we can ignore this. The networks which interest us run across many types of physical layer. The application layer represents, as its name suggests, the application which we are running. In our case this application is the Web and the application layer is HTTP. I will examine HTTP in Section 16.3.

Figure 16.1 shows the data path between applications. This path is *logical*: there is not a real permanent connection between the two applications. Clearly data passes between the applications but the data is sent as a series of packets. Each packet is free to find its own way across the network. When transmitting across complex networks, such as the telephone system, packets may be routed along many different paths.

A useful analogy here is to consider postal systems. If you wanted to send 20 large items to an individual you might package them all into a single box and send them with the postal service. However, if the items are really large it might be better to send each one individually. Once you have sent them, you have no way of knowing how the postal service handles them. They may all travel together in the same truck, but equally they may travel in a number of trucks whose drivers all take different routes to the destination. The route taken does not matter to you or to the person who is receiving the parcels. All that matters is that the are sent safely and that they arrive safely.

When we say that a connection is logical we therefore mean that, to the applications there is a real connection, but at the physical layer that connection is not present. The multilayer model means that application developers, for instance, can concentrate on developing their own programs without having to consider the complexities of getting data from one machine to another.

16.2.1 Internet Protocol

In the Internet layer of a sending machine the data is split into packets which also contain addressing information about the recipient. Implementations of the Internet Protocol[2] are probably the most common way of generating and addressing data packets in widespread use today. IP packets have between 20 and 60 bytes of header information and up to 65 515 bytes of data. Figure 16.2 shows the structure of the header, which as you can see, contains all of the information that might be needed to get a packet from point A to point B.

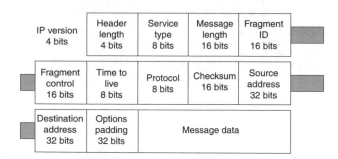

Figure 16.2 The Internet Protocol packet header

Why do all IP packets not take the same route? When most people encounter these ideas for the first time they tend to think that opening a physical connection between the machines and funneling all of the data through that connection would be the most efficient approach. Well it might, although sending lots of data across a busy network like this is pretty inefficient, but the designers of IP had other criteria to satisfy. IP was one of the many useful computing ideas which grew out of the Cold War years. IP was designed to be used in military networks which had the ability to survive catastrophic failures of some nodes. If you built a network in which all data passed through a single point in, for instance, Sheffield

---

[2] In discussing protocols, we usually refer to the protocol even if we really mean *implementations* of it.

and that point was terminally damaged in some way then your whole network would be rendered useless. IP does not work like that. If Sheffield was destroyed, data would simply find a way to its destination which did not involve passing through there. Of course data intended *for* Sheffield would still experience problems.

IP has relatively limited functionality. The protocol makes no guarantee of delivery: just because a packet of data is sent, there is no reason to expect that it will arrive. Large messages, which means any over 65 515 bytes, must be sent as a series of packets. Because these packets may be sent along different routes, they can arrive in a different order from that in which they were sent. Further functionality is needed to provide sequencing and guaranteed delivery. These functions, and more, are supplied in most Internet systems by the Transmission Control Protocol.

16.2.2 Transmission Control Protocol

Abstraction means only having to deal with complexity when you need to. When a system is receiving data across a network, it has no reason to spend time preparing that data for use by applications. IP gets the data onto and off the network but on its own it provides no support for applications. The data packets are not sequenced. TCP fills in some of the gaps left by IP. A packet sent from a system which uses TCP has another set of headers in addition to the IP headers. These provide control information for use by TCP. A typical structure is shown in Figure 16.3.

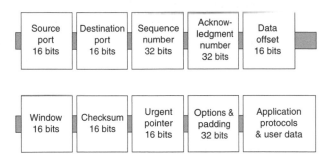

Figure 16.3 The Transmission Control Protocol header

When a host receives a data packet, the IP code removes the IP header and passes the packet onto TCP code. If only one packet was sent, the TCP headers are removed and the packet is passed onto the application. If several packets were sent, TCP must store them as they arrive until the whole data set is stored. As each packet is stored, TCP sends an acknowledgment message back to the sending machine indicating which packet it now has. If an acknowledgment is not received by the server for a specific packet it will transmit that packet once more.

Using TCP places a significant processing load on both sender and recipient. Each must buffer the outgoing message, i.e., store it in local memory, until all packets are received and acknowledged. The recipient must then strip the headers from the packets and reassemble the original message. TCP is, frankly, slow. It is very widely used because the benefits massively outweigh the costs. Large volumes of data can be sent and their safe arrival is guaranteed, as far as is technically possible.

16.2.3 Internet Addresses

Networking only happens if machines can identify each other and so send data to the correct place. All machines connected to the Internet and using IP have a unique address. Some machines, such as those on organizational LANs, have fixed addresses. Others, such as home users who have a dial-up connection with an Internet Service Provider, are dynamically assigned addresses each time they log on to the Internet.

The addressing system used by the Internet Protocol gives each machine a unique four-byte numerical address. These addresses are usually written in the form 127.0.0.1. This is the loopback address: the address of the PC when it wants to talk to itself. Each of the four bytes in the address is represented by an integer in the range 0 to 255. As you have already seen in this section, the IP packet header includes the address of the sending machine and of the recipient. As the packet is routed through the network, each router chooses the *best* route to the destination address.

Whilst computers have few problems handling numbers (basically that is *all* that they do), human users prefer textual addresses. A system called the Domain Name System, DNS, is used to address hosts. Each numerical address has a textual equivalent, for instance, www.shu.ac.uk maps onto 143.52.2.89. When you enter a text format address into your browser a dedicated machine called a DNS server converts it into the numerical form before the packets are sent.

A further refinement lets a server run a number of Internet connected applications at the same time. Each application is assigned a *port number*. This is simply an area of memory which the application will use for its network connections. Ports can be numbered anywhere from 0 to 65 535 with each one potentially assigned to a different application. HTTP servers usually run on port 80 and FTP servers use port 20 for data transfer and port 21 to receive commands. If you want to know more about ports, any introductory networking text should help.

16.3 HYPERTEXT TRANSFER PROTOCOL

If you look back at Figure 16.1, you will see that the top level of the diagram shows the application layer. Logically, data transfer happens between applications and uses services from the other layers. The World Wide Web has its own special protocol which applications like browsers and Web servers use to talk to each other. This protocol is the Hypertext Transfer Protocol (HTTP).

HTTP runs on top of TCP but changes some of the ways in which TCP works. In particular TCP is *session-oriented*, the server and client maintain a (logical) connection for the duration of a data exchange. HTTP has no concept of a session. Once a message has been sent and received, the two machines forget about each other. This presents application developers with problems. It is very useful to be able to remember who is visiting your site if, for instance, you are running a commercial site and must track transactions through a number of screens.

16.3.1 HTTP Sessions

Under HTTP there are four steps to communicating across the Web:

- make the connection
- request a document
- respond to a request
- close the connection.

I will briefly look at each of these steps in more detail.

Connection Setup

The browser opens a standard TCP connection to the server. Port 80 is used by default but any port which is not required by another application *can* be used. If a non-standard port is used, both client and server must be aware that this will happen. In fact, as the Web has become more and more popular, the use of non-standard ports has almost disappeared. Where ports other than 80 are used, the port number is added to the URL as in this example: http://www.some.server.com:8080.

Any software application may be developed to use HTTP. There is nothing special about the way that Web browsers work and there is no reason why a network-aware word processor, for instance, could not communication using HTTP.

Browser Request

Once the TCP connection is established, the browser requests a given document using its URL. The message will be in the format:

```
GET /first.html HTTP/1.1
```

The command GET tells the server that the browser is attempting to retrieve a document. The document is assumed to be stored on the server and so the fully qualified address which includes the DNS name of the server is not needed. The request ends with the version of the HTTP protocol to be used. The request message is terminated by repeating the characters carriage return and linefeed:

```
\r\r\n\n
```

Browsers can send a variety of other commands including POST which sends form data to the server, HEAD, which gets only the page header and not the data, and PUT, which is used to transmit a data file to the server.

The request can be refined by the addition of more commands. Typically the browser appends an Accept command which indicates the data types it can handle. The name of the application may also be appended using the command User-Agent. Combining all of this into a complete request gives

```
GET /first.html HTTP/1.1
Accept: text/html
Accept: text/plain
User-Agent: Mozilla/4.7[en](win95;i)4
```

with two blank lines appended to the message.

Server Response

The httpd (Web server) process can automatically insert information into the header of a response. Often this is the MIME type of the document which is based upon the file type. Unfortunately, CGI scripts which create HTML documents cannot use this mechanism and must explicitly include this information. The following headers may be returned by your CGI scripts:

- Content-Type: tells the browser how to process the document.
- Location: used to automatically redirect the browser to another URL.
- Set-cookie: set a Netscape style cookie.

The server response begins with a response code. The details of some of these are shown in Section 16.3.2. A typical response in which the file has been successfully found and returned looks like:

```
HTTP/1.1 200 OK
Server: Apache/1.3
MIME-Version: 1.0
Content-Type: text/html
Content-length: 53


<html>
<head></head>
<body>
```

```
<h1>Title</h1>
</body>
</html>
```

Closing the Connection

The client and server can both close the connection. This uses the standard TCP approach.
If another document is required, a new connection must be opened.

Response Code	Meaning
200 OK	This is the commonest code. It indicates that the message contains the requested data including all necessary headers.
201 Created	The server has created a file which the browser should now attempt to load. This code is only used as a reply to POST requests.
204 No Content	The request was processed successfully but there was no data to return to the browser.
301 Moved Permanently	The page has moved to a new URL which the browser should automatically load.
400 Bad Request	The request from the client used invalid syntax and could not be processed.
401 Unauthorized	Some form of authorization information is needed before this resource can be accessed. This authorization was not supplied.
404 Not Found	This is the commonest error response. It indicates that while the request was valid, the server could not find the document.
500 Internal Server Error	The server generated an error which it cannot handle.
501 Not Implemented	The server is unable to process the request due to some missing or unimplemented feature.
503 Service Unavailable	The server is temporarily unable to handle requests.

Table 16.1 HTTP server response codes

16.3.2 HTTP Server Response Codes

Web servers can send *many* different codes to the browser. Some of these get displayed by the browser but users rarely know what they actually mean. The codes are grouped together logically with codes in the 200–299 range indicating a successful request, 300–399 indicating that a page may have moved, 400–499 showing client errors and 500–599 showing server errors. The main codes are listed in Table 16.1.

16.4 COMMON GATEWAY INTERFACE

When the browser submits data to the server (usually from a Web form) the server is unable to fully process that data. The data must be passed onto a dedicated application for processing. As part of the processing an HTML page may be dynamically generated and returned to the browser. The format in which the server passes data to the appropriate program is defined by the Common Gateway Interface protocol.

CGI applications can be written in any language. Chapter 10 demonstrated how to write these in Perl. Each time that the server gets data for a script it initiates the script as a separate process. This places a significant processing load on the server and is the main reason that Active Server Pages *can* run more quickly than CGI scripts, even when written in the same language. There is a big benefit in this model. If the script crashes, the server is unaffected, assuming that a suitable operating system is being used. Additionally the script can only access a limited set of facilities on the machine and hence the model is relatively secure.

16.4.1 The Dangers of Using CGI

If you decide to write a CGI script then you are inevitably going to run a serious security risk.[3] Each CGI script that you write presents its own opportunities for malicious misuse and for accidental bugs. Two basic types of security hole exist:

- scripts may present information about the host system to hackers
- scripts which execute commands from remote users, for instance search scripts, are vulnerable to hackers who attempt to trick them into executing system commands.

On UNIX systems the Web server is never run as user nobody. Instead a special user is created, often called something like www. A special user group is also created to hold www and any ordinary users who want to set up Web pages. The user nobody has minimal privileges but it must still be able to run some commands. These can be used for instance to mail the /etc/passwd file back to a hacker. Application developers will tend to want to keep the CGI scripts somewhere in their own directory tree. This is not inherently dangerous but presents problems from the sys-admin point of view. If you are going to let users develop scripts which are themselves potential security holes then you want to be able to minimize

---

[3] See also The World Wide Web Security FAQ, written by Lincoln D. Stein and widely available on the Web.

the risk that those scripts present. By making developers store their scripts in cgi-bin the system administrator can track which scripts are installed and what they do. The cgi-bin directory can have its access permissions set to further reduce the risk.

In Chapter 9, I suggested that scripting languages are preferable to compiled languages for the development of CGI applications. From a security point of view the compiled script is definitely safer. The source code of interpreted scripts is freely available for any user. If hackers can get to your code then they can examine it for holes which they can exploit; if your application is compiled then no one can get at the source code. When configured properly Web servers should prevent access to any executable program but there are situations in which you can accidentally make source code available. If you edit your script file in the cgi-bin directory, most editors will create a backup copy containing the original source before you edited it. This will be renamed slightly: in Programmers File Editor, backups usually have $$$ appended to the file name; in Emacs, backups have tilde appended. This situation is very easy to avoid by removing editing rights from the cgi-bin directory so that you have to edit your files elsewhere and copy them to that directory, overwriting the previous version.

You should be careful when you download a script from the Internet for use on your own site. Always read the code, make sure it does what the author claims. If you do not understand the code then do not use the script. Follow this rule wherever you get the code from, even Perl code on CPAN sites may have bugs: just because a program is widely used does not mean it is perfect. Look at the number of security holes being found in Microsoft and Mozilla browsers. Check these aspects of each script:

- How large is it? Big scripts are more likely to have bugs.
- Does it read or write to the host file system? Check that your own access restrictions are not breached and that sensitive files are not touched.
- If the script downloads further files from the authors own site *do not use it*. This is a sure way to get *Trojan horse* programs onto a server.
- If the script uses other programs on your system such as sendmail, which is a powerful e-mail delivery mechanism for UNIX systems, does it do so safely?
- Does the script need suid (set-user-ID) privileges? This is very dangerous. Never run CGI scripts like this.
- If the script validates data received from HTML forms, the author has thought about security issues. No guarantee that they got the right solution, of course.
- Does the script rely on the PATH environment variable? This is dangerous and should be avoided.

16.4.2 Environment Variables

Table 16.2 lists some of the environment variables that can be accessed and used by CGI scripts. The script shows how these variables might be used.

SERVER_PROTOCOL	Name and revision of the protocol used to send the request.
REQUEST_METHOD	For HTTP requests valid methods are HEAD, GET and POST.
PATH_INFO	Clients can append path information onto a URL. The server will decode this information before passing parameters to the CGI script.
PATH_TRANSLATED	A physical mapping of PATH_INFO provided by the server.
QUERY_STRING	Information following ? in the URL. Not decoded by the server.
SCRIPT_NAME	Logical path to the current script.
REMOTE_HOST	Hostname making the request. If this information is not available the server leaves the variable unset.
REMOTE_ADDR	IP address of the requesting host.
CONTENT_TYPE	Where information is attached via a POST request this gives the MIME type.
CONTENT_LENGTH	Length of content data in bytes.

Table 16.2 CGI-related environment variables

The following Perl script prints all of the environment variables for your system. Try running it from your command line. Once you know how to write and set up CGI scripts alter the script so that it prints an HTML page containing the values:

```perl
#! /usr/bin/perl -w
$ENV = "";

$ENV{REQUEST_METHOD}="GET";
$ENV{QUERY_STRING}="name=Chris+Bates&email=Chris%40home";

foreach $key (keys %ENV) {
  $val = $ENV{$key};
  printf("Environment variable:\t%s %s\n",$key,$val);
  }
```

16.4.3 The GET and POST Methods

Why are there two methods for getting information from the client to the server? Well first, the HTTP protocol specifies different uses for the two methods, and second, you use them to return different types of information, and hence they trigger different types of response from the CGI application.

GET requests are not supposed to change the state of the server more than once. If a user responds through GET and some file on the server such as guestbook is altered, pressing reload on the browser which triggers a new request should not lead to a change in the guestbook. POST requests do not automatically have this effect, but a browser will usually prompt the user before resubmitting a POST.

A further difference is the amount of data that can be returned with the two methods. The GET returns its data as command-line parameters. Some UNIX systems have a limitation of 256 characters on the command line so, if the length of the URL plus parameters is likely to exceed this, POST should be used. Because POST data is enclosed within the body of the HTTP response it is safer than GET data: it is not displayed as part of the URL and hence less open to snooping.

Finally, the two methods pass data into your script in different ways. POST data arrives from STDIN, the number of bytes is given by the CONTENT_LENGTH variable (see Section 16.4.2). GET data is passed into the QUERY_STRING environment variable.

A sample GET request as you might see it at the browser is shown below:

```
http://myserver.ac.uk/cgi-bin/
query.cgi?page=request&keywords=cgi+scripting+perl
```

16.4.4 Using CGI Scripts

CGI scripts usually perform three tasks, although only one is actually required. Your CGI script must parse the input, whether it comes from GET or POST. You may then have to perform some processing such as reading or writing data files. You will probably want to return an HTML page to the user either because that is what they requested or as a confirmation after a transaction.

Configuring Scripts on the Server

First you need to check some information with the system administrator on your Web server. You need to know which directories you can use for your CGI scripts, what Perl version, module and libraries they have, what extension you should give to your scripts and what operating system they are using. Typically the CGI scripts will go somewhere like ~/cgi-bin, a subdirectory of your home directory. If the server runs Microsoft NT you may have to run your CGI scripts as windows batch files using the WinCGI protocol. Because this is both non-standard and proprietary, and not used even by all NT servers, it is not covered here. The Microsoft Internet Information Server is just one NT Web server which easily runs Perl scripts.

If you are in any doubt, consult the documentation that came with your server software. In fact, because Web servers are very susceptible to attack, you should always read this whether installing or upgrading. If you have a Web server out on the Internet it will be attacked. The only questions are: how often will attacks happen; and how serious will they be?

Put your CGI script on the server using FTP, or whatever tool your ISP provides, and in the appropriate directory. The directory and all scripts that it contains must be executable by any user. That is, you have to set the access permissions so that anyone can run your programs. To do this leave the directory by moving to its parent and type:

```
chmod 755 <directory_name>
```

Enter the directory and, assuming your scripts are called <name>.cgi, type:

```
chmod 755 *.cgi
```

Using your Web browser access your Web pages and check that everything works as you expected. Make sure that you create error conditions as well as running successful operations to fully check your software.

Running Scripts from the Command-line

When creating and debugging scripts you need to run them locally so that you can access all error messages and really see what is happening. This technique assumes that your CGI script is just another Perl script. Anything that can be done as CGI, can be done as a normal Perl program, with two caveats. First, rather than reading the data in from the server, we must actually supply the data in the script or in an input file,[4]; second CGI scripts direct output to STDOUT and error messages to STDERR, so we will be directing the output to a temporary file instead.

Once you have a working script you simply edit it to remove the references to temporary files and it will work perfectly as a CGI script.

16.5 THE DOCUMENT OBJECT MODEL

Dynamic Web pages are a combination of three things:

- formatted page content
- executable scripts embedded within the page
- an interface which lets scripts operate on the elements within the document.

---

[4]CGI.pm provides a mechanism by which we can supply data from the command-line.

You have met, and used, languages which meet the first two requirements in that list, within this book. Those languages are *usually* HTML to format the content and JavaScript to manipulate it. In the near future we may see more *exotic* combinations such as XML and VBScript become widespread. Whatever technologies we use when authoring our pages, one thing is not going to change. The scripts that we develop need to be able to access the elements which make up the document. How do they do this? The simplest answer is that they use an *application programming interface*, API, which is provided by the Web browser itself.

An API is a set of hooks into a library of routines which developers can use from within their own programs. There are APIs for all sorts of things. The computer system you use probably has some sort of window-based interface. The functionality which is required to draw and manipulate those windows is encapsulated in a library which is made available to developers when they write code. The developer simply uses the functions which the library provides so that, for instance, each programmer can draw buttons or menus in the same way. HTML and XML documents are made of objects such as headings or paragraphs which we want to be able to manipulate in our programs.

This is where the Document Object Model, DOM, enters our lives. The DOM is an API for HTML and XML documents. In fact, it is probably one of the key things that you need to understand if you are going to develop DHTML. Because the DOM makes everything on the page into an object, it provides a mechanism through which those elements can be manipulated by programmed scripts. The DOM does not specify any event handling, yet that is a key aspect of any interactive application. According to the W3C Web site, event handling *may* appear in a future version of the DOM.

So what does the DOM provide? Well it describes the *logical* structure of documents formatted with HTML,[5] how those documents can be accessed and how they can be manipulated. Because the DOM exists, developers can create documents, manipulate their structure and modify, delete or add elements within them. Best of all, the DOM is language and system neutral so you should be able to apply the same *ideas* to scripts written in JavaScript for Mozilla browsers on Linux, and VBScript for use in Internet Explorer.

Of course, life is never clean cut. In reality the DOM is implemented by the browser manufacturers and, as an applications developer, you can only access those parts of the API which they provide. All manufacturers seem to implement different parts of the DOM and, worse, to implement parts of it in different ways. That is why you can write some perfect, standards-compliant, JavaScript which runs really well in Mozilla but does nothing useful in Internet Explorer or Opera or some other browser. There is a further complication with Internet Explorer: it is *very* closely tied to the Windows operating system. The DOM

---

[5] I am going to concentrate on HTML in this discussion. In fact, the DOM applies equally to XML documents and applications.

as implemented by Microsoft has been radically extended to include lots of IE-specific functionality. It is not all bad news though, some of those Microsoft extensions make accessing the elements inside a page far easier, others are being widely adopted. Netscape 6, for instance, included `innerText` and other useful Microsoft developments. In the rest of this chapter I want to look briefly at the DOM, describe some of the API as defined by W3C and delve into some of the features that you will find in Internet Explorer.

16.6 INTRODUCING THE DOCUMENT OBJECT MODEL

The DOM model of an HTML document is a hierarchical structure which might reasonably be represented as a tree. However, this structure does not imply that DOM-compliant software must manipulate the document in a hierarchical manner; it is simply a representation. The relationship between some HTML code and the DOM is shown in Figure 16.4.

One benefit of establishing the DOM is that any two implementations of the same document will arrive at the same structure. The sets of objects and relationships between those objects will be compatible. In turn this means that a script associated with the document which is used to manipulate those objects should perform consistently in both cases. There is no suggestion that the visual representation of the document will be identical in both cases as implementation is left to the browser developers.

The DOM models, but does not implement:

- the objects that comprise a document
- the semantics, behavior, and attributes of those objects
- the relationships between those objects.

Although the DOM is now central to the development of DHTML, its development was actually preceded by that of DHTML. The specification for the DOM came from the need to create an independent set of objects that could be used by JavaScript programmers as they develop dynamic Web pages.

Unfortunately, the standardization of the DOM has not fed back into a standard approach to object implementation from Microsoft and Netscape. They both lag behind the standard. The single biggest difficulty that JavaScript and JScript developers face is the inconsistencies that Mozilla and Microsoft Internet Explorer exhibit in their approaches to the DOM. For the foreseeable future these differences will remain. Scripts can be developed which work under both browsers, but this is difficult and leads to lots of redundant code. Alternatively, developers may decide that as most of the users of a site have a particular browser, they will use just the DOM for that system. If you are developing for a corporate Intranet or other relatively closed system then this is the best choice to make. If you develop for the world at large then you have little choice but to struggle with these complexities or adopt a minimal approach to scripting and use only that subset of objects which both browsers support in the same way.

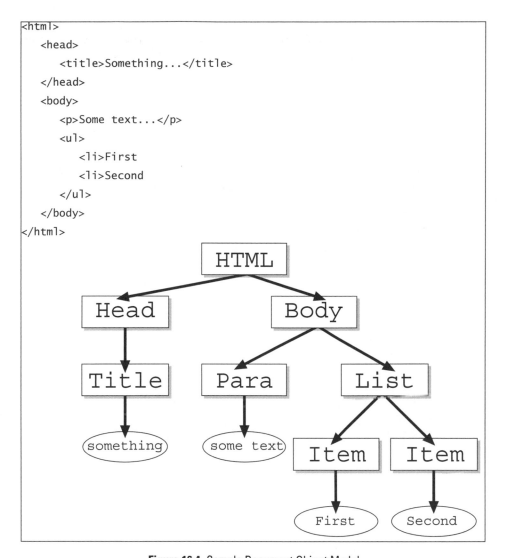

```
<html>
   <head>
      <title>Something...</title>
   </head>
   <body>
      <p>Some text...</p>
      <ul>
         <li>First
         <li>Second
      </ul>
   </body>
</html>
```

Figure 16.4 Sample Document Object Model

EXERCISES

1. Why are protocols necessary when different types of system try to communicate?
2. What is the relationship between the Internet Protocol and the Transmission Control Protocol?

3. Can you think of a reason why the IP header contains the addresses of both the sender and the recipient?
4. What is the CGI protocol?
5. What is meant by the terms CGI script and CGI scripting?
6. How do CGI scripts differ from other types of application program?
7. List five dangers that are inherent to CGI scripts.
8. What are the GET and POST methods of the HTTP protocol?
9. Why is it generally thought better to use POST than GET in Web applications?
10. List six of the environment variables that you can use in your CGI scripts.

Case Study

The SweatHut Fitness and Sporting Club (SFASC) has decided that it requires a presence on the World Wide Web. SFASC is a medium-sized members-only club which caters to individuals, families, and block memberships for companies. The club currently has 12 000 members with approximately 250 people leaving and joining each year.

Having decided to develop a Web site, the committee which runs SFASC has realized that they totally lack the necessary skills and experience in-house. After a series of acrimonious meetings they have decided to engage a contractor to design and build their site. You are that contractor.

The committee members are hesitant about the Web. Some remain unsure that SFASC has any use for the Web or that it has anything to offer to them. Consequently, prudently and sensibly they have decided to start off slowly and to gradually build a more complex site if the need arises. A friend of the club secretary has suggested a work plan which is similar to one successfully used by her company.

17.1 THE PLAN
You are instructed to follow the plan step-by step.

Step One
Create a simple homepage which gives contact details for the club and lists the activities which they run. Suitable images may be included and an appropriate logo designed. The page should be nicely formatted using colors and fonts of your choice. It is felt important that the homepage is in no way garish or startling.

Step Two

The homepage having been successful, you are to move on to creating a more comprehensive Web site. The pages on this site should all have a small logo in the top right-hand corner of the page and copyright and contact information at the foot of each page. The latter information should be in a 9-point monospaced font such as Courier and must be centered on the page. Your site needs a front page which provides a welcome to the site and has links to these other pages:

- the names of the committee members and their roles
- contact information
- activities which the club runs
- membership information: how to join, the levels of fees, etc.
- links to useful external sites.

All pages should use consistent formatting styles.

Step Three

If you have not done so before, you should move all formatting information into styles.

Step Four

Add meta tags to the head section which can be used by search engines.

Step Five

To make the site slightly more dynamic you should create JavaScript powered rollover buttons for all of the main links.

Step Six

The time has come to add some interactivity using CGI scripts and Perl. The first scripts will let people apply for membership on-line and then check the status of their application. To achieve this you will need to create a simple HTML form which has the following fields:

- name
- type of membership (annual, lifetime, family)
- address
- e-mail address
- forms of exercise undertaken (running, weight training, cycling, swimming, tennis, bad-minton, aerobics, other, none)
- frequency of exercise
- proficiency (expert, proficient, beginner).

When the form is submitted, the content of all fields should be checked using JavaScript. This check will ensure that all fields are completed. On the server, data should be converted to XML and written to a text file. You will need to create your own XML DTD for this.

Step Seven

Club members should be able to book activities on-line. Your site needs to display a weekly schedule for each activity which includes the number of places available and the instructor at each session. Users should enter their name into a form along with details of time and activity. Again data needs to be saved in a suitable XML file. The format of all screens and data structures is left to your discretion.

17.2 THE DATA

The committee has provided you with some information about the club. As always, when working in a dynamic medium such as the Web, this data is very fluid. You will want to store it in files which can be easily manipulated. You have not been provided with information about the club accounts but everything else which you need should be here. *As this is an exercise in prototype development you should invent further data if you need it.*

Address
The SweatHut Fitness and Sporting Club,
345 Greengage Lane,
Small Town, Florida.
Email
secretary@sfasc.com

Telephone
555 123 1234

Committee Members and Officials

Role	Name
Chair	Mrs Emiline Tibbins
Secretary	Mr Jonathon Sneer
Treasurer	Mr Roger Thornton
Restaurant Manager	Mrs Jane Greer
Chef	Mr Anthony T. Jones
Chief Instructor	Miss Amy Baxter
Gardener	Mr Walsh

Membership Information

Type	Duration	Price
Individual	Annual	$ 90
Individual	5 Years	$ 350
Individual	Lifetime	$ 500
Child	Annual	$ 25
Child	Five Years	$ 100
Family	Annual	$ 200
Family	Five Years	$ 750
Corporate	Annual	$ 500 (per 10 memberships)

Activities

Activity	Instructor	Price(non-members)
Squash	Mr E. Forsyth	$ 5.00
Running (treadmill)	Mrs G. Harrison	$ 2 per hour
Aerobics	Miss A. Baxter	$ 2.50
Aerobics (Women Only)	Miss A. Baxter	$ 2.50
Aerobics (Under 15s)	Miss A. Baxter	$ 1.00
Swimming	Mr F. Williams	$ 1.20
Swimming (Children)	Mr F. Williams	$ 0.60
Swimming (Women Only)	Miss A. Baxter	$ 1.20
Swimming (Families)	Mr F. Williams	$ 5.00
Weight Training	Mr E. Forsyth	$ 5.00
Weight Training (Women Only)	Mrs G. Harrison	$ 5.00
Circuit Training	Mr E. Forsyth	$ 2.50
Circuit Training (Women Only)	Mrs G. Harrison	$ 2.50

Background

The SweatHut Fitness and Sporting Club was founded in 1983 as a small members-only fitness club. The club founder was Mrs Jenny Abraham who funded the initial development using a legacy left by her late father. She purchased an area of land on the edge of the city which was ripe for development. A Sports Center and Restaurant complex was designed and built by 1984. The first members enrolled in February of that year. Part of the land was sold in 1990 for a housing development providing sufficient income to enlarge the existing club facilities so as to allow more members. By the late 1980s the Committee which runs the club had decided that more members were required. As a consequence membership was open to any individual or family who wished to join. Two years later a simple form of corporate membership was created. This caused trouble on the committee which only ended when Mrs Abraham resigned. Since then the club has continued to grow due to its combination of good facilities and low fees.

Facilities

The Club owns its own spacious facilities. The purpose-built center stands in 15 spacious acres of land on the edge of the city. Within the sports center the accommodation is luxurious. The club has its own 25 meter swimming pool, 4 squash courts, a large gymnasium which accommodates badminton, netball, and basketball matches and can also be used for circuit training. The well-appointed weight training room has modern equipment, treadmills, rowing machines, and static bikes for spinning sessions.

For the less energetic, two sauna rooms are provided alongside a jacuzzi and tanning room which has four sunbeds. The center also has separate spacious changing rooms for men and women which are equipped with secure lockers for personal possessions. Showering, washing and toilet facilities complete the changing room accommodation.

No members club would be complete without a restaurant, and SFASC is no exception here. A very highly praised restaurant provides healthy eating at lunchtimes and in the evening. Lunches are typically light meals such as salads while in the evening the chef provides a range of quality three-course meals. The restaurant is licensed to sell alcohol and a large selection of wines is available.

The grounds have been landscaped. Relaxing walks among their seasonal planting schemes are a popular activity with members. It is hoped that the gardener, Mr. Walsh, will soon be able to offer classes in plant care for those who are interested.

PART VII

Appendices

Glossary

%ENV	A Perl hash which holds details of the environment in which a script is being executed.
$_	Array of parameters passed into a Perl subroutine.
$ARGV	Array of values passed into a Perl script from the command line.
Applet	A Java program which executes inside a Web browser. Applets usually have restricted functionality.
Array	A data structure in which items are stored sequentially.
ASP	Active Server Pages is a Microsoft Web server technology in which scripting commands can be embedded within HTML files.
Browser	A piece of software used to view HTML documents. Internet Explorer from Microsoft and Netscape Navigator are the two most popular examples.
CGI	Common Gateway Interface described the format of data when it is passed from a Web server to a server-side script.
CGI Script	Application which processes data passed from Web servers using the CGI protocol.
Client	A system usually running on a desktop PC which accesses services and data from other machines on a network.
Command Shell	A text-only interface to an operating system.
Cookie	A piece of text which Web servers may store on users PCs so that those surfers can be tracked through a Web site.
DHTML	Dynamic HTML: a combination of scripts and HTML which executes inside a Web browser. Used to build complex and dynamic Web pages.
DOM	Document Object Model is the set of elements which make up an HTML or XML document.
DOS	The underlying operating system on many Microsoft Windows products. DOS can be accessed through a primitive command shell.

ECMAScript	International standard for a particular scripting language. Implemented as Javascript by Netscape and as JScript by Microsoft.
Environment Variable	A variable which can be assigned in a command shell to change the way that operating systems or applications operate. Examples include the PATH which is a set of directories the operating system searches when trying to find an application.
Event	Something which triggers a response from a program. May be initiated by a user or by another application.
FTP	File Transfer Protocol is the standard way of tramsferring files between servers which use IP.
Function	A piece of program code which achieves a single task. These code fragments are called functions in Perl. See also *subroutine* and *method*.
Hash	A Perl data structure in which values are associated with unique keys. The data value can be accessed via the key.
HTML	Hypertext Markup Language is the language used to format documents for use on the World Wide Web.
Hypertext	Documents can be linked together based upon context and meaning.
Internet	The collection of servers around the world which can share data. These servers all use the Internet suite of protocols.
IP	Internet Protocol defines the basic network functionality which the Internet uses.
Java	An object-oriented programming language developed by Sun Microsystems. Java is very useful when building applications which operate across networks.
JavaScript	The Netscape implementation of ECMAScript.
JScript	The Microsoft implementation of ECMAScript.
Linux	A freely available (and free) operating system for PCs. Works very much like UNIX.
Markup	Commands placed within text documents to define how they are structured or presented.
Method	A piece of program code which achieves a single task. These code fragments are called methods in object-oriented languages. See also *subroutine* and *function*.
Microsoft	The largest comapny in the world. Manufacturers of the Windows family of operating systems.
MIME	Multipurpose Internet Mail Extensions let email systems exchange application data such as spreadhseets.

Object	Data structure within a running programming which encapsulates the functionality of a real-world item.
Object Orientation	A software development technique in which programs are based around objects.
ODBC	Object Database Connectivity is a technology which connects PC applications to relational databases running on those systems.
Perl	A programming language which is most commonly used for systems administration and Web scripting.
Perldoc	Documentation system which comes with Perl.
PHP	Popular server-side scripting languages used to create dynamic Web pages.
POD	Plain Old Documentation is the standard documentation format for Perl.
Script	A small program which is usually written in an interpreted language such as Perl or VBScript.
Scalar	Simple Perl variable which can be either a number or a text string.
Server	A system which provides services to other machines on a network.
Servlet	A Java application which interacts with a Web server through the CGI protocol.
SGML	Standard Generalized Markup Language is a complicated markup scheme which can be used to format any document.
Subroutine	A piece of program code which achieves a single task. These code fragments are called subroutines in Javascript. See also *function* and *method*.
Sun Micro-systems	Californian networking company who developed the Java programming language.
Tag	An individual piece of HTML or XML.
TCP	Networking protocol which provides session oriented services to applications. Runs on top of IP.
Telnet	A protocl which allows access to remote computers through authenticated logons.
UNIX	A powerful operating system which was developed in the mid 1970s. Still widely used on servers.
Variable	A named data item in a program.
VBScript	A cut down version of Visual Basic which can be used to add scripting to applications including Web pages.
W3C	The World Wide Web Consortium is a voluntary group which creates and approves standards for Web applications.

World Wide Web	A hypertext system which links documents on millions of servers around the globe.
WYSIWYG	What You See Is What You Get editors display documents whilst you edit them in the same way as they will appear when finished.
XHTML	The latest W3C recommendation for HTML. Applies the rules of XML to HTML pages.
XML	Extensible Markup Language is a subset of XML. It is designed to create grammars which describe documents so that they can be used over networks such as the Internet.

Accessing a Database From PHP Using `mysqli`

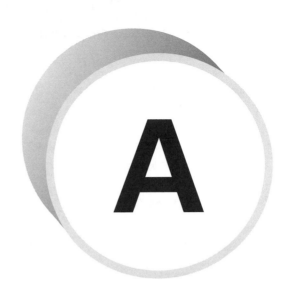

```php
1   <?php
        $db = mysqli_connect('hostname', 'user', 'password', 'database');
        if (!$db) {
            die("Unable to connect to database: ". mysqli_connect_error());
5       }
    ?>

    <html>
        <head><title>Accessing MySQL Databases</title></head>
10      <body>
            <h1>Accessing MySQL Databases</h1>

            <?php

15  if ($_POST['__handle__']) {
        handleForm();
    } else {
        printForm("", "", "", "");
    }
20
```

```php
    function handleForm() {
        global $db;

25      $forename = $_POST['forename'];
        $surname = $_POST['surname'];
        $email = $_POST['email'];
        $role = $_POST['role'];

30      $f = $s = $e = $r = "";

        if ($_POST['save']) {
            // save one record
            $statement = "INSERT INTO user (forename,surname,email,type) VALUES
                ('$forename','$surname','$email','$role')";
35          if ($result = mysqli_query($db, $statement)) {
                echo "<h3 style='color: green'>One row added to the
                    database</h3>";
            } else {
                echo "<h3 style='color: red'>There was a problem saving your
                    data</h3>";
            }
40
        } elseif ($_POST['amend']) {
            // alter one record
            $statement = "UPDATE user SET forename='$forename',
                surname='$surname', type='$role' WHERE email='$email'";
            if ($result = mysqli_query($db, $statement)) {
45              echo "<h3 style='color: green'>Database updated
                    successfully</h3>";
            } else {
                echo "<h3 style='color: red'>There was a problem updating your
                    data</h3>";
            }

50      } elseif ($_POST['delete']) {
            // delete one record
            $statement = "DELETE FROM user WHERE email='$email'";
            if ($result = mysqli_query($db, $statement)) {
```

```
                    echo "<h3 style='color: green'>One row successfully deleted from
                        the database</h3>";
55          } else {
                    echo "<h3 style='color: red'>There was an error whilst deleting
                        the row. Please check that you entered the correct email
                        address</h3>";
            }

        } elseif ($_POST['view']) {
60          // show one record
            $statement = "SELECT * FROM user WHERE email='$email'";
            if ($result = mysqli_query($db, $statement)) {
                    echo "<h3>Your query returned</h3>";
                    $data = mysqli_fetch_object($result);
65                  $f = $data->forename;
                    $s = $data->surname;
                    $e = $data->email;
                    $r = $data->type;
            } else {
70                  echo "<h3 style='color: red'>There was a problem finding the
                        row. Please check that you entered the correct email
                        address</h3>";
            }

        } else {
            // must be showall
75          $statement = "SELECT * FROM user";
            if ($result = mysqli_query($db, $statement)) {
                    echo "<h3>Your query returned</h3><table border='1'>";
                    while ($data = mysqli_fetch_object($result)) {
                        echo "<tr><td>$data->forename</td><td>$data->surname
                            </td><td>$data->email</td><td>$data->type</td></tr>";
80                  }
                    echo "</table>";
            } else {
                    echo "<h3 style='color: red'>There was a problem retrieving
                        data.</h3>";
            }
```

```
85
        }

        printForm($f, $s, $e, $r);

90  } // checkForm


    function printForm($f,$s, $e, $r) {
        echo <<<_DONE
95      <form action="$_SERVER[PHP_SELF]" method="post">
            <table>
                <tr>
                    <td>Your First Name</td>
                    <td><input type="text" length="32" name="forename"
                        value="$f" /></td>
100                </tr>
                <tr>
                    <td>Your Family Name</td>
                    <td><input type="text" length="32" name="surname"
                        value="$s" /></td>
                </tr>
105                <tr>
                    <td>Your Email Address</td>
                    <td><input type="text" length="64" name="email" value="$e"
                        /></td>
                </tr>
                <tr>
110                <td>Choose Your Role</td>
                    <td>
                        <select name="role" size="1">
    _DONE;
        if ($r == 'owner') {
115            echo "<option value='user'>User</option>
                <option value='guest'>Guest</option>
                <option value='administrator'>Administrator</option>
                <option value='owner' selected>Owner</option>";
        } elseif ($r == 'guest') {
```

```
120         echo "<option value='user'>User</option>
                <option value='guest' selected>Guest</option>
                <option value='administrator'>Administrator</option>
                <option value='owner'>Owner</option>";
        } elseif ($r == 'administrator') {
125         echo "<option value='user'>User</option>
                <option value='guest'>Guest</option>
                <option value='administrator' selected>Administrator</option>
                <option value='owner'>Owner</option>";
        } else {
130         echo "<option value='user' selected>User</option>
                <option value='guest'>Guest</option>
                <option value='administrator'>Administrator</option>
                <option value='owner'>Owner</option>";
        }
135
        echo <<<_DONE
                    </select>
                </td>
            </tr>
140         <tr>
                <td><input type="submit" name="save" value="Save
                    Record"/></td>
                <td><input type="submit" name="amend" value="Amend
                    Record"/></td>
                <td><input type="submit" name="view" value="View
                    Record"/></td>
                <td><input type="submit" name="delete" value="Delete
                    Record"/><td>
145             <td><input type="submit" name="showall" value="Show All
                    Records"/><td>
            </tr>
            <input type="hidden" name="__handle__" value="1" />
        </table>
        </form>
150 _DONE;

    } // printForm
```

```
             ?>
155     </body>
    </html>
```

Accessing a Database From PHP Using Pear DB

```php
1   <?php
        require 'DB.php';
        $db = DB::connect("mysqli://user:password@hostname/database");
        if (DB::isError($db)) {
5           die("Unable to connect to database: ". $db->getMessage());
        }
        // handle errors automatically with pear DB
        //$db->setErrorHandling(PEAR_ERROR_DIE);
        // returned values are available as object
10      $db->setFetchMode(DB_FETCHMODE_OBJECT);
    ?>

    <html>
        <head><title>Accessing MySQL Databases</title></head>
15      <body>
            <h1>Accessing MySQL Databases</h1>

            <?php

20  if ($_POST['__handle__']) {
        handleForm();
    } else {
```

```php
        printForm("", "", "", "");
    }
25


    function handleForm() {
        global $db;

30      $forename = $_POST['forename'];
        $surname = $_POST['surname'];
        $email = $_POST['email'];
        $role = $_POST['role'];


35      $f = $s = $e = $r = "";


        if ($_POST['save']) {
            // save one record
            $statement = $db->query("INSERT INTO user
                (forename,surname,email,type) VALUES
                ('$forename','$surname','$email','$role')");
40          if (! DB::isError($db)) {
                echo "<h3 style='color: green'>One row added to the
                    database</h3>";
            } else {
                echo "<h3 style='color: red'>There was a problem saving your
                    data</h3>";
            }
45

        } elseif ($_POST['amend']) {
            // alter one record
            $statement = $db->query("UPDATE user SET forename='$forename',
                surname='$surname', type='$role' WHERE email='$email'");
            if (! DB::isError($db)) {
50              echo "<h3 style='color: green'>Database updated
                    successfully</h3>";
            } else {
                echo "<h3 style='color: red'>There was a problem updating your
                    data</h3>";
            }
```

```php
55      } elseif ($_POST['delete']) {
            // delete one record
            $statement = $db->query("DELETE FROM user WHERE email='$email'");
            if (! DB::isError($db)) {
                echo "<h3 style='color: green'>One row successfully deleted from
                    the database</h3>";
60          } else {
                echo "<h3 style='color: red'>There was an error whilst deleting
                    the row. Please check that you entered the correct email
                    address</h3>";
            }

        } elseif ($_POST['view']) {
65          // show one record
            $statement = $db->query("SELECT * FROM user WHERE email='$email'");
            if (! DB::isError($db)) {
                echo "<h3>Your query returned</h3>";
                while ($data = $statement->fetchRow()) {
70                  $f = $data->forename;
                    $s = $data->surname;
                    $e = $data->email;
                    $r = $data->type;
                }
75          } else {
                echo "<h3 style='color: red'>There was a problem finding the
                    row. Please check that you entered the correct email
                    address</h3>";
            }

        } else {
80          // must be showall
            $statement = $db->query("SELECT * FROM user");
            if (! DB::isError($db)) {
                echo "<h3>Your query returned</h3><table border='1'>";
                while ($data = $statement->fetchRow()) {
85                  echo "<tr><td>$data->forename</td><td>$data->surname
                        </td><td>$data->email</td><td>$data->type</td></tr>";
```

```php
            }
            echo "</table>";
        } else {
            echo "<h3 style='color: red'>There was a problem retrieving
                data.</h3>";
        }
    }

    printForm($f, $s, $e, $r);

} // checkForm


function printForm($f,$s, $e, $r) {
    echo <<<_DONE
    <form action="$_SERVER[PHP_SELF]" method="post">
        <table>
            <tr>
                <td>Your First Name</td>
                <td><input type="text" length="32" name="forename"
                    value="$f" /></td>
            </tr>
            <tr>
                <td>Your Family Name</td>
                <td><input type="text" length="32" name="surname"
                    value="$s" /></td>
            </tr>
            <tr>
                <td>Your Email Address</td>
                <td><input type="text" length="64" name="email" value="$e"
                    /></td>
            </tr>
            <tr>
                <td>Choose Your Role</td>
                <td>
                    <select name="role" size="1">
_DONE;
    if ($r == 'owner') {
```

```
120         echo "<option value='user'>User</option>
                <option value='guest'>Guest</option>
                <option value='administrator'>Administrator</option>
                <option value='owner' selected>Owner</option>";
        } elseif ($r == 'guest') {
125         echo "<option value='user'>User</option>
                <option value='guest' selected>Guest</option>
                <option value='administrator'>Administrator</option>
                <option value='owner'>Owner</option>";
        } elseif ($r == 'administrator') {
130         echo "<option value='user'>User</option>
                <option value='guest'>Guest</option>
                <option value='administrator' selected>Administrator</option>
                <option value='owner'>Owner</option>";
        } else {
135         echo "<option value='user' selected>User</option>
                <option value='guest'>Guest</option>
                <option value='administrator'>Administrator</option>
                <option value='owner'>Owner</option>";
        }

140
        echo <<<_DONE
                    </select>
                  </td>
                </tr>
145             <tr>
                    <td><input type="submit" name="save" value="Save
                      Record"/></td>
                    <td><input type="submit" name="amend" value="Amend
                      Record"/></td>
                    <td><input type="submit" name="view" value="View
                      Record"/></td>
                    <td><input type="submit" name="delete" value="Delete
                      Record"/><td>
150                 <td><input type="submit" name="showall" value="Show All
                      Records"/><td>
                </tr>
                <input type="hidden" name="__handle__" value="1" />
```

```
            </table>
        </form>
155 _DONE;

    } // printForm


            ?>
160     </body>
    </html>
```

HTML Color Codes

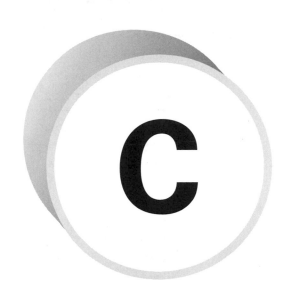

Name	Red	Green	Blue	Hex Value
aliceblue	240	248	245	f0f8ff
antiquewhite	250	235	215	faebd7
aqua	0	255	255	00ffff
aquamarine	127	255	212	7fffd4
azure	240	255	255	f0ffff
beige	245	245	220	f5f5dc
bisque	255	228	196	ffe4c4
black	0	0	0	000000
blanchedalmond	255	235	205	ffebcd
blue	0	0	255	0000ff
blueviolet	138	43	226	8a2be2
brown	165	42	42	a52a2a
burlywood	222	184	135	deb887
cadetblue	95	158	160	5f9ea0
chartreuse	127	255	0	7fff00
chocolate	210	105	30	d2691e
coral	255	127	80	ff7f50
conflowerblue	100	149	237	6495ed
cornsilk	255	248	220	fff8dc

(continued overleaf)

(continued)

Name	Red	Green	Blue	Hex Value
crimson	220	20	60	dc143c
cyan	0	255	255	00ffff
darkblue	0	0	139	00008b
darkcyan	0	139	139	008b8b
darkgoldenrod	184	134	11	b8860b
darkgray	169	169	169	a9a9a9
darkgreen	0	100	0	006400
darkkhaki	189	183	107	bdb76b
darkmagenta	139	0	0	8b008b
darkolivegreen	85	107	47	55662f
darkorange	255	140	0	ff8c00
darkorchid	153	50	204	9932cc
darkred	139	0	0	8b0000
darksalmon	233	150	122	e9967a
darkseagreen	143	188	143	8fbc8f
darkslateblue	72	61	139	483d8b
darkslategray	47	79	79	2f4f4f
darkturquoise	0	206	209	00ced1
darkviolet	148	0	211	9400d3
deeppink	255	20	147	ff1493
deepskyblue	0	191	255	00bfff
dimgray	105	105	105	696969
dodgerblue	30	144	255	1e90ff
firebrick	178	34	34	b22222
floralwhite	255	250	240	fffaf0
forestgreen	34	139	34	228b22
fuchsia	255	0	255	ff00ff
gainsboro	220	220	220	dcdcdc
ghostwhite	248	248	255	f8f8ff
gold	255	215	0	ffd700
goldenrod	218	165	32	daa520
gray	128	128	128	808080
green	0	128	0	008000

(continued)

Name	Red	Green	Blue	Hex Value
greenyellow	173	255	47	adff2f
honeydew	240	255	240	f0fff0
hotpink	255	105	180	ff69b4
indianred	205	92	92	cd5c5c
indigo	75	0	130	4b0082
ivory	255	255	240	fffff0
khaki	240	230	140	f0e68c
lavender	230	230	250	e6e6fa
lavenderblush	255	240	245	fff0f5
lawngreen	124	252	000	7cfc00
lemochiffon	255	250	205	fffacd
lightblue	173	216	230	add8e6
lightcoral	240	128	128	f08080
lightcyan	224	255	255	e0ffff
lightgoldenrodyellow	250	250	210	fafad2
lightgray	211	211	211	d3d3d3
lightgreen	144	238	144	90ee90
lightpink	255	182	193	ffb6c1
lightsalmon	255	160	122	ffa07a
lightseagreen	32	178	170	20b2aa
lightskyblue	135	206	250	87cefa
lightslategray	119	136	153	778899
lightsteelblue	176	196	222	b0c4de
lightyellow	255	255	224	ffffe0
lime	0	255	0	00ff00
limegreen	50	205	50	32cd32
linen	250	240	230	faf0e6
magenta	255	0	255	ff00ff
maroon	128	0	0	800000
mediumaquamarine	102	205	170	66cdaa
mediumblue	0	0	205	0000cd
mediumorchid	186	85	211	ba55d3

(continued overleaf)

(continued)

Name	Red	Green	Blue	Hex Value
mediumpurple	147	211	219	9370db
mediumseagreen	60	179	113	3cb371
mediumslateblue	123	104	238	7b68ee
mediumspringgreen	0	250	154	00fa9a
mediumturquoise	72	209	204	48d1cc
mediumvioletred	199	21	133	c71585
midnightblue	25	25	122	191970
mintcream	245	255	250	f5fffa
mistyrose	255	228	225	ffe4e1
mocassin	255	228	181	ffe4b5
navajowhite	255	222	173	ffdead
navy	0	0	128	000080
oldlace	253	245	230	fdf5e6
olive	128	128	0	808000
olivedrab	107	142	35	6b8e23
orange	255	265	0	ffa500
orangered	255	69	0	ff4500
orchid	218	112	214	da70d6
palegoldenrod	238	232	170	eee8aa
palegreen	152	251	152	98fb98
paleturquoise	175	238	238	afeeee
palevioletred	219	112	147	db7093
papayawhip	255	239	213	ffefd5
peachpuff	255	218	185	ffda69
peru	205	133	63	cd853f
pink	255	192	203	ffc0cb
plum	221	160	221	dda0dd
powderblue	176	224	230	b0e0e6
purple	128	0	128	800080
red	255	0	0	ff0000
rosybrown	188	143	143	bc8f8f
royalblue	65	105	225	4169e1
saddlebrown	139	69	19	8b4513

(continued)

Name	Red	Green	Blue	Hex Value
salmon	250	128	114	fa8072
sandybrown	244	164	96	f4a460
seagreen	46	139	87	2e8b57
seashell	255	245	238	fff5ee
sienna	160	82	45	a0522d
silver	192	192	192	c0c0c0
skyblue	135	206	235	87ceeb
slateblue	106	90	205	6a5acd
slategray	112	128	144	708090
snow	255	250	250	fffafa
springgreen	0	255	127	00ff7f
steelblue	70	130	180	4682b4
tan	210	180	140	d2b48c
teal	0	128	128	008080
thistle	216	191	216	d8bfd8
tomato	255	99	71	006347
turquoise	64	224	208	40e0d0
violet	238	130	238	ee82ee
wheat	245	222	179	f5deb3
white	255	255	255	ffffff
whitesmoke	245	245	245	f5f5f5
yellow	255	255	0	ffff00
yellowgreen	154	205	50	9acd32

HTML
Entities

HTML supports several sets of character entities. These are often used inside Web pages to produce characters which are not part of the ANSII character set. The following table lists these entities. I have shown the text string which most people use in their pages, a numerical string which is equivalent to the text one and which can be used interchangeably. I have also included a short description taken from the HTML 4 recommendation document. Where possible I have given an example of the character which the entity produces. Because this is a book, not a Web page, the set of characters I can show is restricted by my typesetting software.

ISO 8859-1 Characters

Textual Name	Numeric Name	Description	Example
		non-breaking space	
&iexcl;	&#161;	inverted exclamation mark	¡
&cent;	&#162;	US cent	¢
&pound;	&#163;	British currency pound	£
&curren;	&#164;	currency	¤
&yen;	&#165;	yen	¥
&brvbar;	&#166;	broken vertical bar		
&sect;	&#167;	section sign	§
&uml;	&#168;	diaresis	ö
&copy;	&#169;	copyright	©
&ordf;	&#170;	feminine ordinal indicator	
&laquo;	&#171;	left double angle quotation	

Textual Name	Numeric Name	Description	Example
&not;	&#172;	not sign	¬
&shy;	&#173;	soft hyphen	
&reg;	&#174;	registered trademark	®
&macr;	&#175;	spacing macron	
&deg;	&#176;	degree sign	°
&plusmn;	&#177;	plus or minus	±
&sup2;	&#178;	superscripted 2	x^2
&sup3;	&#179;	superscripted 3	x^3
&acute;	&#180;	acute accent	
&micro;	&#181;	micro	μ
&para;	&#182;	paragraph	¶
&middot;	&#183;	middle dot	·
&cedil;	&#184;	cedilla	
&sup1;	&#185;	superscripted 1	x^1
&ordm;	&#186;	male ordinal indicator	
&raquo;	&#187;	right double angle quotation	
&frac14;	&#188;	fraction one quarter	$\frac{1}{4}$
&frac12;	&#189;	fraction one half	$\frac{1}{2}$
&frac34;	&#190;	fraction three quarters	$\frac{3}{4}$
&iquest;	&#191;	inverted question mark	¿
&Agrave;	&#192;	A with grave accent	À
&Aacute;	&#193;	A with acute accent	Á
&Acirc;	&#194;	A with circumflex	Â
&Atilde;	&#195;	A with tilde	Ã
&Auml;	&#196;	A with diaresis	Ä
&Aring;	&#197;	A with ring	Å
&AElig;	&#198;	Latin capital AE	Æ
&Ccedil;	&#199;	C with cedilla	Ç
&Egrave;	&#200;	E with grave accent	È
&Eacute;	&#201;	E with acute accent	É
&Ecirc;	&#202;	E with circumflex	Ê
&Euml;	&#203;	E with diaresis	Ë
&Igrave;	&#204;	I with grave accent	Ì

(continued overleaf)

(continued)

Textual Name	Numeric Name	Description	Example
&Iacute;	&#205;	I with acute accent	Í
&Icirc;	&#206;	I with circumflex	Î
&Iuml;	&#207;	I with diaresis	Ï
&ETH;	&#208;	Latin capital ETH	Đ
&Ntilde;	&#209;	N with tilde	Ñ
&Ograve;	&#210;	O with grave accent	Ò
&Oacute;	&#211;	O with acute accent	Ó
&Ocirc;	&#212;	O with circumflex	Ô
&Otilde;	&#213;	O with tilde	Õ
&Ouml;	&#214;	O with diaresis	Ö
&times;	&#215;	multiplication sign	×
&Oslash;	&#216;	O with a stroke	Ø
&Ugrave;	&#217;	U with grave accent	Ù
&Uacute;	&#218;	U with acute accent	Ú
&Ucirc;	&#219;	U with circumflex	Û
&Uuml;	&#220;	U with diaresis	Ü
&Yacute;	&#221;	Y with acute accent	Ý
&THORN;	&#222;	capital THORN	Þ
&szlig;	&#223;	sharp s	ß
&agrave;	&#224;	a with grave accent	à
&aacute;	&#225;	a with acute accent	á
&acirc;	&#226;	a with circumflex	â
&atilde;	&#227;	a with tilde	ã
&auml;	&#228;	a with diaresis	ä
&aring;	&#229;	a with ring	å
&aelig;	&#230;	Latin ae	æ
&ccedil;	&#231;	c with cedilla	ç
&egrave;	&#232;	e with grave accent	è
&eacute;	&#233;	e with acute accent	é
&ecirc;	&#234;	e with circumflex	ê
&euml;	&#235;	e with diaresis	ë
&igrave;	&#236;	i with grave accent	ì
&iacute;	&#237;	i with acute accent	í

Textual Name	Numeric Name	Description	Example
&icirc;	&#238;	i with circumflex	î
&iuml;	&#239;	i with diaresis	ï
&eth;	&#240;	Latin eth	ð
&ntilde;	&#241;	n with tilde	ñ
&ograve;	&#242;	o with grave accent	ò
&oacute;	&#243;	o with acute accent	ó
&ocirc;	&#244;	o with circumflex	ô
&otilde;	&#245;	o with tilde	õ
&ouml;	&#246;	o with diaresis	ö
&divide;	&#247;	division sign	÷
&oslash;	&#248;	o with a stroke	ø
&ugrave;	&#249;	u with grave accent	ù
&uacute;	&#250;	u with acute accent	ú
&ucirc;	&#251;	u with circumflex	û
&uuml;	&#252;	u with diaresis	ü
&yacute;	&#253;	y with acute accent	ý
&thorn;	&#254;	lowercase thorn	þ
&yuml;	&#255;	y with diaresis	ÿ

Symbols, Mathematical Symbols and Greek Letters

Textual Name	Numeric Name	Description	Example
&fnof;	&#402;	small Latin f	
&Alpha;	&#913;	capital alpha	
&Beta;	&#914;	capital beta	
&Gamma;	&#915;	capital gamma	Γ
&Delta;	&#916;	capital delta	Δ
&Epsilon;	&#917;	capital epsilon	
&Zeta;	&#918;	capital zeta	
&Eta;	&#919;	capital eta	
&Theta;	&#920;	capital theta	Θ
&Iota;	&#921;	capital iota	

(continued overleaf)

(continued)

Textual Name	Numeric Name	Description	Example
&Kappa;	&#922;	capital kappa	
&Lambda;	&#923;	capital lambda	Λ
&Mu;	&#924;	capital mu	
&Nu;	&#925;	capital nu	
&Xi;	&#926;	capital xi	Ξ
&Omicron;	&#927;	capital omicron	
&Pi;	&#928;	capital pi	Π
&Rho;	&#929;	capital rho	
&Sigma;	&#931;	capital sigma	Σ
&Tau;	&#932;	capital tau	
&Upsilon;	&#933;	capital upsilon	Υ
&Phi;	&#934;	capital phi	Φ
&Chi;	&#935;	capital chi	
&Psi;	&#936;	capital psi	Ψ
&Omega;	&#937;	capital omega	Ω
&alpha;	&#945;	small letter alpha	α
&beta;	&#946;	small letter beta	β
&gamma;	&#947;	small letter gamma	γ
&delta;	&#948;	small letter delta	δ
&epsilon;	&#949;	small letter epsilon	ε
&zeta;	&#950;	small letter zeta	ζ
&eta;	&#951;	small letter eta	η
&theta;	&#952;	small letter theta	θ
&iota;	&#953;	small letter iota	ι
&kappa;	&#954;	small letter kappa	κ
&lambda;	&#955;	small letter lambda	λ
&mu;	&#956;	small letter mu	μ
&nu;	&#957;	small letter nu	ν
&xi;	&#958;	small letter xi	ξ
&omicron;	&#959;	small letter omicron	
&pi;	&#960;	small letter pi	π
&rho;	&#961;	small letter rho	ρ
&sigmaf;	&#962;	small letter sigma	ς

Textual Name	Numeric Name	Description	Example
&sigma;	&#963;	small letter sigma	σ
&tau;	&#964;	small letter tau	τ
&upsilon;	&#965;	small letter upsilon	υ
&phi;	&#966;	small letter phi	ϕ
&chi;	&#967;	small letter chi	χ
&psi;	&#968;	small letter psi	ψ
&omega;	&#969;	small letter omega	ω
&thetasym;	&#977;	small letter theta	θ
&upsih;	&#978;	greek upsilon with hook	
&piv;	&#982;	pi	π
&bull;	&#8226;	bullet	•
&hellip;	&#8230;	horizontal ellipses	...
&prime;	&#8242;	prime/minutes/feet symbol	′
&Prime;	&#8243;	double prime/seconds /inches symbol	″
&oline;	&#8254;	overline	
&frasl;	&#8260;	fraction slash	/
&weierp;	&#8472;	script capital p	℘
&image;	&#8465;	blackletter I	ℑ
&real;	&#8476;	blackletter R	ℜ
&trade;	&#8482;	trademark symbol	™
&alefsym;	&#8501;	alef symbol	ℵ
&larr;	&#8592;	leftwards arrow	←
&uarr;	&#8593;	upwards arrow	↑
&rarr;	&#8594;	rightwards arrow	→
&darr;	&#8595;	downwards arrow	↓
&harr;	&#8596;	left right arrow	↔
&crarr;	&#8629;	down arrow with corner left	
&lArr;	&#8656;	double left arrow	⇐
&uArr;	&#8557;	double upwards arrow	⇑
&rArr;	&#8558;	double rightwards arrow	⇒
&dArr;	&#8559;	double downwards arrow	⇓

(continued overleaf)

(continued)

Textual Name	Numeric Name	Description	Example
&hArr;	&#8560;	double left right arrow	⇔
&forall;	&#8704;	for all	∀
&part;	&#8706;	partial differential	∂
&exists;	&#8707;	there exists	∃
&empty;	&#8709;	empty set	∅
&nabla;	&#8711;	backward difference	∇
&isin;	&#8712;	element of	∈
&notin;	&#8713;	not an element of	∉
&ni;	&#8715;	contains as member	∋
&prod;	&#8719;	n-ary product	∏
&sum;	&#8721;	n-ary summation	∑
&minus;	&#8722;	minus sign	−
&lowast;	&#8727;	asterix operator	∗
&radic;	&#8730;	square root	√
&prop;	&#8733;	proportional to	∝
&infin;	&#8734;	infinity	∞
&ang;	&#8736;	angle	∠
&and;	&#8743;	logical and	∧
&or;	&#8744;	logical or	∨
&cap;	&#8745;	intersection	∩
&cup;	&#8746;	union	∪
&int;	&#8747;	integral	∫
&there4;	&#8756;	therefore	∴
&sim;	&#8764;	similar operator	∼
&cong;	&#8773;	approximately equal to	≅
&asymp;	&#8776;	almost equal to	≈
&ne;	&#8800;	not equal to	≠
&equiv;	&#8801;	idemtical to	≡
&le;	&#8804;	less than or equal to	≤
&ge;	&#8805;	greater than or equal to	≥
&sub;	&#8834;	subset of	⊂
&sup;	&#8835;	superset of	⊃
&nsub;	&#8836;	not a subset of	⊄

Textual Name	Numeric Name	Description	Example
&sube;	&#8838;	subset of or equal to	⊆
&supe;	&#8839;	superset of or equal to	⊇
&oplus;	&#8853;	circled plus	⊕
&otimes;	&#8855;	circled times	⊗
&perp;	&#8869;	perpendicular to	⊥
&sdot;	&#8901;	dot operator	·
&lceil;	&#8968;	left ceiling	⌈
&rceil;	&#8969;	right ceiling	⌉
&lfloor;	&#8970;	left floor	⌊
&rfloor;	&#8971;	right floor	⌋
&lang;	&#9001;	left pointing angle bracket	⟨
&rang;	&#9002;	right pointing angle bracket	⟩
&loz;	&#9674;	lozenge shape	◊
&spades;	&#9824;	spade suit	♠
&clubs;	&#9827;	clubs suit	♣
&hearts;	&#9829;	heart suit	♡
&diamonds;	&#9830;	diamond suit	◇

Markup-significant Characters

Entity Textual Name	Entity Numeric Name	Description	Example
&quot;	&#34;	Quotation mark	"
&amp;	&#38;	Ampersand	&
&lt;	&#60;	Less than sign	<
&gt;	&#62;	Greater than sign	>
&OElig;	&#338;	Latin capital ligature OE	Œ
&oelig;	&#339;	Latin small ligature oe	œ
&Scaron;	&#352;	Capital S with caron	Š
&scaron;	&#353;	Small letter s with caron	š
&Yuml;	&#376;	Capital Y with diaresis	Ÿ
&circ;	&#710;	Modified cirumflex accent	ˆ

(continued overleaf)

(continued)

Entity Textual Name	Entity Numeric Name	Description	Example
&tilde;	&#732;	Small tilde	~
		En space	
		Em space	
		Thin space	
&zwnj;	&#8204;	Zero width non-joiner	
&zwj;	&#8205;	Zero width joiner	
&lrm;	&#8206;	Left to right mark	
&rlm;	&#8207;	Right to left mark	
&ndash;	&#8211;	En dash	–
&mdash;	&#8212;	Em dash	—
&lsquo;	&#8216;	Left single quotation mark	'
&rsquo;	&#8217;	Right single quotation mark	'
&sbquo;	&#8218;	Single low-9 quotation mark	‚
&ldquo;	&#8220;	Left double quotation mark	"
&rdquo;	&#8221;	Right double quotation mark	"
&bdquo;	&#8222;	Double low-9 quotation mark	„
&dagger;	&#8224;	Dagger	†
&Dagger;	&#8225;	Double dagger	‡
&permil;	&#8240;	Per mille sign	‰
&lsaquo;	&#8249;	Left angle quotation mark	‹
&rsaquo;	&#8250;	Right angle quotation mark	›
&euro;	&#8364;	Euro symbol	

Index